All About Faith

One-Volume Edition

Gill & Macmillan Ltd
Hume Avenue
Park West
Dublin 12
with associated companies throughout the world
www.gillmacmillan.ie

© Niall and Ann Boyle 2005
© Artwork by Karen Allsop and Design Image
© Maps by Design Image

ISBN-13: 978 07171 3857 9
ISBN-10: 0 7171 3857 7

Colour reproduction by Typeform Repro
Print origination in Ireland by Niamh Lehane Design
Imprimatur: Most Rev. Michael Smith DCL, Bishop of Meath

The paper used in this book is made from the wood pulp of managed forests. For every tree felled, at least one tree is planted, thereby renewing natural resources.

All rights reserved.
No part of this publication may be copied, reproduced or transmitted in any form or by any means without written permission of the publishers or else under the terms of any licence permitting limited copying issued by the Irish Copyright Licensing Agency.

All About Faith
One-Volume Edition

Niall & Ann Boyle

Gill & Macmillan

Syllabus outline

N.B. Syllabus sections may be taught in *any* order; it is *not* necessary to follow the sequence outlined below.

This course consists of *two* parts:

This Book

These topics are dealt with principally in the following parts of this book:

PART 1
Students take *any two* of the following:

Section A   Communities of Faith

- Community
- Communities at work in Ireland
- Communities of Faith
- Relationships between Communities of Faith
- Organisation and Leadership in Communities of Faith (H/L only)

Part 1 (Chapters 1 and 2)
Part 2 (Chapter 4)
Part 5 (Chapters 29, 30 and 31)

Section B   Foundations of Religion – Christianity

- The Context
- Evidence about Jesus
- The Person and Preaching of Jesus
- The Death and Resurrection of Jesus
- Faith in Christ (Titles of Jesus – H/L only)

Part 3 (Chapters 6 to 23)
Part 4 (Chapter 24)

Section C   Foundations of Religion – Major World Religions

- The Context
- Sources of Evidence
- Rites of Passage and Other Rituals
- Development of Tradition
- Tradition, Faith and Practice Today (H/L only)

Part 2 (Chapters 4 and 5)
Parts 6, 7 and 8 (Chapters 32 to 36)

PART 2
Students take *all* of the following:

Section D   The Question of Faith

- The Situation of Faith Today
- The Beginnings of Faith
- The Growth of Faith
- The Expression of Faith
- Challenges to Faith (H/L only)

Part 1 (Chapters 1 to 3)
Part 9 (Chapters 37 to 40)

Section E   The Celebration of Faith

- The World of Ritual
- The Experience of Worship
- Worship as Response to Mystery (H/L only)
- Sign and Symbol
- Prayer

Part 2 (Chapter 5)
Part 4 (Chapters 25 to 28)
Parts 6, 7 and 8 (Chapters 33, 34 and 36)

Section F   The Moral Challenge

- Introduction to Morality
- Sources of Morality
- Growing in Morality
- Religious Morality in Action
- Law and Morality (H/L only)

Parts 10 and 11 (Chapters 41 to 49)

Picture Credits

For permission to reproduce photographs and other material, the author and publisher gratefully acknowledge the following: 43R, 305 © akg-images; 14TR, 14BR, 44, 143L, 148B, 169, 177, 192, 196, 214, 240R, 250L, 288 © Alamy Images; THE ART ARCHIVE: 29 © Private Collection/Dagli Orti, 93 © Dagli Orti, 186 © Turkish and Islamic Art Museum Istanbul/HarperCollins Publishers, 188 © Topkapi Museum Istanbul/HarperCollins Publishers, 261 © Museo del Prado Madrid/Dagli Orti, 265 © Abbey of Monteoliveto Maggiore Siena/Dagli Orti, 278 © Scrovegni Chapel Padua/Dagli Orti; 17, 163, 172, 255, 279, 291, 296 © Associated Press; 180B Photo S. Leutenegger © Ateliers et Presses de Taizé, F-71250 Taizé - Communaté; BRIDGEMAN ART LIBRARY: 10, 275 © Galleria Sabauda, Turin, Italy, Alinari, 15, 236 © Musée d'Orsay, Paris, France, Giraudon, 16T, 83, 94 © Brooklyn Museum of Art, New York, USA, 30 © Palazzo Pubblico, Siena, Italy, Alinari, 33 © Ancient Art and Architecture Collection Ltd, 35 © Galleria d'Arte Moderna, Venice, Italy, Alinari, 51, 232, 311R © Vatican Museums and Galleries, Vatican City, Italy, 53 © Bibliotheque Municipale, Epernay, France, Giraudon, 54, 282 © Private Collection, Bonhams, London, UK, 55 © Palazzo Ducale, Urbino, Italy, 56, 112 © Prado, Madrid, Spain, Giraudon, 122 © Prado, Madrid, Spain, 58 © Museum of Fine Arts, Budapest, Hungary, 59 © Santa Maria Gloriosa dei Frari, Venice, Italy, Giraudon, 71R © The Barnes Foundation, Merion, Pennsylvania, USA, 72 © National Gallery of Victoria, Melbourne, Australia, 79 © Kunsthistorisches Museum, Vienna, Austria, 82, 234 © Stapleton Collection, UK, 84 © Musée des Beaux-Arts, Nantes, France, Giraudon, 86 © Musée des Beaux-Arts, Dunkirk, France, Giraudon, 95, 111 © Scrovegni (Arena) Chapel, Padua, Italy, 96 © Louvre, Paris, France, Giraudon, 98 © Alte Pinakothek, Munich, Germany/Interfoto, 100 © Biblioteca Reale, Turin, Italy, Alinari, 103B © Hamburg Kunsthalle, Hamburg, Germany, 105 © Palazzo Pitti, Florence, Italy, Alinari, 107 © Museo di San Marco dell'Angelico, Florence, Italy, 110 © Leeds Museums and Galleries (City Art Gallery) UK, 117 © Private Collection, 118 © Sudley House, Liverpool, Merseyside, UK, National Museums Liverpool, 119 © Coventry Cathedral, Warwickshire, UK, 120 © Walters Art Museum, Baltimore, USA, 124 © Pushkin Museum, Moscow, Russia, 129 © Galleria degli Uffizi, Florence, Italy, 137T © Koninklijk Museum voor Schone Kunsten, Antwerp, Belgium, Giraudon, 137B © Battistero Neoniano, Ravenna, Italy, 143R © National Gallery of Art, Washington DC, USA, 147, 242 © Louvre, Paris, France, 164 © Gemaeldegalerie Alte Meister, Dresden, Germany/Staatliche Kunstsammlungen Dresden, 227 © Louvre, Paris, France, Peter Willi, 233 © State Russian Museum, St. Petersburg, Russia, 237 © Pavlovsk Palace, St. Petersburg, Russia, 240L © Galleria dell' Accademia, Venice, Italy, Giraudon, 243 © Musée Rodin, Paris, France, 268 © Manchester Art Gallery, UK, 276 © Casa y Museo del Greco, Toledo, Spain, 277 © National Gallery of Scotland, Edinburgh, Scotland, 280 © Private Collection, Lawrence Steigrad Fine Arts, New York, 293 © Worcester Art Museum, Massachusetts, USA, 297 © Victoria & Albert Museum, London, UK, 298T © Ackermann and Johnson Ltd., London, UK, 306 © Christie's Images, London, UK, 307 © Musée des Beaux-Arts, Tours, France, Lauros, Giraudon, 311L © Narodni Galerie, Prague, Czech Republic, Giraudon, 314 © Museo Bandini, Fiesole, Italy, Alinari; 16BL, BC, BR © www.brickbats.co.uk; 135, 191 © Camera Press Ireland; CORBIS: 11B © David Lees, 11T © Philip James Corwin, 18 © Bill Binzen, 22, 114 © Bettmann, 43L © Richard T. Nowitz, 76 © Archivo Iconografico, S.A., 89 © Geoffrey Clements, 103T © David Lees, 113 © Christie's Images, 121 © National Gallery Collection, By kind permission of the Trustees of the National Gallery, London, 148TR © Nik Wheeler, 162 © Hanan Isachar, 166 © Michael St. Maur Sheil, 231R © Kevin Schafer, 285 © David Turnley, 313 © Elio Ciol; 182 © The Corrymeela Community, reproduced by kind permission. For more information visit www.corrymeela.org or email belfast@corrymeela.org; 174L © Irish Times/Peter Thursfield; 152B, 262 © John McElroy; 48 © Reproduced by courtesy of the University Director and Librarian, The John Rylands University Library, The University of Manchester; 298B © The Kobal Collection/20th Century Fox; 75, 187, 189, 294, © Mary Evans Picture Library; 239 © Mary Evans/Ida Kar Collection; 286 © PA Photos/David Jones; 174R, 180T © Pacemaker Press; PANOS PICTURES: 215 © Mark Henley, 283R © Andrew Testa, 290 © Paul Lowe; 14BL © Photocall Ireland; 4B, 134, 179, 310 © Reuters; 199, 203, 269T © Rex Features; 178 © Salvation Army/Gary Freeman; SCIENCE PHOTO LIBRARY: 250R © John Cole, 287 © Edelmann; 73, 80, 175, 229, 231L © Topfoto; 71L © Topfoto/AAAC; 269B © Topfoto/AP; 266 © Topfoto/PA; 284 © Topfoto/Photonews; 41, 148TL, 176, 206, 207, 241 © Topfoto/The Image Works; 264 © Topfoto/UPPA.

The author and publisher have made every effort to trace all copyright holders, but if any has been inadvertently overlooked we would be pleased to make the necessary arrangements at the first opportunity.

Contents

PART ONE **FOUNDATIONS**
Chapter 1	Communities of Faith: An Introduction to Religion	3
Chapter 2	The Elements of Religion	10
Chapter 3	Faith and Prayer	15

PART TWO **JUDAISM**
Chapter 4	The Origins of Judaism	25
Chapter 5	Judaism: Sacred Text and Worship	33

PART THREE **THE ORIGINS OF CHRISTIANITY**
Chapter 6	The Bible	47
Chapter 7	The Gospels: Similarities and Differences	52
Chapter 8	The Birth of Jesus	55
Chapter 9	Life in Palestine	62
Chapter 10	Under Roman Rule	66
Chapter 11	Jesus Prepares for His Mission	70
Chapter 12	Jesus Begins His Public Ministry	74
Chapter 13	The Kingdom of God	78
Chapter 14	Teaching by Parables	81
Chapter 15	The Miracles of Jesus	84
Chapter 16	Jesus' Entry into Jerusalem	88
Chapter 17	Jesus in the Temple	92
Chapter 18	The Arrest and Interrogation of Jesus	96
Chapter 19	The Trial and Death of Jesus	100
Chapter 20	The Resurrection of Jesus	105
Chapter 21	The Expansion of Christianity	111
Chapter 22	The Identity of Jesus	117
Chapter 23	The Trinity	122

PART FOUR **CHRISTIANITY: BELIEFS AND WORSHIP**
Chapter 24	Christianity: Creed and Traditions	129
Chapter 25	Growing Closer to God in the Sacraments	136
Chapter 26	Place of Worship: The Church	147
Chapter 27	The Liturgical Year	154
Chapter 28	Pilgrimage	159

Contents

PART FIVE COMMUNITIES OF FAITH IN IRELAND TODAY

Chapter 29	Catholicism	169
Chapter 30	Protestantism	174
Chapter 31	Ecumenism	179

PART SIX ISLAM

| Chapter 32 | The Origins of Islam | 185 |
| Chapter 33 | Islam: Belief and Worship | 191 |

PART SEVEN HINDUISM

| Chapter 34 | Hinduism: Origins, Beliefs and Worship | 203 |

PART EIGHT BUDDHISM

| Chapter 35 | The Origins of Buddhism | 213 |
| Chapter 36 | Buddhism: Sacred Text, Beliefs and Worship | 216 |

PART NINE CHALLENGES TO FAITH

Chapter 37	Religion and Science: The Origins of the Conflict	223
Chapter 38	Interpreting the Bible	229
Chapter 39	Religion and Science in Partnership	235
Chapter 40	Religion in Contemporary Society	238

PART TEN MORALITY

Chapter 41	Introduction to Morality	247
Chapter 42	Love One Another	253
Chapter 43	Discipleship	262
Chapter 44	Making Moral Decisions	271
Chapter 45	Sin and Forgiveness	277
Chapter 46	Law and Morality	283
Chapter 47	Exploring Moral Issues	287

PART ELEVEN LIFE AFTER DEATH

| Chapter 48 | Reasons for Hope | 305 |
| Chapter 49 | The Life Beyond | 311 |

Glossary 317

Part One

FOUNDATIONS

Chapter One

Communities of Faith: An Introduction to Religion

Robinson Crusoe

In 1719, Daniel Defoe published a best-selling novel entitled *Robinson Crusoe*. It is a classic tale of adventure and survival against the odds. It tells the story of the sole survivor of a shipwreck, a man named Robinson Crusoe, who finds himself cast away on a remote, uninhabited island, far from the regular shipping routes.

At first Crusoe is in despair at his predicament.

> 'I am cast upon a horrible desolate island, without any hope of recovery.'

Slowly, however, with patience and considerable ingenuity, Crusoe not only survives but also gradually transforms this remote island into a tropical paradise.

How is Crusoe able to survive? Fortunately, the island has a freshwater spring and an abundance of wild animals. Further, Crusoe discovers that the sailing vessel on which he had been travelling has run aground on the island's shoreline. From this ship he salvages all the tools and materials he needs to build a fortified home, as well as the seeds to plant crops and the means to make his own clothes.

For the next twenty-four years, Crusoe lives alone on the island. Then one day, a group of cannibals arrives from a neighbouring island. Crusoe uses the muskets he had recovered from the ship all those years ago to drive them off and to rescue one of their victims. Crusoe names this man *Friday*, because that is the day of the week on which he rescues him.

At first, Crusoe treats Friday as his servant. Later, the two men become good friends. Crusoe teaches Friday to speak English and convinces him to become a Christian. Finally, after Crusoe has spent twenty-eight years, two months and nineteen days on the island, he and Friday are rescued. A merchant vessel passes within visual range of the island. It spots their signal fire and sends a shore party to investigate. Crusoe and Friday finally escape from the island.

Reflection

When Daniel Defoe wrote *Robinson Crusoe*, he intended to show that any individual human being could achieve almost anything on his/her own. But if one looks carefully at the story, one can see that Defoe *failed* entirely to prove his claim.

Consider the following points:

○ Robinson Crusoe could not have survived without the items he salvaged from the shipwreck. These things, e.g. tools and weapons, were made by *other people*.

○ In the novel, Defoe says that Crusoe found his long years of isolation a terrible ordeal. He was extremely lonely. If Friday had not arrived to provide *friendship*, Crusoe might well have lost the will to live on alone.

○ Without outside help, Crusoe would have been unable to escape from the island and return safely home. *Other people* had to come and rescue him.

The meaning of community

The story of *Robinson Crusoe* clearly demonstrates:

○ *no one is an island*

○ people *need* each other

○ we need to live in *community*.

Community exists wherever people:

○ *live or work together*

○ *share similar interests*

○ *hold broadly similar views about life*.

There are many different kinds of community, for example:

○ the family ○ the parish
○ the school ○ the sports club.

In this book, however, we shall examine what are called *communities of faith*, i.e. *where a group of people have a religion in common*.

Questions

1. Who wrote the novel *Robinson Crusoe*?
2. Who was Robinson Crusoe?
3. How did Robinson Crusoe survive?
4. How long did he live on the island?
5. How did he eventually escape from the island?
6. Read this statement: *The author of Robinson Crusoe believed that a human being can achieve anything on his/her own.* Do you think that the story of Robinson Crusoe really demonstrates this? Give reasons for your answer.
7. What is meant by *community*?
8. Why do people *need* to live in communities?
9. Identify any three kinds of community.
10. What is a *community of faith*?

The meaning of religion

It is difficult to find a single, adequate definition of *religion*. This is because:

○ there are many different religions

○ a religion can be either *monotheistic* (teach that there is only one God) or *polytheistic* (teach that there is more than one god).

The following definition, however, is offered as a guide:

Religion involves belief in and worship of a God or gods.

We shall explore the meaning of this definition and its implications for people's lives throughout this book.

The importance of religion

Consider the following:

○ Religion can be found in one form or another in *every* part of the globe.

○ Religion has been and continues to be one of the *most* influential factors in human history. The teachings of the different religions have shaped the lives of countless millions of people over the centuries.

○ Although religion has divided some people, it has brought many more *closer* together and made them aware of how much they have *in common*.

○ Religion has been and continues to be *a great force for good* by providing hope and encouragement to people.

○ Religion has been the *inspiration* for many magnificent buildings and beautiful works of art and music.

It is clear that religion plays an important role in human affairs. Like art and technology, *religion is one of the things that sets human beings apart from all the other creatures on this planet*. Why this is so and what difference this makes are the questions we shall explore in this book.

Questions

1. Explain the meaning of each of the following kinds of religion: (a) *monotheistic* (b) *polytheistic*.
2. What does *religion* involve?
3. State two examples of how religion plays an important role in people's lives.
4. Identify three things that *set human beings apart from all the other creatures on this planet*.

The need for religion

The wonders of the universe should cause us to stop and reflect on the meaning and purpose of human life.

Consider the following questions:

○ *How is electricity generated?*

○ *How can an aeroplane fly?*

○ *How did the dinosaurs become extinct?*

○ *How can illnesses be cured?*

Communities of Faith: An Introduction to Religion

These are described as *problems*. Why? Because, given sufficient time and effort, people can find complete *solutions* to them.

However, there are other, very different types of questions to which people also seek answers. For example:

- *How can a person find true happiness?*
- *Why do bad things happen to good people?*
- *What happens to people when they die?*

These are described as *mysteries*. Why? Because people *cannot find complete solutions to them*. This is why so many people see the *need* for and are attracted to religion.

All the major religions offer to help people gain insights into and grow in their understanding of life's mysteries. While the guidance given may differ from one religion to another, these religions offer meaning, purpose and hope to many people.

Questions

1. Explain the difference between a *problem* and a *mystery*. Give an example of each.
2. Why do so many people see the *need* for and are attracted to religion? What do the different religions have to *offer* them?

The origins of religion

The precise date when people began to practise religion is not known. However, archaeologists have shown that it started very early in human history.

Religion most likely began as an attempt by our early ancestors to explain the workings of the natural world around them. They were curious about the weather, the changing of the seasons and the movement of the sun and the moon. They sought an explanation for these events.

At first our early ancestors seem to have

Light illuminating the passage and chamber at the Newgrange passage tomb, Co. Meath.

believed that the different aspects of nature, e.g. the sun or the wind, were some kind of higher powers and looked up to them as *gods*. Later, however, our ancestors came to believe that these forces of nature were themselves not gods, but were actually controlled by powerful, invisible beings who were *gods*. Since these gods *lived apart from* and *ruled over* the natural world, they were called *supernatural* beings. People hoped that if they showed how much they respected the gods, then the gods would treat them well and allow their crops to grow.

In the beginning, most people were probably *polytheists*, i.e. they believed in more than one god. In time, some people became *monotheists*, i.e. they believed in one God only. Eventually, five major religions emerged. They are listed here in order of their historical emergence.

6 All About Faith

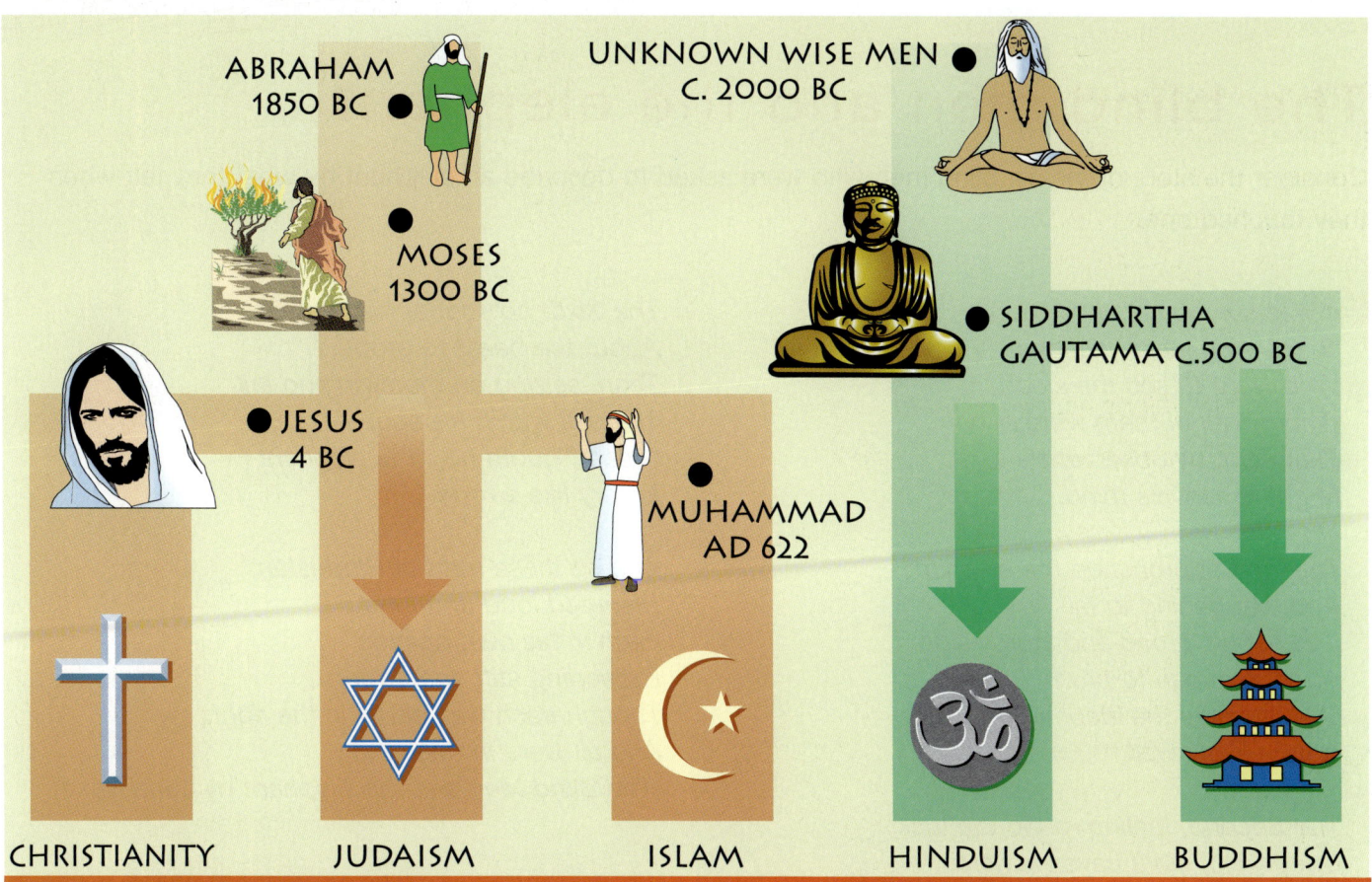

Hinduism	2000 BC
Judaism	1850 BC
Buddhism	500 BC
Christianity	4 BC
Islam	AD 622

N.B. Concerning dates:
BC = Before Christ
AD = *Anno Domini* (a Latin phrase meaning 'in the year of Our Lord').

Alternatively, the abbreviations BCE (before the common era) may be used instead of BC and CE (common era) may be used instead of AD.

Each of these major world religions can trace its origin back to very small and fragile beginnings. While the name of Hinduism's founder(s) has been lost with the passage of time, the other four religions can trace their origins back to one extraordinary person in each case. They are:

Judaism	Abraham
Buddhism	Siddhartha Gautama
Christianity	Jesus
Islam	Muhammad

Questions

1. How did religion most likely begin?
2. What did our early ancestors first believe about different aspects of nature, such as the sun or the wind?
3. What did they *later* come to believe about these forces of nature?
4. Why did our early ancestors try to show how much they respected their gods?
5. (a) List the five major world religions in order of their historical emergence.
   (b) State the *date* when each was founded.
   (c) Name the *founder* of each major religion.

Communities of Faith: An Introduction to Religion

The blind men and the elephant

Consider the story of the six blind men who were asked to describe an elephant by what they felt when they touched one.

It was six men of Hindustan,
To learning much inclined,
Who went to see the elephant
(Though all of them were blind)
That each by observation
Might satisfy his mind.

The First approached the elephant
And, happening to fall
Against his broad and sturdy side,
At once began to bawl:
"I clearly see the elephant
Is very like a wall."

The Second, feeling round the tusk,
Cried: "Ho, what have we here,
So very round and smooth and sharp?
To me, 'tis mighty clear
This wonder of an elephant
Is very like a spear."

The Third approached the animal,
And, happening to take
The squirming trunk within his hand
Thus boldly up and spake;
"I see," quoth he, "the elephant
Is very like a snake."

The Fourth reached out his eager hand
and felt about the knee,
"What most this wondrous beast is like
Is mighty plain," said he,
"'Tis clear enough, the elephant
Is very like a tree."

The Fifth, who chanced to touch the ear,
Said "E'en the blindest man
Can tell what this resembles most;
Deny the fact who can
This marvel of an elephant
Is very like a fan."

The Sixth no sooner had begun
About the beast to grope,
Than, seizing on the swinging tail
That fell within his scope,
"I see," quoth he, "the elephant
Is very like a rope."

And so these men of Hindustan
Disputed loud and long
Each in his own opinion
Exceeding stiff and strong,
Though each was partly in the right,
And all were in the wrong!
(*The Blind Men and the Elephant* by John Saxe)

8 All About Faith

Revelation

If left to our own devices, human beings would know very little about God.

People would perhaps be no closer to understanding God than the six blind men of the story were to describing the elephant. This is because God is so utterly different from anything else in human experience. Indeed, it has been said that human beings can no more imagine a being like God than a baby in its mother's womb can imagine her face.

Yet the different world religions all claim to possess important insights into who God is and how God wants us to live. How, then, can they claim to know these things?

The three great monotheistic religions – Judaism, Christianity and Islam – teach that human beings did *not* discover important truths about God by their own efforts. Rather, they say that at different moments in history, God* called out to certain chosen people and each one of them responded to God's call in their own particular way.

This way in which God communicates with human beings and tells them things about who God is and how they should live, which they would otherwise not know, is called *revelation*.

*N.B.
The word '*God*' is thought to have originally meant '*a call*'.

Questions

1. What is the important lesson about God that we can draw from the poem *The Blind Men and the Elephant*?
2. What is meant by God's *revelation*?

Communities of Faith: An Introduction to Religion

Chapter Two

The Elements of Religion

Introduction

Each of the major world religions offers its *own* set of answers to life's great mysteries. Each has its own *separate* identity.

Yet while recognising that there are many *differences* between the major world religions, we can also see that they all have certain elements *in common*. These are:

- creed
- sacred text
- code
- worship
- symbol
- calendar.

We shall examine each of these in turn.

Creed

The Eternal Father by Guercino.

The word '*creed*' comes from the Latin '*credo*', meaning '*I believe*', i.e. I accept something as being true. We may define a *creed* as a set of beliefs shared by the members of a religion about God and the meaning of life.

Some religions, notably Judaism, Christianity and Islam, have a set creed expressed in the form of a prayer. For example, all Muslims are expected to recite the Shahadah, which states:

There is no God but Allah and Muhammad is his prophet.

The earliest Christian creed is known as the *Apostles' Creed*, which dates from the third century AD (see Chapter 24).

The advantages of having a set creed are that it:

- preserves the true *doctrine* (teaching) of a religion
- helps to prevent the spread of *heresy* (false teachings)
- can be easily memorised.

Sacred text

Each of the major world religions has its own *sacred text* (holy book), which its members are expected to study carefully and treat with great respect. They are as follows.

Religion	Sacred Text
Hinduism	The Vedas
Judaism	The Tenakh
Buddhism	The Pali Canon
Christianity	The Bible
Islam	The Qur'an

10   All About Faith

These sacred texts usually contain the important stories and key teachings of the particular religion. This information is written down to ensure that it is *accurately* handed on from one generation to the next.

Code

Moses receives the Tablets from the Lord.

All religions teach that certain things, such as human life and the world itself, are *sacred*, i.e. deserving of our total respect. Each of the major world religions offers its own particular *code*, i.e. a set of guidelines for living. This code helps people to decide whether an action is the right or the wrong thing to do.

An example of a code would be the *Ten Commandments*, which is accepted by Jews, Christians and Muslims.

Questions

1. What does it mean to say '*I believe*'?
2. Define the word '*creed*'.
3. What are the advantages of a religion having a set creed?
4. State the title of the earliest known Christian creed.
5. (a) What is a *sacred text*?
   (b) What does it contain?
   (c) Why were sacred texts written?
6. Match the correct sacred text with its religion.

Hinduism	The Tenakh
Judaism	The Qur'an
Buddhism	The Bible
Christianity	The Vedas
Islam	The Pali Canon

7. Explain the meaning of the following statement: *All religions teach that certain things are sacred.*
8. What is meant by a *code*?
9. How does a code help people?
10. Give an example of a code accepted by Jews, Christians and Muslims.

The Elements of Religion

Worship

The word 'worship' means 'to recognise worth'. When people worship God, this means that they recognise the supreme importance of God as the creator and sustainer of the universe.*

Each of the major world religions has places specially set aside where its members can gather to worship God. For example, a Jew worships in a *synagogue*, while a Muslim worships in a *mosque*.

In each of these places, the members of a religion take part in *rituals*, i.e. religious ceremonies which give a regular pattern to their worship of God.

Rituals celebrate the mysterious presence of God in people's lives. God, however, is *invisible*, so rituals seek to make God *visible* and *accessible* to people. They do this through the use of *symbols*.

> *N.B.
> *Idolatry* refers to the worship of anyone or anything *other* than God. Idolatry is considered to be a grave *insult* to God because *God alone is worthy of worship*.

Symbol

A *symbol* needs to be carefully distinguished from a *sign*, as the two are often confused with each other. A *sign* is a concrete image, word or gesture that points beyond itself, but has only *one* fixed, clear and unambiguous meaning. For example, a green light at a road junction is a simple sign that means 'proceed ahead'.

A *symbol* is also a concrete image, word or gesture that points beyond itself but has *more* than one meaning. For example, consider the lights on a Christmas tree. They are *symbols* because they remind Christians that:

- Jesus, whose birth Christmas celebrates, is the *Light of the World*.
- Christmas is also a time when those who have much should share generously with those who have little.
- Christmas is a holiday season intended to brighten the dark days of winter.

A symbol also has a *much richer content* than a sign. A symbol enables people to express ideas that are very difficult to put into words. For example, consider the experience of *joy*. Joy itself cannot be seen because it is *abstract*, i.e. it has no size, weight, colour or shape. It cannot be described like a concrete object such as a chair. But joy can be expressed in poetry, music or art through the use of *symbol*.

A rocky mountain. This can be a symbol of either steadfastness or a great obstacle to overcome.

A strong breeze stirring the grass. This can be a symbol of either change or refreshment.

Water. This can be a symbol of either life or hope.

12 All About Faith

Symbols play an important role in many aspects of people's lives. Consider the following.

> A nation's flag usually includes certain colours and details that symbolise or represent important beliefs about that country.
>
> Consider the flag of the Republic of Ireland. It is a *tricolour*.
>
> This design and these three colours were chosen to express an important aspiration. Let us consider each colour in turn.
> - Green: Represents the Nationalist tradition.
> - Orange: Represents the Unionist tradition.
> - White: Expresses unity.
>
> The founders of the Irish state hoped that Ireland would be a place where the members of both traditions, Nationalist and Unionist, could live together in peace and mutual respect.

Symbols play an important role in all religions. An *awareness* of symbol can enrich people's experience of life by helping them to look beyond surface appearances and discover the different, deeper meanings in things. They can also help people to be more aware of and focus their minds upon the invisible presence of *God* in their lives.

The Symbols of the Major Religions

Religion	Symbol	Explanation
Judaism		The menorah, a seven-branched candlestick, stood in the Temple in Jerusalem in ancient times and its design is described in the Torah. The central branch is said to represent the Sabbath, the day on which God rested after creating the world.
Christianity		Jesus died on the cross, the normal method of execution in the Roman Empire at that time. It was a shameful and painful death, but Christians believe that through it Jesus showed his power over sin, suffering and death.
Islam		Muslims say that Islam guides a person's life just as the moon and stars guide a traveller at night in the desert. This symbol on a country's flag often indicates that it is a Muslim state.
Hinduism		This is the written form of the sacred sound 'Aum' (sometimes spelled 'Om'). According to the sacred Hindu texts, *Aum* was the first sound, out of which the rest of the universe was created.
Buddhism		The Buddha spoke of an Eightfold Path to enlightenment. This is traditionally represented as an eight-spoked wheel. The path is a guide to living life compassionately and non-violently.

The Elements of Religion

Calendar

Each of the major world religions has its own *calendar*. Each marks the course of the year by holding special ceremonies on what are referred to as holy days. These *holy days* are important because they:

○ *reinforce* people's sense of belonging to a *distinct* religious community, united by certain shared beliefs

○ help people to *understand* where their community has come from and *remind* them of the kind of person they should try to be

○ help to *strengthen* people's resolve to put their beliefs into practice in their daily lives.

In many nations across the globe, these holy days are also recognised as state holidays.

Questions

1. What does it mean to *worship God*?
2. (a) What is a *ritual*?
   (b) What do rituals celebrate?
   (c) What do rituals seek to do?
3. (a) What is a *sign*?
   (b) Draw and explain the meaning of any two signs.
4. (a) What is a *symbol*?
   (b) Draw and describe one symbol which has a special meaning for you. It could be a team badge, sculpture or painting, etc.
5. In each case below, identify whether it is a sign or a symbol.
   (a) A Christmas tree.
   (b) A country's flag.
   (c) An ambulance's flashing blue light.
   (d) A poster in a shop window announcing a sale.
   (e) A photograph of a waterfall.
6. Why is an awareness of symbols important for all religions?
7. Identify the major world religion associated with each of the following symbols. Then explain the *meaning* of each symbol.

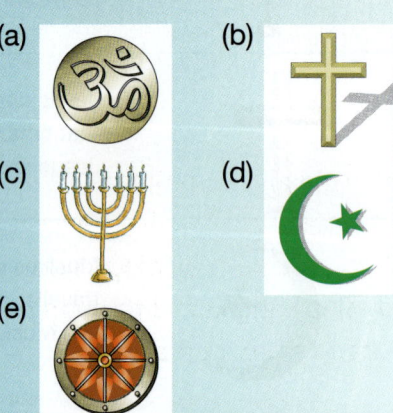

8. Why are *holy days* important for each of the major religions?

14   All About Faith

Chapter Three

Faith and Prayer

Introduction

The Angelus by Jean François Millet.

Judaism, Christianity and Islam teach that God *loves* human beings. As a result, these religions are deeply concerned with helping people to grow closer to God. This is achieved through *prayer*.

Prayer has been described as

> *a conversation from the heart between God and human beings.*

Prayer is vitally important for building a strong and lasting relationship with God. However, building such a relationship requires continuous effort and long-term commitment. Only then can a person develop a deep *faith* in God.

The meaning of faith

Faith involves:
○ *belief in God*
○ *love of God*
○ *belief in the truth of God's revelation*
○ *trust in God's goodness.*

Faith is of vital importance for understanding the meaning of prayer. However, it is important to note that *faith is a gift from God*.

This means that human beings do *not* initiate (start) their relationship with God. Rather, it is *God* who initiates this relationship. God *invites* people to have faith in him. It is for people *to respond* to this invitation.

The development of faith

God is our loving guide and friend.

As a person grows from childhood to adulthood, his/her faith should grow and develop too. He/she should begin asking questions about the meaning

Faith and Prayer 15

of life and seek to grow in understanding of life's mysteries.

A person of *mature* faith, i.e. one whose faith has grown deeper and stronger, is one who has come to realise that:

○ God has a *plan* for the universe and offers each person his/her *own role* in bringing this plan to completion
○ God is an *everlasting friend* who offers to *guide* each person through life's many challenges and who will always be there to give comfort and strength when it is needed.

The Lord's Prayer by James Jacques Joseph Tissot.

Images of God

As a person's faith matures, this causes his/her image of God to undergo important changes.

A *child* might imagine God as either an old man with a white beard seated on a throne in the clouds *or* as someone who is only interested in catching people doing wrong and then punishing them.

An adult, however, should come to realise that God is neither of these things. Rather, God is a loving friend and guide through both the good times and the bad times in life.

Questions

1. What is meant by *prayer*?
2. What does *faith* involve?
3. Explain this statement: *Faith is a gift from God*.
4. What is meant by a *person of mature faith*?
5. Consider the following images of God, then answer the questions that follow.

Image 1 Image 2 Image 3

(a) What kind of image of God is presented in Image 1?
(b) What kind of image of God is presented in Image 2?
(c) How is the image of God presented in Image 3 different from that in Images 1 and 2?

16 All About Faith

The importance of prayer

The importance of prayer. US Marines praying over a comrade who died of his wounds in Fallujah, Iraq.

Many people seem to go about their daily lives with the view that prayer has no real role to play in a dog-eat-dog world.

A person who has developed a deep faith, however, believes that prayer has *everything* to do with his/her day-to-day living. For example:

- It is the relationship with God that a person builds through prayer that gives him/her the encouragement and strength needed to face life's many challenges.

- Through prayer, a person can come to have an ever stronger awareness of God's loving presence in his/her life. This sustains that person in difficult times.

How do people pray?

A person can pray to God on his/her own. However, one should pray with other members of one's community of faith on a regular basis. Worshipping together as a community helps to keep people's faith alive because it reminds them that prayer cannot be separated from other areas of their lives.

A person cannot be a friend of God if he/she ignores the needs of others.

Prayer itself can take many different forms, such as vocal or silent prayer.

Vocal prayer

For instance, people can recite a *formal* prayer, i.e. one with a fixed format that has been taken from a sacred text, such as the *Our Father* or the *Hail Mary*, or one decided upon by religious authorities, such as the *Apostles' Creed*.

Alternatively, people can say an *informal* prayer, i.e. one which they compose themselves.

People can also *sing* hymns or *play* an instrumental piece of music. The great Christian thinker Augustine of Hippo once wrote:

To sing is to pray twice.

Silent prayer

People can *meditate* (silently read and reflect) on a passage of sacred scripture and see how its message can be applied to their daily lives (see page 20).

Faith and Prayer 17

Why do people pray?

'Be still and know that I am God.'
(Psalm 46:10)

People often turn to God in prayer for the following reasons:

- they experience suffering in their own lives
- they are sorry for letting someone down in an important matter
- they are thankful when something important goes well
- they feel powerless when they are unable to help someone they love
- they experience the love of another person
- they are awed by an encounter with the beauty and power of nature
- they realise how short and swiftly ended life can be.

Each of these different circumstances gives rise to a different kind of prayer. If we rearrange their order we can identify *six* types of prayer:

1. *Adoration*: A sense of mystery and wonder.
2. *Intercession*: Love for other people and a wish to help them in practical ways.
3. *Petition*: An awareness of our own needs.
4. *Contrition*: A realisation of where we have gone wrong in our lives and a desire to live better lives.
5. *Protection*: A sense of the power of evil and an awareness of the suffering it causes.
6. *Thanksgiving*: A deep-seated gratitude to God for all those people and things that are important to us.

As we can see, prayer often consists of giving thanks and praise *to* God and seeking help and forgiveness *from* God.

Questions

1. Read this statement: *Prayer has no role in a dog-eat-dog world.* How would a person of deep faith respond to this statement?
2. Why should people pray with other members of their community of faith on a regular basis?
3. Explain the difference between (a) *formal prayer* and (b) *informal prayer*.

18   All About Faith

Questions

4. Match the description in column B with the type of prayer in column A.

A	B
1. Adoration	Love for other people and a wish to help them in practical ways.
2. Intercession	A realisation of where we have gone wrong in our lives and a desire to live better lives.
3. Petition	A sense of the power of evil and an awareness of the suffering it causes.
4. Contrition	A deep-seated gratitude to God for all those people and things that are important to us.
5. Protection	A sense of mystery and wonder.
6. Thanksgiving	An awareness of our own needs.

Example of a formal prayer

The Lord's Prayer

The *Lord's Prayer*, or the *Our Father*, is the only example in the New Testament (see Matthew 6:7–16) of a prayer taught by Jesus himself. It has been described as the most perfect of prayers because it beautifully expresses so much of Jesus' teaching.

Prayer	Explanation
1. Our Father, who art in heaven,	God is the Father, i.e. loving parent, of all people and He invites all people to share eternal life with Him.
2. hallowed be thy name.	God's name is to be respected.
3. Thy kingdom come. Thy will be done on earth, as it is in heaven.	People should work with God to bring His plan for creation to fulfilment.
4. Give us this day our daily bread,	God will provide us with what we need.
5. and forgive us our trespasses, as we forgive those who trespass against us,	Being forgiven by God depends on forgiving those who have offended us.
6. and lead us not into temptation, but deliver us from evil.	God is to be trusted. God will strengthen people in times of crisis or temptation.

Questions

1. Match each explanation in column B with the appropriate statement from the *Lord's Prayer* in column A.

A	B
Our Father, who art in heaven,	People should work with God to bring His plan for creation to fulfilment.
hallowed be thy name.	God will provide us with what we need.
Thy kingdom come. Thy will be done on earth, as it is in heaven.	God is the Father, i.e. loving parent, of all people and He invites all people to share eternal life with Him.
Give us this day our daily bread,	God is to be trusted. God will strengthen people in times of crisis or temptation.
and forgive us our trespasses, as we forgive those who trespass against us,	God's name is to be respected.
and lead us not into temptation, but deliver us from evil.	Being forgiven by God depends on forgiving those who have offended us.

2. The *Lord's Prayer* is a beautiful summary of all Christian prayer. It contains prayers of:

    ○ praise   ○ thanksgiving   ○ sorrow   ○ petition.

    Read it once more and find an example of each of these different kinds of prayer.

Meditation

Read the following extract.

Most of us in our contemporary, fast-paced society are restless human beings. When faced with a chance to just be quiet for a while, we typically fidget or jump up to do something like turn on the television or play a computer game. We let our thoughts race through our heads like cars on a motorway. We prefer noise over silence, motion over stillness, being scattered over being focused. We desperately need to calm down and get ourselves together.

Meditation is **an inner quieting so that a person can come together within and focus attention on something.** *Athletes use meditation as a way to boost their performances. Doctors recommend meditation to patients as a way to reduce stress and lower their blood pressure.*

These are all good uses of meditation. However, as a form of prayer, Christian meditation has a different purpose. Its goal is to focus on God and the mystery of God's love given to us in Jesus, using our thoughts, feelings and imagination. That kind of focus requires inner quieting, much like the calming and centring techniques people might do to reduce stress and improve their work performance. But Christian meditation aims to clear 'inner space' for us **to make room for God in** *our heart*. It is not about achieving something like health or success, but about consciously growing closer to God.

A passage in the **Bible** describes well what it means to meditate. 'Be still, and know that I am God!' (**Psalm** 46:10). If you have ever tried to empty your mind of thoughts, you know how difficult being still can be. It takes self-discipline, practice and patience to learn how to meditate.

The **first step** is to calm the body by consciously relaxing the muscles and breathing deeply and rhythmically. The **next step** is to introduce some way of focusing attention. A method might be as simple as slowly repeating a word, like **Jesus** or **love**. Or one might read a Bible passage and reflect on it, or put oneself into a Gospel story as one of the characters, imagining one's feelings and reactions towards Jesus.

Sometimes mediation is so deep that it is purely an experience of the heart – no thoughts or words at all, just the sense of being in union with God. This type of meditation is called contemplation.

Adapted from T. Zanzig and B. Allaire, *Understanding Catholic Christianity*.

Questions

1. What is *meditation*? Why do doctors recommend it?
2. What is the purpose of *Christian* meditation?
3. In order to be able to meditate, a person must be willing to do certain things. What are they?
4. State the two steps in meditation identified in the extract.
5. What is *contemplation*?

When it is difficult to pray

Even when people want to pray, it might be hard to do so. If they are upset about something or if they have had a row with someone, they can find it difficult to concentrate. Their thoughts seem to crowd in. Since it is not possible to exclude them from their minds, the best thing is to *include* these thoughts in their prayers.

> Lord, I have had a row with X today. I am very upset. My mind keeps going back to the quarrel and she was wrong. But was she? Isn't that my pride speaking? And even if she was wrong, am I not ready to forgive? Lord, how often have I wronged others, how often have I wronged you? You did not hold back your forgiveness, so why should I now? Help me, Lord, to take the first step, to hold out a hand of friendship. She probably feels as bad about it as I do. Lord, give me the courage to forgive.

T. McGivern, *Day-dreaming or Praying?*

A distraction need *not* be a distraction. It can help a person to grow closer to God and to find the courage to show forgiveness and kindness.

Does God listen?

Sometimes people think that their prayers are not answered, that God does not listen to them. But is this really the case?

A person of deep faith would respond by saying that people need to take three things into account when praying to God:

1. **They must be willing to play their part.**

    Some people have a *magical* view of prayer. They do not realise that to pray for something means that they must be prepared to take responsibility for their *own* part in bringing it about.

For example, if a person became seriously ill, he/she might pray for the strength to *endure* the pain and worry of it. But he/she would still have to go to a *doctor*, follow the advice given and undergo medical treatment. He/she would have to *co-operate* with those trying to treat the illness.

2. **They must be willing to change.**

   Sometimes prayers may go unanswered because people's own behaviour may be getting in the way of *God's answer*. They are *not* willing to play their part, when to get what they want would involve a change in their way of life. They do not want to make the effort needed.

3. **They must trust in God.**

   Prayer is not so much a matter of persuading God to do things, rather it is more a matter of people agreeing to put their *trust* in God's plan for the world.

Questions

1. How would a person of deep faith respond to the claim that *if people's prayers are not answered, it is because God does not listen to them?*

2. Consider the story of the great American president, Abraham Lincoln. In his life he endured much disappointment and suffering.

   Mark Link SJ writes:

   Abraham Lincoln knew failure. For thirty years it dogged his every footstep. It walked the streets with him during the day. It kept him awake at night.

   A partial list of his failures reads like this:

   1832 defeated in the election for the legislature
   1833 failed in business
   1836 defeated in nomination for House of Representatives

Abraham Lincoln.

1854 defeated for Senate
1856 defeated in nomination for vice-president

However, in 1860 Abraham Lincoln was elected president of the United States.

Abraham Lincoln was well prepared for the defeats and setbacks that battered and bruised America during the terrible Civil War years. A lesser man would in all likelihood have collapsed under the enormous strain of leading the USA. Throughout it all, however, his faith in God gave him the strength to face each new challenge.

Of himself, Lincoln said: **'God selects his own instruments, and sometimes they are strange ones; for instance, he chose me to steer the ship [America] through a great crisis.'**

What do you think a person can learn about the importance of faith and prayer from Abraham Lincoln's life story? Give reasons for your answer.

Part Two

JUDAISM

Chapter Four

The **Origins** of Judaism

Introduction

Judaism is the world's oldest monotheistic religion.

The Jewish people's faith in God has been tested many times in their long history, never more so than in the nightmare years of Nazi Germany. Between 1933 and 1945, some six million Jewish people, 1.5 million of them children, were systematically murdered in concentration camps.

Yet even throughout this horrific and terrifying ordeal, a large core of Jewish people kept their faith in God. Despite the vicious treatment they received, they still believed that God cared for them and loved them. They saw their suffering as the work of hate-filled people, *not* God.

The achievement of the Jewish people is quite extraordinary. As Loretta Pastva has written:

> *No people, so widely dispersed and as often persecuted as the Jews have been, has ever kept a faith alive for so long.*

The patriarchs

All *devout* Jews, i.e. those who take their religion seriously, are familiar with the stories about the great people and events of their religion. The Jews trace their origin as a distinct people to about 1850 BC, when the era of the patriarchs began. Abraham is recognised as the first *patriarch*, i.e. *founding father*, of the Jewish people, or as they were originally known, the *Hebrews*.

At that time, the Hebrews were just a small group of travelling merchants who led long trains of camels and donkeys loaded down with goods from one trading post to another. This was the source of their name. As they walked, their leather sandals and their animals' hooves kicked up a lot of dust, which settled on them. Other people began calling them *Abiru*, meaning 'dusty ones'. In time *Abiru* became *Hebrew*.

It is believed that Abraham was inspired by God to lead a small group of Hebrews across the Fertile Crescent from Ur in Mesopotamia to settle in the place they came to call The *Promised Land*.

Abraham and his family, servants and animals moved through the Fertile Crescent, camping near water points.

THE PROMISED LAND

Name

The *Promised Land* has been known by several different names down through the centuries:

- In the time of Abraham it was known as the *Land of Canaan*.
- When David and Solomon ruled as kings, it was called *Israel* (meaning 'God strives'). This is the name by which it is known today.
- In the time of Jesus it was known as *Palestine*, a name taken from the Philistines, an ancient people who had once occupied the area.

Size

The Promised Land measured just 150 miles in length and anywhere from thirty miles to fifty miles in width from its western coast to its eastern border. Its total area was only about 7,000 square miles. Today, this whole area can easily be travelled from one end to the other by car in just a few hours. Indeed, a Jewish person 2,000 years ago could have walked the same journey in less than five days.

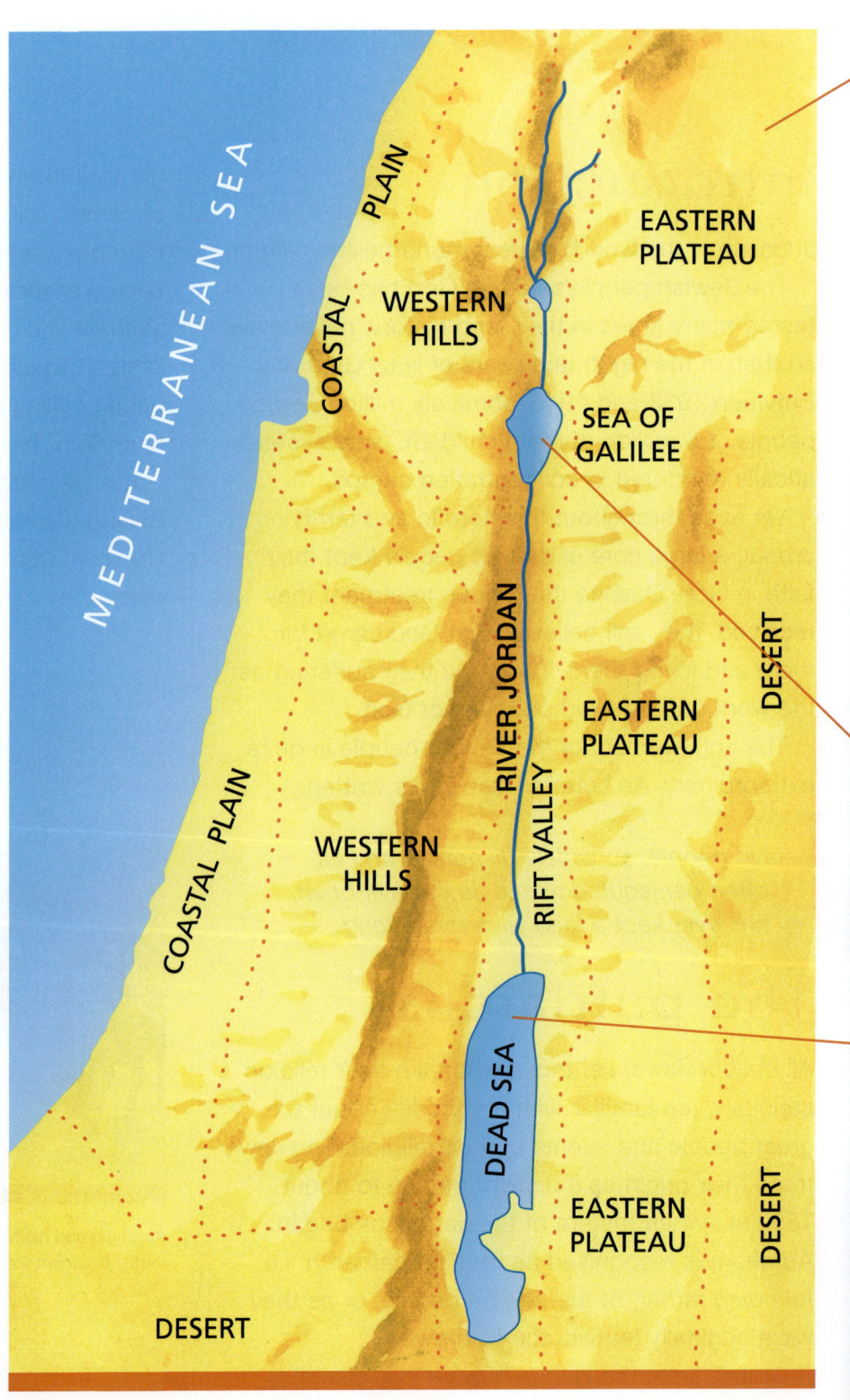

26 All About Faith

Landscape and climate

The terrain falls into three almost parallel zones. From west to east they are:

- the coastal plain
- the western hills
- the rift valley through which the River Jordan flows.

To the east of this lies a great plateau and beyond this and to the south there are vast expanses of scorching desert.

There are basically two seasons: the hot, dry summer (May to September) and the cool, wet winter (October to April).

Land of contrasts

Though small in size, it remains a land of remarkably diverse landscapes.

- The land around the Sea of Galilee in the north is generally green and fertile. This area remains home to many thriving farming and fishing communities.
- In contrast, the area around the Dead Sea in the south is a harsh wilderness with temperatures reaching 50°C.

The God of the Hebrews

At first the Hebrews believed, like other nations at that time, that each people had its *own* God. Only gradually did they come to realise that there was only *one* God, *their* God, who was the God of *all* people.

They came to believe that God* is:

- a *pure spirit* (a being who does not have a physical body)
- a *person* (someone with whom people can form a relationship)
- *faithful* (worthy of people's trust)
- *perfect* (completely good)
- *merciful* (one who loves and forgives the repentant sinner)
- a *guide* (one who offers people love and support in the face of life's challenges)
- *the creator* (the one who made the universe)
- *universal* (the God of all people)
- *all powerful* (nothing is beyond God's power)
- *eternal* (one who lives outside of time, was never born, does not age and will never die).

*This view of God is shared today by Jews, Christians and Muslims.

The covenant

The Hebrew sacred texts tell the story of how God made a *covenant* (a sacred agreement) with Abraham and his descendants. God promised that if the Hebrews faithfully worshipped him and kept his laws, then he would guarantee their ownership of the Promised Land.

Abraham and his descendants would be God's *chosen people*. This did *not* mean that God was declaring them to be better than any other people. Rather, God had selected them and invited them to fulfil a *special mission* in human history – they were to tell the whole world that there was only *one* God and, by living good lives, encourage others to believe this too. In doing this they would prepare the world for the time when *all* people would come to know and worship God.

Questions

1. By what name were the Jews originally known?
2. What does the word '*patriarch*' mean? Who was given this title?
3. Why did Abraham lead his followers to the *Land of Canaan*?
4. Explain the meaning of the name given to the modern state of *Israel*.
5. Where was the name *Palestine* taken from?
6. What was the size of Palestine?
7. Describe the terrain and climate of Palestine.
8. What did the Hebrews come to believe about God?
9. What is a *covenant*?
10. Explain the *covenant* God made with Abraham and his descendants.
11. What is meant by describing the Hebrews as *God's chosen people*?

From guests to slaves

When Abraham and his followers settled in the Promised Land, they had hoped to build a better life there. However, their descendants had to endure great hardships caused by long droughts that ruined their crops and devastated the grasslands which supported their livestock.

Around 1700 BC, the Hebrews decided to migrate into the fertile Nile Delta region of Egypt, which was rich in grain.

At first the Hebrews were made welcome and the pharaohs (Egyptian kings) employed them as craftsmen. Later, however, the Hebrews were forced into slavery.

For the next three centuries the Hebrews in Egypt suffered terrible hardships. The one thing that kept them going, however, was their unique and deep faith in God. They trusted that God would not desert them. They were not disappointed. It seemed that God had finally sent someone who would lead them to freedom – Moses.

Moses

Moses was a man of great intelligence and goodness. He had an extraordinary experience of the power and mystery of God, which changed his whole outlook on life. God appeared to Moses in the form of a bush that was on fire but did not burn.

After this, Moses found that his faith in God gave him the courage needed to lead the movement seeking freedom for the Hebrews. God called on Moses to lead his chosen people back to the Promised Land.

The Exodus

According to the Hebrews' sacred texts, God gave Moses the power to make miracles. Moses confronted the Egyptian pharaoh and demanded that he set the Hebrew people free. When the pharaoh refused, Egypt was struck by a series of disasters.

These events shattered the pharaoh's confidence and he finally gave in, allowing the Hebrews to leave Egypt altogether. This great movement of the Hebrew people back to the Promised Land is called the *Exodus* (meaning '*the going forth*').

Moses and the burning bush from which God spoke to him.

The law of God

The Exodus was the most important event in Hebrew history. While journeying home to the Promised Land, the Hebrews had to pass through the harsh, scorching terrain of the Sinai desert. During this time, the Hebrews *renewed* their covenant with God.

God promised them the Land of Canaan. In return, the Hebrews promised to faithfully love and serve God by keeping his laws. These laws were summarised in ten short and simple *commandments* which the Hebrews believed God himself had given to Moses. These *Ten Commandments*, as they have been called ever since, are at the very heart of not just the Jewish religion, but of Christianity and Islam as well. (For a listing of the Ten Commandments, see Chapter 42.)

Questions

1. What event led many Hebrews to move from the Land of Canaan to Egypt?
2. Why did the pharaoh change his mind, set the Hebrews free and allow them to return to the Promised Land?
3. What is the meaning of the word '*exodus*'?

Israel established

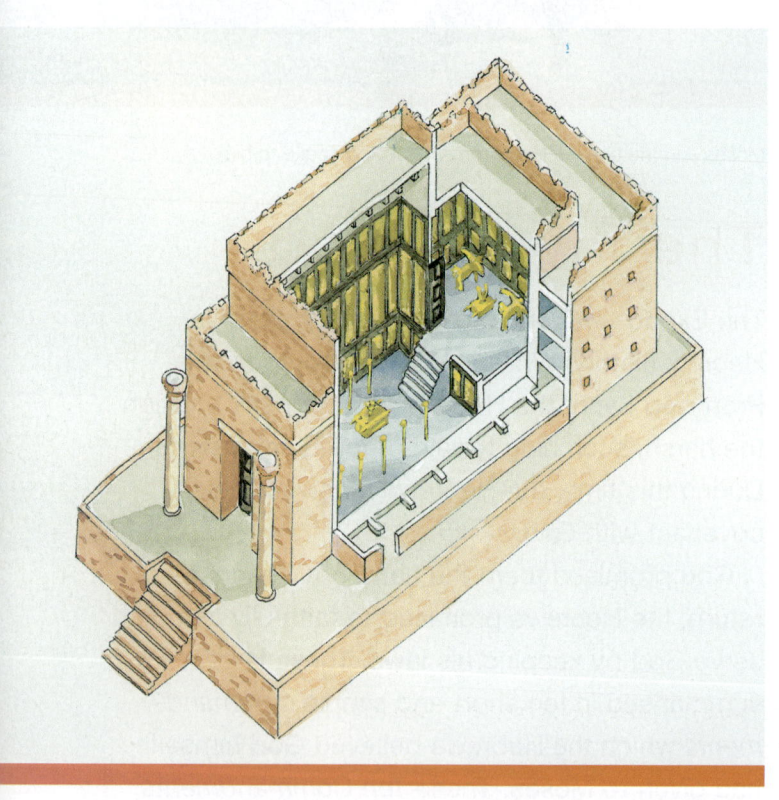

An artist's impression of Solomon's Temple. The main room was the Holy Place and contained the incense altar, the table of showbread and five pairs of candlesticks. The Holy of Holies was the smaller room furthest from the main doors and was entered by a priest just once a year. It housed the Ark of the Covenant, which was overshadowed on either side by winged creatures. All interior walls were lined with pine covered with gold.

For almost 200 years after they had reached the Promised Land, the Hebrews had to fight a series of wars before they gained control of the area. Finally, they established an independent kingdom called *Israel*. For a time it prospered. They were ruled over by a series of kings, the most important of whom were David and Solomon.

David established Israel's capital city, Jerusalem. There his son, Solomon, built a Temple. This served as a resting place for the *Ark of the Covenant*, the casket in which, it was said, the stone tablets on which God had carved the *Ten Commandments* were kept.

Many Hebrews, however, grew unhappy with Solomon. After Solomon died in 930 BC, the kingdom split in two: *Israel* to the north and a separate state called *Judah*, with its capital at Jerusalem, in the south.

The prophets

The Prophet Isaiah by Simone Martini.

Today, the word '*prophet*' is often used to describe someone who claims that he/she can accurately predict future events. For the ancient Hebrews, however, a prophet was

> *a holy man who had received messages from God which he then preached to the people.*

30 All About Faith

In the years following the division of the kingdom into two separate and often quarrelling states, a number of prophets, most notably *Elijah*, *Amos*, *Hosea*, *Jeremiah*, *Ezekiel* and *Isaiah*, came forward to offer guidance to the Hebrews.

These prophets reminded the people of their duty to love God and do good to one another and warned the Hebrews about the dangers of fighting amongst themselves.

A tempting target

The Hebrews grew so preoccupied with their own internal problems that they forgot that their land had always been a tempting target for their powerful neighbours.

Why? Though covering only a small area, the Hebrew kingdoms occupied a geographical position of great military and economic importance. Their land was the meeting point for three continents, a crossroads where the great overland trade routes of the ancient world – from Europe to the north, Asia to the east and Africa to the south – met.

Disaster

The Hebrews refused to listen to the prophets' warnings. The rival Hebrew kingdoms of Israel in the north and Judah in the south were each, in turn, easily conquered by more powerful neighbours:

○ The Israelites were conquered and scattered throughout the Assyrian empire and simply ceased to exist as a people, disappearing into the mists of time.

○ The *Jews*, as the inhabitants of Judah were now known, witnessed the destruction of their Temple and were marched away into exile to work as slaves in the great city of Babylon.

There, without the Temple, a homeland or a king, the Jews learned to depend upon God as their only refuge.

Half a century later, however, the Jews were freed from slavery, returned to the Promised Land and rebuilt the Temple.

Jews being led away as slaves to Babylon.

The promised Messiah

In the years following their return, the Jews suffered many setbacks at the hands of successive conquerors: Persians, Greeks and Romans. The once-great kingdom of David and Solomon was reduced to a pale shadow of its former glory. It existed merely as a small province of someone else's vast empire. The Jews themselves divided once more into rival groups. *They needed a leader* – someone who would unite them. The prophets told them that God had promised to send them one. They gave this promised leader the title *Messiah*.

The title 'Messiah' comes from the Hebrew '*Moshiach*', meaning '*anointed one*'. In ancient times, kings and high priests were anointed with oil to show that they had been chosen by God to fulfil an important task.

The Jewish people believe that the Messiah has yet to come. Christians, however, believe that in Jesus of Nazareth the Messiah has already arrived and that he will return again at the end of time.

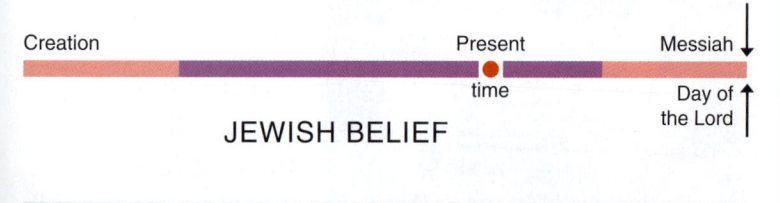

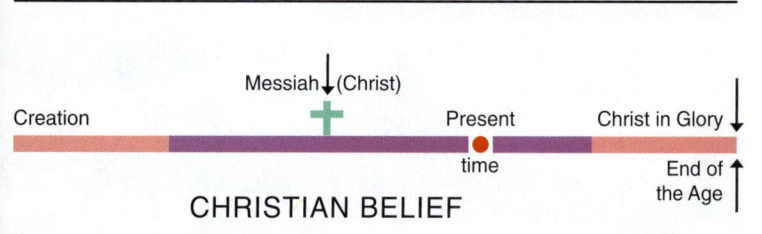

Creation — Present time — Messiah / Day of the Lord
JEWISH BELIEF

Creation — Messiah (Christ) — Present time — Christ in Glory / End of the Age
CHRISTIAN BELIEF

The coming of the Messiah according to the beliefs of Jews and Christians.

Years of trial

In AD 70 the Jewish people rose up against their Roman rulers. This rebellion was swiftly and ruthlessly crushed and the rebuilt Temple was destroyed.

Then, in AD 135, the Jews were forcibly dispersed throughout the world, thus beginning what is known as the *Diaspora* (dispersion).

After many centuries of persecution and upheaval, the greater majority of modern Jews have settled in the state of *Israel*, the land which they believe God promised to Abraham and his descendants. There are also Jewish communities scattered across the globe, most notably in North America and Europe.

Questions

1. Name the two most important and successful Hebrew kings.
2. What was the *Ark of the Covenant*?
3. What happened to the kingdom after Solomon's death?
4. What did the Hebrews believe about their prophets?
5. What kind of things did the prophets say to the Hebrews?
6. Why were the Hebrew kingdoms of Israel and Judah tempting targets for their powerful neighbours?
7. Why did the Jews believe they needed a great leader?
8. What title did they give to this great leader?
9. (a) What event happened in AD 70?
   (b) What was the *Diaspora*?
   (c) When did it occur?

Chapter Five

Judaism: Sacred Text and Worship

The Dead Sea Scrolls

Caves in the Qumran wilderness.

In 1947 some Bedouin Arabs were smuggling goats into southern Israel. As they passed through the desolate Qumran wilderness near the Dead Sea, one of their goats strayed away from the herd.

A young boy was sent to bring the animal back. He had to climb along steep, rocky hillsides to catch up with it. As he passed the opening of a large cave, the boy paused for a moment. He picked up a stone and threw it into the cave's dark interior. To his great surprise he then heard the sound of something breaking. The boy summoned up his courage and went in to explore the cave.

Inside the cave he found a row of tall clay jars. Each jar contained bundles of *manuscripts* (handwritten documents). These manuscripts were sewn together in long scrolls and wrapped in linen. They are now known as the *Dead Sea Scrolls*.

When these scrolls were carefully unrolled and examined by scholars in Jerusalem, they proved to be a find of enormous importance. The scrolls were discovered to be handwritten copies of the Hebrew *scriptures* (sacred texts). They had been hidden in the cave by Jewish scholars some time in the middle of the first century AD. The identity of the people who put them in this hiding place has been a matter of some controversy among scholars. However, they were most likely hidden to prevent their destruction by the Romans.

Questions

1. Who discovered the *Dead Sea Scrolls*?
2. Where were they discovered?
3. How had they been stored?
4. What was written on the Dead Sea Scrolls?
5. When were they hidden?
6. Why were they hidden?

The Tenakh

In the beginning, the Jews passed on important stories and teachings from one generation to the next by word of mouth (by *oral tradition*). Eventually, Jewish scholars began to write these stories and teachings down. Their sacred writings came to consist of thirty-nine books. These were finally gathered into one volume, which is called the *Tenakh*.

The Tenakh is written in Hebrew and has traditionally been divided into three sections:

○ the *Torah*

○ the *Nevi'im*

○ the *Ketuvim*.

It was from the initial letters of each of these three sections – *T*, *N* and *K* – that the title Tenakh was derived.

The oldest complete manuscript of the Tenakh was discovered near the Dead Sea. Today, it is housed and displayed in the building known as the *Sanctuary of the Book* in Jerusalem.

We shall now examine each of the *Tenakh's* three sections.

1. The Torah

This can be translated as either *'instruction'*, *'law'* or *'teachings'*. The Torah is also known as the *Pentateuch*, from the Greek word for 'five', because it consists of five books: *Genesis*, *Exodus*, *Leviticus*, *Numbers* and *Deuteronomy*.

The Torah contains:

○ the story of the Jewish people from the time of Abraham until their return to the Promised Land after their escape from Egypt

○ the rules according to which all Jews should try to live their lives.

The Torah is considered by most Jews to be the holiest part of the Tenakh. This is because they believe that it was given directly by God to Moses.

2. The Nevi'im

This means *'the prophets'*. The Nevi'im consists of two parts:

○ *The Former Prophets* (four books) traces the story of the Jews after the death of Moses

○ *The Latter Prophets* (also four books) is concerned with encouraging the Jews to live up to their part of the covenant Abraham and Moses made with God.

3. The Ketuvim

This translates as *'the writings'*. The Ketuvim contains the *Proverbs* (wise sayings) and the *Psalms* (poems and songs).

According to tradition, most of the Psalms were supposed to have been composed by King David. The Psalms speak in loving terms to God, who they praise as the ruler of the universe.

Questions

1. What is meant by *oral tradition*?
2. What is the Tenakh?
3. In what language is the Tenakh written?
4. Where does the name '*Tenakh*' derive from? What does it refer to?
5. (a) Where was the oldest complete manuscript of the Tenakh discovered?
   (b) Where is it now housed and displayed?
6. What does the title '*Torah*' mean?
7. Why is the Torah considered by many Jews to be the holiest part of the Tenakh?
8. What are the contents of the Torah?
9. What does the title '*Nevi'im*' mean?
10. What matters is the Nevi'im concerned with?
11. What is contained in the Ketuvim?
12. According to Jewish tradition, who is supposed to have composed most of the *Pslams*?

Prayer

Portrait of a Rabbi by Marc Chagall.

Jews pray to demonstrate their commitment to keeping the *covenant* (sacred agreement) which God made with their ancestors.

Following the example of the patriarchs, Jews pray three times a day:

- *in the morning*, because Abraham prayed early in the morning
- *in the afternoon*, because Isaac stopped his work to pray in the afternoon
- *in the evening*, because Jacob thanked God in the evening.

Judaism: Sacred Text and Worship 35

The symbols of prayer in Judaism

The yarmulke

This is a *skullcap* worn by Jewish men to demonstrate respect for God. It reminds Jews that God's wisdom is vastly greater than that of humans. While there is no religious rule requiring Jewish males to wear the *yarmulke*, most do so because they believe that praying bareheaded shows serious disrespect to God.

The tefillen

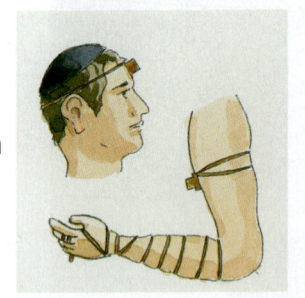

These are two cube-shaped leather boxes, each of which contain four passages from the Tenakh, i.e. Exodus 13:1–10 and 11–16, and Deuteronomy 6:4–9 and 11:13–21. One box is strapped to a Jewish person's forehead to remind him/her to *think* about what his/her religion teaches. The other box is tied around his/her upper forearm, next to his/her heart, to remind him/her to *act* on what his/her religion teaches.

The tallit

This is a prayer shawl made of silk or wool. It is usually coloured blue and white, with fringes attached to its four corners, as laid down in Numbers 15:37–41. The *tallit* is worn at morning prayers only and is draped across a man's shoulders. This man is reading from the *siddur*, the official Jewish prayer book.

Questions

1. Why do Jews pray?
2. (a) How often are Jews expected to pray each day?
   (b) Why do they pray at these times?
3. Explain the meaning of the following symbols worn by Jews when praying:
   (a) the yarmulke
   (b) the tefillen
   (c) the tallit.
4. What is *the siddur* (see illustration)?

The synagogue

A Jewish place of worship is a simple rectangular building called a *synagogue*. The word '*synagogue*' may have its origin in the Greek word '*synagein*', which means '*to gather together*'.

After the destruction of the Temple in Jerusalem by the Romans in AD 70 and the scattering of the Jewish people in AD 135, the synagogue became the centre of Jewish community life.

Certain features of a synagogue recall Jewish worship in the long-destroyed Temple:

○ *the layout of a synagogue's prayer hall*, which is based on that of the Temple

○ *the direction in which the synagogue faces*, i.e. towards Jerusalem, where the Temple once stood.

A synagogue serves *three* main functions. It acts as:

1. *a house of prayer*, where services are held each Sabbath and festival day
2. *a place of education*, where children learn Hebrew and study the Tenakh
3. *a community centre* where Jews can meet for a variety of purposes, such as youth groups, women's groups or charitable organisations.

All About Faith

Jewish males are expected to attend the synagogue as often as possible. This is because public congregational prayers can only be said if there is a *minyan* (a group of no less than ten adult males) present.

Shabbat

According to the Tenakh, God made the world in six days and rested on the seventh day (see Genesis 2:1–4). God commanded that the seventh day of the week should be a day for prayer and relaxation for all Jews (see Exodus 20:8–11).

Jews refer to the seventh day of their week as *Shabbat*, i.e. the *Sabbath day*.

In summary, *Shabbat* is the name given to the Jewish weekly day of prayer and rest, which begins at sundown on Friday and runs through until nightfall on Saturday.

Shabbat is of vital importance to Jews because it:

○ reminds them that God is the creator of all life
○ encourages them to keep the covenant that God made with their ancestors
○ provides them with time for worship and the study of the Torah.

Many devout Jews believe that all business activities, shopping, housework and the use of most technology should be avoided on the Sabbath day.

Most Jews attend a service in the synagogue on Saturday morning, while some do so on Friday evening. The service consists of:

○ readings from the Torah
○ prayers and hymns
○ a sermon on the readings.

The rabbi

The title 'rabbi' means '*my master*' or '*my teacher*'. A rabbi is someone employed by a Jewish community to have authority over running its synagogue. A rabbi is usually male, but some Jewish communities employ a female rabbi.

It is important to note that a rabbi is *not* a priest. The Jewish priesthood died out after the Temple was destroyed in AD 70. A rabbi is a *layperson* who has studied for several years to assume a leadership role in the Jewish community.

The rabbi performs weddings and conducts funeral services, visits the sick and may act as chaplain to a school, hospital or prison. Although the rabbi gives the sermon at synagogue services, another person called the *cantor* leads the congregation in singing hymns and chanting prayers.

Questions

1. Explain the possible origin of the word '*synagogue*'.
2. Identify the different features of a synagogue that recall the Temple in Jerusalem.
3. What are the main functions of a synagogue?
4. Why are Jewish males expected to attend a synagogue as often as possible?
5. What is Shabbat? When does it begin and end?
6. Why is Shabbat important to Jews?
7. What kind of activities do many devout Jews believe should be avoided on Shabbat?
8. When do Jews attend the synagogue on Shabbat?
9. What does a Shabbat service in the synagogue consist of?
10. Explain the meaning of the title '*rabbi*'.
11. Who employs the rabbi?
12. What is the rabbi's role?
13. What is the role of the *cantor*?

Judaism: Sacred Text and Worship

The synagogue

Seating

In traditional synagogues, men and women sit separately, though in some they may sit together. Here the women are seated in the gallery.

Symbol of Judaism

This is the *Magen David*, the six-pointed star or shield of David.

Memorial

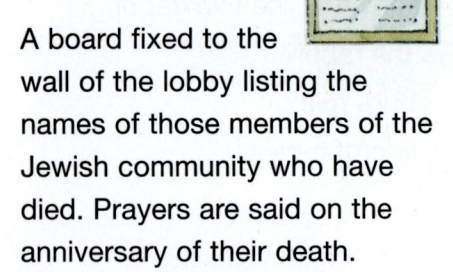

A board fixed to the wall of the lobby listing the names of those members of the Jewish community who have died. Prayers are said on the anniversary of their death.

Rabbi and cantor

Each has a role to play in Jewish worship:

○ the rabbi gives the sermon
○ the cantor leads the congregation in singing the hymns and chanting the prayers.

38   All About Faith

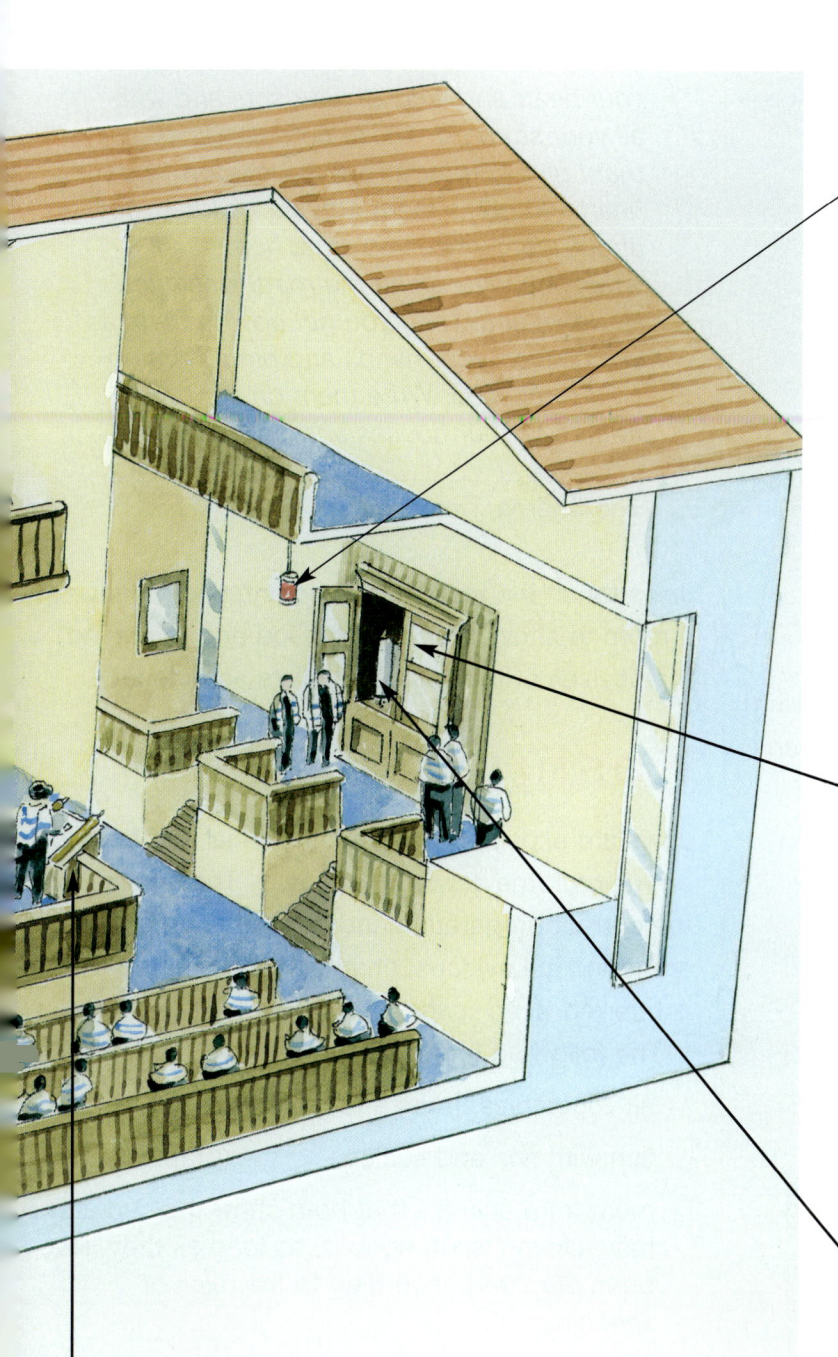

Ner Tamid

Ner Tamid means 'the perpetual lamp' or 'the eternal light'. It hangs above and before the Ark and represents the *menorah* (the seven-branch candlestick), which was always lit in the Temple.

Aron Hakodesh

This translates as '*the Ark*'. It is a special alcove or cupboard fitted with doors and set into the wall of the synagogue that faces Jerusalem. It contains the *Sefer Torah*.

Sefer Torah

This is a set of parchment scrolls on which the Torah has been hand-written. These scrolls are treated with great respect. A silver pointer called a *yad* is used when they are being read to avoid finger contact with the precious parchment and to show respect.

Bimah

This is a reading desk on a raised platform that is positioned near the centre of the hall. It is from here that the Torah and prayers are read and the sermon preached. Seating is usually arranged around three sides of the Bimah.

Judaism: Sacred Text and Worship

Questions

1. What is the *Magen David*?
2. How are people seated in a synagogue?
3. Explain each of the following features of a synagogue.
   (a) Ner Tamid
   (b) Aron Hakodesh
   (c) Sefer Torah
   (d) Bimah
   (e) memorial.
4. Why is a *yad* used when reading the Torah?

The home

Although the synagogue plays a very important role, it is the *home* that is the main focus of Jewish life. This is because Jews view the home as *much more* than just a place in which people live. The home is a place into which God is invited and welcomed. As such, Jews consider the home to be a special, *sacred* place.

The most visible symbol of this belief is the *mezuzah*, which is found throughout Jewish homes.

The mezuzah

The *mezuzah* is a small decorated container which is fixed to the upper third of all doorposts in a Jewish home, with only the following exceptions:

- the toilet
- the bathroom
- the garage.

The mezuzah contains the verses of the *Shema*.

A mezuzah.

Here, O Israel: The Lord our God, the Lord is one. Love the Lord your God with all your heart and with all your soul and with all your strength. These commandments that I give you today are to be upon your hearts. Impress them on your children. Talk about them when you sit at home and when you walk along the road, when you lie down and when you get up. Tie them as symbols on your hands and bind them on your foreheads. Write them on the doorframes of your houses and on your gates.

The Shema, Deuteronomy 6:4–9

Jews touch the mezuzah when entering or leaving a room to show their love for God and to remind themselves of their Jewish beliefs and identity.

Kashrut

Jews are expected to follow a special diet based on *Kashrut* (the Jewish food laws). These rules for the correct preparation and consumption of food are found in Leviticus, chapter 17. Permitted food is referred to as *kosher*.

The following foods are kosher:

- all vegetables, fruits and grains
- fish with fins and scales
- meat from animals that both chew the cud and have cloven (split) hooves, as long as they have been prepared according to the rules of *shechita*.

Shechita involves slaughtering an animal with only one cut across the throat with a razor-sharp blade. Then all the blood is drained from the dead animal.

It is *forbidden* to eat meat and dairy products together or for some time after eating one or the other. However, foods that are not meat or dairy may be eaten with either. Separate utensils should be used in kitchens to prepare meat and dairy products.

It is also forbidden to eat either pork or meat from the hindquarters of any animal.

Jews believe that keeping *Kashrut* helps them to preserve their distinct identity and to encourage obedience to God's laws.

Questions

1. Where is the *main focus* of Jewish life?
2. Why do Jews view the home as *much more* than just a place in which people live?
3. What is a *mezuzah*? What does it contain?
4. Why do Jews touch the mezuzah when entering or leaving a room?
5. What is *Kashrut*?
6. What is the name given to *permitted food*?
7. Name three types of permitted food.
8. What is involved in *shechita*?
9. What is *forbidden* to eat?
10. Why do Jews believe that keeping *Kashrut* is important?

Naming and circumcision

Jews consider children to be a blessing and a gift from God (see Psalm 127). Children are seen as the hope for a better future and as the inheritors of the *covenant* (sacred agreement) God made with Abraham.

When a baby boy is eight days old, he is formally named at a ceremony held in the local synagogue. The name chosen always has a meaning. For example, *Isaiah* means '*God is salvation*' and *Joshua* means '*saviour*'.

On the same day the ritual of *Brit Milah* (*the Covenant of the Circumcision*) takes place. This involves the boy being *circumcised*, i.e. the loose foreskin over the penis is cut off. This operation is carried out by a specially trained man called a *mohel*.

Jews believe that circumcision is necessary for all *male* members because it is taught that God demanded it of them when he made the covenant with Abraham (see Genesis 17:9–14).

Jewish *girls* usually receive their names on the first Sabbath following their birth. However, in some Jewish communities, girls receive their names at a special ceremony called *Zeved Habet* (meaning 'the gift of a daughter') when they are seven days old.

Becoming an adult

Coming of age. A Jewish girl surrounded by family and friends in the synagoge reads from the Torah to show she is grown up enough to be *bat mitzvah*.

Judaism: Sacred Text and Worship

Judaism recognises that girls generally mature *earlier* than boys. As a result, girls are considered adults at the age of *twelve*, while boys are declared adults at *thirteen*. Each take part in separate public ceremonies to mark their new status as *adults*:

- a boy becomes *bar mitzvah* (Son of the Commandments)
- a girl becomes *bat mitzvah* (Daughter of the Commandments).

Boys and girls spend several years studying in preparation for this day. They must learn Hebrew so that they can read from the Torah (the first five books of the Tenakh) and be able to lead a prayer service.

Following these ceremonies in the synagogue, family and friends share a celebratory meal.

The *bar mitzvah* and *bat mitzvah* are important occasions intended to mark people's willingness to commit themselves to faithfully living out the teachings of Judaism in daily life.

Questions

1. What is the Jewish attitude to children?
2. When and where is a male child named?
3. Explain the meaning of the following male names: (a) *Isaiah* (b) *Joshua*.
4. What is *Brit Milah*?
5. Explain the following terms: (a) *circumcision* (b) *mohel*.
6. What is *Zeved Habet*?
7. When are (a) *girls* and (b) *boys* considered adults in Judaism? Why?
8. Jewish boys and girls each take part in separate ceremonies to mark their passage into adulthood. What is the name of the ceremony for (a) a girl (b) a boy? State the meaning of each.
9. How do Jewish boys and girls prepare for these ceremonies?
10. What usually happens *after* these ceremonies?

Jewish festivals

Right The religious festivals of the Jewish year.

Rosh Hashanah	This marks the start of the Jewish New Year.
Yom Kippur	A period of fasting lasting for twenty-four hours. Jews reflect on their lives and seek forgiveness from God and from anyone they have harmed or offended.
Sukkot	Also referred to as *Tabernacles*, this commemorates the time when the Hebrews lived in temporary shelters in the desert as they travelled to the Promised Land and how God cared for them during this time.

42 All About Faith

Hannukah   This eight-day *Festival of Lights* is held in winter. Jews remember their victory over foreign invaders and the rededication of the Temple in 165 BC. An eight-branch candlestick is lit for this festival to celebrate how the *menorah* (the Temple's seven-branch candlestick) stayed alight for eight days, even though it should only have done so for *one* day. This festival also symbolises the survival of Judaism in spite of all its people have had to endure.

Shavuoth   Also known as the *Feast of Weeks*, this celebrates God giving the Ten Commandments to Moses. Children usually begin their study of the Torah at this time.

Pesach   Also referred to as *Passover*. For Jews in Israel it is a seven-day festival, while it lasts eight days for Jews living elsewhere.

The name 'Passover' comes from the story of how the angel of death '*passed over*' (left unharmed) the Hebrew children in the last of the ten plagues. This forced the Egyptian pharaoh to release the Hebrews from slavery and allow them to return to the Promised Land.

The high point of this festival is the *Seder* (the Passover meal), which is held in Jewish homes on the first evening of the festival. Families make a special effort to come together to share this meal.

Special synagogue services are held to mark this festival. The account of the Exodus in the Torah is read and Psalms praising God are chanted.

Rosh Hashanah and Yom Kippur are ushered in with the sound of a ram's-horn trumpet, or *shofar*.

The Seder at Pesach.

Yom Kippur in the Synagoge by Bernard Picart.

Question

1. Write a brief note on each of the following Jewish festivals.
   (a) *Rosh Hashanah*   (d) *Hannukah*
   (b) *Yom Kippur*   (e) *Shavuoth*
   (c) *Sukkot*   (f) *Pesach*

The Seder

The Passover meal is called the *Seder* (meaning 'order') because it always follows the same set pattern that has been handed down from one generation to the next.

In preparation for the Seder, Jewish families remove all traces of *hametz* (leavened/yeast

Judaism: Sacred Text and Worship   43

bread) from their homes. Special plates, glassware and cutlery which have had no previous contact with yeasted bread are used.

The Seder begins with the head of the household saying a prayer called the *Kiddush*. Everyone takes parsley which has been dipped in salt water. The head of the household then breaks the *matzah* (a loaf of unleavened bread) and shares it out among those present.

During the meal, wine is consumed with the food. However, one glass of wine is poured but left *untouched*. This symbolises (represents) the belief that, at some future time, the prophet Elijah will return and announce the arrival of the Messiah.

The youngest person present then asks:

Why is this night different from all other nights?

The head of the household responds by reading the story of the Passover and the Exodus, telling of how God freed their Hebrew ancestors from slavery in Egypt.

A Seder plate

This is a traditional Seder plate. It is used at Pesach (Passover) each year. It has a special place for each of the *six* dishes prepared for this occasion. They are:

1. *Matzah* (unleavened bread): This symbolises the fact that the Jews left Egypt in a hurry and did not have time to bake yeasted bread.
2. *Parsley dipped in salt water*: This represents the tears of the Hebrew slaves.
3. *Bitter herbs*: This is a reminder of the bitterness of 400 years of slavery.
4. *Haroset*: A mixture of apples, nuts, cinnamon and wine. It symbolises the mortar Jews used to make bricks for the Egyptians, but it tastes sweet, like freedom from slavery.

Two other dishes are prepared but *not* eaten:

5. *Roasted shank-bone of lamb*: This was the meat the Hebrews ate on their last night in Egypt.
6. *An egg*: This is a symbol of new life in the Promised Land, made possible by the goodness of God.

Questions

1. Why is the Passover meal called the *Seder*?
2. How do Jewish families prepare for the Seder?
3. Why is a glass of wine left *untouched* on the table during the Seder?
4. What question does the youngest person ask?
5. What is the response to this question?
6. (a) Name each of the six dishes prepared for the Seder.
   (b) Explain the meaning of each one.

Part Three

THE ORIGINS OF CHRISTIANITY

Chapter Six

The Bible

Introduction

The word 'bible' comes from the Greek word 'biblia', meaning 'books'. The Bible is not really one book but an entire library of books that have been bound together in a single volume. The Bible is divided into two parts: the Old Testament* and the New Testament.

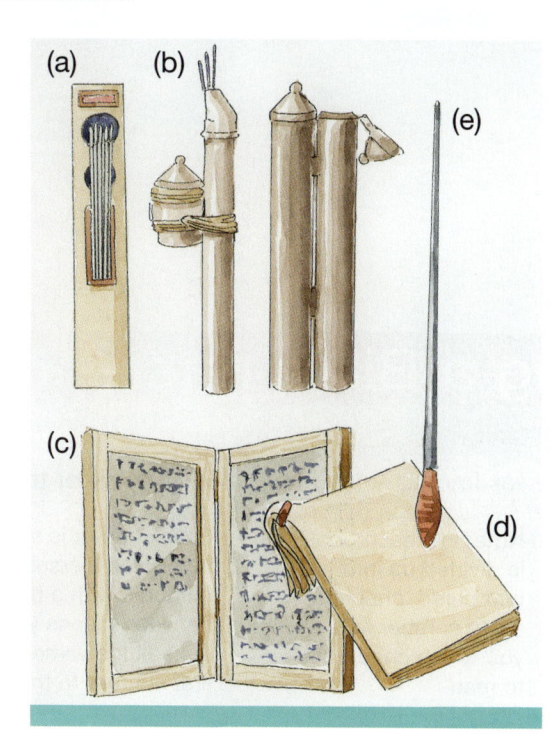

Utensils used for writing: (a) a holder for pen and ink (b) two types of containers for ink, the second one for two colours of ink (c) a writing tablet (d) a booklet of papyrus sheets (e) a metal pen.

*N.B.
The Old Testament is basically the same as the Jewish Tenakh, except that its parts are arranged in a different order.

The meaning of 'testament'

The word 'testament' is derived from the Latin 'testamentum', which means 'covenant', i.e. a solemn and binding agreement between two parties, in this case between God and human beings.

In the Old Testament, the Jews are identified as God's chosen people.

Christians believe that the birth of Jesus of Nazareth marked the beginning of a new covenant, or New Testament, between God and *all* people. It is for this reason that the authors of the New Testament emphasise that *all nations are God's people, if they live according to God's ways*.

The New Testament

The New Testament consists of twenty-seven books, written during the latter half of the first century AD, which are divided up as follows:

- *The Four Gospels* record Jesus' life and teachings as remembered by those who knew him.
- *The Acts of the Apostles* describe the rapid spread of Christianity beyond Palestine.
- *The Epistles* are twenty-one letters written by the leaders of the early Christian churches offering guidance to their communities, encouraging them to remain faithful, resolving disputes and clarifying Christian teachings.

- *The Book of Revelation* (or *Apocalypse*) is a series of visions depicting the battle between the forces of good and evil, which predict the triumph of God and the final judgment of humanity at the end of time.

The earliest manuscripts

We do *not* possess a complete original manuscript of the New Testament that dates from the first century AD. The modern printed New Testament is based on later copies of the original documents. The earliest complete manuscript of the New Testament is the *Codex Sinaiticus*, which was preserved in the monastery of St Catherine in the Sinai Desert and which dates from the fourth century AD.

Archaeologists have discovered fragments of copies of the New Testament that were produced before the Codex Sinaiticus. The earliest known undisputed fragment is the *Rylands Papyrus*, which dates from AD 134.

Rylands Papyrus.

Questions

1. What does the word '*bible*' mean?
2. Name the two parts of the Bible.
3. Explain the meaning of the word '*testament*' as used in the Bible.
4. List the four parts of the *New Testament* and write a brief description of each.
5. (a) What is the name given to the oldest known *complete manuscript* of the New Testament?
   (b) Where was it preserved?
   (c) How old is it?
6. What is the name given to the *earliest* known undisputed *fragment* of the New Testament?

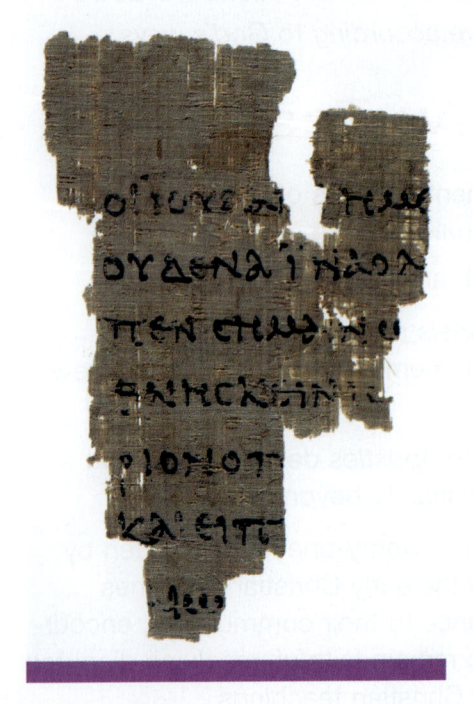

Finding a Bible reference

There is a code for finding your place in any book of the Bible.

This is the name of the particular book.

Note how each book is divided up into numbered 'chapters' – this number tells you which chapter to read.

Each chapter is split up into numbered 'verses' – two numbers with a dash between means you have to read all the verses from the first number to the second.

Luke 11:9–13

Meaning: God cares as deeply for everyone as the best parents do for their children.

48 All About Faith

The four Gospels

The New Testament begins with the four Gospels. The word 'gospel' is derived from the Old English 'God-spell', meaning 'good news'.

Since earliest times, Christians have associated the four Gospels with the names of *Mark*, *Matthew*, *Luke* and *John*. There are good reasons for accepting them as the authors, though some scholars have voiced reservations.

Each author offers a different version of the *same* story:

- *Mark* is thought to have accompanied the apostle Peter to Rome.
- *Matthew* was a tax collector whom Jesus chose as one of his twelve apostles.
- *Luke* was a Greek doctor.
- *John* was the youngest and perhaps closest friend to Jesus among the twelve apostles.

The Gospel writers are also referred to as the four *evangelists* (*proclaimers of the good news*).

Dates

It is difficult to give precise dates for the writing of the Gospels. The following are the dates accepted by many Christian scripture scholars.

circa AD 30	The death and resurrection of Jesus.
64	The Gospel of *Mark* was written.
70–80	The Gospels of *Matthew, Luke* and the *Acts of the Apostles* were written.
90	The Gospel of *John* was written.

Matthew: an angel   Mark: a lion
Luke: a bull   John: an eagle

Each of the four evangelists is associated with a particular symbol, each based on a figure mentioned in the Old Testament book of Ezekiel.

Questions

1. Explain the meaning of (a) *gospel* (b) *evangelist*.
2. Name the four evangelists.
3. Identify the figure associated with each of the four evangelists.
4. When were each of the four *Gospels* written?

Why the Gospels were written

The early Christian community needed to compile and accurately record the sayings of Jesus and any important stories about him for several reasons:

- As time passed, those Christians who had known Jesus began to die. There was a fear that vital information might be lost.
- The Gospel accounts explained the meaning of Christianity to interested people and corrected any mistaken ideas about what Christians believed.

The Bible

- They provided readings for use at Christian worship. To the present day the Christian Churches give priority or a special place of honour to the Gospels over the other parts of the New Testament because the Gospels are our principal sources of information about the life of Jesus.

Why four?

Christians believe that there is really only one Gospel (Good News) but that the evangelists just produced four different versions of it. Why?

By the time the Gospels came to be written in the latter half of the first century AD, there were Christian communities scattered across the Middle East, north Africa and southern Europe. Each evangelist wrote his own version of Jesus' story to help his own community cope with the particular problems it faced. For example:

- Scholars believe that *Mark* wrote his version of Jesus' story with the intention of giving encouragement to Christians at a time when they were being persecuted by the Romans.
- *Matthew* probably wrote his Gospel to help people in his community who had *converted* (changed) from Judaism to Christianity to understand the meaning of Jesus' life and what they would be expected to believe.
- Of all the Gospels, the Gospel of *Luke* offers us the fullest account of Jesus' life. It forms the first half of an unfinished history of Christianity's beginnings. The second half of the story is recorded in *the Acts of the Apostles*, also written by the same author.

  Luke was the only Gospel to have been written by a *gentile* (non-Jew) and was written particularly to explain Jesus' life and teachings to other gentiles who had become Christians. *Luke* was concerned to show that Jesus is the *saviour* of all people, both *Jews and non-Jews*.
- The Gospel of *John* was the last one to be written. Its author seems to assume that his readers already know the details of Jesus' life.

John was chiefly concerned with the question of who Jesus is and why people should follow him. This is because by the time this Gospel came to be written, these were the questions that were important for Christians.

Questions

1. State three reasons why the early Christians wanted to record the story and teachings of Jesus in the *Gospels*.
2. Why did each evangelist write his own version of Jesus' story?
3. Which Gospel offers the fullest account of Jesus' life?
4. Which Gospel was the last to be written?
5. What was the intention behind *Mark's* Gospel?
6. Why did *Matthew* write his Gospel?
7. Which other *New Testament* book was written by the author of *Luke*?
8. For whom did *Luke* write his Gospel?
9. What question was the author of *John* chiefly concerned with?

Inspired by God

Jesus seems to have taught only by word of mouth, not by writing. How much, then, of the teaching recorded in the Gospels is actually Jesus' own words, and how much is put into his mouth by the four evangelists? This is a difficult question and scholars disagree among themselves on how to answer it.

Christians believe that the *Bible* is *the inspired word of God*. This does not necessarily mean, however, that Jesus' words are recorded in the Gospels exactly as he said them. Christians believe that while God inspired the evangelists, God did not directly tell them what to write. Rather, God guided them to use their human

Saint Matthew by Guido Reni.

talents and the normal means of communication to faithfully record the *meaning* of what Jesus said.

For example, it is quite acceptable today for a TV news programme to report an important person's speech, not in the person's actual words, but in the words of the reporter. While the reporter may not use exactly the same words as the person who made the speech, the reporter will try to accurately communicate the *meaning* of what was said in the speech.

It was just the same in Jesus' time. The evangelists concentrated on reporting the *message* of Jesus rather than the exact literal way in which he said it.

Christians believe that God inspired the evangelists to faithfully record the meaning of what Jesus taught.

The Gospels are accepted by Christians as *substantially reliable records of what Jesus taught*.

The focus of the Gospels

A reader of the Gospels will quickly discover that:

- They are *not* diaries of day-to-day events in Jesus' life.
- They do *not* offer us a biography of Jesus in the modern sense of the word. For example, they do not include a detailed description of Jesus' appearance, nor do they tell us about his school days.

Why?

The reason for this is that the evangelists *never intended* to write down the entire life story of Jesus, so they were not interested in recording the kind of personal details which might interest the modern reader. Rather, the Gospel authors were more concerned with explaining the *meaning* and *importance* of Jesus' life.

The evangelists believed Jesus to be the *Son of God* and wrote their Gospels to help others to believe this too. They recorded only what they considered to be the *vital* facts about Jesus. That is why even though Matthew and Luke briefly discuss the events surrounding Jesus' birth, the main focus of all four Gospel writers is on Jesus' miracles, teachings, death and resurrection.

Questions

1. What do Christians mean when they say that *the Gospels are the inspired word of God*?
2. If the evangelists did not always record the exact words of Jesus every time, what was their main aim when writing their accounts?
3. Do the Gospel writers offer us biographies of Jesus in the modern sense of the word? Explain your answer.
4. What was the main concern of the evangelists?
5. What parts of Jesus' story did the evangelists mainly focus on?

Chapter Seven

The Gospels: Similarities and Differences

Parallel passages

Read the following extract from three different Gospels.

Then he called the crowd to him along with his disciples and said: 'If anyone would come after me, he must deny himself and take up his cross and follow me. For whoever wants to save his life will lose it, but whoever loses his life for me and for the Gospel will save it.

What good is it for a man to gain the whole world, yet forfeit his soul? Or what can a man give in exchange for his soul? If anyone is ashamed of me and my words in this adulterous and sinful generation, the Son of Man will be ashamed of him when he comes in his Father's glory with the holy angels.'

And he said to them, 'I tell you the truth, some who are standing here will not taste death before they see the kingdom of God come with power.' (Mark 8:34–9:1)

Then Jesus said to his disciples, 'If anyone would come after me, he must deny himself and take up his cross and follow me. For whoever wants to save his life will lose it, but whoever loses his life for me will find it. What good will it be for a man if he gains the whole world, yet forfeits his soul? Or what can a man give in exchange for his soul? For the Son of Man is going to come in his Father's glory with his angels, and then he will reward each person according to what he has done. I tell you the truth, some who are standing here will not taste death before they see the Son of Man coming in his kingdom.' (Matthew 16:24–28)

Then he said to them all: 'If anyone would come after me, he must deny himself and take up his cross daily and follow me. For whoever wants to save his life will lose it, but whoever loses his life for me will save it. What good is it for a man to gain the whole world, and yet lose or forfeit his very self? If anyone is ashamed of me and my words, the Son of Man will be ashamed of him when he comes in his glory and in the glory of the Father and of the holy angels. I tell you the truth, some who are standing here will not taste death before they see the kingdom of God.' (Luke 9:23–27)

Analysis

These extracts are so alike that it might seem that someone is copying from someone else! One can find many examples of such parallel passages in the Gospels of Mark, Matthew and Luke, which largely agree in:

○ their basic outline of the main events in Jesus' life

○ the sequence in which they organise these events

○ their wording of many of Jesus' statements.

It is because they share so many similarities that Mark, Matthew and Luke are called the *Synoptic*

52   All About Faith

Gospels ('synoptic' meaning 'seen together'). Why is this the case? Consider the following diagram:

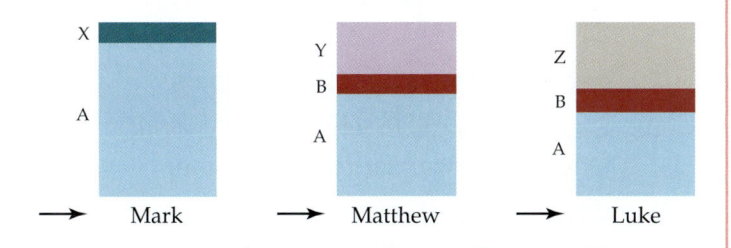

[Diagram showing three bars: Mark (X, A), Matthew (Y, B, A), Luke (Z, B, A)]

Notice how the three Synoptic Gospels share the identical material, marked A above. This is because Mark was the first Gospel to be written and both Matthew and Luke included material written by Mark in their accounts of Jesus' life.

Differences

However, despite so much common material, differences remain between the three Synoptic Gospels. For example:

- Some events are placed in a different order.
- Each Gospel mentions events and records statements made by Jesus which the others do not. For example, only Matthew and Luke offer any information about Jesus' birth, while Mark says nothing at all on this topic.
- Only Luke records the story of how Jesus, as a twelve-year-old boy, became separated from Mary and Joseph while in Jerusalem.

Why differences?

Again, consult the diagram above. You will notice the following:

- Both Matthew and Luke share a common source, marked B above. Scholars believe that both Matthew and Luke consulted a long since lost collection of Jesus' sayings, known as the Q document. Mark did not use the Q document when writing his account.
- Each of the three Gospels include material not found in the others, marked X, Y and Z above. They each probably drew upon different eye-witness accounts.

These points help to explain the differences between the three Synoptic Gospels.

St Luke at Work on His Gospel, miniature in the ninth century *Ebbo Gospels*.

The Q Document

Between AD 30 and 50, the sayings of Jesus were handed on mainly by word of mouth. Then, between AD 50 and 64, the sayings of Jesus were collected and written down. One of these early collections has been identified and named Q. The title Q is derived from the German word '*Quelle*', meaning '*a source*'.

The Gospels: Similarities and Differences

John's Gospel

St John the Evangelist by Guido Reni.

John's Gospel was written some years after the Synoptics. It differs from them in the following ways:

- John did not copy material from either Mark or the Q document
- John only recorded certain events and sayings of Jesus because he was mainly interested in explaining important truths about *who Jesus is*, rather than what he did.

For example, John is the *only* Gospel to record the story of how Jesus restores the gift of sight to a blind man. This is because John wanted to help people see that Jesus is '*the light of the world*'.

Questions

1. What is the meaning of the term '*synoptic*'?
2. Name the three Synoptic Gospels.
3. State two ways in which the Synoptic Gospels are *similar* to one another.
4. Which evangelists included material first recorded by Mark?
5. Identify the *differences* between the Synoptic Gospels.
6. What was the Q document?
7. Which Synoptic Gospel did not use the Q document?
8. Identify one way in which John's Gospel is different from the other three.

Chapter Eight

The **Birth** of Jesus

Introduction

Madonna and Child by Il Sassoferrato.

No other person in human history has attracted more attention and interest than Jesus Christ. People of all religions, as well as those who are members of none, have been fascinated by his story.

Though Jesus never travelled far, never achieved great political power, never amassed a vast fortune and died while still a young man, his impact on the history of our world since has been enormous. Just consider:

- Today, Christianity, the religion he founded, is numerically the largest religion in the world, with approximately 2 billion members.
- No other figure in history has been the focus of more discussion or the subject of more works of art than Jesus.
- We date the years of our world's history from Jesus' birth:
  BC = *Before Christ*
  AD = *Anno Domini*, meaning '*In the year of our Lord*'.

Non-Christian sources for the life of Jesus

Both Jewish and Roman writers all testify to the fact that *Jesus did exist* and that he founded a new religion.

Jewish sources

- *The Talmud* contains references to Jesus. It states that he was put to death on the eve of the feast of Passover.
- *The Antiquities of the Jews*, written by Josephus around AD 90, describes Jesus as a wise teacher and miracle worker who was condemned to death by Pontius Pilate,

The Birth of Jesus   55

and that his followers believed that he had risen from the dead.

Roman sources

- In a letter written in AD 110, a Roman governor in Asia Minor named Pliny complained to the Emperor Trajan about the Christians in his province who *sang hymns to Christ as to a god*.

- In his *Annals*, the historian Tacitus, writing around AD 115, states that Jesus was a troublemaker who was executed on the orders of Pontius Pilate during the reign of Emperor Tiberius.

Unfortunately, neither Jewish nor Roman sources offer much more detail. To find out more about Jesus' life, we must turn to the *Gospel* accounts.

The story

Adoration of the Kings by Velásquez.

The story of Jesus' birth is one of the most memorable and attractive stories ever written, and has been the inspiration for many beautiful works of art. By combining materials from the Gospels of Luke and Matthew we can offer the following account.

Jesus was born during the reign of the Roman emperor Augustus, who called a census of the Jews to find out which of them were eligible to pay taxes. Everyone had to state their name, social rank, occupation and so on, but they could not fill in their census details in the place where they normally lived. Instead, all Jews had to go to the place from which their family originally came. Joseph, husband of Mary, was a descendant of King David, who came from Bethlehem. Mary and Joseph were forced to leave their home in Nazareth and travel to Bethlehem, and it was there that Jesus was born.

On the night of his birth, shepherds visited the infant Jesus and worshipped him. They were later followed by *Magi* (wise men) from the east who had followed a star, believing it would lead them to a great king whose birth they were expecting. They brought with them three gifts:

- *gold* – to demonstrate that they recognised Jesus as a king

- *frankincense* – to show that they had come to worship Jesus

- *myrrh* – as a warning that they believed Jesus would have to suffer much.

But the Magi were not the only ones seeking Jesus. Ever fearful of any threat to his throne, King Herod, the Roman-appointed ruler of Palestine, ordered his soldiers to kill all male children in Bethlehem aged two years or younger. However, Jesus, Mary and Joseph escaped this massacre and took refuge in Egypt. After Herod's death they returned to Nazareth, where Jesus grew up.

56   All About Faith

Naming the event

There are three names Christians use for the birth of Jesus:

- *the Nativity*, which is derived from the Latin '*natus*', meaning '*the birth*'
- *Christmas*, meaning '*Christ's mass*' or '*Christ's festival*'
- *the Incarnation*, which means '*becoming flesh*' and refers to the Christian belief that God actually became a human being in the person of Jesus.

Dating the event

We cannot say with certainty the exact date of Jesus' birth. This date was not recorded in the Gospels and early Christians did not appreciate its importance for some time. Only gradually did they come to realise that Jesus' birth had marked a whole new era in human history.

To show this clearly, the years before Jesus' birth were termed BC and those afterward AD.

The task of working out the date of Jesus' birth was given to a monk named Denis. He is responsible for our current system of numbering the years, taking the birth of Jesus as occurring in year AD 1. This system has been in use since the sixth century AD. However, it is now generally acknowledged that Denis arrived at the *wrong date* for Jesus' birth. How?

It seems that Denis interpreted the statement that Jesus was '*about thirty years old when he began his ministry*' (Luke 3:23) as though it meant that he was exactly thirty years old. This led him to miscalculate. Scholars today believe that Jesus was born at least four or perhaps even six years earlier than Denis had thought. Why?

Using the information contained in the Gospels and matching it with non-Christian sources, we can see that Jesus was most likely born sometime in the period 6 BC to 4 BC by our calendar.

Consider the following:

- King Herod died in 4 BC. Since he ordered all boys up to the age of two to be put to death (Matthew 2:16), this means that Jesus would have to have been born sometime in the period 6 BC to 4 BC.
- Chinese astronomical records state that in the year 5 BC, a brilliant star appeared in the eastern sky. Some scholars believe that this was a super nova, i.e. a brilliant light caused by an exploding star, and that this may be the origin of the Star of Bethlehem mentioned in Matthew 2:1–10.

Why 25 December?

The early Christians lived under Roman rule. Their Roman overlords worshipped many gods, but perhaps the most widely worshipped of all these gods was *Mithras*, also known as *Sol Invicta* (meaning '*the invincible sun*'). Mithras' birth date was 25 December and it was celebrated near the time of the *winter solstice* (the shortest day of the year). As the hours of sunlight grow longer after the solstice, many Romans believed that this was because Mithras, the sun god, was regaining his strength.

When Christianity became the official religion of the Roman empire in the fourth century AD, its leaders decided to take over this date, considering it to be an appropriate date on which to celebrate Jesus' birth. This was because Christians believed that Jesus, not Mithras, is '*the rising sun from on high who has come to visit us*' (Luke 1:78) and that Jesus alone should be called '*the light of the world*' (John 9:5).

However, not all Christians accepted this date. Christians in the Orthodox tradition chose a different date: 6 January. They combined two important events in Jesus' life, his birth and his baptism, and celebrate them on the *same* day of each year.

Questions

1. Who was the Roman emperor when Jesus was born?
2. Why did Mary and Joseph have to travel to Bethlehem for the census?
3. Explain the meaning of each of the three gifts given by the Magi.
4. Why did Herod order the murder of all male children of two years and younger in Bethlehem?
5. Explain the following: (a) *Nativity* (b) *Christmas* (c) *Incarnation*.
6. How did Denis arrive at the wrong date for the birth of Jesus?
7. Why do modern scholars think that Jesus was most likely to have been born sometime in the period 6 BC to 4 BC?
8. By what other name did the Romans worship the god Mithras?
9. What led many Romans to believe that Mithras' strength returned to him *after* the winter solstice?
10. Why did Christians come to believe that 25 December was a more appropriate date than any other on which to celebrate Jesus' birth?

The Annunciation by El Greco.

Comparing accounts

The story of Jesus' birth is found in two Gospels: Luke and Matthew. They both agree on the following details.

Luke 1:5	The story is set during the reign of Herod the Great.	Matthew 2:1
Luke 1:27, 2:5	Mary was a virgin who had been formally engaged to Joseph.	Matthew 1:16
Luke: 1:27, 2:4	Joseph was descended from King David.	Matthew: 1:16
Luke 2:7	Jesus was conceived in Mary's womb, not through sexual intercourse with Joseph, but through the power of God. This is called 'the virginal conception' or 'the virgin birth'.	Matthew 1: 18–20
Luke 2:7	Mary gave birth to Jesus in Bethlehem.	Matthew 1:25
Luke 1:31	Jesus was given his name before his birth.	Matthew 1:21
Luke 2:51	Jesus, Mary and Joseph, sometimes called 'the holy family', finally settled down in Nazareth.	Matthew 2:23

All About Faith

Most scholars, however, believe that each evangelist wrote his account *separately*. They hold this view because Luke includes details in his account that Matthew does not and vice versa.

Consider the following:

- Luke and Matthew each give a different genealogy (family tree) for Jesus.
- Whereas Luke tells us the story of how the angel Gabriel appeared to Mary (the *annunciation*), Matthew tells us how an angel spoke to Joseph in a dream.
- Luke's version of the nativity has shepherds visiting the baby Jesus, but he never mentions the Magi (the three wise men).
- However, while Matthew does mention the story of the Magi, he makes no mention of the shepherds.

Common purpose

It is very easy to get caught up in the details of the Christmas story, but to do so is to miss the important truths that the evangelists were trying to communicate about the *meaning* of Jesus' birth:

- Luke wanted his readers to know that Jesus came to bring God's love and forgiveness to people of *all* social classes, whether they were poor shepherds or wealthy nobles.
- Matthew used the story of the Magi to drive home the point that Jesus had come into the world to show the power of God's love not just to the Jewish people, but to *all* humankind.

Questions

1. On what points of the Nativity story do Luke and Matthew agree?
2. Why do most scholars believe that each evangelist wrote his account separately? Give reasons for your answer.
3. Explain (a) *genealogy* (b) *annunciation*.
4. Beyond the differences in their accounts of the Nativity, what important messages did Luke and Matthew want to get across to their readers about the birth of Jesus?

Mary: the mother of Jesus

The Catholic Church teaches that Mary lived a life of total devotion to Jesus. She is described as the *model* of how Christians today are called to bring the healing and loving presence of God into the world.

Although she did not understand exactly how God was at work in her life (see Luke 1:34), the Gospels present Mary as trusting God completely. She agreed to bring the Son of God into the world (see Luke 1:38). Through Mary, humanity and divinity were brought together. It was for this reason that the Council of Ephesus (AD 431) gave Mary the title *Theotokos* (a Greek word meaning '*God bearer*' or '*Mother of God*').

Mary's importance has been acknowledged by the Catholic Church in three important doctrines (teachings). All of these emphasise Mary's closeness to God – something all Christians hope to one day enjoy.

Assumption of the Virgin by Titian.

1. The Virgin Birth

Both Catholics *and* Protestants accept the Virgin Birth. They teach that Jesus was conceived in Mary's womb through the power of the Holy Spirit and born to her while she was still a *virgin* (had not had sexual intercourse with a man). This means that Christ was born into the world *not* as a result of human effort but as a totally undeserved gift of love from God.

> N.B.
> However, Catholic teaching about Mary includes two doctrines that most Protestants do not accept. These have been declared *dogmas* of the Catholic Church, i.e. *infallible teachings that must be accepted by all Catholics.*

2. The Immaculate Conception

This was proclaimed a dogma of the Catholic Church by Pope Pius IX in 1854. This means that from the moment of her conception in her mother's womb, Mary was without sin of any kind. She was totally pure of heart, gentle and loving. As a result, Mary was a fit person to be the mother of the Son of God.

3. The Assumption

This was proclaimed a dogma of the Catholic Church by Pope Pius XII in 1950. This means that because of her unique role in human history as the mother of Jesus, Mary was *assumed*, i.e. taken bodily from this world, and instantly united with God in heaven.

The Catholic Church does not say whether or not Mary died first before her assumption into heaven. Many early Christians believed that Mary was taken directly into heaven before her death because she was so totally good – *full of grace* (filled with God's love).

Mary gives Catholics hope that one day, all those who have faithfully lived according to the Gospel message will also share eternal life with Jesus.

Questions

1. Explain the term '*Theotokos*'.
2. What is a *dogma*?
3. Match the doctrine in column A with the explanation in column B.

A Doctrine	B Explanation
The Virgin Birth	From the moment of her conception Mary was without sin of any kind.
The Immaculate Conception	Mary was *assumed*, i.e. taken bodily into heaven, and instantly united with God.
The Assumption	Jesus was conceived in Mary's womb through the power of the Holy Spirit and born to her while she was still a virgin.

Formal prayer: the Hail Mary

One of the most familiar prayers for Catholics is the *Hail Mary* (from the Latin *Ave Maria*). This beautiful prayer may be divided into two parts, as set out below, with an explanation of each part accompanying it.

I
Hail Mary, full of grace,
The Lord is with thee,
Blessed art thou among women,
And blessed is the fruit of thy womb, Jesus.

Prayer of Praise

This recalls the Annunciation (Luke 1:26–38) when the angel Gabriel gave the joyful news to Mary that God was with her and that she would be the mother of the Messiah. It also recalls the Visitation (Luke 1:39–45), when Mary's cousin Elizabeth greeted her and declared the child in Mary's womb *blessed*.

II
Holy Mary, Mother of God,
Pray for us sinners, now
And in the hour of our death.

Prayer of Petition

This calls upon Mary to care for us as she cared for her son, Jesus. We admit that we are *sinners* (people who have done wrong). We seek God's mercy and compassion. We ask Mary to be with us each day and to guide us safely to the end of our lives, so that we may share eternal life with God.

This ancient prayer emphasises Mary's deep faith and calls on Christians to follow her example.

Questions

1. What are the two types of prayer found in the Hail Mary?
2. Explain the following terms: (a) *the Annunciation* (b) *the Visitation*.
3. What is the purpose of the ancient prayer the *Hail Mary*?

Chapter Nine

Life in **Palestine**

Introduction

In the first century AD, the Promised Land was known as *Palestine*. By that time, it was merely one small province of the vast Roman empire, which had conquered the area in 63 BC.

Political regions

The principal political regions of Palestine were *Galilee* in the north, *Samaria* in the centre and *Judaea* in the south. When Jesus was born all three regions had been united for many years under the rule of King Herod the Great. Herod was allowed to rule the area on behalf of Rome, but only as long as he kept it peaceful and collected taxes for the emperor.

After Herod's death, Emperor Augustus appointed a Roman official to act as *procurator* (governor) of Samaria and Judaea. One of Herod's sons, Herod Antipater, was appointed *tetrarch* (commander) of the least important part of Palestine – Galilee.

Communities

The people of Palestine lived in one or other of the following types of community:

- the long-established Jewish cities and towns such as Jerusalem, Bethlehem and Nazareth
- the more recent Roman-built urban centres such as Caesarea and Tiberias
- the small rural farming communities dotted across the more arable areas of the region.

Nazareth

Although Jesus was born in Bethlehem in Judaea, he grew up in the old Jewish town of Nazareth, in Galilee in northern Palestine. The latter region is hilly and mountainous, especially the further south one travels.

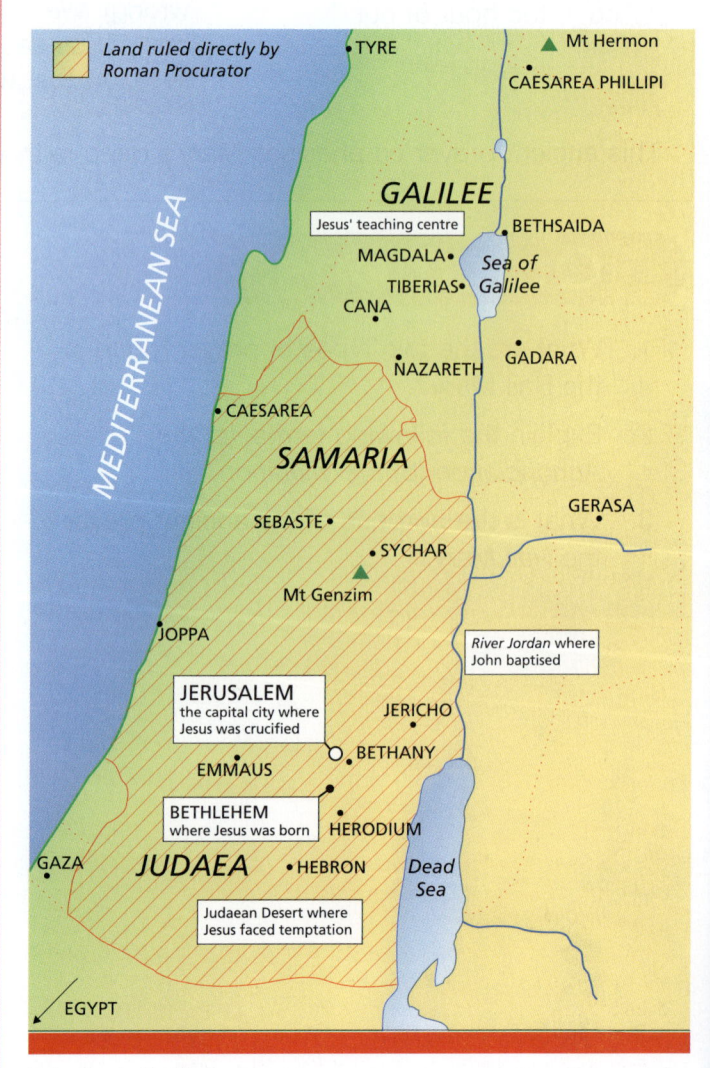

Palestine in the first century AD.

62 All About Faith

Today Nazareth is a large, thriving urban centre with a population of about 60,000 people. However, 2,000 years ago it was just a small village built around a spring well. Nazareth was close to a number of important trade routes, so while it was somewhat out of the way by our standards, it was not completely remote. Indeed, its inhabitants traded with other towns and villages which, although heavily populated by their fellow Jews, also included Arabs, Greeks, Phoenicians and Syrians too.

Work

Despite all the great political upheavals caused by successive waves of invaders and occupiers which struck Palestine over the centuries, the lives of most ordinary people remained *relatively unchanged*. Most Jews found employment in farming, fishing or craft work.

Farming

In the time of Jesus, Jews of both sexes wore a linen undergarment and a woollen tunic that covered the body from the lower neck to well below the knees. Over these was draped a cloak that served variously as topcoat, blanket, bedroll, carpet and even as collateral for loans – provided the borrower was allowed the use of it at night. To keep the voluminous tunic from billowing awkwardly, men and women wore belts of rope, leather or cloth, sometimes highly decorated. Even the poorest Jews, as with the peasant family here, deemed footwear essential and wore sandals of camel hide or wood.

The average Jewish farmer did not live on his farm, but in a village nearby where he had access to a water supply.

Farmers and their workers generally endured lives of back-breaking toil and hardship. This was because although Palestine had been called a *'Promised Land'*, a large part of its landscape was rock and sand, unsuited to agriculture. Even in its more arable areas, farmers had to contend with such challenges as:

- *drought*
- *the sirocco*, i.e. strong winds from the east that could strip away the dry topsoil
- *plagues of locusts* which would devour crops.

The professional class

While most people earned their living by manual labour, there was a professional class that did not. This consisted of a relatively small group of educated people who instead earned their living as administrators, doctors and merchant traders. Among the most influential were the *scribes* (professional copyists) and the religious teachers, who were addressed as *rabbi* (meaning '*my master*').

Questions

1. What were the three types of community in Palestine?
2. What were Palestine's three principal political regions?
3. On what conditions did the Romans allow Herod the Great to rule Palestine on their behalf?
4. Explain the following terms: (a) *procurator* (b) *tetrarch*.
5. Who was appointed tetrarch of Galilee?
6. Where did Jesus grow up? Briefly describe it.

Life in Palestine

Questions

7. State the three categories of work in which most Jews found employment.
8. Who were members of the *professional class*?
9. What was a *scribe*?
10. Explain the meaning of the title '*rabbi*'.

Cut-away drawing of a Jewish home circa first century AD.

○ While the well-to-do minority lived in comfortable Roman-style houses (villas), the average house in a town like Nazareth was whitewashed, both inside and out. There were no bathing facilities inside.

○ Fixed to the right-hand doorpost at the entrance to the house was a little wooden or leather case called a *mezuzah*. It contained a tiny scroll with the words of the *Shema*, a prayer taken from the Old Testament book of Deuteronomy 6:4. A devout Jew would always touch the mezuzah before entering and leaving the house.

○ The family slept upstairs. Most family members slept on mats which were rolled up and stored when not in use.

○ The lower level was used at night as a stable to keep the family's animals safe. The family members themselves lived on a raised

All About Faith

- platform of beaten earth covered with straw. Sometimes stone chippings were pressed into the earth to form a floor.
- As there were no windows, the interior was cool but dark, as there was no natural light. So an oil lamp was always kept burning in a little alcove in the family's upper living area to provide light.
- At meal times the family sat cross-legged on the floor around a circular mat or low table on which their food was placed. They were not served individual portions. Instead they shared a common bowl, dipping in and taking their food with their right hands.
- The house had a flat roof made from mud-caked reed mats which were spread over and secured to rows of parallel wooden beams which supported the roof. When it rained heavily and for a long period of time, such a roof was liable to severe leaking.
- There was no real fireplace as such. A fire was kept lit in a shallow pit in the floor or in a large earthenware pot. Charcoal, thorns and dried animal dung were used to fuel the fire. There was no chimney, so during the colder winter months the house was often filled with smoke. In summer the smoke from the fire helped ward off insects.
- There was very little furniture, perhaps a few stools. Utensils were hung from hooks on the roof beams. Water drawn from the local well was stored in porous earthenware jars in which the water remained cool by a process of slow evaporation.
- The diet consisted of goat's cheese, eggs, porridge, beans, lentils, cucumber, dates, figs and pomegranates. Those living near waterways ate fish. Watered-down wine was served at meal times, as was goat's milk.

Questions

1. In what kind of house did the well-to-do minority live?
2. What is a *mezuzah*?
3. Describe life in a typical Jewish home in first-century Palestine. In your answer mention each of the following: (a) wall colour (b) bathing facilities (c) sleeping arrangements (d) roof (e) use of oil lamps (f) diet and meal times (g) advantages and disadvantages of not having a chimney (h) storage of water.

Chapter Ten

Under Roman Rule

Making an impression

In the summer of AD 26, the newly appointed Roman *procurator* (governor) of the provinces of Judaea and Samaria stepped ashore at the great sea port of Caesarea. His name was Pontius Pilate. His mission was to:

○ ensure that the local population paid their taxes promptly to the emperor

○ keep the area peaceful and the trade routes open.

A Roman procurator.

For anyone observing the large display of Roman troops which greeted Pilate's arrival at Caesarea, there would have been no doubting the power of the empire.

The rows of men in shining armour would have looked very impressive. They had earned a fearsome reputation. Everyone knew that the Roman army had easily conquered Palestine.

What everyone did *not* know, however, was that the Roman garrison at Pilate's disposal was never more than 3,000 men. The nearest reinforcements were hundreds of miles away in either Egypt or Syria.

The key to Roman power in Palestine and throughout their empire was twofold.

○ *Threat elimination*: Pilate had to keep almost 750,000 people convinced that it was pointless trying to oppose Roman rule. A large network of informants was set up throughout Palestine to spy for the Romans, and these helped the Roman authorities to quickly identify and eliminate anyone who might pose a threat. This discouraged any ideas of rebellion.

○ *Ruling by co-operation*: The Romans recognised the importance of having the co-operation of influential figures from among the peoples they had conquered. If Pilate wanted to administer Palestine in the smooth and efficient way the emperor demanded, he needed the help of the Sanhedrin.

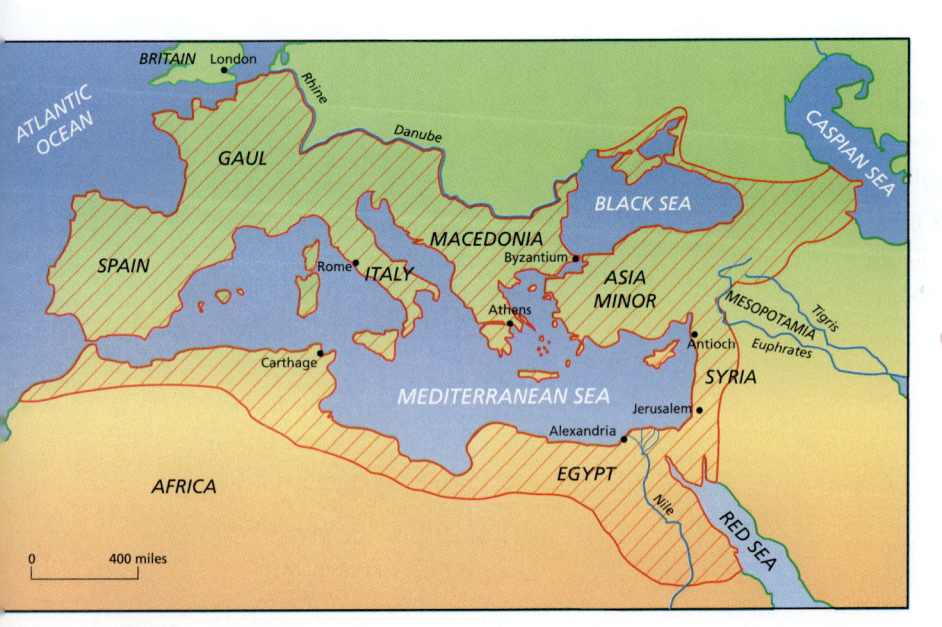

The Roman empire in the first century AD.

66   All About Faith

The Sanhedrin

The *Sanhedrin* was the ruling council of the Jewish religion. It consisted of seventy elders, and the high priest directed its activities.

The Sanhedrin's members were divided into two rival groups: the *Sadducees* and the *Pharisees*.

Each group claimed to uphold the true ideals of the Jewish religion and they competed with one another for control of the Sanhedrin.

The Romans demanded and received the loyal support of the Sanhedrin. In return, the Jews were allowed a considerable degree of self-rule. The Romans permitted the Sanhedrin to:

- serve as a court of law for the Jewish population
- have its own Temple guards to keep order
- punish Jews who broke the laws of their own religion.

However, the Sanhedrin was *not* allowed to impose the death penalty.

Questions

1. What was Pontius Pilate's mission as procurator?
2. What was the key to Roman power? Explain how it worked.
3. What was the *Sanhedrin*?
4. Name the Sanhedrin's two rival groupings.
5. Who directed the Sanhedrin's various activities?
6. Describe the Sanhedrin's power.

Reactions to Roman rule

A Roman soldier.

The Jewish people were never allowed to forget that they were subjects of the Roman emperor. Different Jewish groups reacted to this situation in different ways.

- The *Sadducees* accepted Roman rule, adapted to it and made an unwritten agreement to use their influence to keep order.
- The *Pharisees* rejected Roman rule but did not oppose it. Instead they devoted all their energies to practising their religion.
- The *Essenes* rejected Roman rule, but instead of opposing it, opted out of society altogether. They set up religious communities in remote desert areas.
- The *Zealots* rejected Roman rule and formed a resistance movement to violently oppose it.

The four most influential Jewish groups

The Sadducees

- Were wealthy aristocrats and included the Temple priests.
- Dominated the Sanhedrin and controlled the key office of high priest.
- Adopted non-Jewish lifestyles.
- Interpreted the Torah rigidly and literally. Refused to accept any development of new ideas. Rejected belief in angels and in life after death.
- Did not expect a Messiah to deliver them from Roman rule.

The Pharisees

- Were laymen, not priests. Included the *scribes* (teachers of the law), who expected to be called '*rabbi*'.
- Controlled local synagogues.
- Name means '*the separated*'. Were dedicated to preserving the purity of the Jewish religion and tended to keep themselves apart from ordinary Jews.
- Open to development of new religious ideas. Believed in angels and in life after death.
- Expected a Messiah to free them from Roman rule and establish a kingdom, as in the days of King David.

The Essenes

- Were communities of *monks* who settled in remote places. Believed they were obeying the word of God (see Isaiah 40:3).
- Thought to have set up a community at Qumran, near where the *Dead Sea Scrolls* were found.
- Felt that the Jewish religion was being corrupted by outside influences. Believed that they alone had the correct interpretation of the Torah.
- Followed strict rules of life. Three-year training period. New members had to swear to keep their teachings and practices secret.
- Placed great emphasis on bathing. May have influenced John the Baptist.

The Zealots

- Were deeply religious Jews who believed violent action was justified if it was in defence of the Jewish religion.
- Possibly an offshoot of the Pharisees.
- Hated the Sadducees for working with the Romans. One group of the Zealots, known as the *Sicarii* (cut-throats), engaged in a campaign of assassination.
- Caused a great deal of unrest among the Jewish people. Jesus was viewed with suspicion for having a Zealot (Simon the Patriot) among his apostles.

Questions

1. Briefly explain the reaction of each of the following to Roman rule of Palestine:
   (a) the *Sadducees* (b) the *Pharisees* (c) the *Essenes* (d) the *Zealots*.
2. Which group dominated the Sanhedrin and controlled the key office of high priest?
3. What is the meaning of the title '*Pharisee*'?
4. State two differences between the Sadducees and the Pharisees.
5. What was the name given to the communities of Jewish monks who settled in remote areas such as Qumran?
6. Which group believed that violent action was justified in defence of the Jewish religion?

The tax collectors

Tax collector.

A number of Jews were willing to work for the Romans. These people were generally detested by their fellow Jews. The *most* despised job, however, was that of tax collector.

Most Jews earned just enough to provide for the basic necessities of life: food, clothing and shelter. Few were wealthy. Yet the Romans imposed heavy taxes, which, though they bitterly resented them, the Jews had no choice but to pay.

Those Jews who supervised and carried out the collection of these unfair taxes were considered *traitors*. Further, because some of these tax collectors kept a proportion of the money they collected for themselves, they were also denounced as *thieves*.

Most Jews treated tax collectors as social outcasts. Tax collectors were disqualified from holding any religious office and they were not allowed to give evidence in a Jewish court, because they were considered cheats and liars.

Jesus horrified many of his followers and angered his critics when he even held a conversation with a tax collector. Imagine, then, the reaction there must have been when Jesus invited a tax collector named Matthew to join his close circle of friends.

Questions

1. Why did most Jews resent paying taxes to the Romans?
2. What did most Jews think of those who collected taxes?
3. Is it true to say that tax collectors were treated as social outcasts? Give reasons for your answer.

Under Roman Rule

Chapter Eleven

Jesus Prepares for His Mission

Introduction

The Gospels tell us very little about either the childhood or early adulthood of Jesus. This is because the evangelists were more interested in recording the events of the last three years of Jesus' life on Earth, which they believed revealed him to be the Messiah they had hoped God would send.

The promised Messiah

The title '*Messiah*' comes from the Hebrew '*Moshiach*', meaning '*anointed one*'. In Old Testament times, kings and high priests were anointed with oil to show that they had been chosen by God to fulfil an important task.

By the first century AD, most Jews hoped that the Messiah would be a *warrior king* who would:

- bring God's peace and justice among them
- free them from foreign domination
- set up a new independent Jewish kingdom.

Devout Jews daily recited the following prayer:

> I believe with perfect faith in the coming of the Messiah and, even if he delay, still will I await his arrival every day.

The Christ

When the Bible was first translated from Hebrew into Greek, the Greek word used in place of the Hebrew Messiah was '*Christos*'. From this we get the title '*Christ*', which also means '*anointed one*'. So when someone says *Jesus Christ* it means *Jesus the Messiah*.

The Jewish people believe that the Messiah has yet to come. Christians, however, believe that in Jesus of Nazareth the Messiah/Christ *has arrived* and that *he will return again at the end of time*.

Questions

1. Explain the meaning of the title '*Messiah*'.
2. By the first century AD, what kind of messiah did most Jews expect God to send?
3. How did the title '*Christ*' come to be given to Jesus?
4. Explain the difference between the Jewish and the Christian belief about the Messiah.

John the Baptist

John the Baptist was a cousin of Jesus. It seems that John began his work about AD 28–29.

The four Gospels clearly identify John the Baptist as the *herald of the Messiah*, i.e. the one who forewarns the people and prepares them for the Messiah's arrival.

John was an *ascetic*, i.e. someone who lives a life of self-denial. He lived in hostile desert areas, wore a robe of camel hair tied with a leather belt and survived by eating only locusts and wild honey.

St John the Baptist (Russian icon).

Questions

1. What does it mean to say that John the Baptist was the *herald of the Messiah*?
2. What is an *ascetic*?
3. What does it mean to *repent*?
4. Why did John baptise people with water?
5. Why was John the Baptist executed?

The baptism of Jesus

Baptism of Christ by Paolo Veronese.

Large crowds flocked to the Jordan valley to hear John the Baptist preach. John told them that God had sent the promised Messiah at last. He urged them to *repent* (show sorrow for their sins and change their way of living). Those who did so were then *baptised* – with water from the River Jordan poured over their heads. This was done to show that their sins (past wrongdoings) had been washed away by God's forgiveness. God was offering each person a fresh start and a chance to prepare for the coming of the Messiah.

John was not afraid of challenging powerful and dangerous people. He criticised Herod Antipas, tetrarch of Galilee, for marrying Herodias. He said that Herod's action was wrong because Herodias had been the wife of Herod's brother Philip, who was still alive. Herod had John imprisoned and later executed.

Jesus went to John the Baptist and asked to be baptised like everyone else. John was very reluctant to do this because he realised that Jesus was the promised Messiah. John did not feel worthy and asked Jesus to baptise him instead.

Jesus Prepares for His Mission

Jesus gently insisted with his request, however, so John relented and baptised him.

The Gospels tell us that when Jesus was baptised the *Holy Spirit* descended on Jesus in the form of a *dove* (this was meant to represent the peaceful presence of God) and that a voice spoke to Jesus from heaven.

By being baptised, Jesus was not admitting that he had ever sinned. Rather, Jesus was showing how he wanted to completely identify himself with the lives and daily struggles of human beings. Jesus would share in all the joys and sorrows of those around him. He was ready to *do all that righteousness demanded*, even if it eventually meant dying for what he believed.

Questions

1. Why was John the Baptist unwilling at first to baptise Jesus?
2. What do the Gospels say happened when Jesus was baptised?
3. What did Jesus want to show by being baptised?

The temptations

After his baptism, Jesus withdrew into the harsh landscape of the Judaean wilderness. There he fasted and prayed alone for a period of forty days. According to the Synoptic Gospels, it was during this time that Satan* attempted to turn Jesus away from his mission.

Jesus had gone into the wilderness to pray about the kind of Messiah he would be. There Satan tempted him three times. On each occasion, Jesus *rejected* what Satan offered him.

According to the Gospels:

1. Jesus was tempted to use his power for himself by turning stones into bread. Jesus knew, however, that while food is a basic necessity, people need more than just food to live a truly human existence. He responded by saying: *Man cannot live on bread alone*.

2. Then Jesus was tempted to turn his back on his mission and worship Satan instead. In return for doing this, Satan said that he would give Jesus all the wealth and power necessary to make people follow and obey him. Jesus rejected this offer. He stated: *You must worship the Lord your God and serve him alone*.

3. Finally, Jesus was tempted to use his power to impress people by throwing himself from the highest point of the Temple (a 450-foot drop) and have God send his angels to save him. Jesus saw no value whatsoever in such a stupid gesture. He firmly dismissed Satan by stating: *You must not put the Lord your God to the test*.

Once Satan realised that he had failed to tempt Jesus, he left him alone. However, this was *not* the end of the matter. Jesus would have to face these temptations again and again during his ministry.

The Temptation of Christ by Ary Scheffer: 'The devil took Him to a very high mountain and showed Him all the kingdoms of the world…' (Mt 4:8–11).

*N.B.
Christian teaching about Satan

St Michael overcoming the Devil by Jacob Epstein, Coventry Cathedral, England.

- The name '*Satan*' comes from the Hebrew word meaning '*slanderer*' or '*enemy*'. Its Greek equivalent is '*Diablos*' or '*devil*'.
- Satan is a *pure spirit*, i.e. a being without a physical body.
- Satan is *not* the equal of God.
- Satan was created good, but abused God's gift of free will and rebelled against God.
- Satan was condemned to hell for eternity.
- Satan does *not* have the power to force anyone to do things. However, Satan can *tempt* people to do evil things.

Question

1. State each of the temptations Jesus faced in the Judaean desert. Then, in your own words, explain why Jesus resisted each of them in turn.

Jesus Prepares for His Mission

Chapter Twelve

Jesus Begins His **Public Ministry**

Introduction

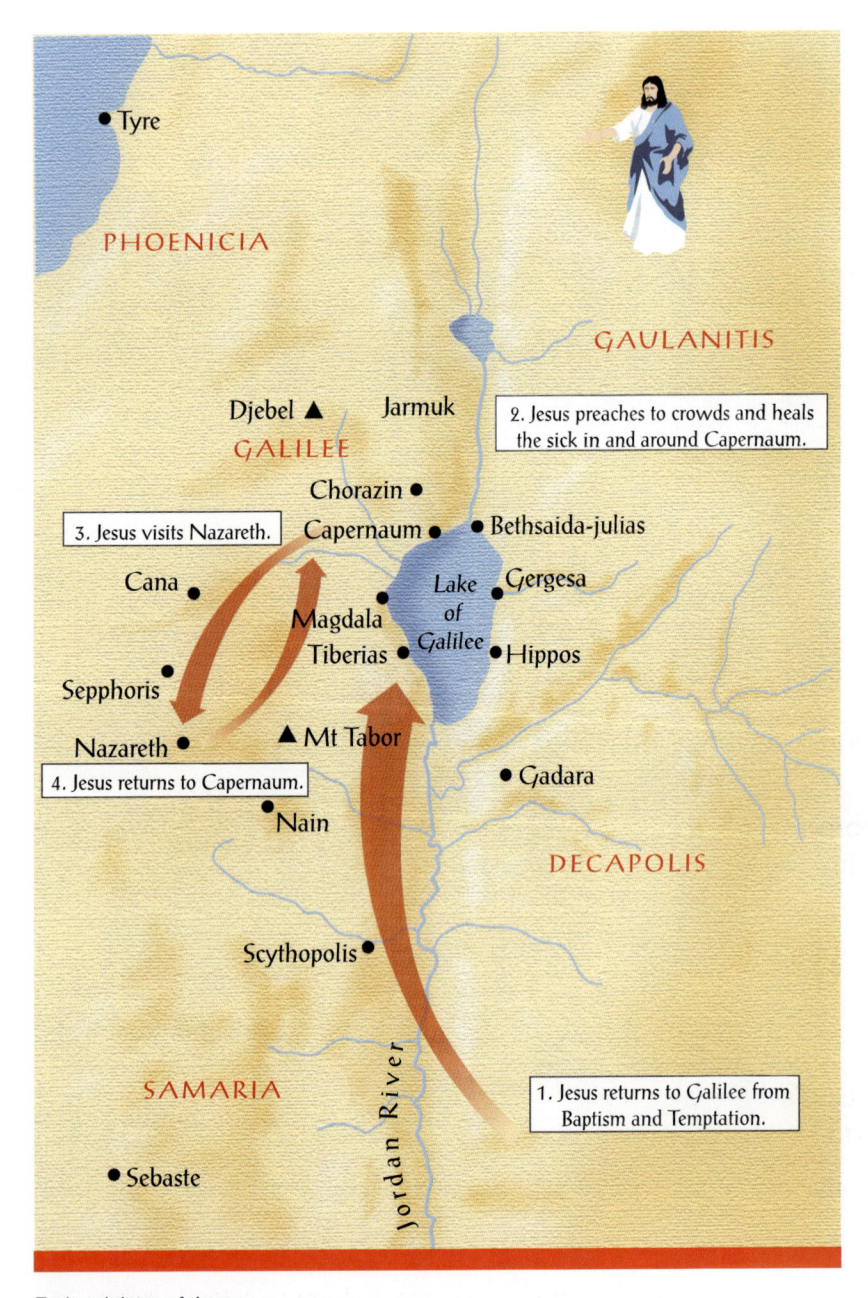

Early ministry of Jesus.

After his experience in the Judaean desert, Jesus returned to Galilee, where he began his ministry of healing and preaching. He visited his hometown of Nazareth but was rejected by its people. After this he moved to Capernaum on the shores of the Sea of Galilee. There he began to draw large crowds as word spread about the extraordinary things he said and did.

Teaching with authority

Throughout his preaching, Jesus made use of the Tenakh (what Christians call the Old Testament). Jesus' words had a profound effect on many of those who heard him preach.

> *His teaching made a deep impression on the people because he taught them with authority, and not like their own scribes.* (Matthew 7:28–29)

Clearly, Jesus was an extraordinary person.

74 All About Faith

Portrait of Jesus. The early Church was more concerned with symbols than with portraits and so no genuine portrait of Jesus, or even a description in words, of his physical appearance is known to exist. Although we shall therefore probably never know what Jesus really looked like, artists have often tried to imagine his appearance and to depict it.

This ancient portrait was painted not later than about AD 150 on the ceiling of the tomb of Saints Achilleus and Nereus in the catacombs at Rome. The illustration shown here is a copy, made by Thomas Heaphy around 1847, of the painting in the tomb. The original is very faded and although the copyist worked with great care, it is by no means certain that this closely resembles the original or that the original itself was a genuine likeness of Jesus.

The personality of Jesus

If we carefully study the Gospels, they offer us the following insights into his personality.

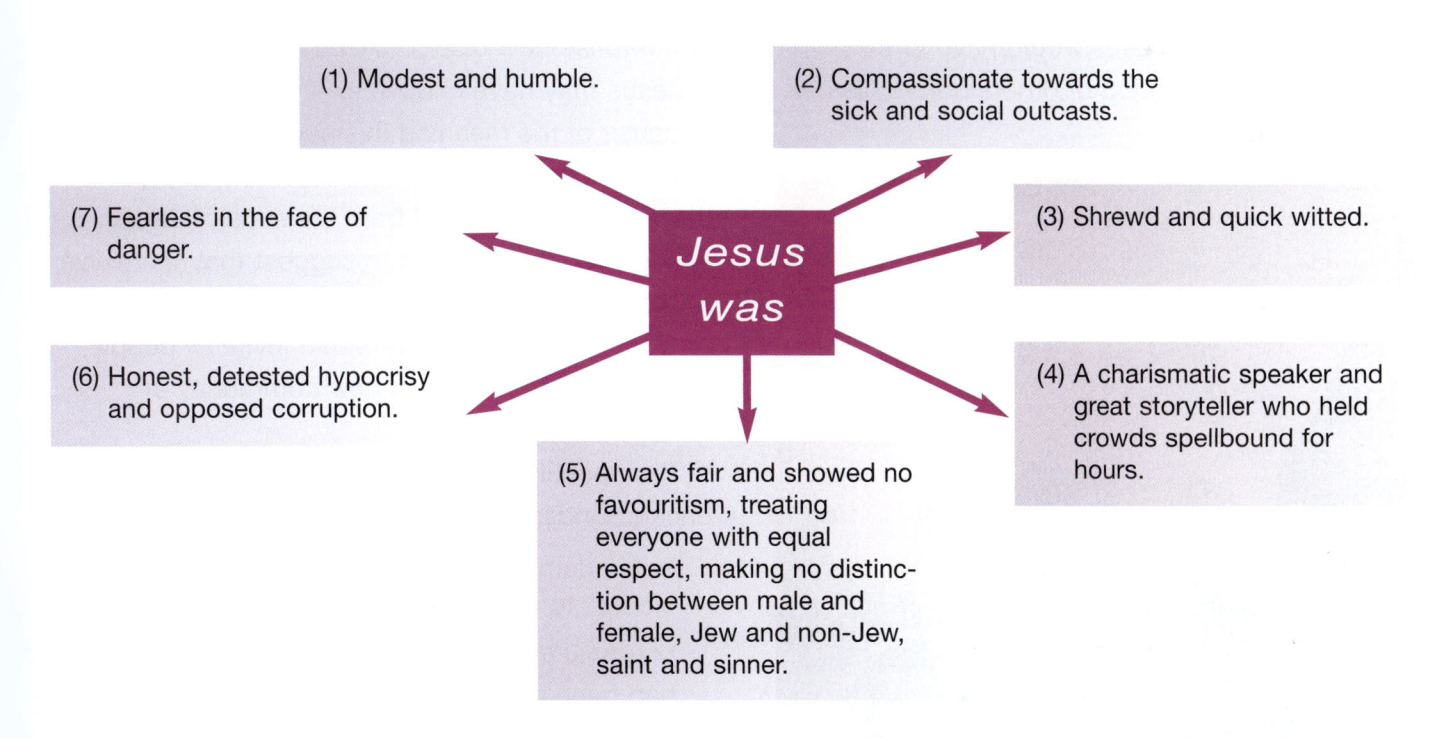

Jesus was

(1) Modest and humble.

(2) Compassionate towards the sick and social outcasts.

(3) Shrewd and quick witted.

(4) A charismatic speaker and great storyteller who held crowds spellbound for hours.

(5) Always fair and showed no favouritism, treating everyone with equal respect, making no distinction between male and female, Jew and non-Jew, saint and sinner.

(6) Honest, detested hypocrisy and opposed corruption.

(7) Fearless in the face of danger.

The Gospels portray Jesus as a uniquely good and charismatic person who practised what he preached. Little wonder that many of those who encountered him believed that Jesus taught with authority and developed a deep and lasting love for him (see John 11:1–6).

Questions

1. Why did Jesus move his home from Nazareth to Capernaum?
2. In your own words, write your own description of Jesus' personality.

The disciples

A reader of the Gospels will quickly realise that Jesus enjoyed the company of people and made many friends. However, these people were more than just friends of Jesus, they were also his *disciples* (from the Latin '*discipulus*', meaning '*student*' or '*learner*'). These disciples were expected to learn from Jesus and follow his example.

The disciples were invited to be *co-workers* of Jesus. However, they were told that by following Jesus they would have to face many challenges to their faith. They were encouraged to pray so that God would give them the strength they needed. Finally, a disciple of Jesus would have to be humble and put the good of others before his/her own interests.

The Calling of the Apostles Peter and Andrew by Duccio di Buoninsegna.

The Gospels present Jesus' call to become his disciple as a huge step in a person's life, involving a complete break with the way a person has lived his/her life up until then. It demands a '*metanoia*', a Greek word meaning '*a complete change of heart*'. See Mark 2:13–17 and Luke 9:57–60.

The apostles

The Gospels mention Jesus sending out seventy-two disciples in pairs to preach and heal. However, within this wide circle of followers, Jesus had a smaller and closer group of disciples who Christians call the *apostles*, although they are usually referred to in the Gospels as *the twelve*.

The word '*apostle*' comes from the Greek word meaning '*to send forth*'. Jesus selected them to be his constant companions as he travelled throughout Palestine. He gave them a special task which set them apart from the other disciples. After Jesus ascended into heaven, the apostles were to lead his followers and, in his name, *preach*, *heal* and *baptise* new disciples (see Matthew 28:16–20).

Jesus may have chosen exactly *twelve* apostles because of the meaning this number had for the Jews. At one time there had been *twelve tribes* of Jews, each descended from the sons of Jacob. Jesus may have wanted to suggest that *his twelve apostles would be the foundation for a new people of God*. Through them he would invite *all* people, Jews and gentiles, into a new community of believers – *Christianity*.

The apostles came from a variety of different backgrounds:

- Peter, James and John, the disciples who were closest to Jesus, were fishermen
- Matthew (or Levi, as he was sometimes called) had been a tax collector
- Simon had been a Zealot.

At first glance, the apostles do not appear to have been very worthy of the trust Jesus put in them.

76   All About Faith

Consider how:

○ sometimes they completely failed to understand Jesus' message (Mark 4:13)

○ sometimes they needlessly quarrelled among themselves (Mark 9:33–35)

○ they deserted Jesus after his arrest on Holy Thursday (Matthew 26:56)

○ one of them, Judas, betrayed Jesus to his enemies (Luke 22:1–6).

However, in each one of the apostles Jesus saw the potential to do great things. Even when they deserted him, Jesus forgave them. After they had experienced Jesus risen from the dead, the apostles justified his trust in them and became outstanding leaders who led heroic lives.

Questions

1. Explain each of the following terms: (a) *disciple* (b) *metanoia* (c) *apostle*.
2. Why might Jesus have chosen precisely *twelve* apostles?
3. Identify the background of each of the following apostles: (a) Peter (b) Matthew (c) Simon.

Chapter Thirteen

The Kingdom of God

Introduction

Teaching was a vital part of Jesus' work as he travelled around the towns and villages of Palestine. He himself described it as *making God known*.

One phrase occurs again and again in Jesus' preaching: *the Kingdom of God*. This idea can be traced back to the Old Testament writings, but Jesus put it at the very centre of his teaching.

Difficulties

1. The very word '*kingdom*' conjures up an image of a clearly identifiable area of land, marked out on a map and ruled over by a king or queen. Many Jews in Jesus' time hoped that the Messiah would set up an independent Jewish kingdom. This was *not* the kind of kingdom Jesus was talking about.

2. Jesus never offered a precise definition of the *Kingdom of God*. Instead, he used a number of powerful and puzzling images and stories to illustrate its meaning.

   Jesus may have done this to force his listeners to think hard about his message and what it demanded of them. He wanted his followers to be serious-minded and committed people.

The meaning of the Kingdom of God

Throughout his teaching, Jesus made it quite clear that the Kingdom of God is *not* a place on a map. He taught that:

○ The Kingdom of God is *in the future*. It exists as the ideal or perfect community in which people truly realise that they are all God's children, members of the one family, and live lives committed only to goodness, justice and peace.

○ The Kingdom of God is *in the present*. Through the life and teaching of Jesus, the Kingdom of God has already come. It exists wherever God's love reigns in people's hearts and where they struggle to live their lives by God's standards.

78   All About Faith

- The Kingdom of God is a *very deep mystery*. It is so profound that only God fully understands it. Although people can gain insight into it through prayer and good works, they can never hope to understand it fully.

Questions

1. Why might Jesus have used puzzling images and stories when preaching about the *Kingdom of God*?
2. Explain each of the following statements:
   (a) The Kingdom of God is *in the future*.
   (b) The Kingdom of God is *in the present*.
   (c) The Kingdom of God is a *mystery*.

The Beatitudes

The Feeding of the Five Thousand by Hendrick de Clerck. The Gospels record how Jesus fed the 5,000 who flocked to see him with just five loaves of bread and two fish.

Jesus declared that the Kingdom of God had arrived *in him*. He called on people to reform their lives in order to enter the kingdom. In the *Beatitudes* (from the Latin '*beati*', meaning '*happy*' or '*blessed*'), he set out the qualities people need if they want to be members of the Kingdom of God. They should be:

- *Poor in spirit:* Humble enough to realise that they are weak and selfish and know that they need God's grace (love and strength) to live good lives.
- *Repentant:* Truly sorry for their own sins and dedicated to living good lives.
- *Meek:* Unassuming and modest people who draw all their strength and confidence from their faith in God.
- *Righteous:* People who long for God's rule on Earth and desire that God's will be done in their own lives as well as in society as a whole.
- *Merciful:* Ready to forgive those who offend them.
- *Pure in heart:* Single minded in their devotion to God. They are positive in outlook and do not readily attribute evil motives to others.
- *Peacemakers:* People who are at peace in themselves because of their trust in God and so are able to play a meaningful role in bringing peace to the wider world.
- *Courageous:* Willing to suffer for righteousness's sake and to endure persecution bravely because of their love for God. If they are faithful and loving, then they will share eternal life with God.

Question

1. Briefly list the qualities Jesus insisted should be possessed by those people who strive to be members of the Kingdom of God as set out in the *Beatitudes*.

The Kingdom of God

Jesus and women in the Gospels

Christ and the Woman with the Issue of Blood by Paolo Veronese. The woman depicted may be suffering from a haemorrhage cured when she touched Christ's robe. This scene emphasises the prominent role played by women in Christianity.

Jesus lived in a *patriarchal society*, i.e. one in which men had the dominant role. Women were generally regarded by men as useful possessions and largely treated as second-class citizens. We can see this reflected in the Old Testament. For example:

- the law regarding rape, which said that an unmarried woman was her father's property (Deuteronomy 22:28–29)
- the law which stated that a man could divorce his wife if he wished, but did not say that a wife was equally entitled to divorce her husband (Deuteronomy 24:1).

The evangelists portray Jesus as being very different from his contemporaries in his attitude to women. He did *not* share the view that women were second-class citizens which was so common among men of that era. Jesus treated women as people in their own right, as *equals*. Consider the following:

- Jesus included women among his disciples (see Luke 8:1–3).
- Jesus defied the social conventions of the day by having private conversations with women, where he listened to them, took what they said seriously and treated them with respect (see John 4:5–42).
- Jesus enjoyed the company of women and made no distinctions between his male and female followers (see Luke 10:38–42).
- Jesus accepted and readily acknowledged help from women (see Luke 7:36–50).
- Jesus emphasised equality of respect for women. When he said that a man could commit adultery against his wife, he was saying something *new*. The Jewish rabbis of that time only recognised adultery as being a sin committed by *a wife against her husband*.
- Jesus took a firm stand against the unjust treatment of women, e.g. the adulterous woman (John 8:1–11) and the healing of the crippled woman on the Sabbath (Luke 13:10–17).

Jesus said that he came into the world to free the oppressed and to raise up the humble. He wanted to show that the Kingdom of God breaks down all the barriers that separate people. He taught that all human beings, irrespective of their race, social class or gender, are *equal* in God's sight.

Questions

1. What is meant by a *patriarchal society*?
2. State one way in which women in the time of Jesus were treated as second-class citizens.
3. Identify three ways in which Jesus treated women as *equals*.
4. What did Jesus want to show people about the Kingdom of God?

Chapter Fourteen

Teaching by Parables

Introduction

Much of Jesus' preaching about the *Kingdom of God* was done through parables. They make up about a third of the total content of the Gospels. Therefore, it is necessary to study them carefully if we are to gain a better understanding of Jesus' message.

Meaning

A parable can be defined as

> an image or story in which Jesus illustrates some point of his message by using concrete examples drawn from everyday life.

Main themes

Jesus teaching in the synagogue.

The parables can be divided up into four main themes, where each group of parables is concerned with explaining an important aspect of the Kingdom of God.

1. Descriptions of God – *King of the Kingdom* in the parables of:

   ○ The Lost Sheep (Matthew 18:12–14)

   ○ The Lost Coin and The Prodigal Son (Luke 15:8–32)

   ○ The Labourers in the Vineyard (Matthew 20:1–16).

2. Guidance on how people should act if they hope to enter the Kingdom in the parables of:

   ○ the Pharisee and Tax Collector (Luke 18:9–14)

   ○ The Rich Fool (Luke 12:16–21)

   ○ The Talents (Matthew 25:14–30).

3. Teachings about how people should treat one another in the Kingdom in the parables of:

   ○ The Unforgiving Servant (Matthew 18:21–35)

   ○ The Good Samaritan (Luke 10:25–37).

4. Warnings about the future day of judgment, when God's Kingdom will come in all its fullness in the parables of:

   ○ The Weeds among the Wheat (Matthew 13:24–30)

   ○ The Ten Bridesmaids (Matthew 25:1–13).

Interpreting the parables:

A parable works on *two* levels:

- *On the surface*, a parable is an interesting, easily remembered story which uses images and ideas drawn from everyday life and has a strong human interest.
- *Below the surface*, a parable has a deeper meaning hidden within it which Jesus wants his listeners to work out, think about and apply to their own lives.

Example 1: The Good Samaritan (Luke 10:25–37)

The Good Samaritan by Siegfried Detler Bendixen.

This is the story of how a Samaritan traveller cares for a Jewish man who had been viciously attacked, robbed and left for dead.

The Samaritans were a people who lived in Samaria, the land between Judaea in the south of Palestine and Galilee in the north. Jews travelling between Judaea and Galilee would usually go across to the east bank of the River Jordan to avoid contact with the Samaritans (see John 4:9).

Samaritans came from Jews who had married *foreigners* (non-Jews) and there had been a quarrel between pure Jews and Samaritans for centuries. The Samaritans had built their own Temple at Mount Gerazim and had their own version of the Tenakh. By the time of Jesus, most Jews despised the Samaritans and had nothing to do with them.

Jesus shocked his Jewish listeners by making a Samaritan the hero of this story. However, he did so to make an important point about the Kingdom of God.

There is no place for racial or religious hatred in God's kingdom. The neighbour who God requires each person to love is *anyone in need*.

Example 2: The Sower (Luke 8:4–15)

Here Jesus uses the simple image of a farm labourer sowing seeds to encourage his listeners to reflect on the different ways in which people respond to his message.

- The seed is the word of God.
- Those who *hear* God's word preached to them, who *understand* it and who then *act* upon it are compared to *good soil* where the seed can take root and grow.
- The seeds that fall on the pathway represent the Gospel being preached to those whose hearts and minds are closed.
- The stony ground stands for those who initially receive Jesus' message gladly, but find it makes such big demands on how they behave that they give up trying and reject it.
- The thorns represent all the worldly cares about wealth and power that can smother people's

All About Faith

initial interest in and enthusiasm for Jesus' message.

Example 3: The Prodigal Son (Luke 15:11–32)

The Return of the Prodigal Son by James Jacques Joseph Tissot.

This is one of the best-known and most familiar of the parables. Luke tells us that Jesus told his story after the Pharisees had complained to him that he was spending too much time in the company of *sinners*, i.e. people who had cut themselves off from God.

The parable tells of a wealthy man with two sons, one of whom asked for his share of the family estate and then squandered it all on a wild lifestyle.

After a time the son became completely penniless and worked at the most wretched jobs to earn a living. Eventually he became truly sorry for being so *prodigal*, i.e. wasteful of all he had been given. He swallowed his pride and returned home to ask his father's forgiveness. To his astonishment, his father was delighted to have him home and forgave him. The elder brother, however, was annoyed with his father and resented his younger brother being forgiven.

The whole point of the story is that God cares deeply about all his children – both saints and sinners. God is always willing to forgive someone who is *genuinely* sorry. There are no limits to God's love.

Questions

1. What is a *parable*?
2. In what ways did the parable of *the Good Samaritan* challenge the accepted ideas of most Jewish people in the time of Jesus?
3. What message do you think the parable of *the Good Samaritan* contains for people today? Explain your answer.
4. The *good soil* refers to whom in the parable of *the Sower*?
5. What is the most important point of the parable of *the Prodigal Son*?

Chapter Fifteen

The Miracles of Jesus

Meaning

A *miracle* can be broadly defined as

a wonderful or awe-inspiring event which occurs solely as a result of God's direct action.

Number

The four Gospels record about thirty-five different occasions where Jesus performed a miracle. These miracles were as important to Jesus' ministry as his preaching.

Kinds of miracles

Christ healing the blind man of Jericho.

Jesus' miracles fall roughly into four categories:
- healing miracles
- exorcisms (casting out demons)
- nature miracles
- restorations of life.

Difficulties

For some people, the miracle stories create serious problems. They find it hard to believe such things. It is sometimes said that Jesus would be more 'acceptable' *without* the miracles.

However, it is impossible to extract a miracle-free account of Jesus' ministry from the Gospels, for several reasons:

- the story of Jesus' conception in Mary's womb is a miracle
- much of Jesus' preaching takes a specific miracle as its starting point
- the miracles are presented as inspiring many of those who witnessed them to have faith in Jesus
- Christianity itself is founded on the miracle of Jesus' resurrection.

Did Jesus really work miracles?

Christians believe that Jesus *did work miracles*. They point out that:

- The first-century Jewish historian Josephus described Jesus as a *doer of wonderful deeds*.

84   All About Faith

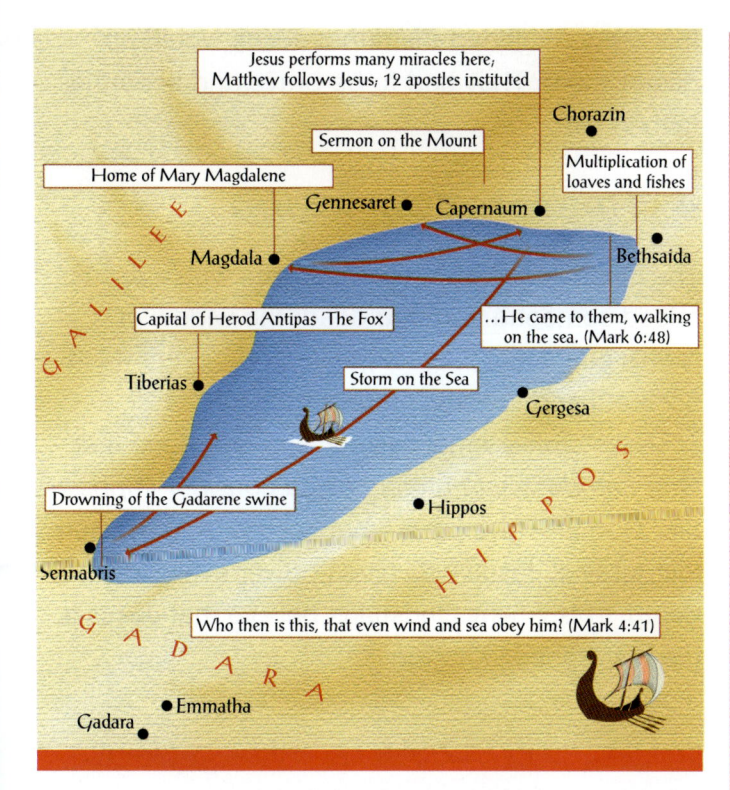

Map labels:
- Jesus performs many miracles here; Matthew follows Jesus; 12 apostles instituted
- Chorazin
- Sermon on the Mount
- Home of Mary Magdalene
- Multiplication of loaves and fishes
- Gennesaret • Capernaum
- GALILEE
- Magdala
- Bethsaida
- Capital of Herod Antipas 'The Fox'
- ...He came to them, walking on the sea. (Mark 6:48)
- Tiberias
- Storm on the Sea
- Gergesa
- HIPPOS
- Drowning of the Gadarene swine
- Hippos
- Sennabris
- GADARA
- Who then is this, that even wind and sea obey him! (Mark 4:41)
- Gadara • Emmatha

- Even Jesus' enemies recognised that he had an extraordinary power to work miracles.
- Many eyewitnesses to the works of Jesus would still have been alive when the Gospels were written. If the Gospel accounts had not been based on actual events, these people would have raised serious objections to them.

Questions

1. How many miracles are recorded in the Gospels?
2. Identify the four kinds of miracle that Jesus worked.
3. The following is a list of some of Jesus' miracles in the Synoptic Gospels:
   - healing a leper
   - healing a centurion's servant
   - calming a storm
   - casting out the Gadarene demoniac(s)
   - healing a paralytic
   - restoring Jairus' daughter to life
   - healing two blind men
   - the miracle of the loaves
   - restoring the widow's son to life
   - walking on water
   - healing a deaf man
   - giving sight to the blind man of Bethsaida
   - expulsion of a demon from a young boy.

   Reorganise these miracle stories under the four categories of:
   (a) *healing miracles*
   (b) *exorcisms*
   (c) *restorations of life*
   (d) *nature miracles*.
4. Is it possible to extract a miracle-free account of Jesus' ministry from the Gospels?
5. What evidence is there to support Christian belief that Jesus performed miracles?

Why did Jesus work miracles?

The Gospel accounts reveal that:

- Jesus was often reluctant to work a miracle
- he frequently instructed the people he had healed not to tell anyone what he had done
- he refused to use his miraculous powers either to win over the powerful or to gain the acceptance of those unwilling to listen to his message.

Christian scholars believe that Jesus worked miracles for three reasons:

1. to strengthen the faith of those people who *already* believed in him

The Miracles of Jesus

2. to reveal God's power in order to show people that the Kingdom of God had begun *in him*
3. to demonstrate God's *unlimited love* for each and every human being, regardless of their race or religion.

Consider the following examples of miracles.

1. Healing miracle

In Luke 5:12–14, Jesus not only healed a man afflicted by leprosy but actually *touched* him. Lepers were social outcasts who were ordered to keep apart from other people because of the contagious nature of their disease. Jesus did something that no one else would have dared to do. He showed that while people may have rejected this man because of his illness, God had not. Jesus' actions revealed the love of God reaching out to and embracing people who were abandoned and suffering.

2. Exorcism

In Mark 5:1–20, Jesus encountered *Legion*, a man said to have been possessed by demons. This man lived in a cemetery, cut off from his family and neighbours, who were frightened by him. Jesus cast out the demons or, as some scholars think, the mental illness that had shattered this man's life and restored him to his right mind. The man was able to live with other people again and could rebuild his life. Jesus' actions brought peace and hope where before there had been only rage and despair.

3. Nature miracle

In Luke 8:22–25, Jesus ordered the winds to cease and the water to be calm. To the amazement of the apostles this immediately happened. This story gave great comfort to the early Christians. In times of terrible suffering, when it seemed that great waves of Roman persecution might drown them, this story reminded them that Jesus would not desert them. They had to be brave and keep their faith in him.

4. Restoration to life

The Gospels tell of three occasions where Jesus raised someone from the dead: the widow of Nain's son (Luke 7:11–17), Jairus' daughter (Mark 5:21–43) and Lazarus (John 11:38–44).

These stories emphasise Jesus' message that *God can do what human beings consider impossible*. God can give back what seems to have been lost forever. Jesus was given power even over death. This is why Christians believe that Jesus is *the resurrection and the life*.

The importance of the miracles

The resurrection of Lazarus.

Without tangible evidence of Jesus' power over sin, suffering and death, his preaching about the Kingdom of God would have been less believable to his Jewish audience.

Consider the story of the healing of the paralysed man (see Mark 2:1–12 or Luke 5:17–26):

- Most Jews at that time regarded physical suffering as a punishment from God for sins committed.
- They would only believe that the man's sins had been forgiven if his paralysis was removed.

By healing the man Jesus showed that his *authority* to forgive sins and his *power* to heal *came from God*, and that what he said was *true*.

Questions

1. In what circumstances did Jesus refuse to work a miracle?
2. Briefly state each of the three reasons why Jesus worked a miracle.
3. Choose one miracle story. Write a brief account of it in your own words.
4. What was the importance of the miracle stories for Jesus' preaching about the Kingdom of God?

Summary

If we draw together all the clues about the *Kingdom of God* found in the Gospels, we can construct the following diagram showing its many aspects.

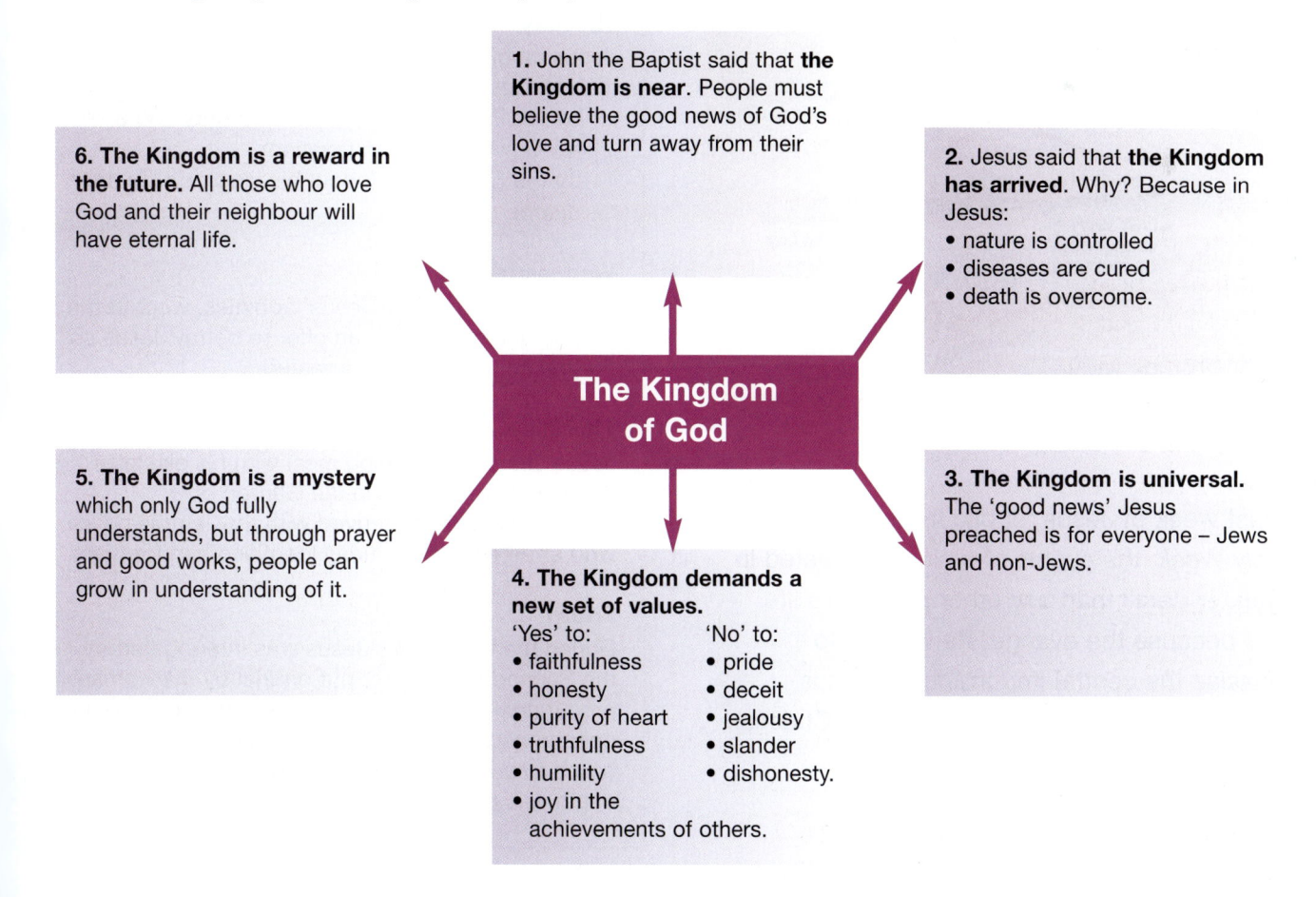

The Kingdom of God

1. John the Baptist said that **the Kingdom is near**. People must believe the good news of God's love and turn away from their sins.

2. Jesus said that **the Kingdom has arrived**. Why? Because in Jesus:
- nature is controlled
- diseases are cured
- death is overcome.

3. The Kingdom is universal. The 'good news' Jesus preached is for everyone – Jews and non-Jews.

4. The Kingdom demands a new set of values.

'Yes' to:
- faithfulness
- honesty
- purity of heart
- truthfulness
- humility
- joy in the achievements of others.

'No' to:
- pride
- deceit
- jealousy
- slander
- dishonesty.

5. The Kingdom is a mystery which only God fully understands, but through prayer and good works, people can grow in understanding of it.

6. The Kingdom is a reward in the future. All those who love God and their neighbour will have eternal life.

The Miracles of Jesus

Chapter Sixteen

Jesus' Entry into Jerusalem

Holy Week

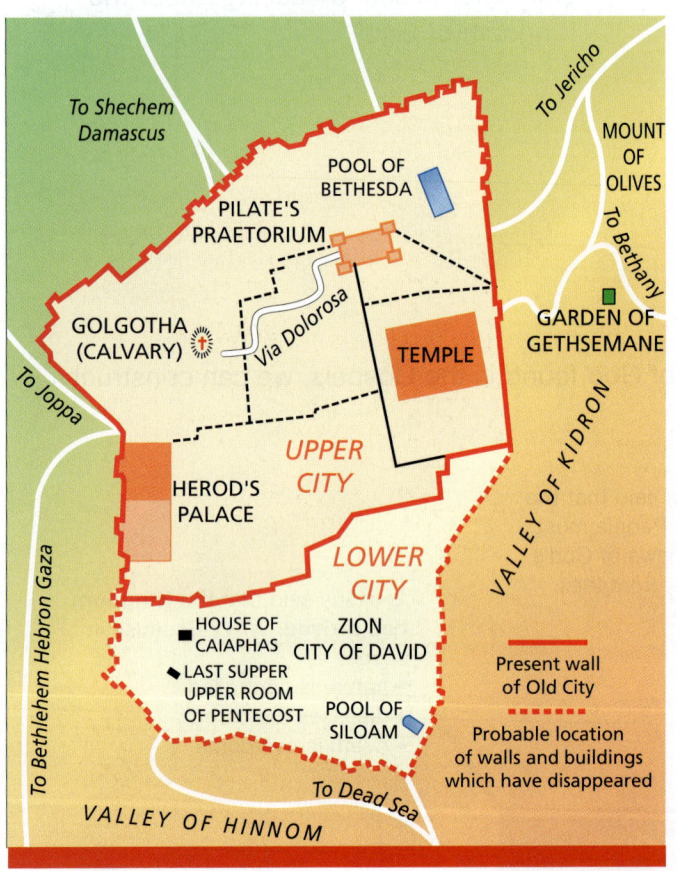

Jerusalem in the time of Jesus.

The last week of Jesus' public ministry is known as *Holy Week*, the events of which are treated in far greater detail than any other part of his life. This is because the evangelists wanted to emphasise the central importance of Jesus' suffering, death and resurrection for the Christian religion.

An Outline of Events

Sunday
Jesus arrived in Jerusalem seated on a colt and was welcomed by cheering crowds waving palm branches and shouting '*hosanna*'.

Monday
Jesus went to the Temple and denounced the traders and money-changers. Jesus overturned their stalls and drove them out of the Temple. The Pharisees and the Sadducees in the Sanhedrin plotted to kill Jesus.

Tuesday
Jesus taught in the Temple and was asked some leading questions intended to trap him:
- by the Pharisees (about his authority and about his views on Roman taxation)
- by the Sadducees (about his views on life after death).

Wednesday
Judas Iscariot, one of Jesus' apostles, went to the Jewish authorities with an offer to betray Jesus so that he could be quietly arrested.

Thursday
Jesus shared an evening meal with his disciples. Judas left early. Later, in the Garden of Gethsemane, Judas arrived with the Temple police, who arrested Jesus. Judas identified him for them.

Friday
During the early hours Jesus was interrogated by the Sanhedrin and later put on trial by the Roman procurator, Pontius Pilate. Jesus was scourged and condemned to death by crucifixion. Jesus was nailed to an upright cross and suffered an agonising death. His body was buried in a tomb nearby.

88 All About Faith

Revealing the Messiah

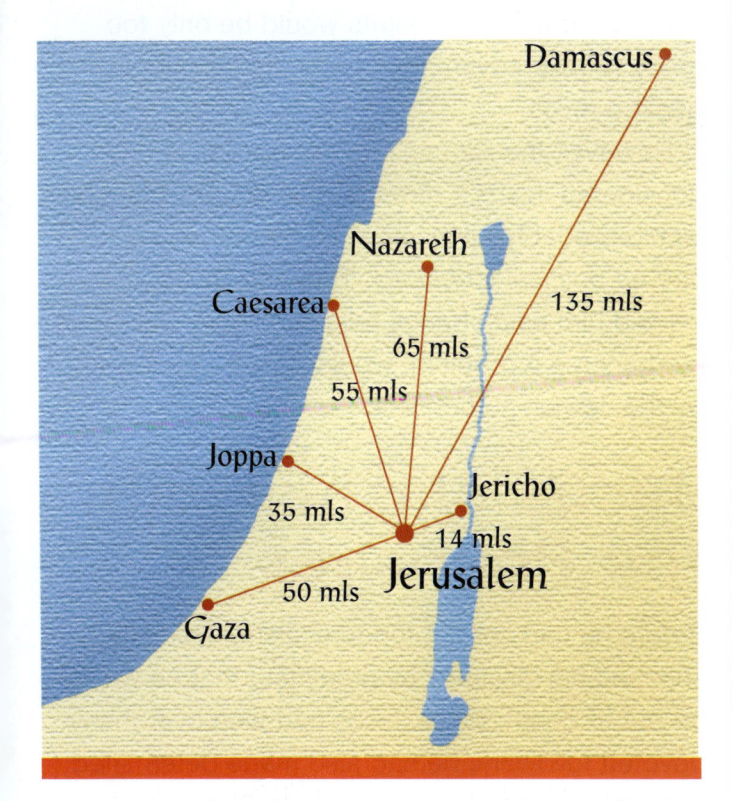

Distances from Jerusalem. The distances shown on this map are 'as the crow flies'. Distances by road were much greater. For example, the traveller from Jerusalem to Jericho would have covered a distance of about twenty-one miles by road.

For several years Jesus healed and taught people. Then, probably in the spring of AD 30, he decided that the time had finally arrived for him to go to Jerusalem and reveal that he was the Messiah.

While journeying to Jerusalem, Jesus had several discussions with his apostles about the meaning of all that he had said and done. It seems that they still did not understand the meaning of the Messiah in the same way as Jesus did. For example, the apostles still seem to have expected Jesus to set himself up as a ruler of a new and powerful Jewish kingdom. However, Jesus made it clear that this was *not* what he wanted to achieve. Instead, Jesus told his followers that:

- he had come into the world *to serve others and not to be served*
- anyone who wanted to be his disciple would have to be *humble* and *willing to endure great suffering*.

It was only *after* Jesus had risen from the dead that his followers began to understand the meaning of what he had said and done.

Questions

1. What is the name given to the last week in Jesus' life?
2. The apostles believed that Jesus was the Messiah. What were they expecting him to do?
3. How was Jesus' own understanding of his mission as Messiah *different* from that of the apostles?

Palm Sunday

Entry into Jerusalem by Sassetta.

Jesus arrived in Jerusalem as preparations were beginning for the annual feast of *Passover*, the time when Jews celebrate God's freeing of their ancestors from slavery in Egypt. As he joined the procession of pilgrims entering the city for the festival, Jesus was well aware of two things:

- most Jews believed that Passover was the time when the long-awaited Messiah would reveal himself

Jesus' Entry into Jerusalem 89

- many Jews expected that the Messiah would be a great warrior king, just like David in the Old Testament.

Jesus made it clear, however, that he had *no* such political ambitions. He did not arrive in glittering style, trying to impress people. Instead, he entered Jerusalem seated on a colt or a young donkey. This was because the colt was a humble animal of peace and *not* a war horse. This made it clear that Jesus would lead by *peaceful* means. He invited people to follow him and never forced them to do so.

Jesus was enthusiastically welcomed by a large crowd of pilgrims. Many of them greeted him by waving palm branches. It is because of this that the event is known as *Palm Sunday*. Jesus was acclaimed *King of Israel* and many people shouted '*hosanna*', meaning '*save now*' (see John 12:13). This welcome was like the coronation procession for a new king.

Questions

1. What is the feast of *Passover*?
2. What did many Jews believe about the Passover and the coming of the Messiah?
3. Why did Jesus enter Jerusalem seated on a colt?
4. Why is the first day of Holy Week known as '*Palm Sunday*'?
5. What does '*hosanna*' mean?

Reactions

While Jesus was enthusiastically greeted by large crowds of pilgrims, others observing this scene would have been far from happy. Influential members of the Sanhedrin would have been worried that Jesus was about to upset the delicate political peace in Jerusalem. The city was crowded with easily excited pilgrims who were very anti-Roman and who longed for the promised Messiah to appear. There was great tension in the air and it was feared that the Zealots would be only too ready to take advantage of any opportunity to begin a revolt.

However, the Romans do not appear to have considered Jesus a threat at this stage. Their spies would probably have informed them that *Jesus had no political ambitions*. They may have just viewed him as a strange religious figure who, if he did become a problem, would best be dealt with by the Jewish authorities.

Jesus clashes with the Pharisees

Before he had set out for Jerusalem, Jesus had shocked his disciples by predicting that he would be put to death. While Jesus had won over many devoted followers, he had also made determined enemies, most notably among the Pharisees.

The Pharisee, shown here at prayer, wears clothing that actually differs little in its essentials from the workaday clothing of a Jewish peasant family. However, he has added a *tallith*, or tasseled prayer shawl. Attached by leather thongs to his forehead and left hand are the *tefillin*.

The evangelists recorded a number of occasions on which Jesus clashed with members of the Pharisees, such as:

- the healing of the paralysed man (Luke 5:17–25)
- the casting out of an evil spirit (Mark 3:20–30)
- the healing of the man with a withered hand (Luke 6:6–11)
- the healing of the man born blind (John 9:13–41).

The Pharisees considered themselves to be *the* greatest experts on God's law. Jesus had shocked most of them by what he had said and done.

While a few Pharisees, such as Nicodemus and Joseph of Arimathea, supported Jesus, most opposed him.

The accusations of leading Pharisees against Jesus	Jesus' response to these accusations
Jesus committed *blasphemy* (showed grave disrespect toward God) by claiming to have the power to forgive sins. Only God could so such a thing.	Jesus stated that as *the son of Man* (a title for the Messiah used in the Old Testament book of *Daniel*), he had the authority to forgive sins.
Jesus received his power to perform miracles from Satan.	Jesus said that his power to restore life and health came from God.
Jesus broke the Sabbath laws prohibiting work when he healed the sick.	Jesus stated that he was the *Lord of the Sabbath*.
Jesus was unfit to be called *rabbi* because he mixed with people they considered outcasts, such as tax collectors, lepers and non-Jews.	Jesus said that his mission was to reveal God's love to all people. Everyone was invited to enter the Kingdom of God – saints and sinners, Jews and non-Jews.

Conflict

Jesus' responses infuriated his enemies. But Jesus went even further. He called these Pharisees *hypocrites* who had replaced love of God with a cold-hearted obsession with petty rule-keeping. This was because by the first century AD all Jews were expected to follow 613 laws that covered every aspect of a person's life. For example, according to strict Jewish law, a person was not allowed to whisk away a fly that landed on his/her body during the Sabbath day. He/she simply had to wait until the fly decided to go away. Devout Jews were expected to know all these laws and follow them without exception. If they did not, then it was believed that they would be punished by God.

Jesus saw how all this *legalism* (harsh and excessive devotion to the precise letter of the law) had become a terrible burden for so many good people. He claimed that many Pharisees, though *not all*, were encouraging legalism because they had closed their hearts to God's message. He offered an alternative to this. His teaching was very challenging, but *positive* and *life giving*. Jesus emphasised love of God rather than fear of God.

It is because of all this that Jesus realised that a showdown between him and his opponents was inevitable.

Questions

1. Why were influential members of the Sanhedrin worried by Jesus' entry into Jerusalem?
2. Was Jesus aware that his life was in danger?
3. Did any Pharisees support Jesus?
4. Imagine you are an influential Pharisee in the Sanhedrin. State your reasons for opposing Jesus.

Chapter Seventeen

Jesus in the Temple

Introduction

There were two great Temples in the history of Judaism. The first Temple was built by Solomon (961–922 BC) but was lost in the destruction of Jerusalem in 587 BC. A second Temple was built around 515 BC. Under Herod the Great this Temple was enlarged. Work had begun in 20 BC, and ten years later the Temple was rededicated. However, it was only finally completed in AD 64.

In AD 70 the Romans destroyed the Temple and reduced Jerusalem to a heap of rubble. The only part of the Temple which survived was a section of the perimeter wall built by Herod the Great. This is sometimes called *the Western Wall* or *the Wailing Wall*. Today, it is the holiest place in Judaism.

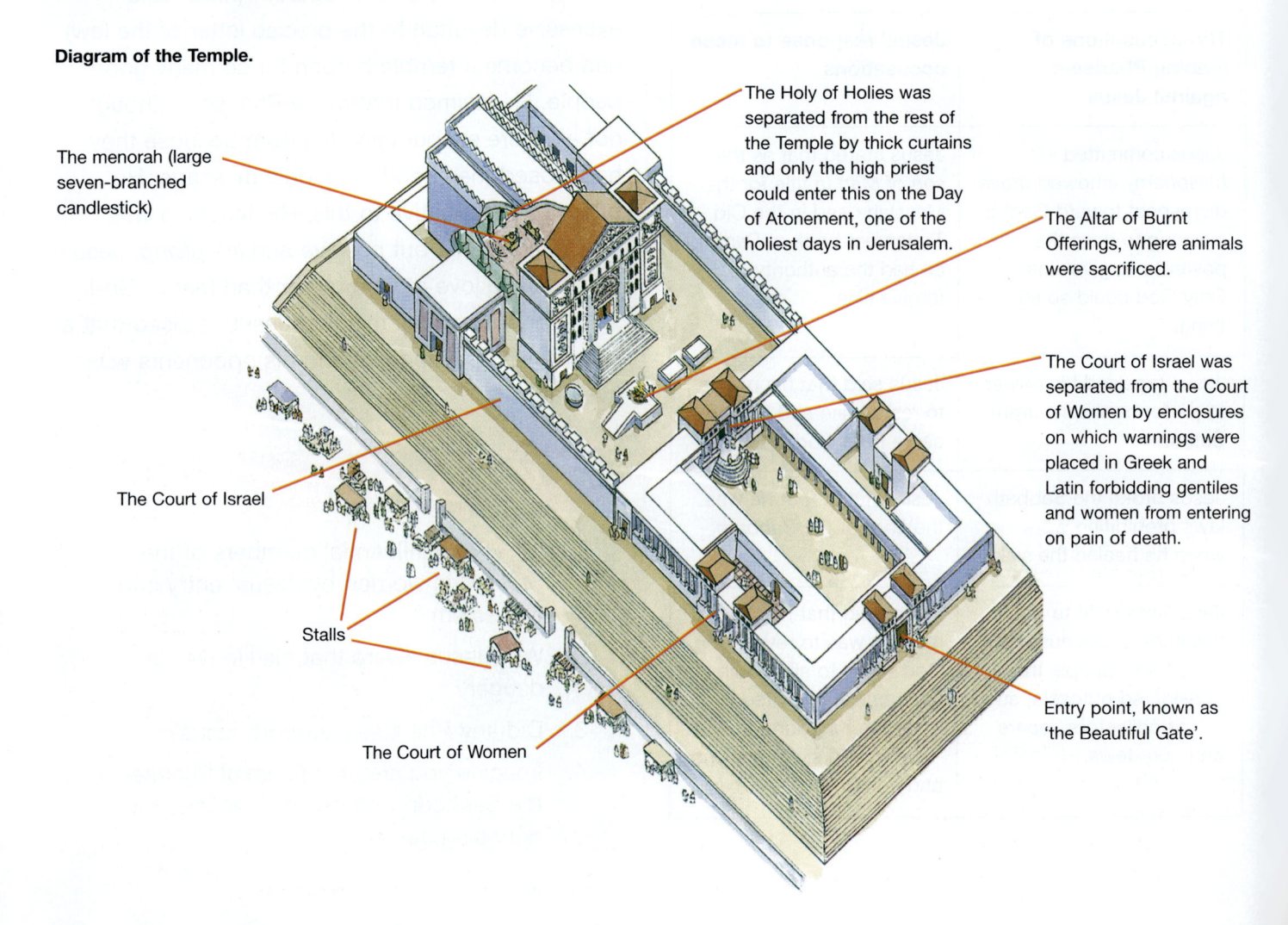

Diagram of the Temple.

- The menorah (large seven-branched candlestick)
- The Holy of Holies was separated from the rest of the Temple by thick curtains and only the high priest could enter this on the Day of Atonement, one of the holiest days in Jerusalem.
- The Altar of Burnt Offerings, where animals were sacrificed.
- The Court of Israel was separated from the Court of Women by enclosures on which warnings were placed in Greek and Latin forbidding gentiles and women from entering on pain of death.
- The Court of Israel
- Stalls
- The Court of Women
- Entry point, known as 'the Beautiful Gate'.

92 All About Faith

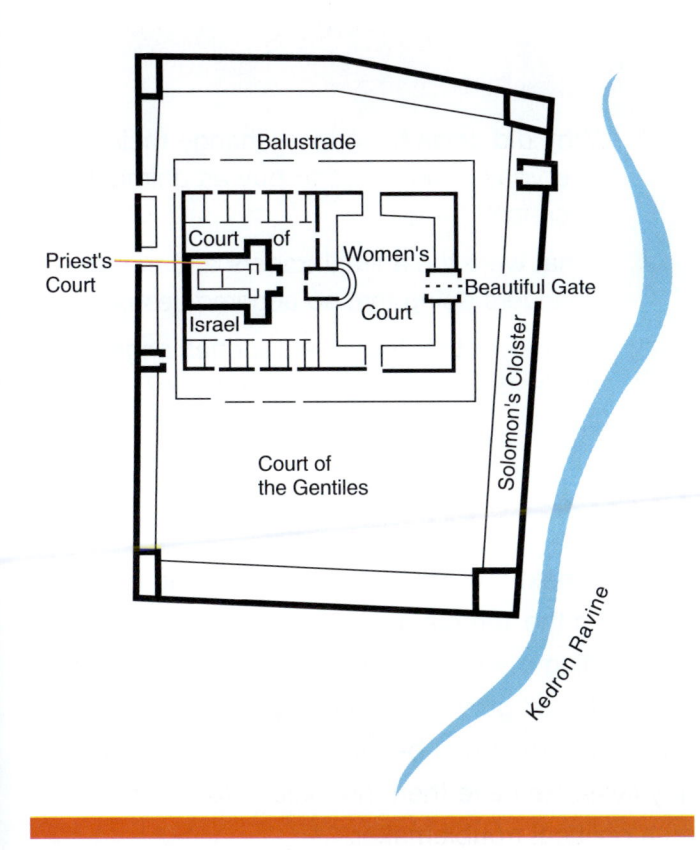

The cleansing of the Temple

According to the earliest Gospel account, Mark 11:15–18, Jesus went to the Temple on the Monday of Holy Week.

What he found there both appalled and deeply angered him. To understand why Jesus reacted in this way, we need to know how the Jews worshipped God in the Temple.

Consider the following:

- All pilgrims to the Temple were expected to give the Temple priests an animal which would then be killed and burned as a *sacrifice* (offering) to God.
- However, only animals *without imperfections* (see Leviticus 1:3) were acceptable as sacrifices. Such animals could only be bought in the market that the Temple authorities had allowed to be set up in the outer area of the Temple, known as the *Court of Gentiles*, but at a higher price than elsewhere.
- However, Jews could not purchase any of these acceptable animals with their everyday money. All silver coins in circulation bore the image of the Roman emperor. Jews were forbidden to make an image of anyone (see Exodus 20:4), especially someone who claimed to be a god. These coins could not be used to buy an animal acceptable for sacrifice.
- Instead, Jewish pilgrims had to go to the stalls of the money-changers who had also been permitted into the Court of Gentiles. These money-chargers exchanged the people's everyday coins for special *Temple coins* with which they could buy an animal for sacrifice. These money-changers charged a high price for exchanging pilgrims' coins.

Seeing how devout pilgrims were being exploited by such unscrupulous people, Jesus decided to drive them out of the Temple area. It was supposed to be a *house of prayer* and a *light to the gentiles*, but they had turned it into a den of profiteering. Jesus overturned their tables and drove out their animals.

Denarius coin with the head of Tiberius (AD 14–37).

Jesus in the Temple

Reaction

Christ Driving Out Them that Sold and Bought from the Temple by James Jacques Joseph Tissot.

This whole scene was undoubtedly observed by the Temple priests, who were among the most influential members of the Sadducees. Jesus had openly attacked the corrupt practices that they had allowed to thrive within the Temple's precincts. Jesus had publicly embarrassed them and had shown them to have failed to uphold the high standards they demanded of everyone else.

The Sadducees agreed with the Pharisees. They could not tolerate anyone who showed them up and challenged their authority in such a manner.

The cleansing of the Temple seems to have finally convinced the leading Sadducees and Pharisees in the Sanhedrin to find some way to have Jesus put to death.

Questions

1. What role did animals play in Jewish Temple worship in the time of Jesus?
2. Where in the Temple did the Jewish authorities allow a market to be set up?
3. Why did Jews have to exchange their everyday silver coins to buy an animal for sacrifice?
4. What were the animal traders and money-changers doing that so angered Jesus?
5. Why were the Jewish authorities angered by Jesus' cleansing of the Temple?

Betrayal

Over the next few days, Jesus taught and healed people in the Temple area, attracting large crowds. The leading members of the Sanhedrin could not ignore Jesus' growing popularity. However, they could not arrest him because he had not broken any laws. He gave them no excuse to brand him as a political troublemaker.

However, the leaders of the Sadducees and the Pharisees were determined to find a way to silence Jesus. Since they feared that any attempt to arrest him in daylight would lead to a major riot in Jerusalem, they decided to arrest him after dark, in a place that was out of public view.

However, they had a problem. No one seemed to know where Jesus stayed at night. To find him they would need inside help. This was provided by one of the apostles – Judas Iscariot.

Explanations

Judas had witnessed all the good Jesus had done. He had been one of Jesus' close circle of friends. Yet in spite of all this, he betrayed Jesus. Why?

Generally, scholars have tended to support one or other of the following explanations for this act of betrayal.

1. **Judas was a greedy and disloyal opportunist who sold out his friend to make money and gain influential contacts in the Sanhedrin.**

94 All About Faith

The Synoptic Gospel accounts all agree that Judas approached the Sanhedrin's key figures and *volunteered* his help:

Judas went to the chief priests and officers of the Temple guard and discussed with them how he might betray Jesus. They were delighted and agreed to give him money. He agreed and watched for an opportunity to hand Jesus over to them when no crowd was present. (Luke 22:4–6)

2. **Judas was not treacherous, but rather *misguided*.**

   Why did Judas commit suicide after hearing that Jesus had been condemned to death? One evangelist offers the following account:

When he found out that Jesus had been condemned, Judas his betrayer was filled with remorse and took the thirty pieces of silver back to the chief priests and elders. 'I have sinned,' he said, 'I have betrayed innocent blood.' 'What is that to us?' they replied. 'That is your responsibility.' And flinging down the silver pieces in the Temple, he went away and hanged himself. (Matthew 27:3–5)

Perhaps Judas *was* horrified to realise what he had done. But what exactly had he intended to do in the first place?

Thirty silver coins was the price of a slave – surely a small sum to receive for handing over someone who the Sanhedrin considered to be such a serious threat. Why did Judas accept such a modest payment? Was the money ever really an issue?

The Payment of Judas by Giotto di Bondone. Judas receives the thirty pieces of silver.

Some scholars believe that a clue might be found in Judas' surname, which may have meant 'man of the Sicarii', a small, violent Zealot group. Did Judas wrongly believe that the Kingdom of God which Jesus had preached would be an independent Jewish kingdom ruled over by Jesus himself? Did Judas conclude that all he had to do was force Jesus to go before the Sanhedrin and that Jesus would convince them that he was the Messiah? Did he think that Jesus would work a miracle if he knew his life was in danger? Could Judas really have been so *blind* to the truth? Perhaps. Perhaps not. We cannot say for certain.

Questions

1. Why did the Jewish authorities want help from someone inside Jesus' circle of followers?

2. (a) Briefly explain the two theories about Judas' betrayal of Jesus.
   (b) Which of these two explanations do you find the most convincing? Give reasons for your answer.

Chapter Eighteen

The Arrest and Interrogation of Jesus

The Last Supper

The Last Supper by Philippe de Champaigne.

On the Thursday evening before the great feast of Passover (which would begin at 6 p.m. on Friday evening), Jesus shared a private meal with his closest friends. It was held in a room loaned to them by a follower in Jerusalem. This event has since become known as *the Last Supper*.

At the end of the meal and according to normal Jewish custom, Jesus said a prayer of thanksgiving to God for the meal they had shared. Then he did something unexpected.

He took the bread, blessed and broke it, gave some to his friends and said:

> *'This is my body given for you; do this in remembrance of me.'* (Luke 22:19)

Then, after they had eaten this, he took a cup of wine and after blessing it, gave it to them and said:

> *'Drink from it, all of you. This is my blood, the blood of the new covenant, which is poured out for many for the forgiveness of sins.'* (Matthew 26:28)

By these words and actions, Jesus forewarned his friends of his approaching death and clearly connected this meal with his death.

The disciples present that evening were puzzled, confused and upset by what Jesus had said. They were well aware of the increasing risk to Jesus' life, but all the confrontations of the previous days seem to have made them more confident that Jesus had come to Jerusalem to assume his role as king. They were not expecting him to be killed. It was only after Jesus' death and resurrection that they came to understand the meaning of what he had said and done that Thursday evening.

Questions

1. On what day of Holy Week did the Last Supper take place?
2. Why were the disciples puzzled by what Jesus had said and done?

96   All About Faith

Betrayal

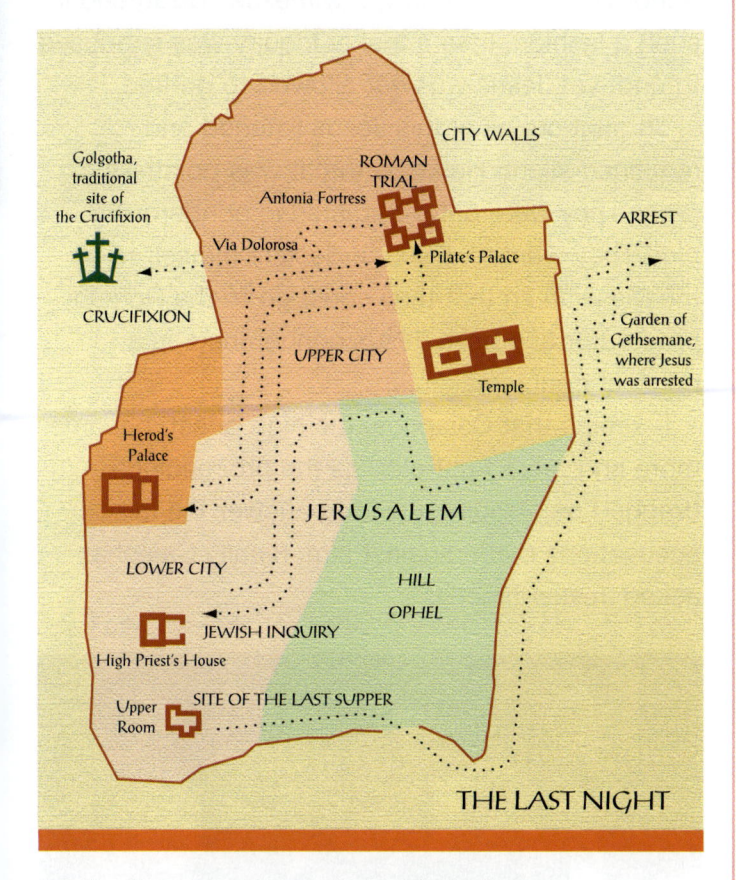

Locating the events of the Passion and death of Jesus.

After the Last Supper, Jesus and his disciples went outside the city to the *Garden of Gethsemane*, near the Mount of Olives, to pray. It was at this point that Judas arrived with a contingent of Temple guards to arrest Jesus.

Jesus challenged their right to do this. He pointed out how he had taught in public each day in the Temple but that none of them had had the courage to arrest him there. Instead, they came to arrest him under cover of darkness when no one could see what they were doing.

Jesus and the disciples could have resisted arrest and might have been able to escape into the night, but Jesus undoubtedly realised that his enemies would never cease to pursue him because he posed such a threat to them. They would simply capture him another day. To save lives, Jesus stopped his disciples from fighting to prevent his arrest.

When Peter drew his sword and cut off the ear of the high priest's servant, Jesus immediately stepped in to halt the violence and healed the wounded man.

Peter's denial

When Jesus was arrested, most of the disciples fled. Peter, however, followed the arrest detail to find out what was going to happen.

Jesus had startled Peter at the Last Supper by predicting that soon *Peter would publicly deny having ever known him*. Peter was so upset at Jesus saying this that he promised to face death alongside Jesus.

When the test came, however, Peter failed. It seems that Peter greatly underestimated the sheer heart-clenching terror he would experience when faced with the threat of interrogation and execution. Jesus, in contrast, was quite aware of all this.

While Jesus was being interrogated by the Sanhedrin, Peter remained in the courtyard outside. When identified as a follower of Jesus on three occasions, Peter vehemently denied it. Luke records something the other accounts do not mention: after Peter had denied Jesus, he turned around to see Jesus looking straight at him. Peter was crushed by the realisation that what Jesus had said had come to pass. Peter had denied ever knowing his closest friend. Peter went away and wept bitterly.

Questions

1. Where was Jesus arrested?
2. Who led the group of Temple guards who arrested Jesus?
3. Why did Jesus allow himself to be arrested?
4. (a) What did Jesus predict about Peter at the Last Supper?
   (b) How did Peter react when Jesus said this?

Jesus before the Sanhedrin

Jesus was brought before the seventy members of the Sanhedrin. They met in the Hall of Hewn Stones in the inner court of the Temple. They sat in a semi-circle and were presided over by Caiaphas, the high priest.

This was more a court of inquiry than a trial. Its main purpose was to decide what charge the Jewish leaders would make against Jesus in the trial that would be held later by the Roman procurator.

According to the Gospels, Jesus was not given a fair hearing by the Sanhedrin.

- Instead of charging Jesus with some offence and calling witnesses, they questioned Jesus in the hope that he would condemn himself by his own words.
- It was *not* considered legal to hold either a trial or an inquiry such as this at night.
- Jesus was beaten and abused both before his questioning and during it.

This is perhaps not surprising. The Sanhedrin's leaders had apparently *already* made up their minds. They wanted Jesus put to death. *Both* the Sadducees and the Pharisees had their reasons for wanting this.

- Jesus had publicly challenged the authority of both the Pharisees and the Sadducees and had exposed their hypocrisy.
- Jesus claimed to be the Messiah. *Both* the Pharisees and the Sadducees feared he might somehow encourage a popular uprising against the Romans.

During his interrogation, Jesus was accused of wanting to destroy the Temple. This was quite obviously *not* what Jesus had wanted to happen. Moreover, the witnesses brought forward to support this allegation *contradicted each other*. According to Jewish law, if witnesses disagreed in such a fashion, then a trial or inquiry was supposed to end, yet Jesus was *not* allowed to go free.

Throughout all of this Jesus listened and remained silent. He knew that it was pointless to reply. They were only interested in condemning him. They wanted Jesus to declare himself to be the Messiah so that they could go to the Roman procurator and have Jesus condemned as a political troublemaker.

It seems that Caiaphas, the high priest, became more and more frustrated as the proceedings dragged on. Jesus refused to answer the false accusations made against him. Finally Caiaphas asked Jesus directly:

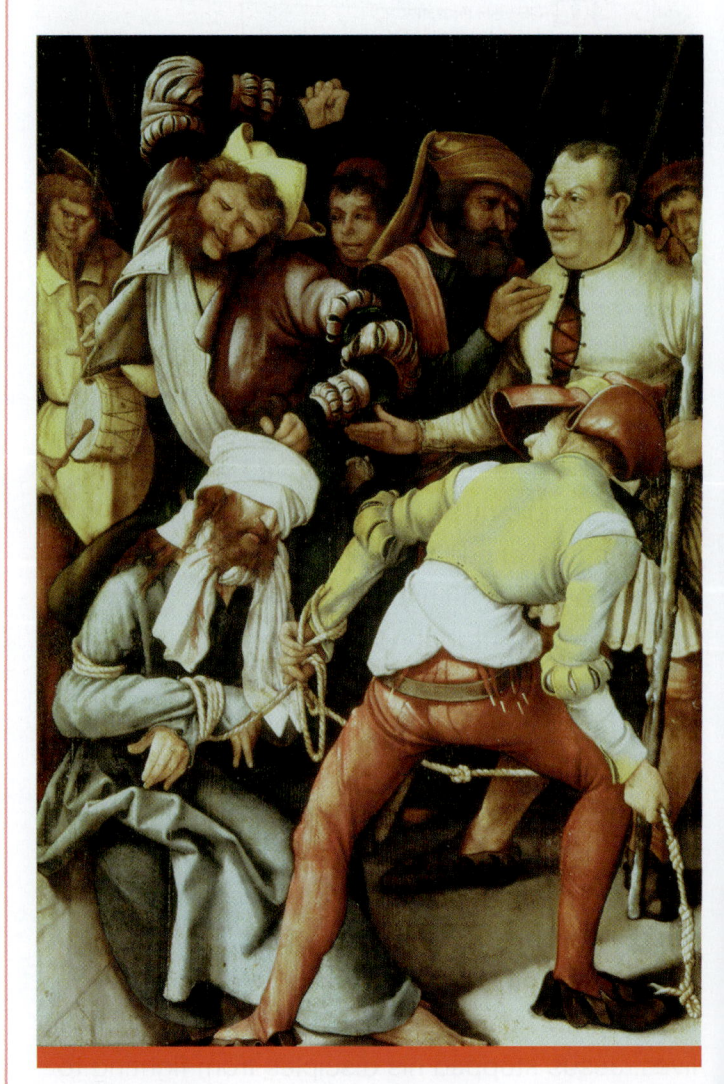

The Mocking of Christ by Matthias Grünewald.

98 All About Faith

'Are you the Messiah, the Son of the Blessed One?' (Mark 14:61)

Jesus chose, at last, to respond, answering:

'I am. And you will see the Son of Man sitting at the right hand of the Mighty One and coming on the clouds of heaven.' (Mark 14:62)

The Sanhedrin leaders were infuriated by this answer. This was because Jesus had not only identified himself as the Messiah, but had also gone on to say that he shared a unique relationship with God, implying that the Sanhedrin had no authority over him.

The Sanhedrin's leaders declared that Jesus had committed *blasphemy* by claiming for himself a dignity due to God alone. Although they wanted to put Jesus to death, they no longer had the legal power to impose the death penalty on him. Only the Roman procurator had the power to order Jesus' execution. For this reason they handed him over for trial by the procurator, Pontius Pilate.

The high priest. The apron-like garment worn by the high priest was covered in part by a breastplate, which hung by gold chains from two stone epaulets and was inset with twelve gemstones. The stones, set in gold and engraved with the names of the children of Israel, were of twelve different colours and symbolised the twelve tribes of the Hebrew nation.

Questions

1. What was the name of the high priest?
2. Do you think that Jesus was given a fair hearing by the Sanhedrin? Give reasons for your answer.
3. Why did many of the Sanhedrin members want Jesus put to death?
4. Why did they accuse Jesus of blasphemy?
5. Why did the Sanhedrin's leaders hand Jesus over for trial by the Roman procurator?

The Arrest and Interrogation of Jesus

Chapter Nineteen

The **Trial** and **Death** of Jesus

Introduction

Pontius Pilate, the Roman procurator, was staying at the Antonia Fortress near the Temple complex. Shortly after dawn on what Christians call *Good Friday* morning, a delegation from the Sanhedrin brought Jesus before Pilate. Although the Sanhedrin had declared Jesus guilty of blasphemy, this was a religious matter which would have been of no interest to Pilate. If the Jewish leaders wanted the Romans to execute Jesus for them, then they would have to convince Pilate that Jesus posed a danger to Roman rule over Palestine.

The charges against Jesus

Christ is brought before Pontius Pilate.

The delegation from the Sanhedrin accused Jesus of *treason*, which was punishable by death. They claimed that Jesus had:

○ proclaimed himself *Messiah* and called himself *King of the Jews*

○ told the people not to pay their taxes to the emperor

○ disturbed the peace and might soon lead a revolt.

Pontius Pilate was not the kind of man who needed much persuading to condemn a person to death if he believed that he/she was a threat. It is estimated that there were 6,000 executions during his ten years as procurator (AD 26–36).

Pilate's response

Pilate was trained in Roman law. The Gospel accounts show that after Pilate had examined the evidence presented by the Jewish authorities to support their accusations, he concluded that *Jesus was innocent*.

Pilate did not want to condemn Jesus, but he was worried about offending the Sanhedrin. On hearing that Jesus came from Galilee, he sent him to be questioned by Herod Antipas, the tetrarch of Galilee (see Luke 23:6–12).

Herod Antipas

Herod had heard about Jesus and tried to force him to work a miracle for him. When Jesus refused either to say or do anything, Herod let his guards

100 All About Faith

dress Jesus in a purple robe and make fun of the idea that Jesus was a king. Then he sent Jesus back to Pilate.

Pilate questions Jesus

The Roman procurator was still satisfied that Jesus posed no threat, but to clarify matters beyond all doubt he asked Jesus a direct question:

> 'Are you the king of the Jews?'

Jesus responded:

> 'Yes, I am a king.' (John 18:37)

However, Jesus explained his words by adding:

> 'Mine is not a kingdom of this world; if my kingdom were of this world, my men would have fought to prevent my being surrendered to the Jews. But my kingdom is not of this kind.' (John 18:36)

Pilate seems to have found Jesus' calm manner both impressive and disturbing. He was quite unsure what to do next. He realised that there was no case against Jesus and *was anxious to set him free* (John 19:12). However, the Sanhedrin's representatives were becoming angrier as each moment passed. In an effort to pacify them Pilate stated:

> 'As you can see, the man has done nothing that deserves death, so I shall have him flogged and then let him go.' (John 23:15–16)

A Roman scourging was a horrific experience: the victim was tied to a post and then repeatedly struck upon the back by a multi-stranded whip, which had pieces of jagged metal inserted into each leather strand so that the lashes not only cut the skin, but tore strips of flesh off each time they made contact. A severe scourging could kill a person.

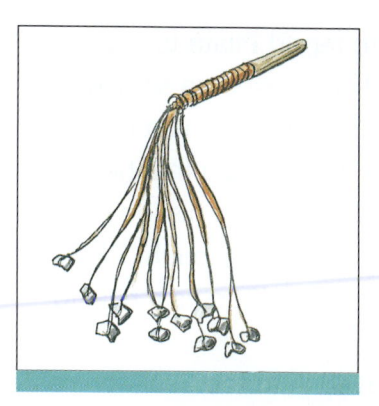

Roman whip of the kind used to scourge Jesus.

Jesus or Barabbas

However, Pilate underestimated the determination of the high priest and the Sanhedrin. They wanted Jesus dead. It was as simple as that. Then, Pilate pulled what he thought was a master stroke. Over the years it had become the accepted practice for the Roman procurator to release a Jewish prisoner during a major religious feast. To honour the feast of Passover, Pilate offered the crowd gathered outside the Antonia Fortress a choice: he would allow them to choose the one to be released. He offered them either Jesus or a violent rebel named Barabbas. Pilate was surprised when the crowd shouted for Barabbas to be set free. One evangelist claims that the crowd had been *put up* or bribed to do this by members of the Sanhedrin.

Pilate was forced to set Barabbas free in order to avoid a riot.

Jesus is condemned to death

Pilate still hesitated to condemn Jesus. Then the Sanhedrin delegates uttered words that seem to have frightened him:

The Trial and Death of Jesus

'If you let this man go, you are no friend of Caesar. Anyone who claims to be a king is an enemy of Caesar.' (John 19:12)

They were threatening to report Pilate to the Emperor Tiberius for failing to execute someone who they claimed was a threat to Roman rule of Palestine. Pilate was no doubt afraid that he might be recalled to Rome and might lose his job or even his life, especially if Tiberius thought Pilate had allowed Jesus to set himself up as a rival to the emperor.

At this point Pilate caved in to the Sanhedrin's demand and declared Jesus guilty of *treason*.

In a dramatic public gesture by which Pilate tried to distance himself from the whole event:

He took water and washed his hands in front of the crowd. 'I am innocent of this man's blood,' he said. 'It is your responsibility.' (Matthew 27:24)

But this gesture could not alter the fact that Pilate was first and foremost interested in saving his job. To do this *he knowingly condemned an innocent man to death*.

Questions

1. When the Sanhedrin brought Jesus before Pontius Pilate, what political offence did they accuse Jesus of committing?
2. If you were Pontius Pilate, how would you have understood Jesus' answer to your question *'Are you the king of the Jews?'* Would you have considered him a threat to Roman rule? Explain your answer.
3. How was Jesus treated by Herod's guards?

Questions

4. Why did Pilate offer the crowd outside the Antonia Fortress a choice between freeing either Jesus or Barabbas?
5. (a) What was the crowd's reaction to this offer?
   (b) Why might they have reacted in this way?
6. (a) In what way did the Sanhedrin delegates threaten Pilate?
   (b) How did he react? Why did he do this?
7. How did Pilate try to distance himself from the condemnation of someone he *knew* to be innocent of treason?

Carrying the cross

Jesus was condemned to death by *crucifixion*.

The story of Jesus' crucifixion is so familiar to us that it is quite easy to forget how truly awful it was to die on a cross. It was a barbaric form of execution reserved for *non-Romans* found guilty of treason. Crucifixion caused the condemned person to suffer an agonising death. This was to deter other people from challenging the authority of Rome.

Contrary to the way in which artists over the centuries have depicted the crucifixion, historians believe that Jesus was actually given the wooden crossbeam to carry, rather than the entire cross.

This was a heavy burden for someone in his seriously weakened state. Jesus had just endured a dreadful scourging and must have lost a lot of blood. Wearing a crown of thorns made for him by mocking soldiers, Jesus was led through the narrow streets of Jerusalem, forced to carry the instrument of his death upon his back.

The Via Dolorosa, the route to Golgotha, where Jesus was crucified.

Most of those who lined the route that Jesus took were horrified and stunned by what had happened:

> *Large numbers of people followed him, who mourned and lamented for him.* (Luke 23:27)

The nailing

Crucifixion by Eduard Karl Franz von Gebhardt. Crucifixion was a form of punishment the Romans had learned from Carthage.

The execution procession finally halted when it reached a small hill outside the city walls, aptly named *Golgotha*, a Hebrew word meaning '*place of the skull*', or in Latin, *Calvary*. Jesus was forced to lie on his back while nails were driven through his wrists (not, as was generally believed until recently, through his hands) to secure him to the crossbeam. Then the crossbeam was lifted up and slotted onto an upright pole that stood permanently on the site. Once fixed in this position, Jesus' feet were nailed to the upright post and his body was probably tied to the cross with ropes to prevent it from tearing free.

The ordeal

Crucifixion was death by slow suffocation. A condemned person was hung by his arms, which cut off the air supply to the lungs. In order to breathe, Jesus had to push down on the nails through his feet, which caused agonising pain. Even the strongest person could not survive this for long. Jesus endured this torture for six hours.

Annoyed at the way the Jewish elders had manipulated him, Pilate decided to have the last word and, deliberately seeking to insult them, he ordered that a placard be nailed on the upright beam above Jesus' head, which read:

Jesus of Nazareth, King of the Jews.

This infuriated the Sanhedrin delegates but Pilate refused to change it.

Jesus was left hanging between two thieves and the Roman guards gambled for his few possessions. All the while he could hear the insults of those who had plotted his death. When faced with this nightmarish test, Jesus stayed true to his beliefs, saying of his enemies:

> '*Father, forgive them, for they know not what they are doing.*' (Luke 23:24)

The Trial and Death of Jesus

The death of Jesus

The Gospels assert that about noon, an unusual darkness *'came over the whole land'* and lasted until about three o'clock that afternoon. Then Jesus was offered a sponge soaked in vinegar diluted with water, which was held up to his lips with the aim of refreshing him and keeping him conscious for as long as possible. But, unexpectedly, after he had taken a drink, he said:

'It is accomplished' and bowing his head, he gave up his spirit. (John 19:30)

Questions

1. Describe the Roman method of crucifixion.
2. What was the name of the place where Jesus was crucified?
3. What was written on the placard Pilate ordered to be nailed to the upright beam of the cross above Jesus' head?
4. How did Jesus react to the insults of his enemies while he was dying on the cross?
5. (a) How long did Jesus suffer on the cross before he died?
   (b) At about what time on Good Friday is Jesus said to have died?

Chapter Twenty

The **Resurrection** of Jesus

The removal and burial of Jesus' body

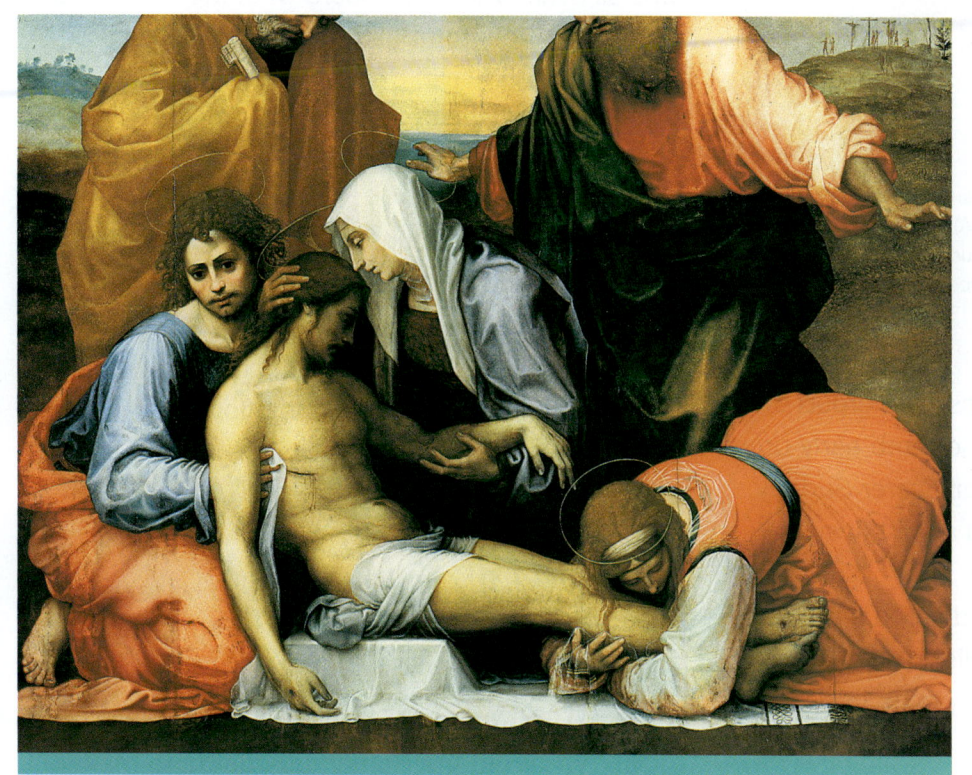

Deposition by Fra Bartolommeo.

According to Jewish religious law, the body of a criminal could not be left displayed on a cross over the Sabbath. It had to be buried before nightfall.

To ensure that Jesus and the two thieves crucified with him would be dead and buried before the Sabbath began that Friday evening at sundown, the Jewish leaders asked the Roman guards to break the prisoners' legs with a hammer so that they could no longer hold themselves up to breathe. However, when the guards came to Jesus they realised that he was already dead. His death was due to a combination of massive blood loss, exhaustion and suffocation. But to be absolutely sure that Jesus was dead, they *pierced* his side with a spear (see John 19:34).

Then Joseph of Arimathea came forward and claimed Jesus' body for burial. Joseph was a member of the Sanhedrin who had supported Jesus.

The burial itself was a rushed affair because of the approaching Sabbath. It was decided that the women present would return on the Sunday morning, once the Sabbath was over, to embalm Jesus' corpse properly. For the time being it was

wrapped in a shroud and put in a tomb, which was hewn in stone in which no one had yet been buried. (Luke 23:53)

The entrance to the tomb was sealed by rolling a large, heavy stone into place. It is believed that the little tomb was in a garden close to the city gates and '*near at hand*' (John 19:42) to where Jesus had been crucified.

The Resurrection of Jesus **105**

The empty tomb

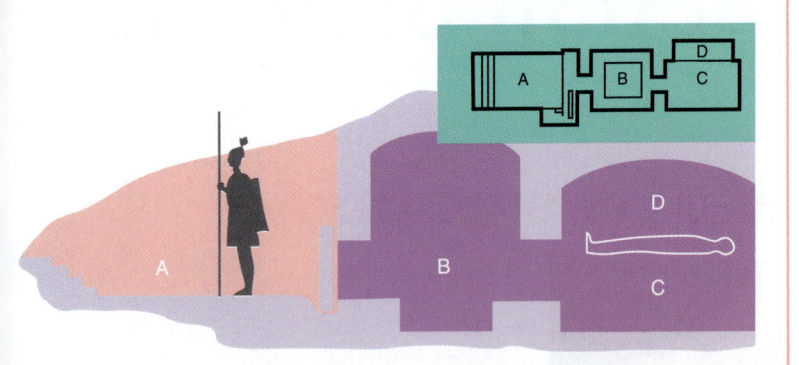

The tomb of Jesus. A profile and plan of a garden tomb. Built into the side of a hill, it was approached by stairs (A), which led to the small, low opening of the tomb. The opening, usually covered by a stone, led to a small anteroom (B). In the last room (C), the body was put in a niche (D).

After the Jewish Sabbath had passed, a group of Jesus' female disciples went to the tomb early on the morning of what Christians call *Easter Sunday*. They brought with them spices to anoint Jesus' corpse.

Although the Gospel accounts differ in certain respects, they do agree on the following points:

- a group of women led by Mary Magdalene went to the tomb
- they discovered that the stone covering the entrance had been rolled back
- they found that the tomb was empty
- they heard an announcement that Jesus had risen from the dead
- they went immediately to where the apostles were hiding and reported what had happened.

> **N.B.**
> It is important to note that no one actually claimed to have seen Jesus rise from the dead. The Gospel accounts only deal with what happened *afterwards*.

The apostles' reaction

The apostles reacted with total disbelief:

When they heard that Jesus had risen...they did not believe it. (Mark 16:11)

The apostles were deeply upset and humiliated by the events of Good Friday. They believed that Jesus' mission had ended in total failure. He was dead. It was all over. When they heard what the women said about an empty tomb and a risen Jesus,

Their words seemed to them like nonsense. (Luke 24:11)

However, Peter was unsure and, accompanied by John, he risked going to the tomb. There they discovered that it was indeed empty. Jesus' corpse was missing and the linen cloths in which it had been wrapped were lying on the floor of the tomb.

Questions

1. Why did Jesus' body have to be taken down from the cross before sundown on Good Friday?
2. What were the causes of Jesus' death?
3. What did the Roman guards do to make certain that Jesus was dead?
4. Who claimed Jesus' body for burial?
5. Describe the tomb in which Jesus' body was placed.
6. Who were the first of Jesus' followers to go to the tomb on Easter Sunday morning?
7. On what points do the Gospels agree concerning the discovery of the empty tomb?
8. Did anyone actually witness Jesus rising from the dead on Easter Sunday morning?

All About Faith

Questions

9. What was the reaction of the eleven apostles when they heard the women's story of the empty tomb?
10. How did Peter react to this news?

The appearances of the risen Jesus

Noli Me Tangere by Fra Angelico, fresco in the Museum of San Marco, Florence.

According to the New Testament, a large number of people actually met and talked with Jesus on several different occasions *after* his death and burial.

Drawing on the different Gospel accounts, we can see that these separate appearances by Jesus include the following elements:

- Jesus unexpectedly appears among his disciples, usually greeting his astonished followers with some reassuring words, such as '*Peace be with you*.' (John 20:21)
- In each case all those present are initially shocked and frightened when they first see the risen Jesus, a perfectly natural reaction in such an extraordinary set of circumstances.
- This shock and fear quickly fades away and is replaced by a great inner peace and joy when they realise that Jesus has risen.
- The disciples realise that although Jesus is alive, he is *not* alive in the same way as before his death. They had seen Jesus bring Lazarus and Jairus' daughter back to life. They make it quite clear that Jesus has *not* been restored to his old earthly life, as had Lazarus and Jairus' daughter.
- Jesus is no longer limited by the physical laws of the universe that limit all human freedom of action. Jesus can walk through bolted doors and appear in two places at the same time. Through his resurrection Jesus has been transformed or '*glorified*' and *is living a completely new kind of life*.
- Jesus tells his followers to spread the news of his resurrection and tells them to '*Go, therefore, make disciples of all nations*.' (Matthew 28:19)

Questions

1. Read John 20:19. What were Jesus' first words to his disciples? Why do you think he said this?
2. What effect did Jesus' sudden appearance among them have on his disciples?
3. Christians believe that after his resurrection *Jesus was living a completely new kind of life*. What do you think this means?
4. What command did Jesus give his disciples?

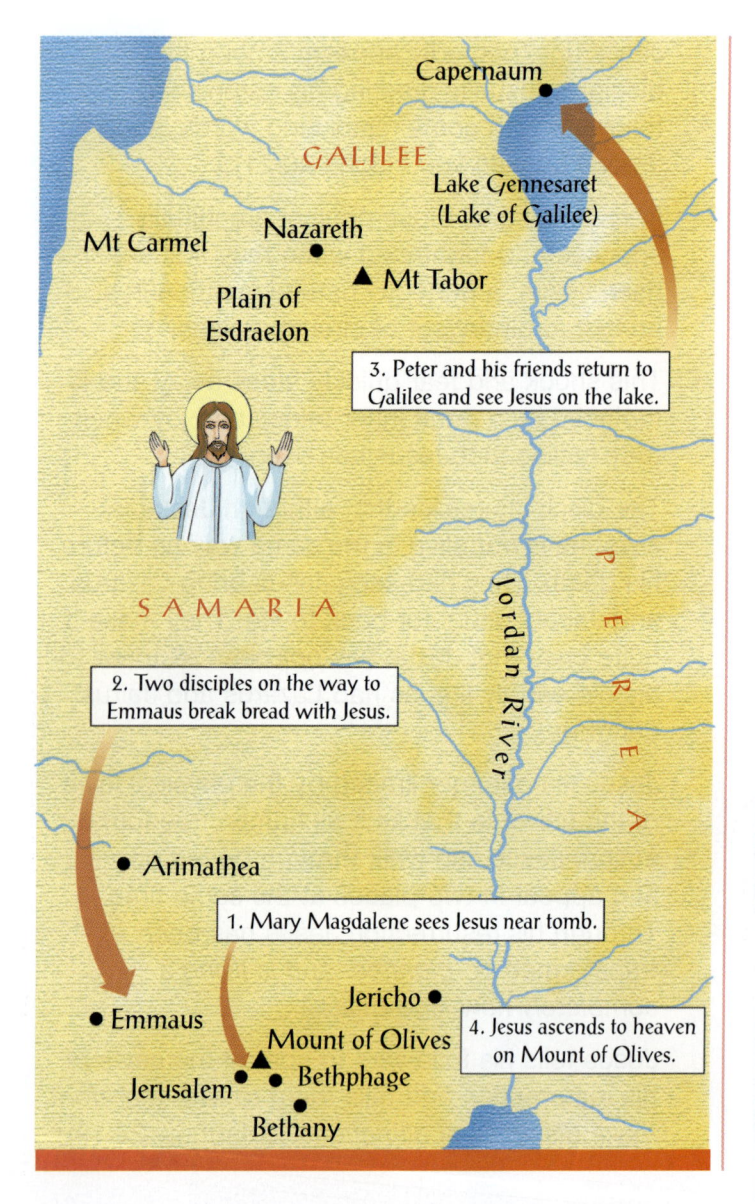

The appearances of the risen Christ.

Did the Resurrection really happen?

Over the centuries, four alternative explanations have been offered for the Christian doctrine of the resurrection. We shall consider each in turn.

Claim 1	Jesus did not die on the cross.
Response	*No. Jesus did die on the cross.*
Consider	○ Both the Roman historian Tacitus and the Jewish historian Josephus accepted that Jesus died on the cross.
	○ Roman executioners were very thorough. They pierced Jesus' side with a spear, puncturing his lungs to ensure his death.

108 All About Faith

Claim 2	The apostles stole the body of Jesus from the tomb.
Response	*No. They would not have stolen the body from the tomb.*
Consider	○ The apostles had deserted Jesus and left him to die alone. His arrest and execution had completely shattered their confidence in him. ○ The apostles did not come forward to claim Jesus' body for burial on Good Friday. They feared that they would be arrested and executed. They would have avoided going anywhere near the tomb for fear of being arrested. ○ All the indications are that the apostles wanted to put the whole event behind them and return to Galilee as soon as possible.

Claim 3	What the apostles experienced after Jesus' death were ghostly apparitions.
Response	*No. They did not experience some disembodied, ghostly apparition. The risen Jesus was physically, tangibly present to the apostles.*
Consider	○ At first glance it might seem that Jesus' visits were merely ghostly apparitions. For example, Jesus could appear suddenly in a locked room and vanish at will. ○ However, Jesus appeared in *solid* form. For example, he ate food with his followers and allowed Thomas to touch the wounds on his body.

Claim 4	The apostles invented the story of Jesus' resurrection.
Response	*No. The resurrection really happened.*
Consider	○ Those Jews who believed in life after death thought that it would only take place at the end of time and be shared by all those people who had lived good lives. ○ The idea of a single individual person rising from the dead was an *unheard of* idea, which most Jews would have found very difficult to accept. ○ Further, if the evangelists had wanted to invent a phoney story about Jesus rising from the dead, then they would never have identified *women* as the first witnesses to the resurrection. According to Jewish law at that time, a woman could not give evidence in court and would have had no credibility as a witness. ○ Finally, their experience of the risen Jesus transformed the apostles from frightened people into courageous missionaries who spread Jesus' message far across Europe, North Africa and even to India. All suffered great hardship and many paid for their devotion to Jesus with their lives. It is most unlikely that they would have gone to such lengths if they had invented the story of the resurrection.

The importance of the resurrection

The Incredulity of St Thomas by Benjamin West.

Christianity makes an extraordinary claim. It teaches that the resurrection of Jesus is an *historical fact* – that Jesus actually died on the cross on Good Friday and rose from the dead on Easter Sunday.

This claim is at the very heart of the Christian faith, for as Paul wrote:

> *If Jesus has not been raised, then our preaching is useless and your believing in it is useless.* (1 Corinthians 15:14)

It is a matter of profound importance, therefore, that Jesus actually rose from the dead to a new and glorified life on Easter Sunday morning. Through his resurrection, Jesus demonstrated that:

○ there is life after death

○ he is the promised Messiah

○ the power of good has triumphed over evil

○ what people do in this life has real meaning and value, and that the good they do in this life will be rewarded in the next.

Questions

1. What is the evidence to support the claim that Jesus died on the cross?
2. Why is it thought to be highly unlikely for the apostles to have gone to the tomb and stolen the body?
3. Why might Jesus' visits with his disciples be thought of as *ghostly apparitions*?
4. What is the evidence in the Gospel accounts to support the belief that Jesus was *not* a ghost?
5. Did the disciples expect that a single, individual person such as Jesus would rise from the dead within two days of his execution?
6. Why is it said that if the evangelists wanted to make up a phoney story then they would not have identified women as key witnesses?
7. Describe the change that came over the disciples in the days after Jesus' death.
8. What extraordinary claim does Christianity make?
9. Identify *four* ways in which the resurrection of Jesus is of profound importance.

Chapter Twenty-one

The Expansion of Christianity

Sources

Most of what is known about the first thirty years of the Christian community is to be found in the *Acts of the Apostles*. The author of *Acts* is the same person who wrote the Gospel of *Luke*. It takes up the story where the Gospel of Luke ends – with the ascension of Jesus into heaven.

The Ascension

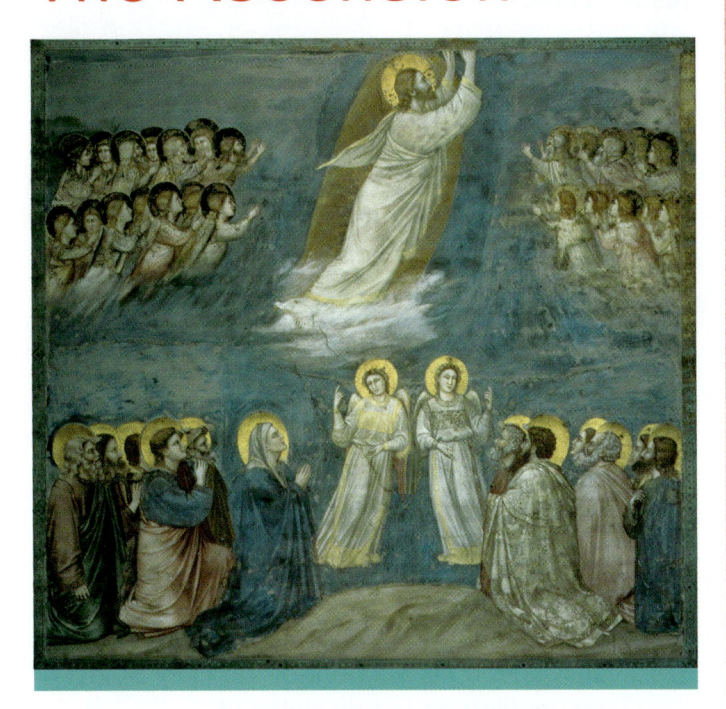

The Ascension, early fourteenth-century fresco by Giotto di Bondone in the Scrovegni Chapel at Padua, Italy.

Forty days after Easter Sunday, Jesus appeared to his disciples for the last time. He told them that although he would no longer be physically present among them, he would send them the *Holy Spirit* to give them the guidance and strength they would need for completing the work he had begun.

> *After saying this, he was taken up to heaven as they watched him, and a cloud hid him from their sight.* (Acts 1:9)

When the evangelist wrote this he did *not* mean this to be taken literally, any more than when we say that someone *moves up* the school at the end of each academic year, we mean that he/she has gone up to the top floor of the building. *Taken up to heaven* means that Jesus was returning to a better or higher form of life with God the Father. Luke used these particular words in an effort to communicate an experience that was very difficult to put into words. The mention of the word '*cloud*' is to be expected here. The Old Testament writers often used the word 'cloud' when they wanted to describe God's presence in some event.

Pentecost

Ten days after the Ascension, the disciples gathered together to celebrate the Jewish harvest festival of Pentecost. They met in a room in Jerusalem. There they waited for the coming of the Holy Spirit as Jesus had promised:

> *When Pentecost day came round, the apostles had all met in one room, when suddenly they heard what sounded like a powerful wind from heaven, the noise of which filled the entire house in which they were sitting: and something appeared to*

The Expansion of Christianity   111

them that seemed like tongues of fire; they separated and came to rest on the head of each of them. They were filled with the Holy Spirit. (Acts 2:1–4)

The Pentecost by El Greco.

This experience of the Holy Spirit of God entering the lives of these disciples was so extraordinary that Luke found it very difficult to express it in words. When writing his account in Acts, he once again had to resort to using *picture-language*:

○ the coming of the Holy Spirit upon the disciples was likened to the rushing of '*powerful wind*'

○ the courage and strength the disciples gained was like '*tongues of fire*'.

These symbols of *wind* and *fire* were frequently used in the Old Testament to convey the idea of God's power and goodness, purifying and renewing those who opened their hearts and minds to his love. Not surprisingly, Pentecost Sunday became a popular date for christening newborn babies because it was associated with the idea of new beginnings.

As a result of this Pentecost experience, the disciples were fired up to begin fulfilling the mission they had received from Jesus. They began openly preaching that Jesus was the Messiah, that he had risen and they began healing the sick in Jesus' name.

Questions

1. (a) In which New Testament book is the story of the first thirty years of the Christian community to be found?
   (b) Who wrote it?
2. Why did Jesus promise to send the Holy Spirit to his disciples after his ascension into heaven?
3. What do scholars believe the phrase '*taken up into heaven*' means?
4. What did Old Testament Jewish writers use the word '*cloud*' to indicate?
5. Why did the author of Acts use *picture-language* in his account of the Holy Spirit descending on the disciples at Pentecost?
6. What did Old Testament writers use the symbols of *wind* and *fire* to say about God?
7. What effect did this Pentecost experience have on the disciples?

Reaction

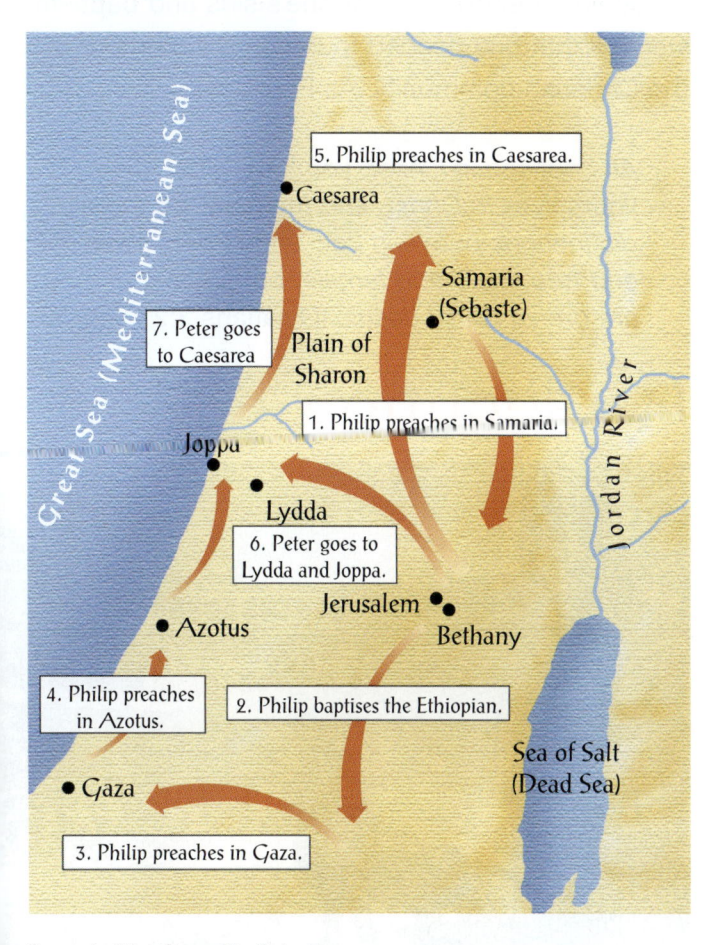

Spread of the Gospel in Palestine.

As more and more people began to ask for baptism and became disciples of Jesus, the Sanhedrin became increasingly worried. They put a young disciple named Stephen on trial. He was accused of *blasphemy*. The trial ended in a riot and Stephen was stoned to death by an angry mob.

After this many *Christians* (meaning followers of *Christ*, from the Greek word for Messiah, '*Christos*') decided to leave Jerusalem. They first spread from Palestine through the network of Jewish communities that existed in other parts of the empire. These Jews living outside Palestine were known as the *Diaspora* (from the Greek word meaning '*dispersion*').

The spreading of the Gospel message throughout the Roman empire was greatly assisted by the excellent road network, which the Romans had built to ensure the safe travel and swift communication necessary for the effective government of such a vast territory.

Paul

St Paul by Etienne Parrocel.

Though the apostles played a vital role in the early success of Christianity, most scholars agree that the most outstanding Christian missionary of the first century AD was Paul (or in Hebrew, Saul) of Tarsus. Before he became a Christian, Paul had been a devout Pharisee who had persecuted Christians in Jerusalem.

While journeying to Damascus in Syria, where he intended to persecute the Christians there, Paul had an extraordinary and sudden conversion to Christianity. Instead of persecuting the Christians, Paul *joined* them.

The Expansion of Christianity

Not surprisingly, the Jewish authorities decided to arrest Paul on a charge of *heresy* (spreading false ideas about God). Paul escaped and set out on the first of three great missionary journeys.

Paul was uniquely well equipped to spread the Christian religion. Though Jewish by religion, he was a Roman citizen by birth. He spoke Aramaic, Greek, Hebrew and Latin and so could communicate with a wide variety of people, both Jews and gentiles (non-Jews).

Paul travelled tirelessly throughout the eastern Mediterranean area, spreading the Gospel message, baptising people and setting up Christian communities in every town and city he visited. His *epistles* (letters written offering advice to these new Christian communities) testify to his wide-ranging influence.

Questions

1. What was the *Diaspora*?
2. What does the word '*Christian*' mean?
3. How did the Christian message quickly spread from Palestine throughout the Roman Empire?
4. What is *heresy*?
5. Write a brief essay on the important role Paul played in the spread of Christianity.

Moment of decision

A problem soon arose for the new Christian converts who had not been Jews beforehand. Did they need to become Jews first *before* they could become Christians? Did they have to be circumcised *before* they were baptised?

A general council of Christian leaders, the first of its kind, was held in Jerusalem in AD 49 to answer these questions. After a long debate, Paul won the support of Peter and the majority of those present to his solution. Peter, as leader of the Christian community, declared that the new converts did *not* have to become Jews first before becoming Christians. Repentance for one's sins and baptism were all that one needed to become a member of the Christian community. As Paul wrote:

> *All baptised in Christ, you have all clothed yourselves in Christ, and there are no more distinctions between Jew and Greek, slave and free, male and female, but all of you are one in Christ Jesus.* (Galatians 3:27–28)

Persecution

Completed in AD 80, the Colosseum became an enduring symbol of Roman persecution of Christians.

It was the sudden and widespread growth of Christianity throughout the empire that first brought it to the attention of the Roman authorities. By the middle of the first century AD, they viewed Christians with growing suspicion for several reasons.

○ The Romans were *polytheists* (believed in many gods). They were tolerant of the religious beliefs of their conquered subjects so long as they worshipped one extra god – the *emperor* – as a guarantee of their loyalty. Only one group – the Jews – had been excused from doing this, in gratitude for Herod the Great once helping Julius Caesar. This exemption had been granted to the Christians too, until the Romans realised that the Christians were no longer Jews but a *new, separate religion*. When Christians refused to worship a pagan god, particularly the emperor, the Romans considered them disloyal.

○ Christians refused to attend the popular, bloodthirsty games in the arena and encouraged others to boycott them.

○ The Roman historian Tacitus mentions how ugly rumours that Christians were cannibals began to circulate, causing them to be '*hated for their abominations.*' (*The Annals*)

When a terrible fire destroyed much of the city of Rome in AD 64, the Emperor Nero, whom many suspected of causing the fire, claimed that the Christians were responsible instead. Cleverly exploiting popular opinion, Nero launched a vicious persecution of the Christians.

The Roman mob was treated to a series of cruel public spectacles in which thousands of Christians were put to death in the arena or crucified and set alight to provide illumination for one of Nero's outdoor banquets. According to Christian tradition, both Peter and Paul were put to death during this persecution.

Despite this horrific episode and other terrible periods of repression over succeeding centuries, the Christian faith did not die out as the Roman authorities had expected. On the contrary, it continued to thrive and survived many periods of uncertainty and persecution, until the Emperor Constantine granted freedom of worship to Christians in the Edict of Milan in AD 313. By then, Christian missionaries had spread Jesus' message as far as Ethiopia, India and China.

Questions

1. What was the problem facing Christians who had not been Jews before their conversion to Christianity?
2. What was decided at the Council of Jerusalem?
3. Imagine you are a Christian living in Rome during the reign of Emperor Nero. Explain why the Roman authorities are persecuting you and your fellow Christians.

The Expansion of Christianity

Formal prayer: the Rosary

The Rosary has been an important part of Catholic prayer life since the Middle Ages. It consists of the repetition of certain prayers – *the Our Father, the Hail Mary* and *the Glory Be* – while one is reflecting on the meaning of key events in the lives of Jesus and Mary.

The Rosary is divided into four main sections, each one containing five *mysteries* or aspects of the Christian story.

The Joyful Mysteries
1. Annunciation
2. Visitation
3. Nativity of Jesus
4. Presentation of the infant Jesus in the Temple
5. Finding the child Jesus in the Temple

The Sorrowful Mysteries
1. Agony in the Garden of Gethsemane
2. Scourging of Jesus
3. Crowning with thorns
4. Carrying of the cross
5. Crucifixion and death of Jesus

The Mysteries of Light
1. Baptism in the Jordan
2. The wedding at Cana
3. The proclamation of the Kingdom
4. The transfiguration
5. The institution of the Eucharist

The Glorious Mysteries
1. Resurrection of Jesus
2. Ascension of Jesus
3. Descent of the Holy Spirit at Pentecost
4. Assumption of Mary
5. Coronation of Mary as Queen of Heaven

Traditionally, Catholics have used a set of prayer beads called *rosary beads* to help them keep track of where they are by running a bead through their fingers each time a prayer is said.

Questions

1. What is the *Rosary*?
2. Name the four main sections of the Rosary.
3. How are rosary beads used?

Chapter Twenty-two

The **Identity** of Jesus

Introduction

We have traced the story of how Christianity sprang forth from Judaism in the first century AD.

Like the Jews, Christians believe in and worship *one* God only. Both religions teach that God is the Supreme Being, the creator of the universe and awesome beyond compare. Yet God is also said to love and care for each and every human being.

As we shall see, however, Christians understand this one God in a *different* way to Jews.

God in the Tenakh

The Jews believed that the name of God was *Yahweh*. However, they considered God's name to be so holy that they agreed that it should *never* be spoken. Whenever speaking about God, Jews substituted the title *Lord* for God's name.

The Tenakh teaches that God – Yahweh – is holy and loving, but also awe inspiring. Yahweh is a *distant* being. Yahweh only appears on Earth to speak to specially chosen people, who are known as the *prophets*.

The following extract illustrates the way in which the authors of the Tenakh thought about God. This extract is taken from the account of how God called *Moses* to begin his mission to free the Hebrews from slavery in Egypt.

> Moses was looking after the flock of Jethro, his father-in-law. He led his flock to the far side of the wilderness and came to Horeb, the mountain of God. Moses looked; there was the bush blazing but it was not being burnt up. 'I must go and look at this strange sight,' Moses said, 'and see why the bush is not burnt.' Yahweh called to him from the middle of the bush. 'Moses, Moses,' he said. 'Here I am,' Moses answered. 'Come no nearer,' Yahweh said. 'Take off your shoes for the place on which you stand is holy ground. I am the God of your father, the God of Abraham, the God of Isaac and the God of Jacob.' At this Moses covered his face, afraid to look at God. (Exodus 3:1–6)

Fear Grew in Moses' Heart by Charles Edmund Brock. In this context, 'fear' means awe and respect.

The Identity of Jesus 117

Questions

1. What did the Jews believe God's name was?
2. How did the Jews show their respect for God's name when speaking about God?
3. Having read the extract from the Tenakh above, what evidence do you find in it to show that the God of Moses was an *awe-inspiring* and *distant* being?

Difference

The Finding of the Saviour in the Temple by William Holman Hunt.

Christians believe that their ideas about God are based on the insights first revealed by God to the Jewish people through the prophets.

However, whereas the Tenakh presents God as being at an unbridgeable distance from human beings, Christians think of God very differently.

Christians believe that God is *not* distant. The New Testament tells the story of how Jesus of Nazareth *bridged* the vast distance between God and human beings. Christians claim that God so loved human beings that *in Jesus, God became a human being* and lived among us. As one evangelist put it:

The Word became flesh and dwelt among us. (John 1:14)

We will now turn to consider *why* Christians came to believe this.

Before the Resurrection

From the beginning of Jesus' public ministry, people were asking:

Who is this? (Mark 1:27)

Jesus seems to have been reluctant at first to encourage speculation about his identity. He probably resisted being publicly identified as the Messiah to avoid raising popular expectations that he was going to lead a revolt against Roman rule.

But Jesus could not stop people from wondering about him. Eventually he asked his disciples, '*Who do they say I am?*' (Matthew 16:4) It was Peter who was the first to realise that Jesus was the Messiah.

After the Resurrection

After the disciples had met the risen Jesus, they reflected on all that had happened. They were confronted with a deep *mystery*. Jesus of Nazareth was a human being. For example:

- he had known what it was to be hungry, thirsty and tired
- he had experienced the full range of human emotions, from joy to sorrow
- he had suffered and died on the cross.

They came to believe that while Jesus was the promised Messiah/Christ, he was much *more* than an exceptionally good person. Jesus was an utterly *unique* person. They found this very hard to

Christ in Glory by Graham Sutherland, Coventry Cathedral, England.

express in words and it took them many years to work out Jesus' identity.

The disciples reflect

1. The disciples remembered how Jesus had:
   - healed those who were sick in mind and body instantly
   - revealed that he had the power to forgive sins
   - raised the dead to life
   - had himself risen from the dead on Easter Sunday
   - promised to return again at the end of time for the final judgment of the human race.

Jesus was able to do things that were proper *only* for *God* to do.

The early Christians concluded that Jesus had revealed that he actually possessed authority and power that belong to God *alone*.

2. The disciples remembered how Jesus had spoken about God. Jesus had constantly referred to God as *my Father*.

This way of speaking about God had startled Jesus' fellow Jews. Indeed, he often referred to God as *Abba*, a word Jewish children used when speaking to their fathers. A modern equivalent would be '*Daddy*'.

In doing so Jesus had made a very profound point. In Jewish thinking, a father is seen in his son, so when Jesus called God *my Father*, he was saying that people could see what God was like through *him*.

The Incarnation

It was clear to the early Christians that Jesus had a *uniquely close* relationship with God. He had told them that:

The Father and I are one. (John 10:25)

They came to realise why Jesus' entire life had revealed such a total oneness with God in *all* he had said and done. They concluded that *in Jesus of Nazareth*, *God became a human being*.

In time, Christians began to refer to Jesus as *the Incarnation* (meaning '*God made man*').

Importance

The Christian *doctrine* (teaching) of the *Incarnation* is complex and easily misunderstood. It does not mean that Jesus is part man and part God. Rather, it means that Jesus is both *fully* human and *fully* divine.

The *Catechism of the Catholic Church* (no. 464) teaches that *Jesus Christ is true God and true man*.

The Incarnation means that God is not distant. God is very near to human beings.

One story that serves to illustrate this is *The Long Silence*, the author of which is unknown. It is set on the Last Day, or as it is sometimes called, *Judgment Day*.

The Identity of Jesus 119

Christ on the Cross by F.V.E. Delacroix.

In this story, people who have suffered terribly in their lives complain that *God leads a pretty sheltered life*. To qualify as their judge, they say, God should be sentenced to live on Earth as a human being.

> Let him be born a Jew. Let him be doubted by his family and betrayed by his friends. Let him face false charges and be tried by a prejudiced jury in front of a hostile crowd. Let him be tortured to death – and as he dies, let him feel abandoned and alone.

When this judgment was pronounced, there was a long silence. Nobody moved, for suddenly all knew that God had *already* served his sentence.

Christians believe in and worship a God who is very close to human beings. That is why Christians have called Jesus *Emmanuel*, meaning 'God–with–us'.

Questions

1. Why was Jesus reluctant to encourage speculation about his identity?
2. Who was the first disciple to identify Jesus as the Messiah?
3. (a) Explain the meaning of the word '*Abba*' in the time of Jesus.
   (b) What point was Jesus making when he referred to God in this way?
4. Explain the Christian doctrine of the *Incarnation*. State:
   (a) The meaning of the word itself.
   (b) What it does *not* mean.
   (c) What it *does* mean.
5. Why do Christians sometimes refer to Jesus as *Emmanuel*?

The titles of Jesus

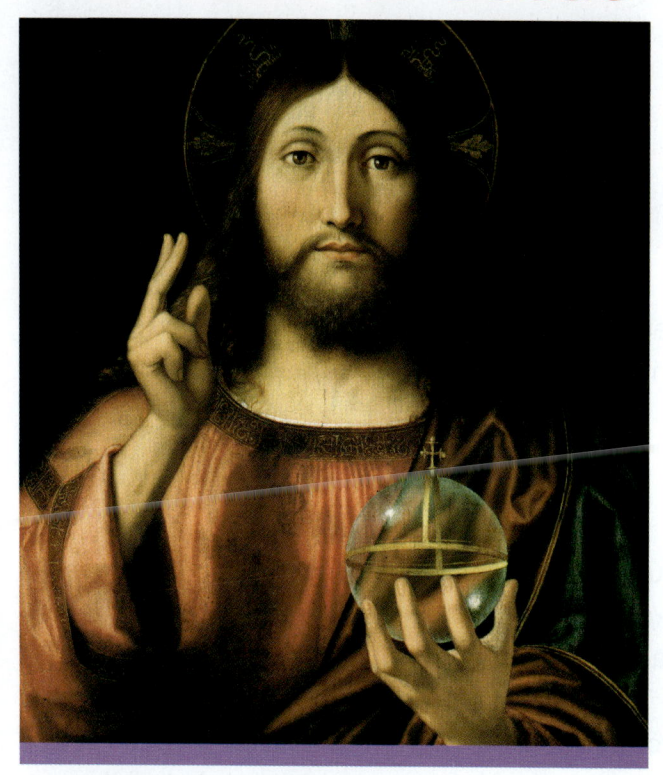

Salvator Mundi by Andrea Previtali.

The Son of Man

This is the title that Jesus used to describe himself in the Gospel of Mark. It is the only specific title that Jesus is recorded as having directly applied to himself.

In the Old Testament book of Daniel, the title *Son of Man* was used to refer to the Messiah, i.e. the saviour who would bring about the Kingdom of God on Earth.

Jesus claimed that he was the *Son of Man* because he could do things that only God could do, such as forgive people's sins.

The Lord

The Jews believed that God's name was *Yahweh*. However, they considered God's name to be so holy that it should never be spoken. So out of respect they substituted the title *Lord* for God's name.

The first Christians were Jews who still worshipped in the Temple. However, they began to refer to Jesus as the *Lord*. This was because they believed that Jesus possessed authority over sin and power over death that belonged only to God.

The Son of God

Sometimes first-century Jews referred to an exceptionally good person as a *son of God*.

By the time the Gospel of John came to be written at the end of the first century AD, the early Christians had had time to reflect on Jesus' many references to God as *his Father*.

They realised that Jesus is not simply a son of God. All Jesus had said and done had shown him to have a *totally unique* relationship with God. His life had revealed his *total oneness* with God, his Father, so much so that he *shares* in God's very nature.

Jesus is not merely *a* son of God. Jesus is *the* Son of God.

Questions

1. In which Gospel did Jesus use the title *Son of Man*?
2. Who did the title *Son of Man* refer to in the Old Testament book of Daniel?
3. Why did Jesus claim to be the *Son of Man*?
4. Why did the Jews substitute the title *Lord* for God's name?
5. Why did the early Christians refer to Jesus as *the Lord*?
6. What kind of person did the first-century Jews sometimes refer to as *a son of God*?
7. Why did the writer of the Gospel of John refer to Jesus as *the Son of God*?

The Identity of Jesus

Chapter Twenty-three

The Trinity

Introduction

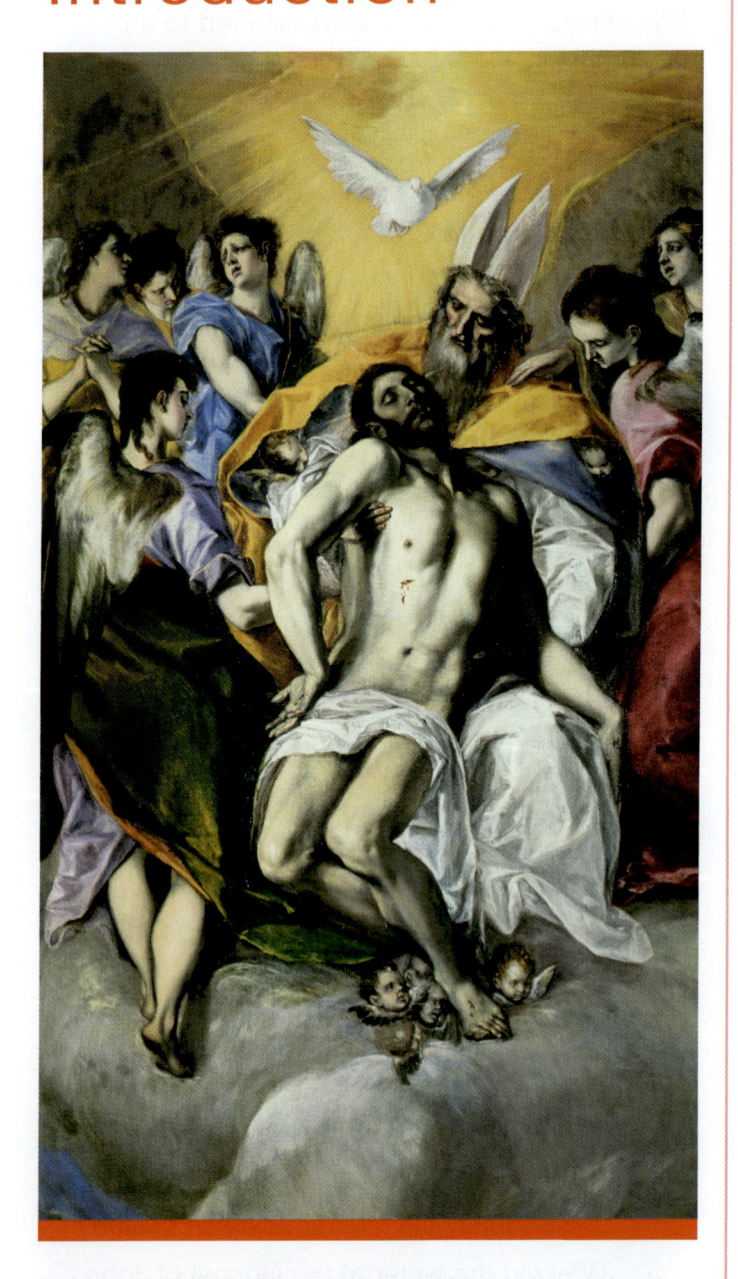

The Trinity by El Greco. The Holy Trinity is depicted in this sixteenth-century painting. The Father is shown holding his crucified Son, with the Holy Spirit hovering as a dove.

Jesus' first followers were devout Jews who uncompromisingly believed that:

> *The Lord, Our God, the Lord is One.*
> (Deuteronomy 6:4)

But their whole understanding of God had been *expanded* and enriched as a result of the time they had shared with Jesus.

They came to believe that Jesus was the *Son of God*. This *raised huge questions* for them as Jews.

In their search for answers as to what all this meant for their belief in *one* God, these early Christians reflected carefully on what Jesus had taught them:

- Jesus referred to God as his *Father*. He frequently prayed to the Father and said that he and the Father were *one*.
- Since he would no longer be physically present after his Ascension, Jesus promised that he would send the *Holy Spirit*.
- On Pentecost Sunday, Jesus *did* send the Holy Spirit.

When Jesus sent his disciples out to spread the Gospel message, he used these words:

> *Go, therefore, and make disciples of all nations; baptising them in the name of the Father and of the Son and of the Holy Spirit.* (Matthew 28:19–20)

Having been brought up as Jews, these early Christians had a deep appreciation for the mystery

122   All About Faith

of God. They believed that God is *beyond* our human ability to ever completely understand. However, they realised that through Jesus, they had been granted a *great insight* into the God they worshipped.

In their prayers they began to refer to God the *Father*, God the *Son* and God the *Holy Spirit*. For example, Paul ends one of his letters with this blessing:

> *May the grace of the Lord Jesus Christ and the love of God and the fellowship of the Holy Spirit be with you all.*
> (2 Corinthians 13:14)

This Christian way of referring to God as *three persons* – Father, Son and Spirit – is called *Trinitarian language*.

The belief that there are *three persons in the one God* is called the doctrine (teaching) of the *Trinity*.

> **N.B.**
> Although the reasons why Christians accept the doctrine of the Trinity are found in the New Testament, the *term 'Trinity'* is not mentioned in it. The *term* itself was not agreed upon until *after* the New Testament had been written.

Importance

The doctrine of the Trinity is *central* to all Christian belief and worship. For example, at both the beginning and the end of the Mass, the priest addresses the congregation in a threefold formula which does not simply refer to *God* but to the Father, the Son and the Holy Spirit.

- In his opening blessing the priest says:

    In the name of the Father and of the Son and of the Holy Spirit.

- In his concluding blessing the priest says:

    May Almighty God bless you, the Father, the Son and the Holy Spirit.

Questions

1. What religion did Jesus' first followers belong to?
2. What had they been brought up to believe about God?
3. Where do we find evidence that the early Christians prayed to God the Father, God the Son and God the Holy Spirit?
4. What is the Christian doctrine of the *Trinity*?
5. Give an example to show how the doctrine of the Trinity is *central* to all Christian worship.

Exploring the Trinity

The Christian doctrine of the Trinity is complex. It is a profound mystery. Sometimes people think that Christians really believe in three Gods, while claiming to believe in one! *No.* Christians are *monotheists*.

Christians worship *one God only*, but they believe that *there are three distinct persons in one God*. This is called the *triune*, or three-in-one God.

Clarification

Christians do *not* believe that:

- one God equals three Gods

    or that

- three Gods equal one God.

Christians *do* believe that:

- each of the three persons of the Trinity is *fully* God, *not* one-third of God
- each member of the Trinity is a separate and distinct person.

Study the diagram on the next page carefully. It is taken from a medieval painting. It seeks to help us understand the doctrine of the Trinity.

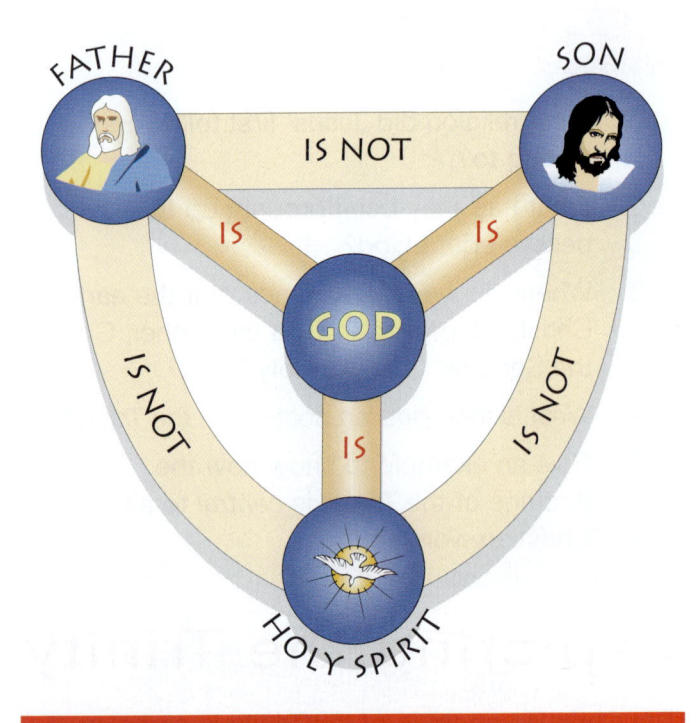

Notice how each member of the Trinity is a distinct person:

- The Father is *not* the Son.
- The Son is *not* the Father.
- The Holy Spirit is *neither* the Father *nor* the Son.
- Each is God, yet still there is only *one* God.

How can this be the case?

Over the centuries, Christian thinkers have sought to help people grow in their understanding of the mystery of the Trinity.

Consider the following explanation. There is the well-known story of how St Patrick used the *shamrock* to help people grow in understanding of the Trinity.

The shamrock has three leaves but is still *one* plant. The Trinity has three persons but there is only *one* God.

Each person of the Trinity reveals God relating to the world in a different way. Yet it is *one* and the *same* God who does so.

Study the diagram, which illustrates each person of the Trinity relating to the world in a different way.

Each person of the Trinity reflects a particular aspect of God. Each person – Father, Son and Spirit – shows God relating to the world in a different way.

Concluding reflection

Alexander Pushkin at the Seashore by Leonid Osipovic Pasternak.

The doctrine of the Trinity is complex, but the Christians who first set out this doctrine were not primarily concerned with what is understandable. Rather, they were concerned with what is *true*.

Consider the following story. It illustrates the kind of difficulties people face when they try to explain what they mean by the word *God*.

One morning, two great scholars were walking along a beach. As they walked they were discussing the meaning of God. Each was convinced that the other was doing a poor job of explaining what he understood God to be. Both were able to raise objections to everything the other said.

Suddenly they came upon a small boy playing by the water's edge. He had dug a small pit in the sand and kept running down to the sea, dipping his toy bucket in the water and running back up the beach to empty the water into the pit. They watched for some time as he ran to and fro. They found the scene amusing. They then went up to him and asked him what he was doing. The child pointed to the sea and told them, very seriously, that he was going to take all the water in the sea and pour it into the pit he had dug out in the sand.

The two men smiled and then continued on their way. They carried on their discussion. Suddenly one of them stopped. 'You know,' he said, 'we were amused just now when that child told us what he was trying to do. Yet what we are trying to do in our discussion about God is just the same.

'It is just as impossible for human beings to fully understand God as it was for that child to put all the sea into the little pit he had dug in the sand.

'Our minds are so limited and small. The reality of God is as great as the ocean.'

However, Christians believe that through prayer, good deeds and study, a person may grow in understanding of the mystery of God.

Questions

1. Explain the following statement: *Christians are monotheists*.
2. What does it mean to say that *Christians believe in and worship a triune God*?
3. Identify which of the following are *true* and which are *false*.
   (a) *The Trinity means that one God equals three Gods*.
   (b) *The Trinity means that each of the three persons is fully God and not one-third of God*.
   (c) *The Trinity means that three Gods equal one God*.
4. Fill in the missing details in your notebook. Each person of the Trinity shows God relating to the world in a different way.

God is

The Father who
_____
_____
_____

The Son who
_____
_____
_____

The Holy Spirit who
_____
_____
_____

Part Four

CHRISTIANITY: BELIEFS AND WORSHIP

Chapter Twenty-four

Christianity: Creed and Traditions

Introduction

The Transfiguration by Giovanni Girolamo Savoldo.

Some people find the divisions among Christians puzzling. They are all said to be followers of Jesus Christ, yet they belong to different groups, some of which have actually fought each other in the past. How did this happen? What are the main differences between them? How are we to understand these divisions within the Christian religion?

Some Christian writers have offered the following approach. They say that we should think of the Christian religion as a *great tree*. The roots of this tree are grounded in the person of Jesus Christ. On two occasions in its history, the trunk of this great tree has *branched off* to produce the three different traditions *within* Christianity today:

○ Catholic

○ Orthodox

○ Protestant.

It is important to remember that the people who belong to these different traditions are *not* members of different religions. On the contrary, they worship the *same* God and *share* certain core beliefs. They are *all* members of the *one* religion – *Christianity*.

With this in mind, this chapter is divided into two parts:
1. An examination of those fundamental beliefs that are held *in common* by all those who identify themselves as Christians.
2. An account of the long and complex process by which Christians *became divided* into three traditions.

Christian belief

The essential beliefs of the Christian religion are expressed in the *Apostles' Creed*.

The Apostles' Creed has been printed below in eight statements of belief. These are the central statements of the Christian faith.

The Apostles' Creed

1. I believe in God, the Father almighty, creator of heaven and Earth.
2. I believe in Jesus Christ, his only Son, our Lord. He was conceived by the power of the Holy Spirit and born of the Virgin Mary.
3. He suffered under Pontius Pilate, was crucified, died and was buried. He descended to the dead. On the third day he rose again. He ascended into heaven.
4. And is seated at the right hand of the Father. He will come again to judge the living and the dead.
5. I believe in the Holy Spirit,
6. the holy catholic church,
7. the communion of saints,
8. the forgiveness of sins, the resurrection of the body and the life everlasting.

Amen.

8. Forgiveness, resurrection and eternal life

People must be willing to forgive others their sins if they want God to forgive them. All will share in the same bodily resurrection from the dead as Jesus.

Those who have unselfishly loved God and neighbour will share unending life and happiness with God in heaven.

7. The communion of saints

This refers to the fellowship of all those, living or dead, who have believed in Jesus and faithfully followed his way of life.

6. The holy catholic church

Both Catholics and Protestants agree that this refers to *the worldwide community of all those who worship and strive to follow Jesus Christ*.

However, Catholics also state that Jesus appointed a visible *leader* of his church on Earth – the apostle Peter. The title given to those who have held this position of authority since is that of *pope*. Catholics look to the pope for leadership and guidance.

All About Faith

1.
God

Christians believe in *one God only*, who is *infinite* (unlimited), *eternal* (everlasting) and *creator of the universe*.

There are *three persons in the one God*: God the Father, God the Son and God the Holy Spirit.

This teaching that God is three persons and yet one God is called the mystery of the *Holy Trinity*.

2.
Jesus Christ

Christians believe that Jesus is the *Incarnation*, i.e. God made man, truly human and truly divine. He is the son of Mary through the power of the Holy Spirit. The teaching that Jesus was born of a virgin mother is important to the claim that he is the Son of God.

3.
Death and resurrection

Jesus really suffered and died on the cross. The resurrection of Jesus on the third day after his burial is the heart of the Christian faith. By rising from the dead, Jesus defeated the power of death over humanity and gave the promise of eternal life to all.

4.
The Judgment

The parables of Jesus make it clear that after their deaths, people will have to account for how they have lived their lives. The three areas on which they will be judged are:
- how they have loved God
- how they have developed the various talents God has given them
- how they have loved other people.

5.
The Holy Spirit

After Jesus returned to heaven, the Holy Spirit descended upon the disciples on Pentecost. They were strengthened in their faith and began fearlessly preaching the Gospel message about the Kingdom of God.

Christianity: Creed and Traditions

The division of Christianity into three traditions

The Orthodox Churches

In the aftermath of the Great Schism, the Orthodox Church came under severe pressure from the expansion of Islam in Asia Minor and North Africa. Although Constantinople itself was conquered by Muslims in 1453, the Orthodox tradition survived. By then it had spread throughout the Balkans and across Russia. As the Orthodox tradition spread, each country acquired its own independent and self-governing Orthodox Church. The principal ones are:

- Armenian
- Greek
- Ethiopian
- Russian.

Each is governed by a *patriarch*, the most senior of whom is the Patriarch of Constantinople. However, unlike the pope in the Catholic Church, he is not the leader of a single united church. Rather, the Patriarch of Constantinople is respected as 'first among equals' and provides leadership at meetings of the different Orthodox Churches. Today, there are about 300 million members of the various Orthodox Churches.

EAST AND WEST

(Map showing ROME, CAPITAL OF THE WESTERN CHURCH; CONSTANTINOPLE, CAPITAL OF THE EASTERN CHURCH; BLACK SEA; ANTIOCH; MEDITERRANEAN SEA; ALEXANDRIA)

The Catholic Church

Spurred on by the great split in the Church, the Pope called the Council of Trent to begin a process of reform. The Catholic Church over the following centuries underwent a massive expansion in the Americas, Asia and Africa. Today it is the largest of the Christian traditions, with over 1 billion members worldwide.

The Reformation

On 31 October 1517, a Catholic monk named Martin Luther posted ninety-five theses (topics for discussion) on the door of Wittenburg Cathedral in Germany. Luther's theses protested against certain corrupt practices that had developed within the Catholic Church (hence the name *Protestant*). Soon Luther began to publicly reject important teachings of the Catholic Church concerning the seven sacraments and the authority of the pope. Finally, Luther was excommunicated (expelled) from the Catholic Church. He established the *Lutheran* church in Germany.

The Protestant Churches

Luther's ideas spread rapidly across Europe and eventually to North America. However, Lutheranism was soon only one of many separate Protestant Churches. Indeed, Protestantism quickly revealed a strong tendency to divide into new *denominations* (separate branches). The chief ones are:

- Lutheran
- Presbyterian
- Methodist
- Anglican
- Baptist
- Quaker.

Split occurs AD 1517

The Catholic Church

In the period following the Great Schism, the Catholic Church grew immensely powerful under the leadership of successive popes. The Catholic Church teaches that the popes are the direct successors of the apostle Peter, to whom Jesus gave a special authority over the whole Christian community (see Matthew 16:18–19). However, with great power comes great temptation. Some churchmen abused the power with which they had been entrusted. This led to a strong desire for reform within the Catholic Church. Tragically, this was not acted upon in time.

132 All About Faith

Rooted in Jesus Christ

The early Christians

From its beginnings there were differences within Christianity as to how the New Testament should be understood. A series of councils discussed and clarified Christian teaching. Most of the difficulties were resolved by the *Nicene Creed*.

The development of two traditions

In AD 313 the Emperor Constantine made Christianity the official religion of the Roman Empire. This decision ended centuries of persecution but had serious long-term consequences for the Christian religion.

In AD 320 Constantine moved the capital of the Roman Empire east to Constantinople (now Istanbul). This led to the development of two traditions within Christianity:

- an Eastern (Greek-speaking) tradition based on Constantinople
- a Western (Latin-speaking) tradition based on Rome.

The Great Schism

The Eastern tradition and the Western tradition had a great deal in common in terms of teaching and worship. However, differences in culture, such as language, and disputes over the leadership of the Christian religion grew stronger.

The two traditions gradually began to move apart. Tragically, they separated from one another in AD 1054 in an event referred to as the *Great Schism*. Christianity was thereafter divided into the Catholic Church* in the West and the Orthodox Church in the East.

Split occurs AD 1054

*N.B.
For Christians, the word 'church' has several meanings:
1. An *organisation* (like the Catholic Church or Methodist Church).
2. The *people* who are members of the whole worldwide Christian community.
3. A *building* for worship.

Christianity: Creed and Traditions 133

Questions

1. Identify the *three* main traditions within the Christian religion.
2. Explain Christians' essential beliefs under each of the following headings:
   (a) God
   (b) Jesus Christ
   (c) death and resurrection
   (d) judgment
   (e) the Holy Spirit
   (f) the holy catholic church
   (g) the communion of saints
   (h) forgiveness, resurrection and eternal life.
3. (a) What was the *Great Schism*?
   (b) When did it occur?
   (c) Why did it happen?
4. (a) What is a *patriarch*?
   (b) Who is the *most senior* patriarch?
   (c) What authority does he have within the Orthodox tradition?
5. Why did a great desire for reform develop within the Catholic tradition by the early sixteenth century?
6. Explain the origin of the name '*Protestant*'.
7. What is a *denomination*?
8. Why did the Pope call the Council of Trent?

Christianity and other religions

All the Christian traditions believe in religious freedom and they all teach that human beings are *invited* and *not* forced to worship God. People have a right to choose whether or not they wish to belong to a particular religion.

However, they should inform themselves about the teachings of a particular religion and reflect seriously on them *before* deciding to accept or reject membership.

Priests and monks of different religions march for peace in Lisbon.

At the Second Vatican Council (1962–1965), the leaders of the Catholic Church stated:

> *The Church condemns, as foreign to the mind of Christ, any discrimination against people or any harassment of them on the basis of their race, colour, condition in life or religion.*

Most Christian churches call on their members to build *bonds of friendship* with non-Christians of good character and agree that Christians should *reject nothing that is true and holy in other religions*.

However, this raises an important question: *Why choose to be a Christian rather than a Jew, Muslim, Hindu or Buddhist?*

Christians answer this question as follows:

- They admit that the founders of other religions taught many profound truths about God and the meaning of life. However, they point out that *none* of these people ever claimed to be *divine*.
- Christians claim that through everything he said and did, Jesus revealed God's love for human beings in a way and in a depth that is utterly *unique*.

134 All About Faith

○ This is because in Jesus God became a human being. He lived on Earth. He suffered and died for people's sins and rose from the dead. God, therefore, is *not* a remote being as in other religions, but very close to us. This is why Christians refer to Jesus as *Emmanuel*, meaning *God–with–us*. Christians claim that there is nothing like this in any other religion.

Jesus is the only Son of God, the second person of the Trinity. He is *the Way, the Truth and the Life* (John 14:6).

Christians respectfully accept that other religions do contain important insights into the mystery of God and the great questions of human life. However, they believe that *only Christianity contains the whole truth about God and the meaning of life.*

Questions

1. What do all the Christian traditions teach about religious freedom?
2. Why should Christians build *bonds of friendship with non-Christians of good character*?
3. Some people today claim that Jesus was a great moral teacher, but *not* God. The Christian writer C.S. Lewis defended Christian belief *against* this claim. He wrote:

C.S. Lewis.

Questions

I am trying to prevent anyone saying the really foolish thing that people often say about Jesus: 'I am ready to accept Jesus as a great moral teacher, but I do not accept his claim to be God.' This is the one thing we must not say. A man who was merely a man and said the sort of things Jesus said would not be a great moral teacher. He would either be a lunatic – on the level with the man who says he is a poached egg – or else he would be the devil of hell. You must make your choice. Either this man was, and is, the Son of God; or else a madman, or something worse. You can shut him up for a fool, you can spit at him and kill him as a demon; you can fall at his feet and call him Lord and God. But let us not come with any patronising nonsense about his being a great human teacher. He has not left that open to us. He did not intend to.

Now answer the following question: What point is C.S. Lewis making about the identity of Jesus?

4. Read the following statement:

The difference between Christianity and the other religions is not basically the difference between truth and error, but between total and partial understanding.

Bishop Stephen Neill (Church of England), quoted *in The Lion Handbook of Christian Belief.*

In light of your reading of the section Christianity and Other Religions, explain what this statement means.

Christianity: Creed and Traditions 135

Chapter Twenty-five

Growing Closer to God in the Sacraments

Introduction

At the heart of religion is the awareness that beyond the visible, tangible world in which humans live, there is a God who gives meaning and purpose to human life.

This awareness of the invisible presence of God in people's lives is called the *sense of the sacred*. It is expressed in symbols and celebrated in rituals (see Chapter 2).

The official public rituals of the Catholic Church are called the *liturgy*.

The liturgy consists chiefly of the *seven sacraments*. These rituals have certain *fixed* features, although they can be modified in a limited way in special circumstances.

Meaning

After his resurrection, Jesus revealed that he was no longer limited by the physical laws of the universe that restrict our human freedom of action. For example:

- Jesus could appear suddenly in a locked room (see John 20:19)
- Jesus could vanish at will (see Luke 24:31).

Jesus revealed that he was free to be *present* at any time, in any place and as he chose to be present. This is a profound *mystery*.

The Gospels portray Jesus as continually seeking to share his love with people. Before his ascension, he promised his disciples that

I will be with you always. (Matthew 28:30)

Catholics believe that Jesus keeps his promise and that he is *present* today when they come together in his name to celebrate the *sacraments*. As St Ambrose of Milan wrote:

You have shown yourself to me Christ, face to face. I met you in the sacraments.

The word 'sacrament' means 'a holy mystery'.

Catholic and Orthodox Christians believe that there are seven sacraments:

- Baptism
- Confirmation
- Eucharist
- Reconciliation
- Matrimony
- Holy Orders
- Anointing of the Sick.

These seven sacraments are *public rituals* in which Catholics recall and re-enact the life, death and resurrection of Jesus Christ. Indeed, Catholics believe that Jesus himself was the *first* sacrament. In his life, death and resurrection, Jesus *revealed* the glory of God's unlimited goodness in all he said and did.

The Altarpiece of the Seven Sacraments, an altarpiece by Rogier van der Weyden in the Musée Royal des Beaux Arts, Antwerp. In the centre panel the artist has depicted the Eucharist; at the left, Baptism, Confirmation and Penance; at the right, the sacraments of the Holy Orders, Marriage and Anointing of the Sick.

Importance

The Gospels show how Jesus was always there to support and strengthen people at important times in their lives. In each of the sacraments, Catholics celebrate the presence of Jesus in the key moments of their lives today.

Baptism	birth
Confirmation	growth to maturity
Eucharist	living and sharing with others
Reconciliation	failure and forgiveness
Matrimony	marriage
Holy Orders	sacred ministry
Anointing	illness, healing and death

Catholics believe that if they offer genuine, heartfelt worship to God in the sacraments, then they will receive God's *grace* (they will experience the loving presence of God in their lives). This grace will nourish their faith and give them the strength to make God's presence felt in the world by the way they live their lives.

This is why the sacraments are called *transformative events*, because they are intended to bring about a *change* in the way people live their lives.

Questions

1. What is the meaning of the word '*sacrament*'?
2. List the seven sacraments.
3. What events do Catholics recall and re-enact in the sacraments?
4. Match the key moments in people's lives in column B with the sacraments listed in column A.

A Sacraments	B Key
Baptism	failure and forgiveness
Confirmation	sacred ministry
Eucharist	illness, healing and death
Reconciliation	growth and maturity
Matrimony	birth
Holy Orders	living and sharing with others
Anointing	marriage

5. What does it mean to *receive God's grace*?
6. The sacraments are described as *transformative events*. What does this mean?

The sacrament of Baptism

Baptism of Christ, mosaic, dome of Orthodox baptistery at Ravenna, c. 450. The figure to the right of Christ is a personification of the Jordan River.

Growing Closer to God in the Sacraments

Introduction

There is a tradition among Catholics of dipping the right hand into a water font and blessing oneself when entering or leaving a church. This gesture is intended to remind Catholics of the first sacrament they receive – *Baptism* (from the Greek word '*baptizo*', meaning '*to dip*').

Baptism is the first of three *sacraments of initiation*, namely *Baptism, Confirmation* and *Eucharist*. They are called *sacraments of initiation* because each of them represents a stage in the process towards *full membership* in both the Catholic and the Orthodox tradition.

History

Until the middle of the fifth century AD, most *catechumens* (candidates for baptism) were adults. They had to undergo a long period of preparation. This is still required of adults who *convert* from non-Christian religions today.

Some Christian denominations, such as the Baptists, will only baptise adults. In the Catholic, Orthodox and most Protestant churches, however, infants are baptised.

Meaning

The sacrament of Baptism may be received only once. It is done so that:

- the child's family can hold a formal naming ceremony and give thanks to God for this precious new life
- the church as a community can welcome the arrival of a new member into its family of faith.

Ceremony (in the Catholic tradition)

- The child is presented for baptism by his/her parents.
- The priest welcomes them and invites them to the baptismal font.
- Also present are specially chosen godparents, who promise to help the parents bring the child up in the Christian faith.
- The priest blesses the child.
- There is a short extract from the New Testament and a brief sermon explaining the importance of baptism.
- The child is anointed with the oil of catechumens.
- The parents and godparents renew their own baptismal promises and make a commitment to make the Christian faith known to the child as he/she grows up.
- Then water that has been blessed is poured over the baby's head. He/she is now formally named, usually after a saint.
- Next, the child is anointed with the oil of chrism.
- A white shawl is wrapped around the child.
- The parents bring with them a candle which is then lit from the large *Paschal* (Easter) *Candle* in the sanctuary.
- The Our Father is recited and the ceremony ends with a blessing by the priest.

The symbols of Baptism

Gesture and words

The priest blesses the child by tracing a cross on his/her forehead, saying *I baptise you in the name of the Father, and of the Son, and of the Holy Spirit. Amen*. This is a reminder that the child belongs to and is a gift from God.

Oil

- **Oil of catechumens:** Symbolises God's grace strengthening the child to face life's challenges.

- **Oil of chrism:** Symbolises the calling of each Christian to live according to God's standards. Fragrant odour reminds all present of the beauty and dignity of each person as a child of God.

The candle

Light is a very important *symbol* in the Christian religion. Jesus once described himself as

the Light of the World.

Light is a symbol of life, goodness and wisdom. *Darkness* is often used as a symbol of death, wickedness and ignorance.

The lighted candle is a reminder to Christians that Jesus' resurrection is their guarantee that death is not the end, but a gateway to eternal life with God.

Water

The sacrament of Baptism may be administered in either of two ways:

- by *infusion*, where a little water is poured over the person's head
- by *immersion*, where the entire person is dipped into water.

Water is a very powerful *symbol*. Water gives life, but it can also cause death. Stormy seas can drown unfortunate sailors. Flood waters can destroy people's homes. But water can also preserve a person's life in the desert. Rain restores life to wilting plants.

In the sacrament of baptism, water is a symbol of death *and* life. Christians remember the central mystery of their faith – Jesus died on the cross on Good Friday but rose to new life on Easter Sunday.

The water of baptism *symbolises* (represents) the purifying power of the Holy Spirit, through which the child *shares* in the death of Jesus, in order to rise with Jesus to new life.

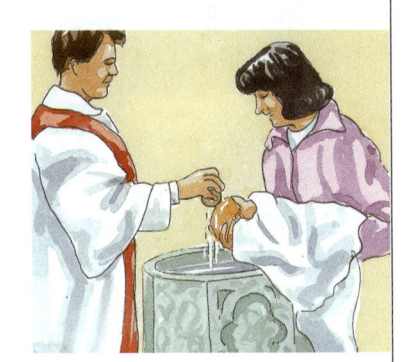

The white robe

In the early Church, a catechumen was clothed in a white robe to show that he/she was *clothed in Christ* and had begun a new life when baptised. This is still done today.

The child is wrapped in a white shawl as a *symbol* that he/she shares in the resurrection of Jesus.

Growing Closer to God in the Sacraments

Questions

1. (a) Name the three sacraments of initiation.
   (b) Why are they called *sacraments of initiation*?
2. Name the Christian denomination that will only baptise adults.
3. Match the explanations in column B with the word in column A.

A	B
font	candidate for baptism
baptism	person responsible for helping in a child's religious upbringing
catechumen	basin holding water for baptism
godparent	ceremony held to initiate a person into the Christian community

4. Write a brief account of the baptismal ceremony.
5. State the two ways in which the sacrament of Baptism may be administered.
6. Explain the use of the following symbols in baptism: (a) *water* (b) *the lighted candle* (c) *the white shawl*.
7. (a) Name the *two* types of oil used in baptism.
   (b) Explain what each symbolises (represents).
8. Suppose you are asked to be a godparent.
   (a) Write down three things you could do to help in a child's religious upbringing.
   (b) What kind of problems might you encounter in fulfilling the role of godparent?

The sacrament of Confirmation

Meaning

Confirmation is also a sacrament of initiation. Like baptism, it may be received only *once*.

The word '*confirmation*' comes from the Latin word '*confirmare*', meaning '*to strengthen*'. This sacrament *strengthens* baptised Christians and through the power of the Holy Spirit helps them as they try to be active, caring followers of Jesus Christ.

History

In the early days of Christianity, when most converts were adults, Christians were usually baptised and confirmed during the *same* ceremony. As Christianity grew and gained new members, however, adult converts as well as infants and children were baptised by priests and *later* confirmed by bishops in a *separate* ceremony.

Since the Middle Ages, the Catholic Church has offered the sacrament of Confirmation to young Catholics who are just entering their teenage years. In the Orthodox tradition, however, people are *still* baptised and confirmed in the same ceremony.

The ceremony (in the Catholic tradition)

The ceremony of confirmation in the Catholic Church is normally held during a special Mass and is usually given by a bishop. He *confirms* (completes) the process of initiation into the Christian community begun at baptism.

140 All About Faith

The ceremony consists of the following:

1. **The renewal of baptismal vows**

   Most Catholics are baptised when they are babies. At that time, they were incapable of understanding what it means to be a Christian. By the time they are presented for the sacrament of Confirmation they are considered to be old enough to understand how challenging it is to follow Jesus' teachings. They are thought to be ready to make the promises made on their behalf at baptism their *own*.

   The candidate for confirmation publicly rejects all that is evil and declares belief in the main teachings of the Catholic Church.

2. **The stretching out of hands**

   The bishop stretches out his hands over the head of each person to be confirmed. This is a gesture dating back to ancient times. It asked for God's grace to strengthen a person to face a special task.

   In the sacrament of Confirmation, each candidate receives his/her *vocation* (from the Latin word '*vocare*', meaning '*to call*'). The bishop calls on them to be witnesses to the values of Jesus Christ, i.e. to be courageous, active, forgiving, generous and positive.

   The bishop reminds them that the Holy Spirit will strengthen them to be true followers of Jesus Christ, just as the disciples were strengthened on the first Pentecost.

   Then the bishop prays that the candidates for confirmation will receive the seven gifts of the Holy Spirit (see page 142).

3. **The anointing with chrism**

   The bishop traces the symbol of the cross on each candidate's forehead with the holy oil of chrism and says

   [Name], be sealed with the gift of the Holy Spirit.

As we have seen, oil is an important Christian symbol and has healing qualities (see Luke 10:34). It is also used to strengthen athletes and make them supple in preparation for a contest.

In the confirmation ceremony, oil symbolises how the power of the Holy Spirit strengthens Christians in their commitment to follow the teachings of Jesus Christ.

Growing Closer to God in the Sacraments

The seven gifts of the Holy Spirit

Christians pray that the Holy Spirit will grant them the seven gifts to strengthen their commitment to follow the teachings of Jesus Christ. They are as follows:

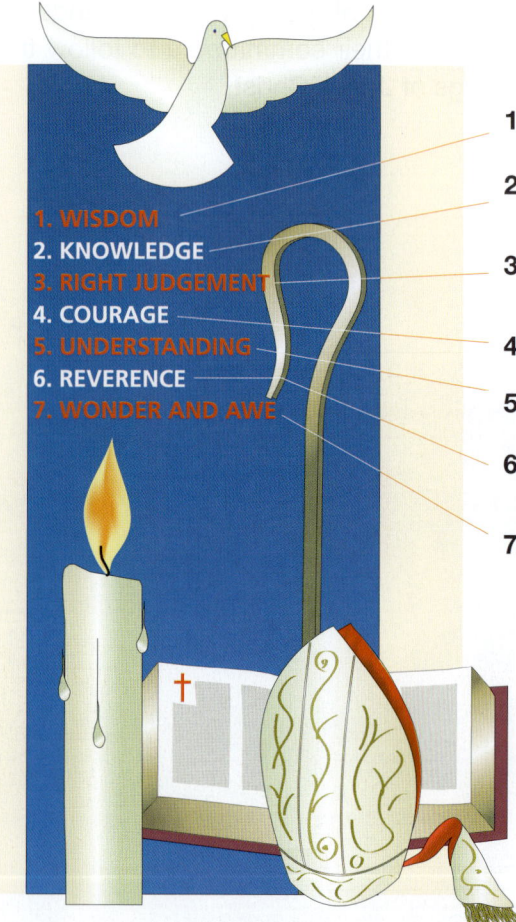

1. WISDOM
2. KNOWLEDGE
3. RIGHT JUDGEMENT
4. COURAGE
5. UNDERSTANDING
6. REVERENCE
7. WONDER AND AWE

1. **Wisdom:** Seeing the world and people as Jesus sees them.
2. **Knowledge:** Knowing and loving God – the answer to all life's great mysteries.
3. **Right judgment:** Knowing what the right thing to do is in difficult situations.
4. **Courage:** Doing what is right, despite opposition.
5. **Understanding:** Realising how to love God and other people.
6. **Reverence:** Taking time to pray and worship with deep respect for God.
7. **Wonder and awe:** Being aware of the great goodness of God and realising that, despite our selfishness and weakness, God loves us.

Questions

1. What is the origin of the word 'confirmation'?
2. Explain the *purpose* of the sacrament of Confirmation.
3. In what way does the Orthodox Church differ from the Catholic Church regarding the sacrament of Confirmation?
4. Who usually administers the sacrament of Confirmation in the Catholic Church?
5. Explain each of the following parts of the ceremony of confirmation:
   (a) *the renewal of baptismal vows*
   (b) *the laying on of hands*
   (c) *the anointing with chrism*.
6. Explain the meaning of *vocation*.
7. Match the description of the seven gifts in column B with the name of each gift in column A.

142 All About Faith

Questions

A Gift	B Meaning
Wisdom	Knowing what is the right thing to do in difficult situations.
Understanding	Knowing and loving God – the answer to all life's great mysteries.
Right judgment	Taking time to pray and worship with deep respect for God.
Courage	Being aware of the great goodness of God and realising that despite our selfishness and weakness, God loves us.
Knowledge	Doing what we know is right despite opposition.
Reverence	Seeing the world and people as Jesus sees them.
Wonder and awe	Realising how to love God and other people.

The sacrament of the Eucharist

Introduction

The sacrament of the Eucharist is *the* focal point of the liturgy of the Catholic Church. It has its origins in the words and actions of Jesus at the Last Supper he shared with his disciples on Holy Thursday evening.

The Eucharist is celebrated every day, but above all on Sunday, as it was on Sunday that Jesus rose from the dead.

The word '*eucharist*' means '*thanksgiving*'. In the sacrament of the Eucharist, Catholics unite in thanksgiving for the good things God has done and continues to do for human beings.

The Mass

The Sacrament of the Last Supper by Salvador Dalí.

When Catholics talk about the sacrament of the Eucharist, they often refer to it as the *Mass* (from the Latin word '*missio*', meaning '*the sending*').

Growing Closer to God in the Sacraments

The Mass

1. Greeting and Penitential Rite
2. Liturgy of the Word
3. Creed
4. Offertory
5. Eucharistic Prayer
6. Our Father and Sign of Peace
7. Communion
8. Blessing — 'Go in peace to love and serve the Lord.'

Roles

Only a Catholic bishop or priest can *preside* (lead the congregation in worship) at a Mass and *consecrate* the bread and wine.

However, the Mass is essentially a *communal* act, as all people present are gathered in Jesus' name to share in celebrating the *Paschal Mystery* (Jesus' death and resurrection).

The laity are called to be *active participants* rather than passive spectators. This can be done by:

○ listening attentively
○ responding appropriately
○ volunteering to act as readers, ministers of the Eucharist, choir members, musicians and altar servers.

Structure

The basic elements and overall structure of the Mass were settled upon as early as the second century AD. The Mass consists of four sections:
1. *The Introductory Rite*
2. *The Liturgy of the Word*
3. *The Liturgy of the Eucharist*
4. *The Concluding Rites.*

Questions

1. What is the origin of the sacrament of the Eucharist?
2. Why is the Eucharist celebrated *above all on Sunday*, the special day of worship for Christians?
3. What is the meaning of the word '*eucharist*'?
4. Who are the only people permitted to *preside* at the Mass and who alone can consecrate the bread and wine?
5. The Mass is described as *essentially a communal* act. What does this mean?
6. List three ways in which a member of a Catholic congregation can be an *active participant* in the Mass.
7. Identify the four sections of the Mass.

144   All About Faith

The Structure of the Mass

1. Introductory rites

This consists of:
- Entrance Procession
- Greeting
- Penitential Rite (confession of sins)
- Kyrie (Gloria)
- Opening Prayer.

The purpose of these rites is to *prepare* the community of those united by their common faith to worship God.

Catholics are expected to *fast* (abstain from consuming any food and liquid) for one hour before Mass.

In the *penitential rite*, Catholics ask God and one another for forgiveness for their *sins* (any deliberate wrongdoing). However, if anyone has committed a very serious sin, he/she must attend the sacrament of Reconciliation *before* the Mass.

2. Liturgy of the Word

This consists of:
- First Reading (Old Testament)
- Responsorial Psalm
- Second Reading (New Testament)
- Gospel Acclamation
- Proclamation Reading of the Gospel
- Homily (sermon)
- Creed (usually *Nicene*)
- Prayers of the Faithful.

Catholics believe that God speaks to people today when their sacred texts are read to them at Mass.

Ideally, the homily should explain the meaning and importance of these texts and show how the messages they contain can be applied to everyday life.

3. Liturgy of the Eucharist

This consists of:
- Presentation of Gifts
- Eucharistic Prayer and *Consecration* (where the bread and wine become the body and blood of Jesus Christ)
- Our Father
- Rite of Peace
- Communion.

In the *Eucharistic Prayer*, the bishop or priest speaks the words Jesus used at the *Last Supper* over the bread and wine. Catholics believe that at the consecration:
- the bread ceases to be bread and becomes the body of Jesus
- the wine ceases to be wine and becomes the blood of Jesus.

This is called the doctrine (teaching) of *transubstantiation*.

This means that when Catholics receive the Eucharist in the form of a *host* (bread wafer) at *Communion*, they are receiving the gift of the risen Jesus himself, who is as *truly present* to them as he was to the disciples 2,000 years ago.

4. Concluding Rites

This consists of:
- Final blessing in the name of the Trinity
- Dismissal (sending out) in the *peace* of Christ to love one another.

When Catholics receive the Eucharist, they undertake to go out from the Mass and show *how much difference* their belief in Jesus really means by the way in which they treat other people in their everyday lives.

Growing Closer to God in the Sacraments

Questions

1. Explain the purpose of both of the following: (a) *penitential rite* (b) *homily*.
2. What does it mean to *fast*?
3. Explain the Catholic doctrine of *transubstantiation*.
4. What do Catholics *undertake to do* when they receive the Eucharist at Communion?

The Mass as sacrifice

'*Sacrifice*' is the word used to describe *anything of value offered to God in worship*.

During the Eucharistic Prayer, Jesus is referred to as the *Lamb of God*. This is because the Mass has its roots in the Jewish Passover meal, which commemorates the delivery of the Hebrews from slavery in Egypt.

The story of the first Passover is told in the book of Exodus. In order to persuade the reluctant pharaoh to let the Hebrews go free, God sent a series of warnings, each of which the pharaoh ignored. Finally, God sent the angel of death to force the pharaoh to set the Hebrews free.

During the first Passover, every Jewish household was instructed to *sacrifice* a lamb and sprinkle its blood on their door posts so that the angel of death would see the blood and *pass over* them.

At the Last Supper, Jesus referred to himself as the *Lamb of God* and the bread and wine he offered as his body and blood. In so doing, Jesus identified himself as the *new and perfect Passover sacrifice*. His blood would be shed and his body broken on Good Friday, but *through his death* something *great* would happen. By giving his life on the cross, Jesus revealed the *limitless* depth of God's love.

Through his sacrifice:
- the broken relationship between God and human beings was healed and restored
- people were freed from slavery to sin and death.

However, the Mass does *more* than simply recall Jesus' sacrifice on Good Friday. Jesus' sacrifice is *not* only something that happened in the past that people remember. While Jesus' death is *over* once and for all,

> *in the Eucharist, Christ gives the very body which he gave up for us on the cross, the very blood which he 'poured out for many for the forgiveness of sins.'*

This means that the same Jesus who offered his life on Golgotha is offered in the Mass. Thus, the sacrifice of Jesus on the cross and the sacrifice of the Mass *are one and the same sacrifice*.

Jesus is *really present* in the Mass, just as he was to the people of Palestine 2,000 years ago. The participants in the Mass encounter him in three ways:
- in the sacred texts
- in the breaking of bread
- in their fellow human beings.

Questions

1. Explain the word '*sacrifice*'.
2. How did Jesus refer to himself at the Last Supper?
3. What did Jesus reveal by sacrificing his life on the cross?
4. What did Jesus achieve *through his sacrifice*?
5. In what way is Jesus *really present* in the Mass?

Chapter Twenty-six

Place of Worship: **The Church**

Introduction

For Christians, the word '*church*' has several meanings. It can refer to:

- an *organisation*, such as the Catholic Church or the Methodist Church
- the members of the worldwide Christian *community*
- a *building* for worship.

We shall consider the word '*church*' in the last sense, i.e. *a building specifically designed and used for the worship of God*.

History

For several centuries, Christians living within the Roman Empire were frequently subjected to brutal persecution for their beliefs. As a result, Christians had to gather for worship in secret.

They usually met in a room in the private house of a fellow believer. The altar was just a simple wooden table. Their clergy did not yet wear any distinctive vestments.

This was necessary because if the Roman authorities should raid this house, all they would find would be a group of friends sharing a simple meal of bread and wine.

Only when the Emperor Constantine granted freedom of worship to Christians in AD 313 could they gather to worship in public without fear of harassment. As a result, the earliest churches built date from the fourth century AD.

The Martyrs in the Catacombs by Jules Eugene Lenepveu. During the early years of Christianity, many believers were killed for their faith or their refusal to renounce it and so had to worship God in secret places, such as the catacombs beneath Rome.

Place of Worship: The Church   **147**

Architectural differences

There are significant differences between the various Christian denominations regarding the architecture and design of their different places of worship.

Non-conformist church.

Christians in the non-conformist tradition, such as Presbyterians, worship in buildings that are usually simple in design and plain in decoration. The *pulpit* (a raised platform on which a minister stands to speak) is the focal point of the building. This is because the main emphasis is on listening to the Word of God.

Art is not forbidden, but the emphasis is on creating a quiet space, free from distraction, where the worshipper can concentrate on what the preacher is saying.

Catholic church.

In contrast, churches in the Catholic and Orthodox traditions are more ornate. They usually have paintings, statutes, stained-glass windows and candlelit shrines. The purpose of these decorations is to help worshippers to reflect on the different aspects of the mystery of God.

Although the pulpit is important, here the *altar* is the focal point of the building.

Orthodox church.

Orthodox churches, however, differ from Catholic ones in two notable ways:

- Unlike Catholics, Orthodox worshippers are expected to *stand* during religious ceremonies. Only the elderly and ill are provided with seats.
- Orthodox churches have a distinctive feature called the *iconostasis*. This is a screen decorated with pictures of the evangelists that separates the main part of the church from the *sanctuary* (the altar area).

148 All About Faith

The typical features of a Catholic church

The tower
Many churches have a spire or a tower, which usually houses the church bells. The tower is a *symbol* of the worshipping community reaching up to God.

The pulpit or lectern
This is where the scriptures are read and the sermon given.

Stained glass
Some churches are richly decorated with paintings, statues and stained-glass windows depicting Biblical scenes. For some Christians, beautiful things inspire prayer and celebrate the beauty of God.

The cross
This is the universal symbol of Christianity.

Sanctuary lamp
This is a red lamp that is only lit when the Blessed Sacrament is in the tabernacle to show that Jesus is present.

The crucifix
This is a cross with the figure of Jesus on it.

The Stations of the Cross

The tabernacle
This is a small safe which holds the Blessed Sacrament. Catholics believe that the Blessed Sacrament, i.e. the consecrated bread, not consumed during Mass but reserved in the tabernacle, is Jesus – really present, to be honoured and adored. The Blessed Sacrament is also called the Eucharist.

The baptismal font
Often placed either to the side of the altar or at the back of the church, this is where babies are christened.

The confessional booth
This is where Catholics go to receive the sacrament of reconciliation. A person confessing (called a *penitent*) has a choice of confessing to the priest face to face or through a screen.

The holy water font
Placed at each entrance to the church, this basin of water is used by church members as they enter the church. They touch the water with their fingers and bless themselves, saying, 'In the name of the Father, and of the Son, and of the Holy Spirit. Amen.' This act recalls one's baptismal commitment and the willingness to live a life for God.

The altar
The focus of the worshippers' attention is always towards the altar. The altar recalls the table around which Jesus gathered his disciples to celebrate the first Eucharist on Holy Thursday evening. Items on the altar include:
- Two candles, always burning during the Mass.
- A cup (chalice) to hold the wine, and a dish (paten) to hold the Eucharist wafers. (A small piece of linen is placed over the wafers of bread to protect them from getting soiled.)
- Decanters (cruets) of water and wine to be mixed together.
- A dish of water for the priest to wash his hands.
- A missal, the Catholic prayer book for priests.

Place of Worship: The Church

Questions

1. Explain the three meanings of the word '*church*'.
2. Why did the early Christians have to worship in secret?
3. How did they worship God?
4. Why do the earliest Christian churches built date from the fourth century AD?
5. Describe a place of worship for a Christian in the *non-conformist* tradition.
6. Describe a place of worship for a Christian in the *Catholic* and *Orthodox* traditions.
7. In what ways does an Orthodox church differ from a Catholic one?
8. Identify the different parts of a Catholic church as indicated in the diagram on page 149. Write the answers in your notebook.

Christian symbols

Christianity is rich in symbols. For example, each of the four evangelists has his own symbol.

Matthew: an angel
Mark: a lion
Luke: a bull
John: an eagle

Symbols commonly used in Christian art and worship include:

The Chi-Rho
This is based on the first two letters of the Greek word for Christ – *Christos*.

The IHS
This is a monogram for the name of Jesus in Greek.

INRI
This is taken from the initial letters of *Iesus Nazarenus Rex Iudaeorum*, meaning *Jesus of Nazareth, King of the Jews*. This was the statement Pontius Pilate ordered to be placed on the cross.

The fish
Perhaps the most popular symbol among early Christians was the *fish*. The Greek word for fish is '*Ichthys*'. Each letter of the word points to a name or title for Jesus.

I	Iesos	Jesus
Ch	Christos	Christ
Th	Theou	of God
Y	Yios	Son
S	Soter	Saviour

Meaning: *Jesus Christ, God's Son, Saviour.*

All About Faith

The meaning of gestures

Gestures are symbols that people *perform*. Christians are expected to reflect upon the *meaning* of certain gestures and keep this in mind while participating in an act of worship.
Consider:

- *Kneeling* — This acknowledges the greatness of God, who alone is to be worshipped.
- *Standing* — This recalls Jesus' rising from the dead on Easter Sunday.
- *Blessing* — By tracing the symbol of the cross a person identifies him/herself as a follower of Jesus Christ.
- *Shaking hands* — This should reveal a genuine desire to be a peacemaker and source of help and encouragement to those one encounters in everyday situations.

The cross

Early Christian paintings, particularly those in the catacombs beneath Rome, focus on the symbol of the fish and upon the idea of Jesus as the *Gentle Shepherd* of his people. The early Christians were reluctant to show Jesus on the cross because it was still considered to be a shameful death reserved for criminals. Later, of course, the cross became *the* Christian symbol above all others.

Without doubt, crucifixion *was* a cruel and vicious form of execution. So why did Christians choose to remember Jesus with such a symbol?

One reason is that the cross gives people a powerful *insight* into what God is like. God *understands* what it is to suffer. But more than this, on the cross God says:

Not only do I know about your suffering, I have shared in it.

For people who are themselves suffering from illness or injustice, their belief in a loving God who suffers too can be a *lifeline*. It helps them to find *purpose* in their suffering, the *strength* to endure it and the *hope* of eternal peace and joy with God beyond it.

The cross is almost always found in a Christian place of worship. Here are three different forms of the cross:

- A *crucifix* is a cross with a figure or image of Jesus hanging from it, either dead or in agony. This represents the *suffering* of Jesus, by which Christians believe they have been saved from sin and death.

- A *plain* cross, i.e. one without a figure or image of Jesus upon it, emphasises the *resurrection* of Jesus, which all Christians believe to be a promise of eternal life for them.

- A *crucifix* that shows Jesus on the cross, but *alive* and *in triumph*. He is dressed in the rich clothes of a king and wearing a crown. This expresses *both* the suffering and the resurrection of Jesus.

Place of Worship: The Church

Questions

1. Identify the symbol associated with each of the four evangelists.
2. Explain the meaning of each of the following four symbols: (a) the *Chi-Rho* (b) *IHS* (c) *INRI* (d) *the fish*.
3. Why were the early Christians reluctant to show Jesus on the cross?
4. Why did Christians later choose to remember Jesus with the symbol of the cross?
5. What is a *crucifix*?
6. Explain the meaning of a *plain cross*.

Icons

The word '*icon*' comes from the Greek word meaning '*an image*'.

Icons are richly decorated paintings of either Jesus, Mary, a saint or an angel or a combination of these religious figures.

Icons are widely used by Christians, especially in the Orthodox tradition, to help them to pray. They are designed to help people focus their minds on the mystery of God.

All the details of an icon are designed to convey important religious teachings. Consider the example of *The Teaching Christ*.

The Teaching Christ, Moscow School.

This is an icon of Jesus, God and man. The belief that Jesus is divine is suggested by the gold and blue colours.

Notice the gold background, the golden border of his robe, the golden light in his face and the deep blue of his outer cloak.

The humanity of Jesus is suggested by the brown, earthy colour of the inner garment.

Music

Music can be *symbolic* when it is written and performed to praise and express belief in God. The music used can be either:

- solemn and dignified or cheerful and lively, depending on the occasion
- instrumental, sung or a combination of both.

Hymns have been sung by Christians since the earliest times, usually inspired by a passage taken from the Bible.

Many great classical composers have written music for worship, such as:

- *The St Matthew's Passion* by Bach
- *The Messiah* by Handel.

Some Christian denominations incorporate *dance* as well as music into their worship. They believe that it demonstrates the presence of the Holy Spirit in the Christian community united in worship.

In contrast, the Society of Friends (Quakers) holds prayer meetings *in silence*.

Questions

1. What is an *icon*?
2. What are the details, e.g. the colours, of an icon designed to do? Use the example of *The Teaching Christ* in your answer.
3. In which Christian tradition are icons particularly used?
4. Why do some worshippers use icons in worship?
5. When can music be regarded as *symbolic* in the religious sense?
6. Where do many hymns take their inspiration from?
7. Name one classical composer who wrote music for Christian worship.
8. Why do some Christian denominations incorporate *dance* into their worship?

Chapter Twenty-seven

The **Liturgical Year**

Introduction

For a Christian, the word '*year*' can have several different meanings. It can refer to:

○ the *calendar* year
○ the *academic* year
○ the *liturgical* year.

The liturgical year is the *annual journey through religious rituals, in which Christians recall the events in the life of Jesus Christ and the beginnings of the Christian religion*. However, the liturgical year is *more* than a *commemoration* of past events. It is also a celebration of Jesus Christ living in the church today and an *invitation* to grow closer to him in worship.

The six parts of the liturgical year.

Advent

Advent wreath. One of the customs associated with Advent is making an Advent wreath. These are rings of evergreens, such as holly and ivy, with five candles in them. One candle is lit on each Sunday of Advent. The final candle is lit during Midnight Mass on Christmas Eve to mark the coming of Jesus.

The liturgical year begins with the season of Advent, from the Latin '*adventus*', meaning '*the coming*'.

Advent is the four-week period leading up to Christmas. During this season, Christians are expected to reflect on the coming of Jesus Christ:

○ In the *past* — 2,000 years ago in Bethlehem.
○ In the *present* — Through the sacraments and the people they encounter.
○ In the *future* — When he will return at the end of time to bring to completion the Kingdom of God on Earth.

154 All About Faith

During Advent, Christians examine their lives and prepare to celebrate Jesus' birth. They seek to demonstrate their love for him through generosity and forgiveness of one another.

Christmas

Most Christians send cards and give presents at Christmas.

The season of Christmas ends with **Epiphany** on 6 January. This festival remembers the visit of the Magi and the gifts they brought to Jesus.

Christmas is the season in which Christians celebrate the birth of Jesus. The *feast* of Christmas itself is set on 25 December and this is a *holy day of obligation* for Catholics, i.e. they are required to attend Mass.

However, the exact time of year in which Jesus was born is *not known*. It is thought more likely to have occurred in the spring rather than in winter. The date of 25 December was set by Pope Gregory I in AD 354. It is believed that he chose that time of year to absorb the existing pagan Roman festival of Mithras, which was set around the winter solstice.

The word *'Christmas'* comes from the Old English expression *'Christes Maesse'*, meaning *'the Mass of Christ'*. For Catholics it begins with a vigil or evening mass on 24 December.

The Christmas season includes the feast of *Ephiphany*, from the Greek, meaning *'to show forth'*. It is celebrated on 6 January. It recalls the worship of Jesus by the *Magi*, the three non-Jews who recognised Jesus as the saviour of *all* humankind (see Matthew 2:1–12). This feast also reminds Christians to think of life as a great journey. Just as the Magi trusted the star to lead them, so too should people allow Jesus to guide them through life.

The Christmas season ends on the Sunday following the Epiphany, when Catholics recall and celebrate the baptism of Jesus and the beginning of his public ministry.

N.B.
Christmas traditions

The practice of having a *crib* (a model of the scene where Jesus was born in a stable) in a church during Christmas was begun by St Francis of Assisi in the thirteenth century.
The practice of giving presents has its origins in two sources:
- the presentation of gifts to the infant Jesus by the Magi
- the charitable work of St Nicholas of Myra, the patron saint of children, who lived in the fourth century AD.

The Liturgical Year 155

Ordinary Time

Ordinary Time covers about sixty per cent of the liturgical year. It is divided into *two* periods, as shown in the diagram on page 154. The *first* is between Christmas time and Lent. The *second* is between Easter and the next Advent.

Each week during Ordinary Time, the liturgy focuses on a different aspect of Jesus' life and teachings. The Gospel readings portray Jesus teaching in parables and performing miracles.

Lent

Lent is the time of preparation for Easter.

The season of *Lent* lasts for forty days, not including Sundays. Lent recalls the time Jesus spent in the Judaean wilderness before setting out on his public ministry.

Shrove Tuesday is the last day before Lent. There is a tradition of people eating pancakes to use up luxury items, such as butter and eggs, before the start of Lent, which begins the next day, *Ash Wednesday*.

However, it is important to realise that Lent is not merely about giving things up. Lent is a time of *preparation* for Easter. It is all about doing *creative* and *positive* things in one's life in order to be *ready* to celebrate Jesus' resurrection.

This preparation should include *fasting* (abstaining from certain luxuries such as alcohol, tobacco and sweet foods), but also involves *prayer* and *good works* (helping other people).

Ash Wednesday is the first day of Lent. Catholics attend Mass and are marked on their foreheads with ashes. This is done to remind them that, though following Jesus involves suffering, the way of the cross is the way to new life, to resurrection with Jesus.

The last week of Lent is called *Holy Week*. The days of this week have a special importance in the Christian calendar: *Palm Sunday, Holy Thursday, Good Friday* and *Holy Saturday*.

The Sunday before Easter is **Palm Sunday**, when Jesus entered Jerusalem.

All About Faith

Easter

The **Ascension** commemorates the moment Jesus ascended into heaven.

Pentecost is the feast which marks the coming of the Holy Spirit upon the disciples.

Although many people today highlight the celebration of Christmas, *Easter* is the *most important* part, the very heart of the liturgical year. This is because all the other events in Jesus' life, from his conception to his ascension, are important *because* he died and rose from the dead.

The celebration of Easter sheds its light on the entire Christian year. Through his death and resurrection, Jesus overcame the power of death and sin so that all people can have the opportunity of sharing eternal life with God.

Easter Sunday is a *moveable feast* in the Catholic Church, i.e. it is *not* always held on the same date each year. It is celebrated on a Sunday between 22 March and 25 April. This occurs because of the decision reached by the Council of Nicea in AD 325 that Easter must be celebrated on the first Sunday after the first full moon after the spring equinox.

In the Catholic and Orthodox tradition, the celebration of Easter begins with the Mass of the Vigil, which takes place in the hours of darkness on Holy Saturday evening. The church is decorated with flowers, which were put away during Lent. In some countries, large religious processions are also held to mark the event.

Forty days after Easter Sunday is the feast of the *Ascension*, which marks the day when Jesus ceased to appear to his disciples and returned to his heavenly Father. Then, ten days later, Christians celebrate the feast of *Pentecost*, which is sometimes called the *birthday of the Christian religion*. Christians recall how the Holy Spirit descended upon the disciples and gave them the courage they needed to publicly preach Jesus' message. Christians pray that the power of God will transform their lives too, so that they will grow ever closer to God.

The Liturgical Year

Questions

1. What is the *liturgical year*?
2. What is the name given to the four weeks of preparation for Christmas?
3. What is meant by a *holy day of obligation*?
4. Why did Pope Gregory I set 25 December as the birthday of Jesus?
5. What is the origin of the word *'Christmas'*?
6. What is celebrated on the feast of the *Epiphany*?
7. Explain the likely origins of the following Christmas traditions: (a) the crib (b) giving gifts.
8. (a) What is *Ordinary Time*?
   (b) When does it occur in the liturgical year?
   (c) What do the Gospel readings focus on in Ordinary Time?
9. (a) How long is the season of *Lent*?
   (b) Why is it this long?
10. How are Christians supposed to prepare during Lent for Easter?
11. Why do Catholics have their foreheads marked with *ashes* on Ash Wednesday?
12. What is the name given to the final week of Lent?
13. Why is *Easter* considered to be the most important part of the liturgical year?
14. How has the date for Easter Sunday been calculated since the Council of Nicaea in AD 325?
15. When does the celebration of Easter begin with a vigil mass?
16. Name the feast which marks the return of Jesus to God his Father.
17. Which feast is sometimes referred to as the *birthday of the Christian religion*?

A baptismal candle (left). A Paschal candle (right).

The Paschal candle is blessed at the Easter vigil. It commemorates the idea of Christ as the beginning and the end (alpha and omega) and the second person of the Holy Trinity. It is lit from a special fire, a fire of renewal representing the Holy Spirit. It is carried into the church to proclaim Easter: *'The light of Christ has come into the world.'* Baptismal candles are lit from this candle as each new member is called to share in the light of Christ.

Chapter Twenty-eight

Pilgrimage

Introduction

We may define a *pilgrimage* as

a journey made by a believer to a place that his/her religion considers holy.

A pilgrimage can be undertaken either by one person travelling alone or by a guided group travelling together. A person who goes on pilgrimage is called a *pilgrim*.

The early Christians understood themselves as a *pilgrim people* on a *journey* through this world towards God. They believed that they were following a route already mapped out for them by Jesus. He had assured them that he was

the Way, the Truth and the Life. (John 14:6)

If they stayed on course by remaining faithful to Jesus, then they would reach their destination – the joy of sharing eternal life with God.

Pilgrimage sites

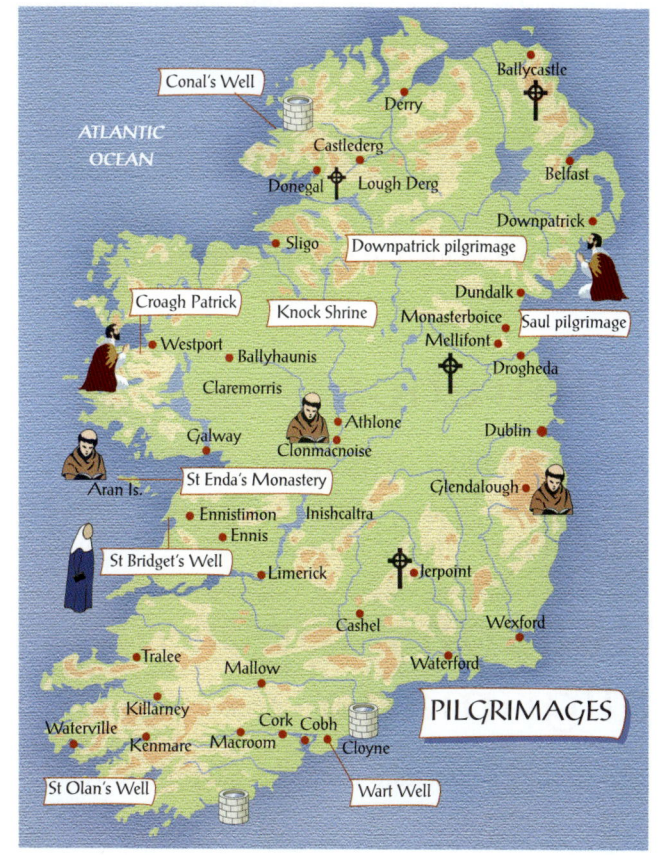

Places of pilgrimage in Ireland.

Pilgrimage 159

Usually each pilgrimage site contains a *shrine*, i.e. a religious monument, sometimes located inside a church, which commemorates an important event or a holy person associated with that place.

A place may become a centre of pilgrimage for any of the following reasons:

- It may be a place associated with the life of Jesus, such as Bethlehem or Jerusalem.
- It may be a place where an *apparition* (appearance) of Mary is said to have occurred, such as Knock or Lourdes.
- It may be a place where a saint (a holy man or holy woman) was buried, such as Downpatrick, the site of St Patrick's tomb.
- It may be a place connected with important events in the life of a saint, such as *Croagh Patrick*, where St Patrick is believed to have fasted and prayed in his desire to grow closer to God.

It is important to remember, however, that while Christians go to such places expecting to meet God in a special way, God is not only present in these official holy sites. Christians believe that God is *everywhere* in life.

When Christians give a certain place a special religious status by referring to it as *holy ground*, they do so to remind themselves that all of the world is holy ground. It is a gift from God that should be treated with *respect*.

Difference

Unlike some other religions, it is *not* compulsory for Christians to go on pilgrimage. It is entirely a matter of personal choice.

Reasons for pilgrimage

People may undertake to go on pilgrimage for a variety of reasons:

- To seek God's *forgiveness* for sin (wrongdoing).
- To ask God's *guidance* before making an important decision.
- To receive the *strength* needed to face a major crisis in life.
- To *strengthen* their faith in God by visiting places connected with the life of Jesus.
- To *revitalise* their faith and encourage them to be more committed to living out their religious beliefs.
- To build bonds of *friendship* with fellow pilgrims.
- To remind themselves that life itself is a great journey. Where this journey ends is decided by the way in which people live their lives.

Questions

1. What is a *pilgrimage*?
2. What is a *pilgrim*?
3. Why did the early Christians see themselves as *a pilgrim people*?
4. What is a *shrine*?
5. For each of the following places, state *why* it has become a place of pilgrimage: (a) Knock (b) Downpatrick (c) Bethlehem (d) Croagh Patrick.
6. When Christians refer to some particular place as a *holy site*, what are they seeking to remind themselves of?
7. How does Christianity *differ* from some other religions in its attitude towards pilgrimage?
8. State any *four* reasons why Christians choose to go on pilgrimage.

Places of pilgrimage

The Holy Land

Christian, Jewish and Muslim shrines in the Holy Land.

- Crusader's Fortress
- Our Lady of Carmel Latin Monastery
- Mary's Well
- Synagogue of Capernaum
- Latin Basilica of the Transfiguration
- Byzantine Church
- Dome of the Rock
- Mosque of El-Askha
- Jacob's Well
- Wailing Wall
- Mosque of the Ascension
- Tomb of Rachel
- Tomb of Moses
- Basilica of the Nativity
- Mosque of Machpelah
- Church of Holy Sepulchre
- Tomb of David
- Greek Monastery

Map locations: Tyre, Mt Carmel, Capernaum, Nazareth, Mt Tabor, Shechem, Djerash, Jerusalem, Mt of Olives, Nebi-musa, Mar-saba, Bethlehem, Hebron

Regions: LEBANON, SYRIA, GALILEE, HAIFA, SAMARIA, JORDAN, ISRAEL, JUDAEA, NEGEB

Mediterranean Sea, Dead Sea

Pilgrimage   161

The *Holy Land* is the name given by Christians to the land where Jesus' extraordinary story unfolded. Two thousand years ago it was the Roman province of Palestine. Today it is divided among the states of Israel, Palestine, Lebanon, Jordan and Syria.

The Holy Land is probably the most frequently visited pilgrimage site for Christians today. Christians are attracted there by the opportunity to retrace Jesus' footsteps on his journey from Galilee to his death and resurrection in Jerusalem.

The main three sites are:

- **Bethlehem:** This is where the Church of the Nativity stands on what is claimed to be the site of Jesus' birth.

- **Nazareth:** Here the Basilica of the Annunciation and the Church of St Gabriel were built to commemorate the angel's message that Mary had been chosen to be the mother of the Messiah.

- **Jerusalem:** The name Jerusalem comes from two words, '*ir shalom*', which means '*City of Peace*'. Jerusalem is unlike other pilgrimage sites because all the Abrahamic faiths consider it sacred. For Judaism and Christianity, Jerusalem is the holiest place on Earth; for Muslims, it's the third-holiest place (after Mecca and Medina).

Christian pilgrims on the Via Dolorosa.

Jerusalem is the principal centre of pilgrimage for Christians, particularly during Easter. The main focus of a pilgrimage is usually the *Via Dolorosa* (the *Street of Sorrows* or the *Way of Grief*). This is the route Jesus took as he carried his cross from Pilate's residence to his place of execution outside the city walls, and ends at his place of burial.

Since the Middle Ages, pilgrims have stopped at fourteen points along the Via Dolorosa for readings, prayers and reflection. Eventually this pilgrim ritual formed the basis for what became known as the *Stations of the Cross* (see box below).

At the end of the Via Dolorosa is the Church of the Holy Sepulchre, which is said to contain the site of Jesus' crucifixion and the tomb where he was buried. Helena, the mother of the first Christian emperor, Constantine, had a church built on this site after she had made her first pilgrimage to the Holy Land in AD 326. This church is usually crammed to capacity on Easter Sunday morning, when Christians celebrate the resurrection of Jesus.

The Stations of the Cross

These are generally found on the walls of Catholic churches. Each marks a stage of Jesus' suffering on Good Friday.

Christians who have been unable to go to Jerusalem and follow the Via Dolorosa have been able to follow the footsteps of Jesus in their local church. By moving around the church and stopping to pray at each station, they have been able to make their own short pilgrimage, as follows:

1. Jesus is condemned to death by Pilate.
2. Jesus receives his cross.
3. Jesus falls beneath the cross for the first time.

4. Jesus meets his mother.
5. Simon of Cyrene helps Jesus to carry the cross.
6. Veronica wipes Jesus' face.
7. Jesus falls a second time.
8. Jesus comforts the women of Jerusalem.
9. Jesus falls a third time.
10. Jesus is stripped and offered a sponge soaked with bitter wine.
11. Jesus is nailed to the cross, between two thieves.
12. Jesus dies on the cross.
13. Jesus is taken down from the cross and laid in his mother's arms. (This scene is depicted by Michelangelo in his *Pieta*.)
14. Jesus is placed in the tomb.

Rome

Rome has been an important centre of pilgrimage for over 1,600 years. It is the place where both Peter and Paul were executed on the orders of Emperor Nero. Peter was the first leader of the Christian community. His successors, who were given the title *pope*, have resided in Rome, except for a few brief periods in exile, ever since.

The headquarters of the Catholic Church are located in the *Vatican*, an independent city-state situated in the heart of Rome. The Vatican occupies slightly more than 100 acres of land and is the smallest country in the world. It has a population of about 1,000 people.

Huge crowds flock to the Vatican to attend one of the Pope's regular public audiences and to receive his blessing.

Rome's many historic churches are packed with pilgrims during the most important religious feasts of the Christian calendar – Easter and Christmas. Three sites in particular draw large numbers of pilgrims:

St Peter's Square, Rome.

- **The Basilica* of St Peter:** Dominating Vatican Square, this massive church occupies more than 163,000 square feet.

  The Basilica of St Peter was constructed over a period of more than 176 years (circa 1450–1626) and built upon the site of the crucifixion of Saint Peter.

- **The Sistine Chapel:** Giovanni de Dolci, under the commission of Pope Sixtus IV, built the Sistine Chapel between 1473 and 1481. Frescos adorn its walls and ceiling. The most famous artwork within the Sistine Chapel is the work of Michelangelo:

  (i) *The Last Judgment*, containing more than 390 figures that surround Jesus.
  (ii) Scenes from the Book of Genesis, including *The Creation of Light*, *The Creation of Stars and Planets* and *The Creation of Adam*.

- **The Christian Catacombs:** The city contains more than 60 catacombs. Constructed over a period of more than 300 years (circa AD 150–450), the Catacombs contain the tombs, sculptures, paintings and inscriptions of the early Christians. Many Christian martyrs and popes are buried within the Catacombs.

*'Basilica' means 'great church'.

Croagh Patrick

Croagh Patrick in Co. Mayo has been a popular place of pilgrimage for Irish people since the Middle Ages. As early as 1113, it was reported that a thunderbolt struck the mountain, killing thirty fasting pilgrims.

Most pilgrimages involve putting up with some kind of hardship. In the case of Croagh Patrick, it is climbing the mountain.

Croagh Patrick is high by Irish standards, rising some 765 metres above the surrounding countryside. The path to the top is four kilometres long. Near the top it is steep and covered with loose rock.

In the past, pilgrimages were always made in one's bare feet. This was considered an act of humility. Although it is no longer felt to be so necessary, some people still climb the mountain in their bare feet to show their sorrow for the ways they have offended God.

Pilgrims climb Croagh Patrick in order to walk where Patrick walked, to kneel where he knelt down and to pray where he prayed. Going on pilgrimage is an act of *devotion* to God.

Questions

1. Why are many Christians attracted to going on pilgrimage in the Holy Land?
2. What is the meaning of the name *Jerusalem*?
3. Where can each of the following places of pilgrimage be found?
   (a) The Christian Catacombs
   (b) The Church of the Holy Sepulchre
   (c) St Peter's Basilica
   (d) The Church of the Nativity

Questions

4. What is the meaning of the street named *Via Doloroso*?
5. What is the purpose of the *Stations of the Cross*?
6. Which Station of the Cross was depicted by Michelangelo in *Pieta*?
7. Why did Rome become an important place of pilgrimage?
8. Write a brief note on *one* important pilgrimage site in Rome.
9. In the past, why were pilgrimages to the summit of Croagh Patrick always made in one's bare feet?

Marian shrines

The Sistine Madonna by Raphael.

Each year huge numbers of pilgrims flock to the many *Marian shrines*, i.e. holy places dedicated to Mary, the mother of Jesus. In terms of specifically Catholic places of pilgrimage, about eighty per cent are dedicated to Mary, or as Catholics have traditionally called her, *Our Lady*. Many of these places have become centres of pilgrimage because it is believed that Mary herself appeared there. Among the most popular are:

- *Aparecida* in Brazil
- *Czestochova* in Poland
- *Fatima* in Portugal.
- *Guadalupe* in Mexico
- *Lourdes* in France.

It needs to be understood, however, that despite the respect shown for Mary at these shrines, the focus of all prayer is not *Mary* but *Jesus*. The Catholic Church teaches that the purpose of pilgrimage is to guide the pilgrim to closer union with

> *Jesus Christ, the Saviour, who is the end of every journey and the source of all holiness.*

Further, Catholics are *not* required by the Church to believe in any of the apparitions of Mary, as they are not considered to be essential elements of their religion.

We shall now consider two Marian shrines, Lourdes and Knock.

Lourdes

Lourdes, in south-west France, only became a place of pilgrimage in the nineteenth century. It is claimed that on 11 February 1858, a fourteen-year-old girl named Bernadette Soubirous had the first of a series of visions of the Blessed Virgin Mary, the mother of Jesus. They are said to have taken place in a little grotto outside the town and occurred on eighteen occasions over a period of six months.

During the ninth apparition, Mary is said to have told Bernadette to dig at a certain place in the grotto. From there a spring of water emerged. Ever since then there have been stories of miraculous healings associated with this spring. Not surprisingly, many Catholics journey to Lourdes in search of healing. Several million people visit Lourdes each year.

Each evening during the pilgrimage season, thousands of pilgrims take part in a torchlit procession through the streets of Lourdes. Prayers and hymns are relayed over loudspeakers. Those who cannot walk are pushed through the streets in wheelchairs by volunteer helpers.

The highlight of the pilgrimage is the visit to the grotto to bathe in its waters. Many pilgrims have claimed that they were completely healed after visiting Lourdes.

Anyone who claims that they have been healed after visiting Lourdes is asked to undergo a series of medical investigations conducted by independent experts. (See page 234.) Out of the reported 5,000 cures, however, only about 2 per cent have actually been declared miracles by the Catholic Church.

Many sick people who have *not* been physically cured at Lourdes, however, claim that their pilgrimage *was* worthwhile. They often say that it brought them closer to God and gave them the courage and strength needed to cope with their illnesses.

Knock

Ireland has its own Marian shrine at Knock in Co. Mayo. Rennie McOwan offers the following account.

> *On the evening of 21 August 1879, a group of local people claimed to have seen an apparition. It consisted of figures of human beings bathed in a great light on the gable-end of the parish church. Word soon spread about the apparition and more people gathered. The figures were believed to be Our Lady, Saint Joseph and Saint John the Evangelist. A life-size altar could also be seen*

and on it stood a lamb and behind it was a cross.

The event was a sensation in the area and people began to flock to the site, including invalids, and some people claimed miraculous cures.

Unlike Lourdes or Fatima, no voices or messages were heard. The Church authorities set up a formal investigation and fifteen witnesses outlined what they saw. After many years of investigation, Catholic Church authorities declared the apparitions to have been genuine. In 1979, Pope John Paul II visited the shrine at Knock and celebrated Mass there, before a congregation of more than 300,000 pilgrims.

The motives of the pilgrims are edifying: the pursuit of a deeper understanding of spiritual things, of personal quests in search of tranquillity, to find support to deal with grief in the face of human tragedies, such as family illness or bereavement. Knock Shrine also promotes reconciliation between people of different traditions.

The tiny shrine has grown and it is now a great centre for prayer, and for Catholics particularly centred on the Eucharist. There is a church, a basilica dedicated to Our Lady, Queen of Ireland, which can hold 10,000 people, a rest home and care unit for invalid pilgrims, a special chapel for the Blessed Sacrament, a Chapel of Reconciliation and the Apparition Chapel, which contains a replica of what the local people saw.

The old church wall was in danger of collapse because it was being touched by so many pilgrims and so a portion of the original wall has been set into the outer wall of the Apparition Chapel. More than 1.5 million people visit Knock Shrine each year and at a time of a decline in formal religious attachment, the Knock numbers have held up.

Adapted from *The Far East*

Knock shrine in Co. Mayo.

Questions

1. What is a *Marian shrine*?
2. *Catholics are devoted to Mary, but they do not worship her*. What does this mean?
3. Who is the focus of all Christian prayer and worship?
4. Are Catholics required by the Church to believe in any of the apparitions of Mary? Why?
5. Who was Bernadette Soubirous?
6. How many people are estimated to visit Lourdes each year?
7. What happens in Lourdes each evening during the pilgrimage season?
8. How many miraculous cures have been confirmed by Catholic Church authorities?
9. What do those who have *not* been physically cured often say about their pilgrimage to Lourdes?
10. Where is Ireland's Marian shrine?
11. What is claimed to have happened there on the evening of 21 August 1879?
12. How was the apparition at Knock different from that of Lourdes or Fatima?
13. What happened in Knock in 1979?
14. State any *two* of the reasons why people go to Knock today.
15. Describe the facilities available to pilgrims at Knock today.
16. How many people are estimated to go on pilgrimage to Knock each year?

166   All About Faith

Part Five

COMMUNITIES OF FAITH IN IRELAND TODAY

Chapter Twenty-nine

Catholicism

Introduction

Since the Second Vatican Council (1962–1965) the Catholic Church has emphasised the idea that *all its members are equal before God*.

Although the Catholic Church is organised on a *hierarchical* basis, i.e. with different levels, one above the other, all baptised people are equal in their membership and responsibility. Clergy, religious and laity together form one community of faith. Together they are called to fulfil the Church's *apostolic mission*, i.e. to make Jesus known and draw others to follow him by the example they set in their daily lives.

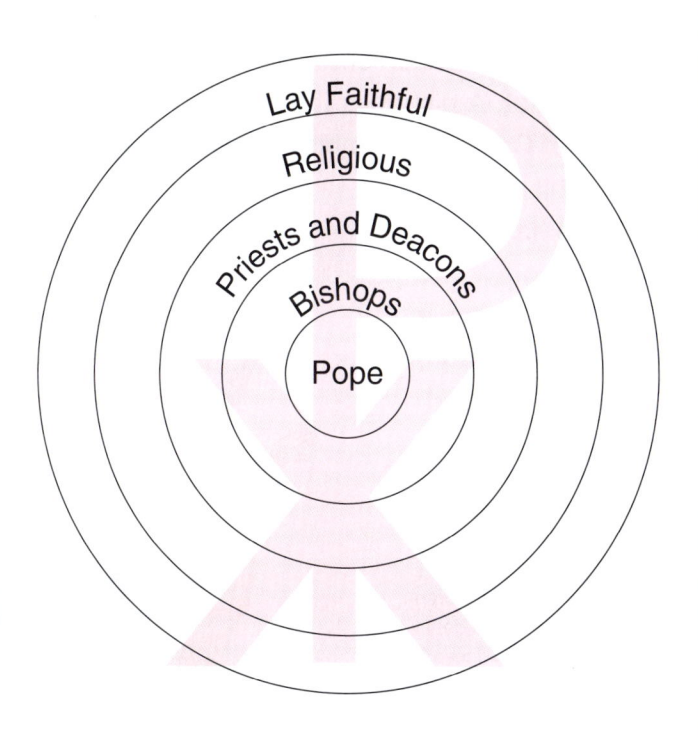

Roles within the Catholic Church. PX is a symbol for Christ. By baptism, every role is connected to Christ's ministry. As the circles get smaller, the roles are more specific.

The Apostolic Succession

The Catholic Church claims that it is the *main trunk* of the Christian family tree. It teaches that it is in *direct continuity* with the first Christian community founded by Jesus Christ himself. Jesus chose the apostles to *continue* his work. The authority of the apostles has been *handed down* from one generation to another over the last 2,000 years in what is called the *Apostolic Succession*. A bishop passes this authority on by laying his hands on the head of another man being made a bishop. As a result, the Catholic bishops claim to be the direct *successors* of the original apostles.

The pope

Statue of the first pope, the apostle Peter, in St Peter's Basilica, Rome.

Catholicism **169**

Jesus made Peter the leader of the disciples and so gave them *unity* (see Matthew 16:18–19). Before his death, Peter passed on his authority to lead the Christian Church to a man named Linus who, in turn, passed this responsibility on to another and so on down to the present day.

Catholics believe that:

- the current pope is in a direct line of succession from the apostle Peter
- the Church is united through the power of the Holy Spirit under the leadership of the pope in Rome
- the pope is the *Vicar of Christ*, i.e. he is Christ's representative on Earth
- the pope is the visible head of the whole Church and his authority extends to all its members.

> N.B.
> Protestants do not accept the authority of the pope, which remains a major point of disagreement between Catholics and Protestants.

The pope lives in Vatican City in Rome.

The First Vatican Council (1870) declared that when speaking on essential matters of faith and morals and after certain strict criteria have been fulfilled, the pope is *infallible* (he cannot err). This topic will be examined further on page 172.

Cardinals

The pope is chosen by a *conclave*, i.e. a secret meeting of the *cardinals* of the Catholic Church. A cardinal is a member of the select group of bishops who may cast their vote when a new pope is being chosen.

In between elections, cardinals offer advice to the pope on important issues. Most countries with a Catholic population have at least one cardinal.

Questions

1. What does the Catholic Church teach about *all baptised people*?
2. (a) What is meant by the *Apostolic Succession*?
   (b) How is it passed on?
3. (a) What is the role of the pope in the Catholic Church?
   (b) Why is the pope referred to as the *Vicar of Christ*?
4. What did the First Vatican Council teach about the pope's authority?
5. How is the pope elected?
6. What is a *cardinal*?

Bishops

Within the Catholic Church there are *local churches* called *dioceses*. Each is led by a *bishop*.

A bishop possesses the *fullness of the priesthood*, i.e. he can confer all seven sacraments, including Confirmation and Holy Orders, which a priest cannot. A bishop is the leader and chief teacher of Catholicism in his *diocese*, i.e. the geographic area over which he has been given authority. The four *archdioceses* in Ireland are Armagh, Dublin, Cashel and Tuam.

A bishop wears particularly recognisable items as symbols of authority. His crosier is a shepherd's crook, as he is shepherd (guide) to the people of the diocese. His mitre, or pointed hat, symbolises the Holy Spirit.

Map of Catholic diocesan boundaries. In Ireland there are four archdioceses (or Provinces): Armagh (north), Dublin (east), Cashel (south) and Tuam (west). In all they contain twenty-six separate dioceses. Each diocese is subdivided into a number of parishes.

In most countries, Catholic bishops meet together on a regular basis to discuss important matters. These gatherings are called *Episcopal Conferences*. In Ireland, they usually take place at St Patrick's College, Maynooth, Co. Kildare.

The Catholic bishops in dioceses scattered across the globe are tasked with working *together* under the pope's leadership to spread the Gospel message and build up the Kingdom of God announced by Jesus. This joint decision making of the pope and the bishops is called *collegiality*.

Priests and religious orders

A Catholic priest.

Each parish is served by a diocesan priest, i.e. a man who has been *ordained* by a bishop to offer spiritual leadership to a local parish. Each priest is expected to:

○ administer the sacraments, e.g. celebrate Mass, hear confession, baptise new members

○ give witness to the love of God by his presence and example, e.g. visit the sick, aid the homeless, counsel those in crisis

○ explain the Church's teaching by sermon or in discussion.

There are also *religious orders* within the Church. These consist of men and women, usually referred to respectively as *brothers* and *sisters*. They form communities dedicated to a particular type of work for the Church, such as caring for the elderly, ill or disabled. All members of religious orders are expected to make solemn *vows* (promises) of poverty, chastity and obedience (see pages 265–6).

The laity

The vast majority of Catholics are members of the laity or *laypeople*, i.e. they are *not* ordained as bishops or priests. With bishops and priests, they come together to celebrate their faith in the

Catholicism 171

sacraments. Both laypeople and clergy are called to give *witness* to God's love by what they say and do in the ordinary surroundings of everyday life (see pages 262–5).

Questions

1. Explain the role of a *bishop* in a diocese.
2. Name the four archdioceses in Ireland.
3. What is *collegiality*?
4. Explain the role of the *priest* in a parish.
5. What are the *religious orders* in the Catholic Church?

The sources of truth

Catholic bishops in Paris.

Jesus commanded his apostles to

Go, make disciples of all the nations…and teach them to observe all the commands I gave you. (Matthew 28:19–20)

Catholics believe that the Gospel message has been faithfully handed on by means of two great sources of truth:

- *Scripture:* The inspired Word of God.
- *Tradition:* The process by which the Church hands on the faith of Catholics from one generation to the next.

The Magisterium

The task of *interpreting* sacred scripture and tradition to guide the belief and behaviour of Catholics is the responsibility of *the Magisterium*. The word '*magisterium*' comes from the Latin word '*magister*', meaning '*teacher*'.

In a broad sense, this teaching role belongs to all members of the Catholic Church, as all are called to communicate the message of Jesus by what they say and do.

Strictly speaking, however, the term '*magisterium*' is used to refer to the pope and the college of bishops under his leadership, who exercise their official role as teachers of the Catholic faith.

Catholics make an important distinction between the *Extraordinary* Magisterium and the *Ordinary* Magisterium.

1. The Extraordinary Magisterium

This occurs on rare occasions when the pope makes a solemn declaration *ex-cathedra*, i.e. using his full authority as successor of the apostle Peter to speak on a matter vital to the Church's *faith* (what people should believe) or *morals* (how people should live).

172   All About Faith

The pope can do so either alone or in an *Ecumenical* (general) Council where the world's Catholic bishops are united under his leadership.

Catholics believe that the decision reached is protected from any error by the power of the Holy Spirit. As a result, the pope is said to be *infallible* (from the Latin meaning '*unable to deceive*') on matters of faith and morals.

Any teachings declared infallible are called *dogmas* of the Church and they must be unreservedly accepted by all Catholics.

2. The Ordinary Magisterium

This consists of the guidance on matters of Church teaching offered by the pope and the bishops by means of public statements and written documents. The most important of these documents is a special letter written by the pope called a *papal encyclical*.

These statements should be treated with respect and carefully studied by Catholics. They provide clear, unified Catholic responses to important moral issues such as abortion, capital punishment, crime, divorce and so on.

Although the statements and documents produced by the Ordinary Magisterium are not considered infallible, Catholics are expected to acknowledge the Ordinary Magisterium as their guide regarding what to believe and how to behave.

Catholics believe that God continues to speak through the teachings of the Catholic Church. As a result, Catholics should respect and accept the teachings of the Ordinary Magisterium.

When a Catholic wants to know whether something is the right or the wrong thing to do, he/she is expected to carefully consider and follow the teaching of the Catholic Church on the matter. (See Chapter 44.)

Importance of the Magisterium

The Magisterium plays a key role in the life of the Catholic Church. As Thomas Zanzig has written:

The teaching authority of the pope with the bishops is one important way that the church has been able to keep unity in the midst of diverse conditions, customs and ways of thinking among Catholic people around the world.

Questions

1. Write a brief note on *the Magisterium* of the Catholic Church. In your answer: (a) explain the origin of the word '*magisterium*' (b) identify who it refers to (c) outline the task of the *Magisterium*.
2. Explain the meaning of the word '*infallible*'.
3. Why do Catholics believe that the pope is infallible when speaking *ex-cathedra* on matters of faith and morals?
4. What is a *dogma*?
5. What is a *papal encyclical*?

Chapter Thirty

Protestantism

Introduction

The term '*Protestant*' is generally applied to those reformist movements within Christianity which, in protest against the authority of the papacy and certain teachings of the Catholic Church, broke away to form several denominations (separate branches) in the sixteenth century.

The principal Protestant Churches in Ireland are:

- the Church of Ireland
- the Presbyterian Church
- the Methodist Church
- the Baptist Church
- the Society of Friends
- the Salvation Army.

The Church of Ireland

The Church of Ireland is the name given to the self-governing Christian denomination which is a member of the international Anglican fellowship of independent churches.

Although the Church of Ireland is in communion with the Anglican Church in England (also known as the Church of England), it is *not* under the authority of the Archbishop of Canterbury. The Church of Ireland is completely *autonomous* and is led by the Archbishop of Armagh, who is referred to as *Primate of All Ireland*.

Church of Ireland Synod.

Church of Ireland Primate Dr Eames.

174 All About Faith

Church of Ireland bishops attend the Lambeth Conference, which is held every ten years. This event draws leaders of the 70 million-strong Anglican communion from around the world. Their discussions produce detailed statements on issues of religious and moral importance which offer guidance to the various member Churches. However, these statements must then be debated and accepted by the individual Anglican Churches before they take effect.

There are approximately 375,000 members of the Church of Ireland, with about 175,000 of them living in the Republic of Ireland.

The *General Synod* is the parliament (the chief decision-making body) of the Church of Ireland. It meets every year and each diocese elects representatives to it. The General Synod consists of two parts:

1. The *House of Bishops*, with twelve members.
2. The *House of Representatives*, which has 216 clergy and 432 lay members.

In recent times, the Church of Ireland has ordained women to the ministry.

The Presbyterian Church

A Presbyterian minister.

This is a worldwide Christian denomination which has some 300,000 members on the island of Ireland. It is the largest Protestant denomination in Northern Ireland.

The Presbyterian Church resulted from the work of John Calvin in Geneva in the sixteenth century. His ideas were brought to Scotland by John Knox in 1559 and then to Ireland by planters in 1642.

Both Calvin and Knox rejected the authority of the pope and the entire hierarchical structure of the Catholic Church. They claimed that such things could not be found in the Bible, so they developed a system of Church government where each local congregation is administered by a council of elected elders, called *presbyters*, instead of a bishop. This council then selects an ordained *minister* to serve their congregation, hence the name *Presbyterian* Church.

At national level, the General Assembly of the Presbyterian Church is the chief decision-making body. It meets once a year under the chairmanship of the *moderator*, who is elected annually to act as the principal spokesperson of the Presbyterian Church.

Presbyterian churches are simple buildings. There are neither stained-glass windows nor any pictures or statues displayed.

A great love of the Bible is encouraged. Presbyterians consider themselves to be *people of the Book*.

The Methodist Church

John Wesley, one of the founders of the Methodist Church.

Protestantism 175

The Methodist Church was founded in the eighteenth century by two Anglican clergymen, John Wesley and his brother, Charles Wesley. They founded a movement aimed at reviving the Anglican Church, which they believed was then losing touch with the needs of ordinary people.

John and Charles faced considerable opposition to their work from the leadership of the Church of England. Their followers were nicknamed *Methodists* because of their very methodical (orderly) approach to prayer, to the study of the Bible and to life in general.

By the end of the eighteenth century, these Methodists separated from the Church of England and formed a new *denomination* (branch) of the Christian tree.

Methodism arrived in Ireland in the 1740s. Over the last 100 years, however, the Methodist population in the Republic of Ireland has fallen from 16,000 to about 5,000.

As with the Presbyterian Church, the Methodist Church is *non-Episcopal*, i.e. there are no bishops in authority. A council of Church members makes decisions and forms policy about Church organisation. A *president* is elected to act as chairperson and spokesperson.

Often a minister has to look after a number of churches, so a system of trained Church members exists to lead services and to preach to the congregation.

Questions

1. Explain what is generally meant by the term '*Protestant*'.
2. What does it mean to say that the Church of Ireland is *in communion* with the Anglican Church in England?
3. (a) What is the Lambeth Conference?
   (b) What role does it play?
4. Explain the role and organisation of the General Synod of the Church of Ireland.

Questions

5. Outline the origins of the name '*Presbyterian*'.
6. What is the role of the *moderator* of the 'Presbyterian'?
7. Describe the interior of a Presbyterian church.
8. Who founded the Methodist Church? Why?
9. Explain the origins of the name '*Methodist*'.
10. What is meant by saying that the Methodist Church is *non-Episcopal*?
11. What is the system adopted in Methodist Churches regarding leading services and preaching to the congregation?

The Baptist Church

Baptists at prayer.

During the sixteenth century, some Christians in the Netherlands became convinced that the traditional practice of baptising babies was wrong. They claimed that only adults should be baptised for two reasons:

- they argued that there was no precedent for infant baptism to be found in the New Testament
- they thought that only those people old enough to make a conscious decision to follow Jesus should be baptised.

Those Protestants who supported these views came together to form a new denomination, known as the *Baptist Church*.

The first Baptist Church was established in England in 1612 by Thomas Helwyn. From there it spread to Ireland, where by 1650 there were Baptist congregations in Dublin, Cork and Waterford.

Each Baptist congregation is self-governing. Baptists teach the *priesthood of all believers*. There are neither bishops nor priests. A council of lay members makes decisions affecting all aspects of Church life.

The Society of Friends

In seventeenth-century England, a small group of Christians led by George Fox became dissatisfied with all existing Church systems, whether Catholic or Protestant.

They believed that religion means each person following his/her personal conviction. They held that *all* formal Church structures and ministers were *unnecessary*. They decided to call themselves the Society of Friends, though they are better known as the *Quakers*.

The name Quaker was a nickname given to Fox himself by Justice Bennett in 1650, after Fox told the judge to *quake in fear at the word of the Lord*. The Friends were initially persecuted by Anglicans and other Protestant denominations. An estimated 15,000 Quakers are thought to have died for their faith between 1650 and 1698. Despite this, the Friends were, and still remain, *pacifists*, i.e. they refuse to use violence or take part in any fighting force.

William Penn, a leading Quaker and founder of the US state Pennsylvania.

As a result of persecution, the Friends settled in North America in large numbers. One of their leading figures, William Penn, founded the colony of Pennsylvania as an experiment in *religious tolerance*, i.e. people of different religions living side by side in peace.

Today there are an estimated 250,000 members of the Society, with about 1,600 in Ireland.

The Friends have always had a great concern for social justice. They did much to help the sick and starving poor of Ireland when the Great Famine devastated the island in the late 1840s.

The Friends have neither ministers nor sacred buildings. They gather together in *meeting houses* to worship God *informally*. Their worship consists of long periods of silent prayer and reflection. They believe that the will of God for each person can be discovered in this way.

The Salvation Army

The Salvation Army at work.

The Salvation Army was founded in 1865 by William Booth, a Methodist minister who worked in the terrible slums of Victorian London.

Booth dedicated his life to the poorest of the poor. Seeing the damage caused by alcohol abuse, he introduced *a total ban* on the consumption of *alcoholic drink* as part of the movement's teachings.

The Salvation Army is organised along military lines. A minister is called an *officer*. Other members are *soldiers*. All wear uniforms. Their meeting place for worship is called a *citadel*. The Salvation Army is highly regarded for its work among the poor and underprivileged.

Questions

1. Explain the origin of the Baptist Church.
2. Where were the first Baptist congregations established in Ireland?
3. Explain how a Baptist congregation is governed.
4. How did the Society of Friends come to be known as the *Quakers*?
5. What are *pacifists*?
6. Why did William Penn found the colony of Pennsylvania in America?
7. How did the Society of Friends reveal its great concern for social justice in Ireland in the 1840s?
8. (a) Who founded the Salvation Army?
   (b) Why did he introduce a *ban* on alcohol consumption for its members?
9. In what way is the Salvation Army organised along military lines?

Chapter Thirty-one

Ecumenism

Introduction

The divisions within Christianity have tragically led to much conflict, bloodshed and persecution over the centuries, all of which has directly *contradicted* the teachings of Jesus Christ.

Since the early twentieth century, however, there has been a growing desire for better relations between the different Christian traditions. The attempt to foster a sense of *togetherness* across centuries-old divisions between Christians is referred to as *ecumenism* (from the Greek work '*oikumene*', meaning '*the world*').

The World Council of Churches

Church leaders listen to a speech during the opening of the meeting of the World Council of Churches in Kuala Lumpur in 2004.

The ecumenical movement has its origins within the Protestant tradition. In 1910, an international conference was held in Edinburgh to discuss ways in which the different Protestant Churches could work together in spreading the Christian faith in Africa and Asia. It was realised that divisions among Christians hindered the effort to spread the Gospel and to win new converts. Eventually, the World Council of Churches (WCC) was established in Geneva in 1945.

The WCC holds a general assembly every six years. It is attended by delegates from many countries. They discuss issues of common concern, such as:

- racism
- the plight of refugees
- the arms trade
- poverty
- advances in technology.

The WCC has been marked by controversy. Some people have claimed that it has become too concerned with political issues. Others, however, say that it should be even more concerned with such matters.

At first, the Catholic Church and the Orthodox Churches were not represented at the WCC. However, the Orthodox Churches have been fully represented since 1961 and the Catholic Church has sent official observers since the general assembly of 1968.

The Catholic Church and ecumenism

Since the Second Vatican Council (1962–1965), the Catholic Church has encouraged shared prayer and dialogue between its members and those of other Christian traditions. There have been significant steps towards healing the rift between the Catholic Church and the Orthodox Churches.

From left to right: Archbishop Dr Sean Brady (Catholic Primate), Archbishop Robert Eames (Church of Ireland Primate), Dr John Reid (then Secretary of State), Rev Winston Graham (President of the Methodist Church in Ireland) and Rev Dr Russell Birney (Moderator of the General Assembly of the Presbyterian Church in Ireland).

Relations have also improved between the Catholic Church and those of many of the Protestant Churches. For example, the leaders of the different Christian Churches in Northern Ireland have co-operated closely in recent years, praying together and producing joint statements.

Discussions have revealed much common ground between the Catholic Church and the Anglican communion. However, important differences remain on such issues as:

- the meaning of the Eucharist
- the authority of the pope
- the ordination of women.

The future of the ecumenical movement

The whole purpose of the ecumenical movement is not to try to make all Christians the same. To do so would be to destroy what is distinctive in each tradition. Rather, its purpose is twofold:

- to promote mutual respect and understanding between the Christian traditions
- to encourage Christians to co-operate with one another to fulfil the very purpose of the Christian community – to be *the Body of Christ on Earth* – and to reveal the love of Christ to the whole world by what they say and do.

Questions

1. What is meant by *ecumenism*?
2. Using the following words, complete this paragraph in your notebook.
   - assembly
   - Geneva
   - observers
   - six
   - 1961
   - 1968

   The WCC was established in _____ in 1945. It holds a general _____ every ___ years. The Orthodox Churches have been represented since _____ . The Catholic Church has sent official _____ since the general assembly of _____ .
3. Identify *three* important areas where differences remain between the Catholic Church and the Anglican Church.
4. What is the purpose of the ecumenical movement?

Ecumenism in action

Brother Roger Schultz.

We shall now consider two examples of the ecumenical movement in action today.

1. The Taizé community

Taizé stands on a hill in Burgundy in France. The small village is surrounded by meadows, vineyards and woods and is where the Taizé community was founded in 1940 by a young man named *Roger Schutz*. At the time, Europe was at war and Brother Roger wanted to do everything he could to help refugees escape from France to Switzerland. Beginning alone, he was joined after the war by others who made their lifelong vows as the first brothers of Taizé in 1949. He intended the community to be a symbol of reconciliation between Christians and of peace, and to be at the service of people in distress.

From the start Brother Roger hoped that the Taizé community would be a focus of unity for all Christians and he worked tirelessly to achieve this. In 1962 a new church was built at Taizé by young volunteers from Germany, which is open to members of all the Christian traditions: Catholic, Orthodox and Protestant. The Taizé community has grown in numbers and is made up of people from many nations. The brothers of the community make a lifetime commitment to celibacy, sharing all goods and accepting the authority of the prior.

There are also small fraternities of Taizé brothers living among the poor on other continents. In church the brothers wear a white habit. Worship is at the heart of Taizé community life and is held three times daily, in the morning, at noon and in the evening. The community's prayer is characterised by the meditative 'songs of Taizé' and by periods of several minutes in complete silence. The Taizé community welcomes young people as pilgrims from all over the world, who come to discuss, share and pray in a climate of openness and simplicity. In the summer months, they can number up to 6,000 people at a time. The community neither accepts donations nor employs staff, as everyone helps with the practical tasks involved in welcoming such large numbers of people.

The pilgrims to Taizé are reminded that prayer and faith in God are never an escape, but involve a commitment to make the world a better place for all to live in. As Brother Roger once stated, 'It is not only the leaders of nations who build the world of tomorrow. The most obscure and humble people can play a part in bringing about a future of peace and trust.'

From the very outset, Brother Roger geared the Taizé community towards fostering ecumenism and expressing the Christian message in modern terms. The community aims to live as a witness to peace and unity through faith in Christ.

Source: Adapted from information provided by the Taizé community

Questions

1. Where is the Taizé community located?
2. Who founded it? When did he do so?
3. Why did he found it?
4. What did he hope the Taizé community would become?
5. Who is invited to join or visit the Taizé community?
6. Describe the way in which the members of the Taizé community pray.
7. What are pilgrims to Taizé reminded of about prayer and faith?
8. From the outset, what was the Taizé community geared to do?

2. The Corrymeela community

The Corrymeela community.

The Corrymeela community was founded in 1965 by *Ray Davey*, a Presbyterian minister, in Co. Antrim, Ireland. He took over a house with a small group of young people, aiming to form a community that would help to heal the social, political and religious divisions in Northern Ireland. Ray Davey had previously been a prisoner of war as well as a chaplain to students, and realised the need to create a centre that would serve the cause of unity between all peoples.

The Corrymeela community offers opportunities for people to come together from all parts of society to share their experiences. The aim is to foster good relationships and for people to spend time together in a relaxed atmosphere. The basic belief is that in this way people will grow to understand each other and this will produce a change in attitude.

The community is open to men and women, laypeople as well as clergy. There is no test of membership and people without religious views or beliefs are also welcome.

Conferences and gatherings for different ages are organised and 'family weeks' are held to encourage whole families to spend time together. A special feature is the international camp for young people and the support that the community gives to groups all over the world. It has also introduced a 'Mixed Marriage Association' to support marriages of mixed religion, and has established links with other organisations such as the Coventry House of Reconciliation. The name Corrymeela means 'hill of harmony' and the community takes its ideal from this name.

Source: Adapted from J.G. Harris, *GCSE Religious Studies*

Questions

1. Where is the Corrymeela community located?
2. Who founded it?
3. Why did he decide to form the Corrymeela community?
4. What is the aim of this community?
5. Who is welcome to join it?
6. What does the name Corrymeela mean?
7. Why do you think that this name was chosen for an ecumenical community?

Part Six

ISLAM

Chapter Thirty-two

The Origins of Islam

Introduction

Islam is an Arabic word that means '*peace through submission to the revealed will of God*'. A follower of Islam is called a *Muslim*, i.e. one who submits.

Birthplace

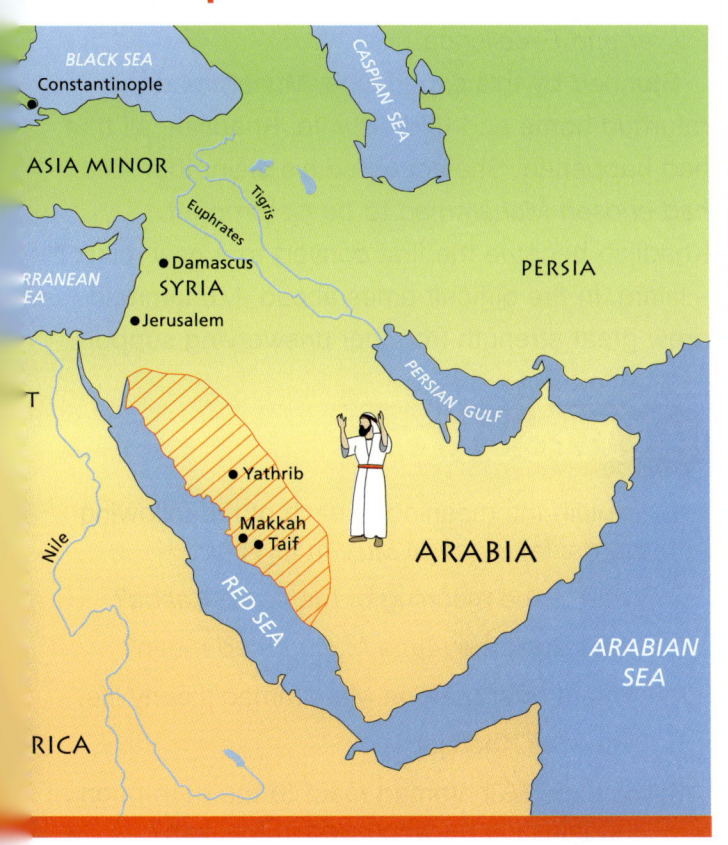

The Middle East in the time of Muhammad.

The birthplace of Islam was the vast Arabian desert peninsula which lies between the north-east coast of Africa and western Asia. The people who lived there were known as *Arabs* (the word 'Arab' means '*nomad*'). A few of the region's inhabitants were Jews or Christians, but the vast majority were *polytheists* (worshipped more than one god).

In the seventh century AD there was no strong, united kingdom in Arabia and the different tribes constantly fought amongst themselves over control of pastures and wells. All this was about to change.

The Kaaba today in the centre of Makkah.

The place where this change began was a town called Makkah (also known as Mecca), which had been built around an oasis in the mountainous area of western Arabia.

Arab pilgrims flocked to Makkah to worship at the *Kaaba* (meaning '*the house of God*'). It contained hundreds of *idols* (statues of pagan gods) at which pilgrims offered sacrifices.

The Origins of Islam **185**

The call of Muhammad

Drawing of the angel Gabriel appearing to Muhammad.

Muhammad (which means '*highly praised*') was born in Makkah around AD 570. Tragedy touched his life from the outset. His father died before he was born and his mother died when he was only six years old. Muhammad was then adopted by his uncle and worked on camel caravans, travelling with his uncle to the great trade centres of the Middle East.

As a young man he became the business manager of a rich young widow named Khadijah. They fell in love, married and were a happy, devoted couple. They had two sons (both of whom died young) and four daughters.

In time, Muhammad became a respected and successful businessman. He was known as *Al-Amin* (meaning '*trustworthy*'). However, he grew increasingly troubled by the corruption and injustice he witnessed in Makkah. He wanted to do something to end this.

Muhammad began spending more and more time alone in a cave on Mount Hira, a few miles outside Makkah. He prayed and *fasted* (went without food and water) for long periods of time.

In AD 610, Muhammad is said to have received a *revelation* (a vision containing a message) from *Allah* (the Arabic name for *God*).

He was alone in the cave on Mount Hira when it is claimed that the angel Gabriel appeared to him and told him that he was to be the *prophet of Allah*, i.e. the one who would tell the people the will of God. This event is known as the *Night of Power and Excellence*.

Stunned by this experience, Muhammad returned home and told his wife, Khadijah, all that had happened. She accepted his claim that *Allah had chosen Muhammad to be his prophet*. Khadijah became the first convert to a new religion – Islam. In the difficult times ahead, Muhammad drew great strength from her unswerving support.

Questions

1. Explain the meaning of each of the following words: (a) *Islam* (b) *Muslim* (c) *Arab*.
2. What is the meaning of the name *Kaaba*?
3. What does the name *Muhammad* mean?
4. Write a brief note on Muhammad's early life.
5. Who was Khadijah?
6. How did Muhammad react to the corruption and injustice he witnessed in Makkah?
7. Where did he often go to pray and fast alone?
8. Describe the event Muslims call the *Night of Power and Excellence*.
9. Muhammad claimed that he had been chosen to be the *prophet of Allah*. What does this mean?

Preaching

In AD 613 Muhammad claimed to have received another revelation from Allah. He was told to begin preaching the message of Allah to the people of Makkah. Muhammad told them that:

- they should abandon polytheism, as there is only *one* God – *Allah*
- people must treat one another honestly and care for the sick, elderly, widowed and orphaned
- Allah will hold people accountable for any harm they have done in their lives.

Reaction

At first Makkah's wealthy businessmen and religious leaders didn't take Muhammad seriously, but soon they began to change their attitude towards him. Muhammad demanded that all idols be removed from the Kaaba. This was a direct threat to the business activities of those who had been making healthy profits from the many pilgrims who came to worship those idols.

Opponents of Muhammad realised that he would not stop until he had destroyed every idol and had reformed the city's government. They accused Muhammad of trying to wreck the local economy and began to persecute him and his followers. Several of his followers were murdered, but Muhammad refused to be intimidated by them.

The departure to Madinah

By the summer of AD 622 Muhammad had been forbidden to preach within the city limits of Makkah. He decided to accept an invitation to go to Yathrib, almost 270 miles north of Makkah, where he and his followers could make a fresh start.

The Hijrah/Hegira.

Muhammad's departure from Makkah is called the *Hijrah* or the *Hegira* (meaning '*the departure*').

Just as Christians mark the beginning of the Christian era with Jesus' birth, Muslims begin their calendar with Muhammad's departure from Makkah. The year AD 622 is the *first* year of the Muslim calendar.

The city of Yathrib was later renamed *Madinah* or *Medina* (the city of the prophet) in honour of Muhammad.

Once in Madinah, Muhammad quickly developed an enormous following and soon took control of that city's government. He proved to be a great political as well as religious leader, reforming the city's administration, uniting its people and providing for all those in need. People began to refer to Muhammad as the *Rasul* (the Messenger of Allah).

Questions

1. What happened to Muhammad in AD 613?
2. What message did he preach?
3. Why did the wealthy businessmen begin to consider Muhammad a threat?
4. What did they accuse Muhammad of trying to do?
5. How did Muhammad's powerful enemies try to stop him?
6. (a) What is the *Hegira* or *Hijrah*?
   (b) Why is this an important date on the Muslim calendar?
7. Why was Yathrib later renamed *Madinah* or *Medina*?
8. (a) What title did Muhammad's followers in Madinah begin to refer to him by?
   (b) What did it mean?

The return to Makkah

Muhammad was determined to return to Makkah. He wanted to:

- convert its people to Islam
- reform its government
- cleanse the Kaaba by removing all the idols.

Muhammad proved to be a highly successful military commander. After a series of battles, he defeated his opponents and led his followers in triumph through the streets of Makkah in AD 630.

Cleansing the Kaaba

Muhammad riding at the head of disciples to Badr to meet the Meccan army.

Muhammad ordered that all the idols be removed from the Kaaba, leaving only a simple cube-shaped building, the size of a small house, which was built of grey stone. Today, this is covered with a huge black cloth and sits at the centre of a large walled enclosure.

Muhammad preserved the Kaaba after removing the idols because he believed that it had originally been built by Abraham*, with the intention that it should be used exclusively for the worship of Allah.

One item was left in the Kaaba. This was the *Black Stone* (thought by some to be a meteorite). This is embedded in one wall of the Kaaba itself.

Muslims believe that Allah gave this stone to Adam, the first human. Originally the stone was *white*, but it turned black after absorbing the sins of all the pilgrims who have touched it.

*N.B.
Muslims believe that Abraham was a Muslim and that Arabs are the descendants of Abraham's son Ishmael, while Jews are the descendants of his other son, Isaac.

The death of Muhammad

By AD 631 Islam had spread across the whole of Arabia. Delegates from all the Arab tribes came to Muhammad, declared their conversion to Islam and accepted his leadership. He had succeeded in uniting the Arabs into one nation, united by a common faith, with a powerful army.

Muhammad fell ill, probably with pneumonia, and died in AD 632. Others continued his work, and within a century of his death, Islam had taken root as far west as Spain and as far east as India.

The Kaaba.

Divisions

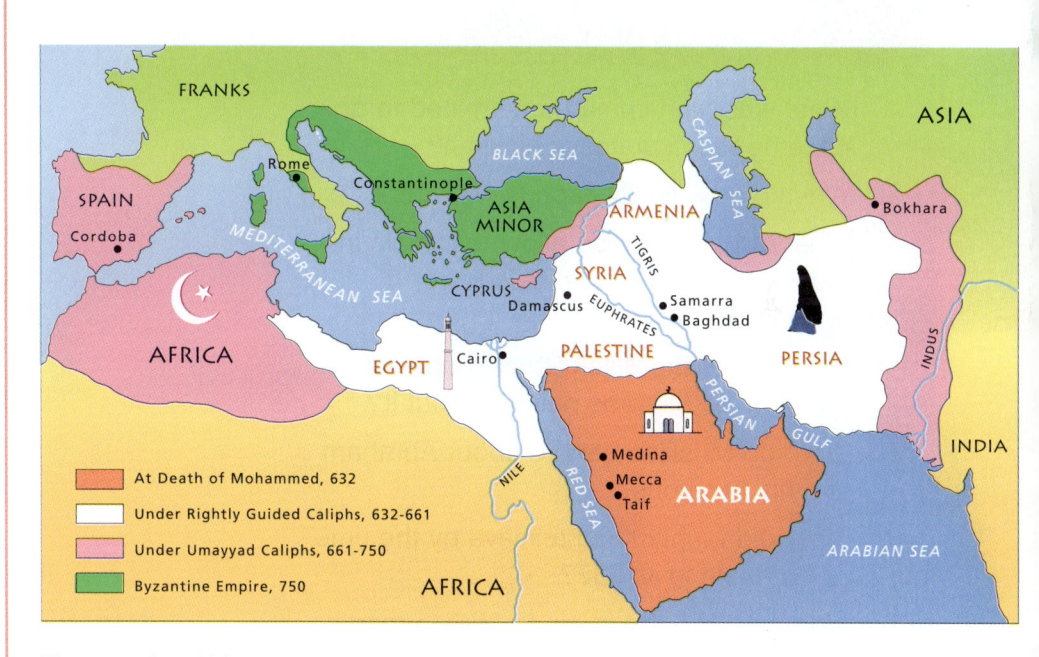

The expansion of Islam.

After Muhammad's death, disputes occurred over who should be appointed *caliph* (successor to Muhammad). The rival factions peacefully agreed to the election of four successive caliphs:

1. Abu Bakr (632–634)
2. Umar (634–644)
3. Uthman (644–656)
4. Ali (656–661).

The Origins of Islam

All four proved to be strong, competent leaders.

However, after Ali's death (he had been husband to Muhammad's daughter Fatimah), a bitter dispute arose over who should succeed him as caliph.

Two groups formed: the *Sunnis* and the *Shias*. Each wanted a *different* person as leader of Islam.

The Sunnis accepted the next caliph, but the Shias (meaning '*Party of Ali*') refused to do so and followed the descendants of Ali.

Sunnis and Shias have been *separate* groups ever since and have periodically fought one another over the centuries.

The majority of Muslims (about ninety per cent) are Sunni. However, the Shias are the dominant group in Iran, Pakistan and Lebanon.

Questions

1. What was Muhammad determined to do once he took control of Makkah?
2. When did he finally capture Makkah?
3. What did Muhammad allow to remain in the Kaaba once all the idols were removed?
4. (a) Where is the Black Stone located?
   (b) What do Muslims believe about it?
5. What do Muslims believe about Abraham and his two sons?
6. What did Muhammad achieve by the time of his death in AD 632?
7. What was the title given to Muhammad's successor?
8. Name the two main groups within Islam. State which is the majority group and which is the minority one.
9. Why did these two rival groups arise after Muhammad's death?

Chapter Thirty-three

Islam: Belief and Worship

Introduction

Muslims believe that *Allah is the Lord of all*. Since the death of Muhammad, Muslims have spread their message from Arabia to every continent, especially Africa and Asia. Today, approximately one-fifth of the world's population is *Muslim*.

The Qur'an

A Muslim boy reading the Qur'an.

The heart of Islam is the sacred text known as the *Qur'an (Koran)*, whose title means *that which is to be read*. Originally written in Arabic about twenty years after Muhammad's death, the Qur'an is a collection of all the messages he was said to have received from Allah.

The Qur'an consists of 114 *surahs* (chapters). It has a very special meaning and importance for Muslims because they believe that every word of it is *literally* the word of God. This explains why Muslims treat each copy of the Qur'an with great respect. For example:

- Muslims try to commit lengthy passages of the Qur'an to memory
- the Qur'an should never be left lying on the ground.

The Qur'an contains the following:

- the basic beliefs of Islam
- clear and strict guidelines as to how Muslims should live
- the forms of punishment to be inflicted for wrongdoing.

Today, the Qur'an rivals the Bible as the world's most widely read book.

The five articles of faith

Every Muslim must accept the following five doctrines:

- Allah is the one, true God.
- Angels are the messengers of Allah.
- The Qur'an is the final and complete revelation of Allah.
- Muhammad was the last and greatest prophet of Allah.
- There will be a final day of judgment, when Allah will reward the good and punish the wicked.

Muslims are expected to uphold these beliefs in their daily lives by practising the *five pillars of faith*.

Questions

1. What does the title '*Qur'an*' mean?
2. In what language was the Qur'an originally written?
3. What kind of collection is the Qur'an?
4. (a) What is a *surah*?
   (b) How many surahs are there in the Qur'an?
5. Why does the Qur'an have a very special meaning and importance for Muslims?
6. State *one* way in which Muslims demonstrate their respect for the Qur'an.
7. What does the Qur'an contain?
8. State the *five articles of faith* for Muslims.

The five pillars

The Qur'an describes the *five pillars of faith* as things which all Muslims are obliged to fulfil. They are as follows:

- The first pillar: *Shahadah*. This is the total acceptance of the belief that there is one and only one God – *Allah*. All Muslims are expected to recite the following creed:

  There is no God but Allah, and Muhammad is his prophet.

The shahadah, written over the entrance to a mosque.

- The second pillar: *Salat*. This involves a commitment to pray each day and to attend a mosque at midday on Friday for communal worship.
- The third pillar: *Zakat*. This concerns the giving of alms (charity). There are *two* kinds of alms. One is the money Muslims donate freely on their own initiative. The other is the part of a Muslim's income (set at one-fortieth) that is collected by the state. This is called *poor-due* and is used to fund education and social services for the poor and sick.
- The fourth pillar: *Saum*. This involves *fasting* during the daylight hours of the holy month of Ramadan, the ninth month of the Muslim year.
- The fifth pillar: *Hajj*. This concerns the commitment every Muslim must make to go on a pilgrimage to the holy city of Makkah at least once in his/her lifetime.

This is a special compass. It enables a Muslim who is not near a mosque to find the direction of the Kaaba, and thus the correct direction to face when praying.

Questions

1. What is meant by the *five pillars of faith*?
2. Match the names in column B with the appropriate pillar of Islam in column A.

A	B
First pillar	Saum
Second pillar	Hajj
Third pillar	Shahadah
Fourth pillar	Salat
Fifth pillar	Zakat

3. Briefly explain each of the five pillars.

Relations with other religions

Muslims believe that Islam did not begin with the prophet Muhammad. The message of Allah was revealed to a number of holy men long before Muhammad was born. Muslims believe that Adam, Abraham, Moses and Jesus were also Allah's prophets. However, Muhammad stands apart from these earlier prophets. They believe that he is the *last*, the *greatest* and the *most decisive* prophet of Allah.

While Muslims recognise that the words of Allah may be found in the Torah, the Psalms and the Gospels, they believe that they are mixed up with too many human additions. Islam teaches that the *pure* word of God is *only* to be found in the Qur'an. As a result they believe that Islam is the only religion with the *complete* truth.

For this reason, devout Muslims believe that it is their solemn duty to encourage others to follow the way of *Islam*, i.e. of submission to the will of Allah. However, the Qur'an expressly *forbids* forcing people to believe what they do not want to believe. This is because Allah has given all people the gifts of reason and free choice. Such gifts are to be respected. As surah 2, verse 257 states:

Let there be no compulsion in religion.

Other religions are to be respected and missionary work should be carried out in such a way as to not give offence.

Questions

1. Name four holy men who lived before Muhammad whom Muslims accept as prophets of Allah.
2. Why do Muslims believe that Muhammad stands apart from the earlier prophets of Allah?
3. (a) What do Muslims believe about the Torah, the Psalms and the Gospels?
   (b) What do Muslims believe about the Qur'an?
   (c) How does this affect the way they view their own religion?
4. Explain the teaching of the Qur'an about respecting the religious beliefs of other non-Muslim peoples.

Islam: Belief and Worship

The mosque

The word '*mosque*' means '*a place of prostration*'. The main function of a mosque is to provide a place in which Muslims can worship Allah. However, it can also serve as a school where children are taught the Qur'an.

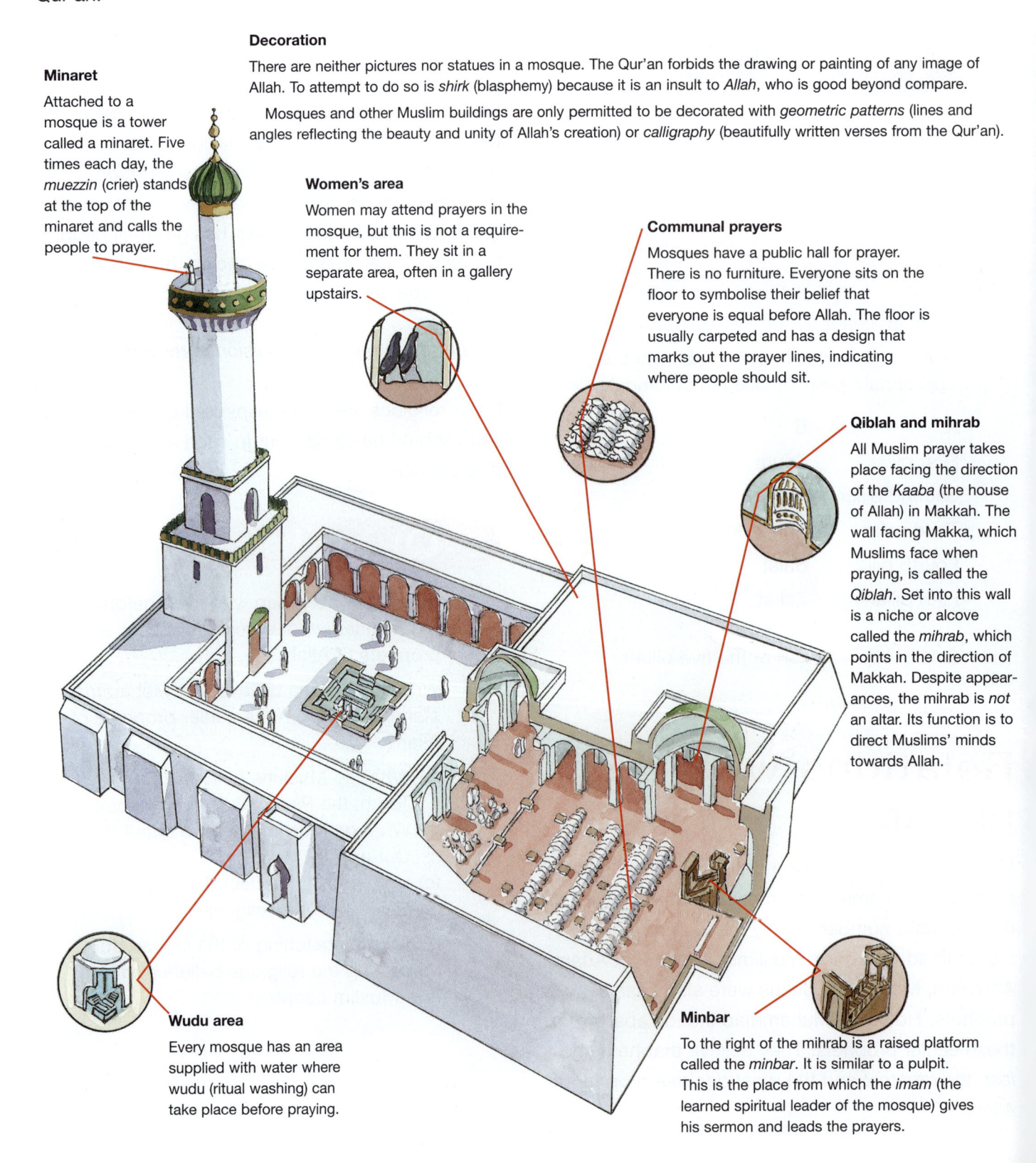

Decoration

There are neither pictures nor statues in a mosque. The Qur'an forbids the drawing or painting of any image of Allah. To attempt to do so is *shirk* (blasphemy) because it is an insult to *Allah*, who is good beyond compare.

Mosques and other Muslim buildings are only permitted to be decorated with *geometric patterns* (lines and angles reflecting the beauty and unity of Allah's creation) or *calligraphy* (beautifully written verses from the Qur'an).

Minaret

Attached to a mosque is a tower called a minaret. Five times each day, the *muezzin* (crier) stands at the top of the minaret and calls the people to prayer.

Women's area

Women may attend prayers in the mosque, but this is not a requirement for them. They sit in a separate area, often in a gallery upstairs.

Communal prayers

Mosques have a public hall for prayer. There is no furniture. Everyone sits on the floor to symbolise their belief that everyone is equal before Allah. The floor is usually carpeted and has a design that marks out the prayer lines, indicating where people should sit.

Qiblah and mihrab

All Muslim prayer takes place facing the direction of the *Kaaba* (the house of Allah) in Makkah. The wall facing Makka, which Muslims face when praying, is called the *Qiblah*. Set into this wall is a niche or alcove called the *mihrab*, which points in the direction of Makkah. Despite appearances, the mihrab is *not* an altar. Its function is to direct Muslims' minds towards Allah.

Wudu area

Every mosque has an area supplied with water where wudu (ritual washing) can take place before praying.

Minbar

To the right of the mihrab is a raised platform called the *minbar*. It is similar to a pulpit. This is the place from which the *imam* (the learned spiritual leader of the mosque) gives his sermon and leads the prayers.

194 All About Faith

Questions

1. Explain the meaning of the word '*mosque*'.
2. What is a *minaret*?
3. Explain the role of each of the following:
   (a) the *muezzin* (b) the *imam*.
4. What is *shirk*?
5. Why are their neither pictures nor statues in a mosque?
6. How is a mosque decorated?
7. (a) What is the *minbar*?
   (b) Who uses it?
8. Which direction must Muslims face when praying?
9. What is the *mihrab*?
10. What is the purpose of the *wudu area*?
11. Why is there no furniture in a mosque?

Praying to Allah

According to the Qur'an, a practising Muslim must pray five times each day – at dawn, noon, mid-afternoon, sunset and evening.

In Muslim countries, one may hear the *muezzin* (prayer caller) summoning the faithful to prayer from the balcony of the *minaret* (the tall, slender tower attached to the mosque). Attendance on Friday, the Muslim holy day, is compulsory. Men and women usually pray in separate areas.

On arrival at the mosque, Muslims remove their shoes and put on skullcaps. There is a fountain for *wudu* (ritual washing) to prepare body and soul for worship of Allah.

Since there are no seats in a mosque, all unroll prayer mats. Kneeling on their mats, Muslims face in the direction of Makkah as indicated by the *mihrab* (recess in one wall of the mosque).

After they have listened to the sermon by the *imam* (leader of the mosque), Muslims recite prayers from the Qur'an according to a set format, with each gesture having a specific meaning.

Prayer beings with Muslims standing with their hands raised to their ears while proclaiming Allah's greatness. Then they recite the opening chapter of the Qur'an, which has been learned by heart.

As they recite other verses from the Qur'an, Muslims change position to indicate something about their relationship with Allah.

Standing: To show alertness.

Bowing: To show respect and love for Allah.

Prostration: To show surrender to Allah.

Sitting: To show tranquillity and acceptance.

Islam: Belief and Worship   **195**

Questions

1. How many times a day must a Muslim pray?
2. Which day of the week is the Muslim holy day?
3. Who gives the sermon in the mosque?
4. Explain the meaning of the following gestures: (a) *standing* (b) *bowing* (c) *prostration* (d) *sitting*.

Aqiqa

A father whispering the adhan to his child.

The birth of a child is regarded as *barakah*, i.e. a blessing from Allah. Indeed, the first word a child should hear is the name *Allah*. The child's father should whisper the *adhan* (the muezzin's call to prayer) in the baby's ear.

> The adhan begins '*Allahu Akbar*...' (God is the Greatest...). It continues, '*I bear witness there is no God but Allah, I bear witness that Muhammad is the Messenger of Allah, Rush to Prayer, Rush to Success, God is the Greatest...*'

On the seventh day after the child's birth, the ritual of *Aqiqa, the naming ceremony*, is held. The child's head is shaved and money is given to charity, by tradition gold or silver of the same weight as the child's hair, but in practice often more. Then sheep are sacrificed (two for a boy and one for a girl). The meat is then sweetened and divided out:

- two-thirds to family and friends
- one-third to the poor.

The child is then *named*. There are two traditional kinds of name:

- the child may be named after either Muhammad or one of his family, such as Fatimah or Ali
- the child may be given a name which reminds him to be obedient to the will of Allah, e.g. *Abdullah* (meaning 'servant of Allah').

Sometimes the parents ask the imam to choose a name for the child.

Boys are usually *circumcised* at Aqiqa. Sometimes this is done in the hospital soon after birth. In some countries, however, circumcision is a separate ceremony held around the age of seven.

Children are considered to be able to distinguish right from wrong by the age of seven and so religious education starts then. Children usually attend Qur'an classes in the local mosque. At this point children learn to read and write Arabic, if the language is not spoken by the family in the home.

196   All About Faith

Questions

1. How do Muslims look upon the birth of a child?
2. (a) What is the *adhan*?
   (b) When does a Muslim first hear it?
3. What is *Aqiqa*?
4. Why is the baby's head shaved for Aqiqa?
5. What are the two traditional kinds of Islamic name?
6. What usually happens to boys at Aqiqa?
7. At what age do Muslim children begin their religious education? Why?

The Hajj

The pilgrimage to Makkah, Islam's holiest place, is called the *Hajj*. It is the duty of every Muslim to make this journey at least once in his/her lifetime. Each year about 1.5 million Muslims undertake the Hajj during Dhu al-hijja, the last month of the Islamic calendar, but only after settling all their outstanding debts and having attended to their family commitments.

Preparations

On arrival at Makkah, Muslims are expected to follow set rituals and there are guides present to *ensure* that they do so:

- They bathe to indicate their intention to complete the pilgrimage.
- Men put on the *ihram* (a seamless white garment) and walk barefoot. Women must ensure that they are modestly dressed, covering everything but their face, hands and feet. The ihram is intended to show the equality of all people before Allah.

Islam: Belief and Worship

The Hajj route

THE HAJJ ROUTE

Hills of Safa and Marwa — The Plain of Arafat — The Mount of Mercy — Mina — The Kaaba

- First, all pilgrims pass around the Kaaba seven times – three times quickly and four times slowly – in an anti-clockwise direction, kissing or touching the Black Stone as they pass.
- Secondly, they pass between the hills of Safa and Marwa seven times, remembering Ishmael's mother, Hagar, who ran there looking for water. Both were near death when Ishmael discovered a spring. The well on this spot is called the *Zamzam*. Pilgrims must drink from it. It reminds them that when things seem bleakest, Allah will not abandon them.
- Thirdly, they proceed on to the Plain of Arafat, near the Mount of Mercy, where they pray from noon to dusk.
- Fourthly, they go to Mina, a small village, where the pilgrims throw stones at a pillar. They recall how Satan tried to tempt Ishmael to turn against his father Abraham, just as Abraham was about to sacrifice him. Ishmael resisted temptation and threw stones at Satan to drive him away. A sacrifice of a sheep is made here, just as Abraham offered Allah a sheep *instead* of Ishmael.*
- Lastly, the pilgrims return to Makkah and walk around the Kaaba again.
- The grand finale of the Hajj is the feast of *Eid-ul-Adha*.

*Jews believe that it was Abraham's other son, Isaac, rather than Ishamel.

Importance

Muslims believe that those who participate in the Hajj in a spirit of *reverence* (deep respect) will have their sins forgiven. Anyone who dies while journeying either to or from Makkah is declared a *martyr* (someone who has died for his/her beliefs) and will be welcomed directly into paradise by Allah.

Questions

1. What is the *Hajj*?
2. How often must a Muslim go on the Hajj?
3. When does the Hajj take place?
4. What do Muslims do to prepare for the Hajj?
5. Write a brief account of what pilgrims must do on the Hajj route.
6. What do Muslims believe happens to a person who, in a spirit of reverence, dies while either going to or coming from Makkah?

Festivals

Muslim pilgrims pray at the Grand Mosque in Mecca.

Islam has its own calendar. It has twelve months, but each month is only twenty-nine or thirty days long because it follows the *lunar cycle*, i.e. the time between one new moon and the next. As a result, the Muslim year is eleven days *shorter* than that of Jews and Christians. Muslims date their era from the year AD 622, when the prophet Muhammad emigrated from Makkah.

Eid or *id* is the Muslim word for a festival. This is a large-scale communal celebration which seeks to engender a spirit of friendship and goodwill. Visitors and strangers are welcomed and special provisions are made for the poor.

The following are the key festivals of Islam.

1. Hijrah

This celebration marks the beginning of the Muslim year and is a time to recall the journey made by the prophet Muhammad from Makkah to Madinah in AD 622. Muslims celebrate the establishment of their religious community and gifts are often exchanged.

2. Eid-ul-Fitr

This festival comes at *the end of* the month of *Ramadan*, the ninth month of the Muslim calendar.

Ramadan is important because Muslims believe that it was during this month that Allah revealed himself to Muhammad through the angel Gabriel. Muslims fast (abstain from food, drink and sexual intercourse) during the daylight hours throughout this month. *Eid-ul-Fitr* marks the end of Ramadan.

Eid-ul-Fitr is also called *the small festival*. It lasts for three days and is celebrated with special prayers. It is a time for visiting friends and holding a large family meal. New clothes are often bought and children also receive presents of money and sweets. The poor are not forgotten. It is customary to send them food.

Eid-ul-Fitr is a celebration not only of the end of a long period of fasting, but of a challenge successfully faced.

3. Eid-ul-Adha

This is known as *the great feast* or *the festival of sacrifice*. It lasts for four days and is held within the final month of the Muslim year.

- In this festival, Muslims celebrate the completion of the annual pilgrimage to Makkah. They rejoice in their shared identity and reflect on their responsibilities as a community of worshippers established by the prophet Muhammad.

- Muslims remember the willingness of Abraham to sacrifice his son Ishmael as an act of complete submission to Allah and how Allah intervened to prevent the boy's death.

As a *symbol* of their own willingness to submit completely to Allah, Muslims traditionally sacrifice a sheep and then enjoy a family meal. There may be an exchange of gifts and cards.

Islam: Belief and Worship

This festival is also a time to give help to those less fortunate. Part of the meat in the celebration meal is traditionally given to poorer families.

Questions

1. From what year do Muslims date their era?
2. Match the correct explanation in column B with the festival name in column A.

A Festival	B Explanation
Hijrah	Marks the end of Ramadan.
Eid-ul-Fitr	Held in the final month of the Muslim year and celebrates the completion of the annual pilgrimage to Makkah.
Eid-ul-Adha	Marks the beginning of the Muslim year.

3. Which festival recalls the journey made by the prophet Muhammad from Makkah to Madinah in AD 622?
4. Why is *Ramadan* important for Muslims?
5. Why is the Eid-ul-Adha also known as the *festival of sacrifice*?
6. In what ways are the poor and less fortunate remembered in Muslim festivals?

Part Seven

HINDUISM

Chapter Thirty-four

Hinduism: Origins, Beliefs and Worship

Introduction

The name '*Hindu*' comes from the *Indus* river. When invading armies from the west arrived at the banks of the Indus, which is located in present-day Pakistan, they simply gave the name Hindu to everything east *beyond* the river.

Hinduism is the most ancient of the major religions. Indeed, Hindus themselves refer to their religion as *sanatana dharma*, which can be translated as '*the ancient religion*'.

Origins

This Hindu temple is in the city of Madurai in southern India, which is believed by some to be the place where Hinduism began.

Many scholars believe that Hinduism was probably founded by one or more unknown *rishis* (wise men) who lived in India around 2000 BC. It has developed over the centuries from the mixing together of beliefs and practices of the many different peoples who settled in India.

Sacred texts

The god Krishna and the warrior Arjuna.

There are many sacred books in Hinduism. All of them are written in *Sanskrit*, the language of ancient India, which is no longer widely spoken and is largely preserved today by scholars. The word '*Sanskrit*' means '*perfect*'. Some Hindus still

Hinduism: Origins, Beliefs and Worship 203

believe that this language was created by the gods themselves.

Among the most important sacred texts are:

1. **The Vedas**
   These are the oldest writings. They contain *mantras* (hymns and chants) and *brahamanas* (explanations of these *mantras*). They also give guidance as to how people should live.

2. **The Upanishads**
   These contain hymns and poems that reflect on the meaning of life, love, suffering and death. They discuss the idea of *reincarnation*, i.e. that human life is an endless cycle of birth, suffering, death and rebirth. Much of Hindu literature is made up of comments and interpretations of them.

3. **The Mahabharata and the Ramayana**
   These are two great epic poems. They teach the importance of courage, honesty and loyalty:
   - The *Mahabharata* is the world's *longest* poem. It concerns the struggles of two families over many years and examines the joys and hardships of everyday life.
   - Within the *Mahabharata* is a section called the *Bhagavad Gita*. It is the most famous and most popular of all Hindu religious writings. It contains the teaching of the god Krishna to the nobleman Arjuna.
   - The *Ramayana* tells the story of how Rama, a prince whose enemies plotted against him, was forced to leave his kingdom and live in exile in a forest. With him went his wife Sita and his brother Lakshmana. Then, Sita was kidnapped by the demon king Ravana.

     In his struggles to rescue Sita, Rama is presented as a model of courage and honour in the face of evil, and as the example Hindus should follow.

     Rama and Lakshmana rescue Sita and defeat Ravana, with the help of the monkey god Hanuman. Rama finally regains his kingdom. This story celebrates the deep love a husband and a wife should have for each other, and the importance of true friendship.

These Hindu religious writings have profoundly shaped Indian art and life.

Questions

1. Explain the origin of the name '*Hindu*'.
2. (a) By what name do Hindus refer to their religion?
   (b) What does it mean?
3. (a) Who founded Hinduism?
   (b) When did it begin?
4. (a) What is *Sanskrit*?
   (b) What does the word mean?
5. What is a *mantra*?
6. Name the oldest Hindu text.
7. What is the title of the most popular of all Hindu religious writings?
8. (a) Who is the hero of the *Ramayana*?
   (b) Why is he said to set an important example for Hindus?

The gods

Hindus can be described as *polytheists* because they believe that there are many different gods. Indeed, Hindus are free to worship any god or goddess of their choice. Some 300 million different gods have been catalogued by scholars. However, the three main gods of Hinduism are *Brahma* (the Creator), *Vishnu* (the Preserver) and *Shiva* (the Destroyer).

Each god fulfils a different role. For example:

- Whenever evil threatens to take over the world, *Vishnu* is said to come to Earth to fight against it and to restore divine order. Each time he has come as a different being, called an *avatar* (meaning '*one who descends*'). It is believed that Vishnu has visited Earth on nine occasions

Some Hindu gods.

Brahma the creator

Vishnu the preserver

Shiva the destroyer

Krishna

Rama

and that he will make his tenth and final visit at the end of this world. Two of Vishnu's best-loved avatars are *Rama* and *Krishna*. There are thousands of Hindu temples dedicated to them.

○ Hindus believe that the universe itself goes through a cycle of birth, growth, destruction and rebirth. *Shiva* is the god who occasionally destroys the universe in order for it to be born again. Shiva is presented as a frightening god who is capable of unleashing great destructive power at any time.

However, Hindus believe that these different gods are only pointers towards something much greater and more mysterious that is *beyond* them.

Hinduism teaches that all the gods, and indeed everything in the universe, emanate or flow out from one mysterious, supreme source of life. They call this *Brahman*.

Brahman

Hindus believe that Brahman contains every characteristic of life in the universe: it is both male and female, beautiful and ugly, creative and destructive, all and nothing.

It is important to note, however, that Hindus do *not* believe that Brahman is a person. Brahman is *impersonal*.

Hinduism: Origins, Beliefs and Worship

Hindu scholars state that it is beyond our human ability to ever fully express what Brahman is in words. It was for this reason that the gods were created to express Brahman's different characteristics.

Genuinely wise people are those who see beyond the different gods to realise that they are merely different ways in which Brahman is expressed.

Hindus believe that the apparent separateness of all things in our world is only an *illusion*. Individuality does *not* really exist. Hindus claim that people, animals, insects, plants, rocks and rivers are merely different aspects of the same thing. They are all merely expressions of the one great *cosmic force* called *Brahman*.

As one Hindu holy man describes Brahman:

> *I am the taste in the water,*
> *the radiance in the sun and moon...*
> *I am the sound in space, I am*
> *the sweet fragrance in the earth.*
> *I am the brilliance in fire.*
> *I am the life in all beings.*
>
> Source: *Bhagavad Gita*

Brahman is in all things and all things *are* Brahman. This belief in the total oneness of the universe is called *monism*.

Questions

1. How many different Hindu gods have been catalogued?
2. Name the three main Hindu gods.
3. What is an *avatar*?
4. When will Vishnu make his tenth and final visit to Earth?
5. Who are Vishnu's best-loved avatars?
6. Explain Hindu belief about *Brahman*. Your answer should cover the following points:
   (a) Brahman's relationship to the gods and the universe.
   (b) What Brahman contains.
   (c) Whether or not Brahman is a person.
7. What do Hindus believe about the differences between people, animals, fish and plants?
8. Explain the term 'monism'.

The Varnas

Hindus washing themselves in the River Ganges. This is a sacred place of pilgrimage for Hindus.

Traditionally, Hinduism has taught that each person is born into a *varna* or *caste* (a social group).

Over the centuries, the caste system has divided Hindus into four main groups.

1. *The Brahmins*   The highest caste, consisted consisted of priests and teachers.
2. *The Kshatriyas*   The ruling noblemen and warriors.
3. *The Vaishys*   The merchants, craftsmen and farmers.
4. *The Sudras*   The peasants and servants.

Below all of these castes and considered the lowliest of all people were the *Outcastes*, or as they are better known, the *Untouchables*.

The Untouchables had to do the most menial jobs, such as handling dead animals and cleaning the streets. The nature of their work led them to be considered *impure* (unclean) and, as a result, they were prohibited from ever touching a caste member or even drinking water from the same well.

The caste system included strict rules about every part of daily life. Each person's job was determined by his or her caste. Members of one caste could not marry, eat with or work with members of another caste. To break these rules was punishable by *expulsion* from the caste system and a life as an Untouchable.

The great Hindu holy man Mohandas Gandhi, known as the *Mahatma* (*Great Soul*), was especially concerned at the way in which the Untouchables were treated. He tirelessly campaigned to improve their position. Instead of calling them *outcastes*, Gandhi called them *Harijans*, which means *Children of God*.

Since India became an independent state in 1947, its government has passed laws protecting the human rights of the Untouchables. Some Hindus have begun relaxing the strict caste system, while others have abandoned it. However, recent reports indicate that the idea and practice of untouchability still remains strong in parts of India.

Questions

1. What is the meaning of the Hindu word '*varna*'?
2. Name the four main groups the caste system is divided into and state who belongs to each caste.
3. Write a brief paragraph on those who exist *outside* the caste system – the *Untouchables*.
4. How does the caste system affect the daily lives of Hindus?
5. (a) Who was the *Mahatma*?
   (b) What did he do for the Untouchables?
6. (a) Who are the *Harijans*?
   (b) What does the name mean?
7. What has the Indian government done for the Untouchables since 1947?

Worship

A Hindu performing a *puju* (an act of worship).

Hinduism: Origins, Beliefs and Worship

Most Hindu worship takes place in the home. Almost every Hindu home has its own shrine, with images of the god or gods worshipped by the family members.

Daily worship is referred to as *puja*. It involves offering flowers, various foods, incense and candles. All these items are kept on a tray near the shrine.

Like the other major world religions, Hindus too have special places where they can gather together to worship as a community. A Hindu temple is called a *mandir* (meaning '*a place of worship*').

A mandir

The temple shown here is a typical village temple in India dedicated to Shiva or Vishnu and has several shrines in an open courtyard shaded by a few trees. It is a place in which Hindus pray and hold village meetings.

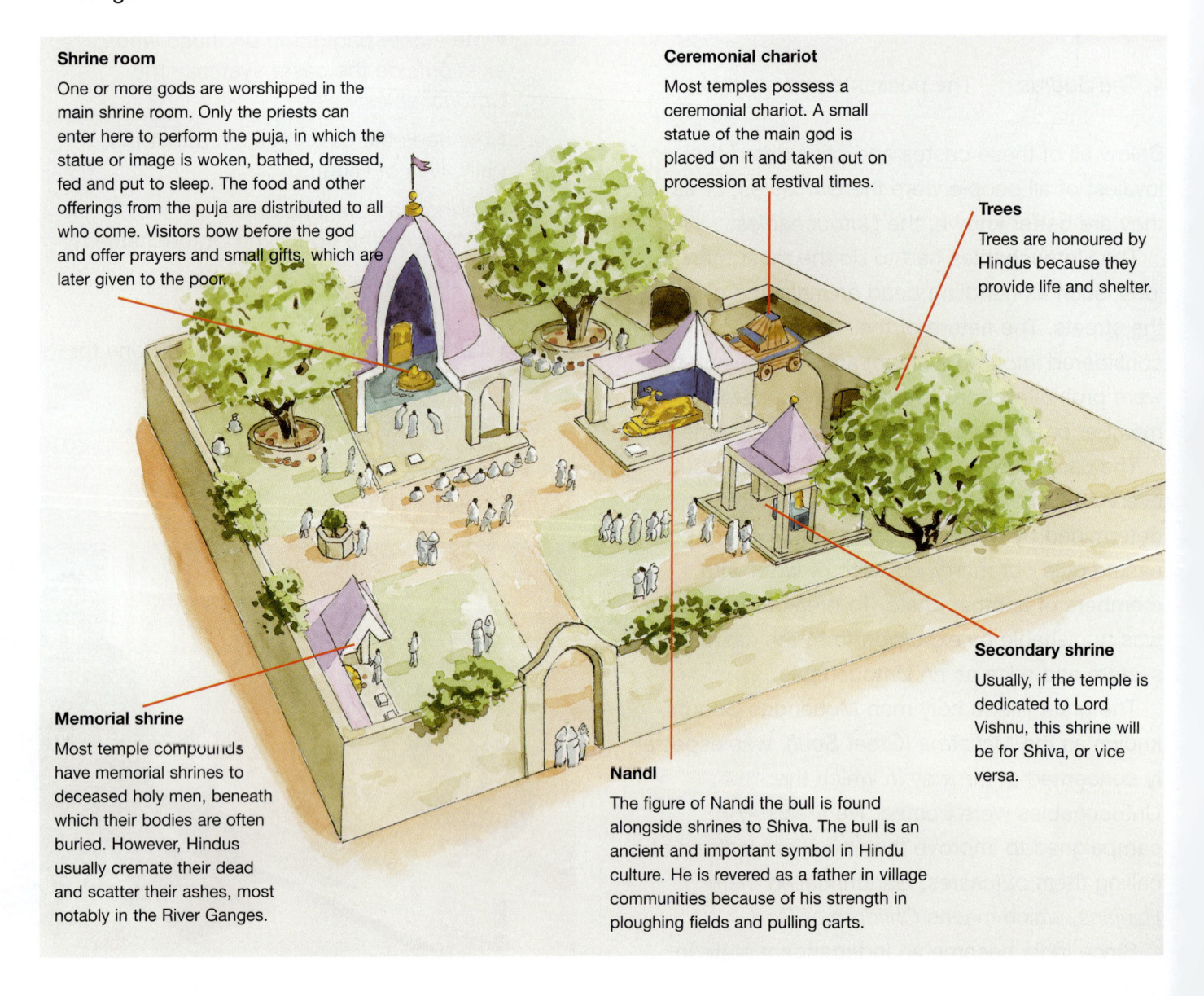

Shrine room
One or more gods are worshipped in the main shrine room. Only the priests can enter here to perform the puja, in which the statue or image is woken, bathed, dressed, fed and put to sleep. The food and other offerings from the puja are distributed to all who come. Visitors bow before the god and offer prayers and small gifts, which are later given to the poor.

Ceremonial chariot
Most temples possess a ceremonial chariot. A small statue of the main god is placed on it and taken out on procession at festival times.

Trees
Trees are honoured by Hindus because they provide life and shelter.

Memorial shrine
Most temple compounds have memorial shrines to deceased holy men, beneath which their bodies are often buried. However, Hindus usually cremate their dead and scatter their ashes, most notably in the River Ganges.

Nandi
The figure of Nandi the bull is found alongside shrines to Shiva. The bull is an ancient and important symbol in Hindu culture. He is revered as a father in village communities because of his strength in ploughing fields and pulling carts.

Secondary shrine
Usually, if the temple is dedicated to Lord Vishnu, this shrine will be for Shiva, or vice versa.

Questions

1. Where does most Hindu worship take place?
2. What is *puja*?
3. What does puja involve?
4. What is a *mandir*?
5. Explain the role of each of the following in a typical Hindu mandir:
   (a) *the shrine room*
   (b) *the memorial shrine*
   (c) *the ceremonial chariot*
   (d) *trees*
   (e) *the secondary shrine*
   (f) *the nandi*.

Part Eight

BUDDHISM

Chapter Thirty-five

The Origins of Buddhism

Introduction

A statue of the Buddha.

Buddhism was founded by an Indian holy man named Siddhartha Gautama who was born in the foothills of the Himalayas around 565 BC. He was raised a Hindu but later, in adult life, rejected it.

Since the Buddhist scriptures were neither organised nor written down until several centuries after his death, one cannot be certain about the exact historical details of his life. However, what follows here is accepted by most Buddhists.

Early life

Siddhartha Gautama was an Indian prince, the son of an incredibly rich nobleman. He grew up within the walls and gardens of his father's magnificent palace, where he was shielded from the unpleasant aspects of life.

As a young man Siddhartha married Princess Yosodhara. For ten years they lived together, wanting for nothing, with servants to cater to their every wish. Eventually a son was born to them. Their lives seemed complete.

The Four Sights

The Four Sights.

By the time Siddhartha was about thirty years old, he realised that despite his rich lifestyle and beautiful surroundings, he was not satisfied. He felt that there must be *more* to life than the pursuit of pleasure.

Restless and frustrated, Siddhartha began travelling outside his palace in search of something that would give his life the meaning and purpose he believed it lacked. He made four trips. What he saw on these journeys deeply shocked him because he had led such a sheltered life.

On his first three journeys he encountered an old man, a man covered in sores and a corpse about to be cremated. For the first time Siddhartha learned about old age, sickness and death. He was deeply disturbed by these experiences and they changed his whole outlook on life. He was now very aware of how fragile human life really is and wanted to know why people have to suffer such tragedies.

On his fourth trip Siddhartha met a wandering *ascetic*, i.e. a person who lived a life of self-denial. Although this man was homeless, with only a few possessions and wearing a simple yellow robe, he looked very happy.

Siddhartha realised that this man's happiness did not depend on money or possessions. He became deeply dissatisfied with his whole way of life.

These four experiences, which profoundly changed Siddhartha's view of life, are known as *the Four Sights*.

The Blessed Night of the Great Renunciation

Siddhartha decided that he could no longer continue his royal lifestyle. More than anything else, he wanted to find answers to life's great mysteries. He decided to slip unnoticed out of his palace, then shaved his head, traded clothes with a beggar and left his family, never to return.

Buddhists celebrate this event, which they call *the Blessed Night of the Great Renunciation*.

Enlightenment

For several years afterwards, Siddhartha lived the life of a wandering monk and sought guidance from the most respected Hindu *gurus* (teachers). He was advised to follow the *ascetic path*, i.e. to

Shrine under the Bo Tree.

starve and pray for long periods in order to gain wisdom. Siddhartha eventually realised that no deeper insight was coming and that he was only injuring himself. He carefully studied the *Vedas* (Hindu scriptures) but could not find the answers to his questions there.

Finally, Siddhartha decided to find life's answers through his own thinking. One day, believed to be his thirty-fifth birthday, Siddhartha wandered into a village and sat down under a banyan tree. He had decided to meditate (quietly reflect) on all he had experienced and learned. By the following day he had '*pierced the bubble*' of the universe. He had at last gained *enlightenment*, i.e. a deep understanding of the meaning of life. The night during which he finally achieved this is called *the Sacred Night*. The banyan tree under which he sat is known as the *Bo Tree* (Tree of Wisdom).

Siddhartha then travelled to Benares, where he gave his first sermon.

He soon attracted many followers and they showed their respect for him by calling him *Buddha*, which means *'the Enlightened One'*. His teachings gave rise to a new religion – Buddhism.

The spread of Buddhism

Buddhist monks.

One of India's most famous kings, Asoka, who ruled during the third century BC, was deeply influenced by the Buddha's teachings. He practised *tolerance and respect for all living things*. Asoka sent Buddhist monks to spread the Buddha's teachings to other lands. Among them were his own son and daughter, who are said to have spread Buddhism to the island of Sri Lanka.

Buddhism soon spread across Asia. It has helped to shape the lives and outlook of millions of people since, in countries such as Thailand, China, Tibet, Cambodia and Burma where, along with India, the greatest number of Buddhists now live. Recently, however, Buddhism has begun to attract followers in Europe and North America.

Questions

1. When and where was Siddhartha Gautama born?
2. Why can we not be certain of the exact details of his life?
3. Describe the kind of life Siddhartha led in his youth.
4. What *four* experiences led Siddhartha to change his way of life?
5. What happened on *the Blessed Night of the Great Renunciation*?
6. Explain the term '*guru*'.
7. What occurred on *the Sacred Night*?
8. What was the *Bo Tree*?
9. Where did Siddhartha give his first sermon?
10. Why did Siddhartha's followers call him *Buddha*?
11. (a) Who was *Asoka*?
    (b) Why is he an important figure in the history of Buddhism?
12. Name three modern countries where the majority of Buddhists live.

Chapter Thirty-six

Buddhism: Sacred Text, Beliefs and Worship

The Pali Canon

Buddhist monk reading the Pali Canon.

At first, the stories and sayings of the Buddha were passed on *orally*, i.e. by word of mouth. Later, during the first century BC, Buddhist monks and nuns on Sri Lanka decided to record them on manuscripts made from palm leaves. They wrote them down in *Pali*, an ancient Indian language probably spoken by the Buddha. As a result, these sacred texts of Buddhism became known as the *Pali Canon*. ('*Canon*' means '*an agreed set of teachings*'.)

The Pali Canon consists of forty-five volumes which are divided into three sections, known as the *Tripitaka* (meaning '*the Three Baskets*'). They are:

○ the *Vinaya* (*discipline basket*), which contains the rules for the Buddhist *Sangha* (community of monks and nuns)

○ the *Sutta* (*instruction basket*), which consists of the Buddha's sermons

○ the *Abhidhamma* (*great teaching basket*), which contains the Buddha's most profound and important teachings.

Questions

1. (a) What is the *Pali Canon*?
   (b) When was it written?
2. What is a *Sangha*?
3. (a) What are the *Tripitaka* of the Pali Canon?
   (b) What does each contain?

Karma and reincarnation

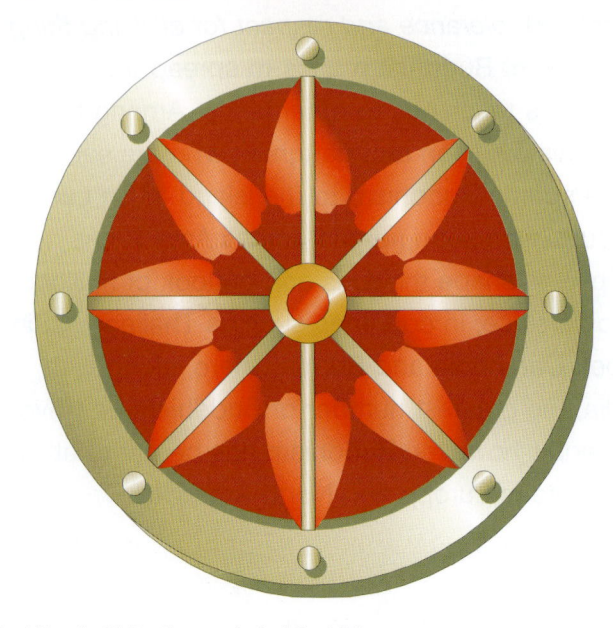

The Wheel of Life, the symbol of Buddhism.

216   All About Faith

Buddha taught that everything that exists in all places and at all times is subject to the law of *karma*, i.e. the law of actions and their effects, which states:

From good must come good, from evil must come evil.

Everything a person thinks, says and does has a profound impact on his/her life.

If a person does something bad it creates *negative* karma, whereas if a person does something good it creates *positive* karma.

Buddhists believe in *reincarnation*, i.e. human beings must endure a long cycle of birth, death and rebirth. People must spend several lives on Earth until they accumulate enough positive karma to free themselves from this long chain of rebirths. Only then can they achieve *nirvana*, i.e. *the state of complete happiness and perfect peace*.

Achieving nirvana

The Buddha taught his followers that if they really wanted to achieve nirvana, then they would have to face up to and take to heart the *Four Noble Truths*, which are:

1. All life is *dukkha* (suffering).
2. The cause of dukkha is *desire* (wanting pleasure and material wealth).
3. Dukkha can only be overcome if people *cease* to desire.
4. The only way to do this is to follow the *Eightfold Path*.

The Eightfold Path

Buddhists believe that they must follow the *Eightfold Path*. This consists of eight steps a person must follow in his/her life. They are the things a person must do in order to end dukkha and achieve nirvana. They are:

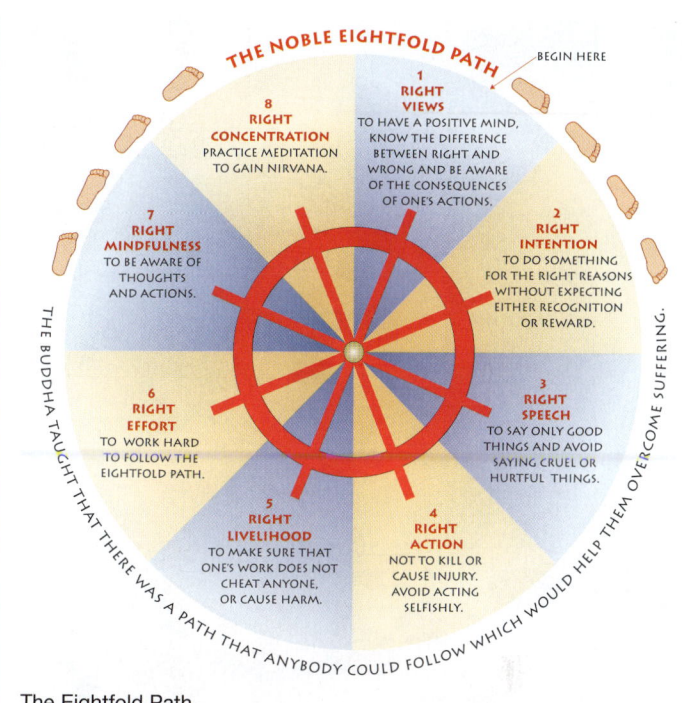

The Eightfold Path.

Questions

1. What did the Buddha teach about the *law of karma*?
2. What does it mean to believe in *reincarnation*?
3. How do Buddhists believe a person can finally be freed from a long chain of rebirths?
4. What does it mean to achieve *nirvana*?
5. What is *dukkha*?
6. State the *Four Noble Truths*.
7. (a) What is the *Eightfold Path*?
   (b) List the steps involved in following the *Eightfold Path*.

Do Buddhists believe in God?

Remarkably, though Buddhism is considered a religion, the Buddha himself appears to have *stayed silent on* the question of whether or not there is a God.

Buddhism: Sacred Text, Beliefs and Worship   217

A Buddhist monk at prayer.

In the centuries that followed, the Buddha's followers debated the question and finally split into *two opposing groups* on this issue:

- Those who were influenced by Hinduism and who, in time, came to consider the Buddha to have been a god. They went on to develop elaborate forms of worship.
- Those who believed that the Buddha wanted his followers to *reject* the whole idea of worshipping an unseen, divine being. They also believed that the Buddha would have been *appalled* at the idea that his followers should worship him as a god.

Buddhist monasteries

Monasteries house a community of monks or nuns who live there permanently, but they are also open to visitors, especially on festival days. The community is known as *the Sangha*. The duty of the Sangha is to uphold and pass on the teachings of the Buddha.

The Buddha

The Buddha drawn here is sitting in the lotus position. His outstretched arm is touching the earth, which symbolises the Buddha's enlightenment.

Devotion

Buddhists usually begin an act of devotion before a shrine by reciting the three refuges:

I take refuge in the Buddha.

I take refuge in the Dharma.

I take refuge in the Sangha.

They may then bow three times before holy images or objects before making offerings or chanting.

Drum and bell

The drum and bell in buildings (shown in cutaway) in the courtyard of the Buddhist temple are mainly used at festival times. Smaller bells in the shrine room are rung during daily devotions.

The temple

In countries where Buddhism is the majority religion, devotion to Buddha is a natural part of people's everyday lives and temples are a familiar part of the landscape.

A Buddhist temple is usually part of a monastery complex. The monks and nuns form a community known as a *sangha*. It is their task to uphold and pass on the Buddha's teachings and to maintain the temple.

The temple itself usually contains a shrine room (in which there is a large statue of the Buddha) as well as meditation and teaching halls.

Offerings

There will usually be various objects placed before the shrine:

Light from candles symbolises understanding.

A *shell* symbolises sound.

Food symbolises taste.

Flowers symbolise sight.

Incense and perfume symbolise smell.

Water – there may be several pots of water symbolising touch, offering, healing, purification, satisfaction of thirst and of desires.

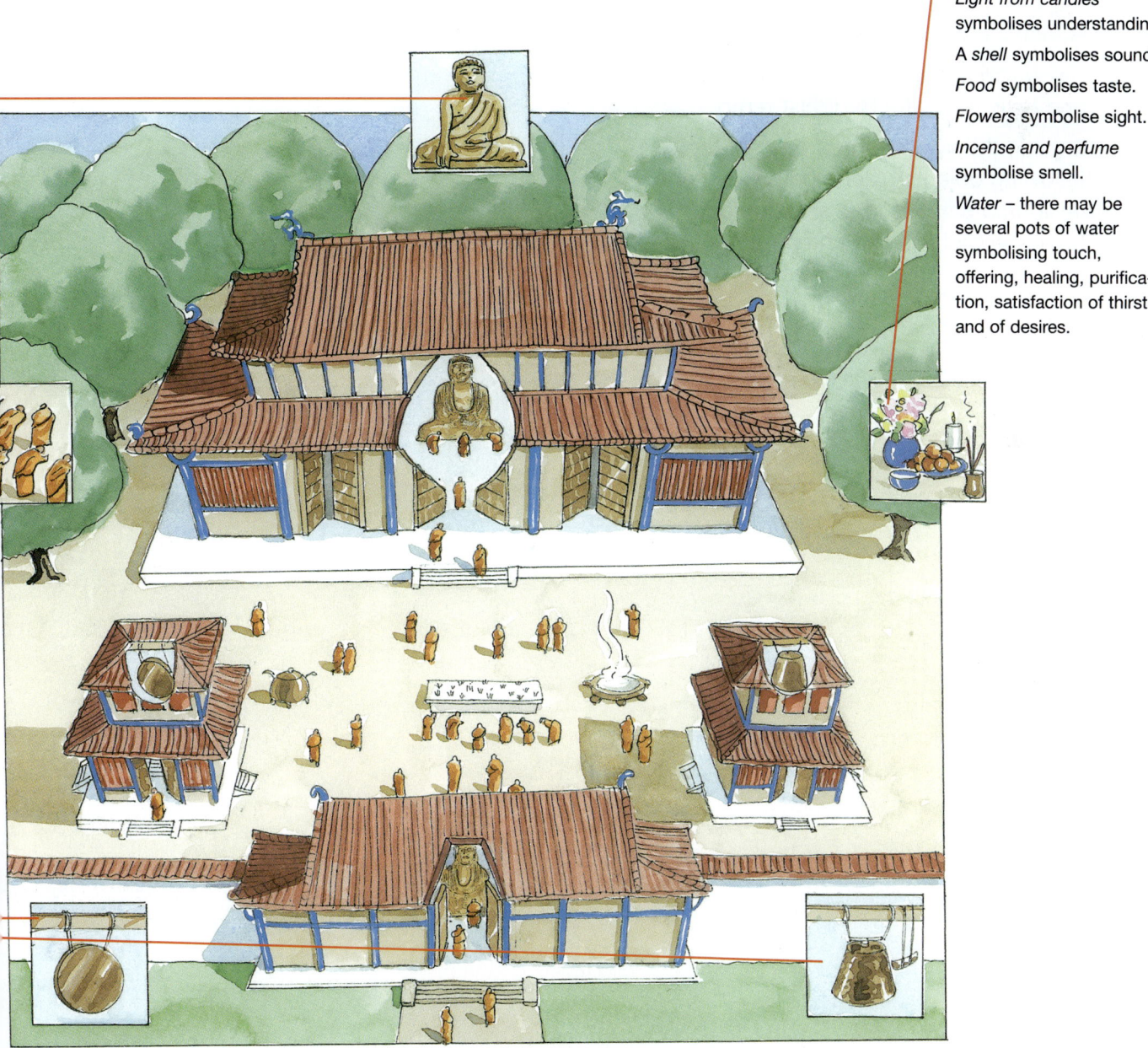

Buddhism: Sacred Text, Beliefs and Worship

Questions

1. What did the Buddha teach about God?
2. Why did the Buddha's followers split into two groups?
3. What is a *sangha*?
4. What is the task of a sangha?
5. What does a Buddhist temple usually contain?
6. How do Buddhists begin an act of devotion before a shrine of the Buddha?
7. Explain the symbolism of showing the Buddha with his arm touching the earth.
8. For which occasions are drums beaten and bells rung at a Buddhist temple?
9. Explain the symbolism of each of the following objects placed before a shrine: (a) *lighted candles* (b) *a shell* (c) *food* (d) *flowers* (e) *incense and perfume* (f) *water*.

A Buddhist Temple.

Part Nine

CHALLENGES TO FAITH

Chapter Thirty-seven

Religion and Science: The Origins of the Conflict

Introduction

Egyptian god Osiris.

Religion has been practised by human beings for many thousands of years. Science, in contrast, is a relative newcomer. It has only made a real impact on how many people think and live in the last 500 years.

For many centuries, the important position religion held in society was unchallenged. Religion seemed to provide people with the answers to most of the questions that concerned them.

For example, consider the farmer who wants a good harvest. This depends on the land he or she works being *fertile*, i.e. able to produce crops.

In ancient times, Egyptian farmers prayed to the god *Osiris* to grant them a successful harvest. They believed that Osiris was responsible for the soil being fertile.

Today, Egyptian farmers would most likely give the credit for a good harvest to fertilizers, pesticides and weed killers. They see things *very differently* from their ancestors. This change is due to the impact of *science* on the way human beings understand the world in which we live.

Science and technology

The term '*science*' comes from the Latin word '*scientia*', meaning 'knowledge'.

Generally speaking, science refers to any area of study where knowledge is gained by:

○ careful *observation* of how things work

○ conducting *experiments* to test our ideas about what we observe

○ only accepting or rejecting any explanation if one has good *reasons* for doing so.

Religion and Science: The Origins of the Conflict

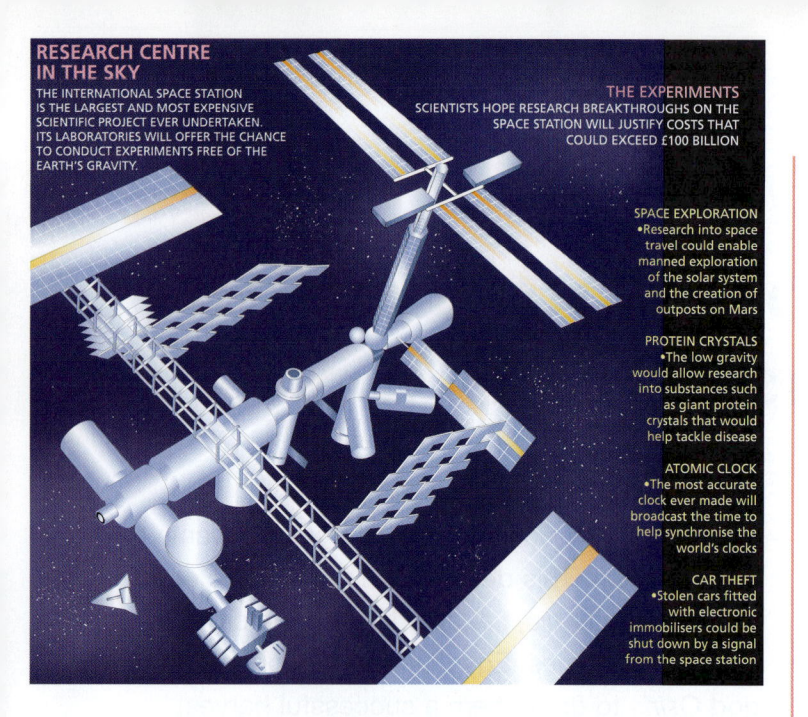

RESEARCH CENTRE IN THE SKY
THE INTERNATIONAL SPACE STATION IS THE LARGEST AND MOST EXPENSIVE SCIENTIFIC PROJECT EVER UNDERTAKEN. ITS LABORATORIES WILL OFFER THE CHANCE TO CONDUCT EXPERIMENTS FREE OF THE EARTH'S GRAVITY.

THE EXPERIMENTS
SCIENTISTS HOPE RESEARCH BREAKTHROUGHS ON THE SPACE STATION WILL JUSTIFY COSTS THAT COULD EXCEED £100 BILLION

SPACE EXPLORATION
• Research into space travel could enable manned exploration of the solar system and the creation of outposts on Mars

PROTEIN CRYSTALS
• The low gravity would allow research into substances such as giant protein crystals that would help tackle disease

ATOMIC CLOCK
• The most accurate clock ever made will broadcast the time to help synchronise the world's clocks

CAR THEFT
• Stolen cars fitted with electronic immobilisers could be shut down by a signal from the space station

Closely linked to science is *technology*, namely

the practical application of scientific discoveries to everyday life.

Science has been very successful in answering a huge range of important questions. Technology has changed the whole way in which many people live.

Just consider the benefits of the following inventions:

○ air transport
○ antibiotics
○ computers
○ organ transplantation
○ space satellites
○ telephones.

Indeed, the very success of science and technology has led some people to wonder if religion has anything worthwhile to contribute today.

The purpose of this chapter is *neither* to question the value of science nor the benefits of technology. However, it does seek to:

○ challenge the view that science *alone* can provide the answers to *all* life's great questions
○ reject the claim that science has shown religion to be worthless.

While some scientists accept that human beings need *both* religion and science, others do *not*. For example, Professor Richard Dawkins of Oxford University has stated that:

Science has nothing to learn from religion and neither has anyone else.

How has this situation come about? To answer this question, we must consider the story of *Galileo*.

Questions

1. (a) Explain the origin of the word '*science*'.
   (b) What does the word '*science*' refer to?
2. What is *technology*? Give some examples.
3. Why have the achievements of science and technology led many people to question the role played by religion in modern society?

The case of Galileo

Galileo Galilei (1564–1642) was an Italian *astronomer*, i.e. a scientist who studied the movement of the planets and the stars in order to build up a more accurate picture of what the universe is like and how it works. Galileo's work has had a profound impact on the way in which human beings view the universe and their place in it.

Aristotle

Until the Renaissance, people accepted a model of the universe found in the writings of the ancient Greek thinker Aristotle. This showed the earth as *stationary* (standing still) at the centre of the universe, with the sun and other planets rotating around the earth.

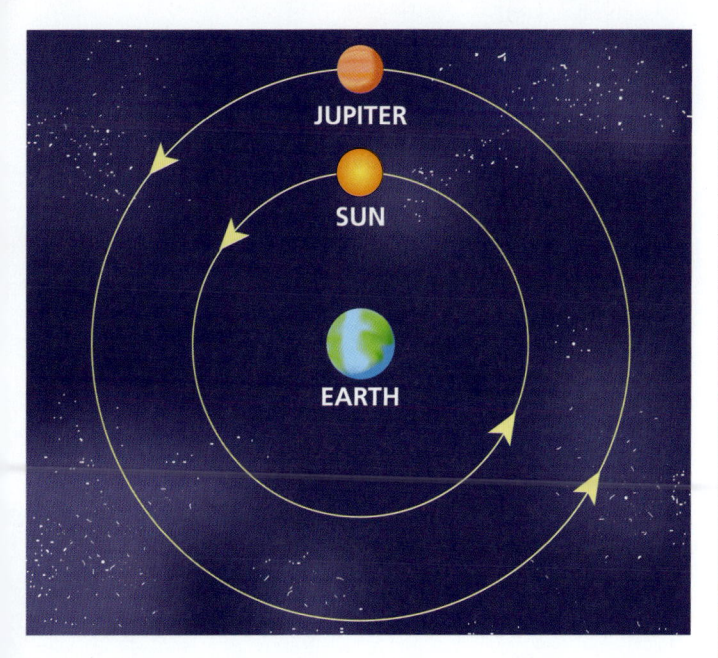

Earth as the centre of the universe.

People accepted this model as an explanation of the universe for such a long time for three reasons.

1. They had learned so many important things from the ancient Greeks, especially Aristotle, that they had begun to consider them *infallible* guides, i.e. ones that could never be wrong.
2. The Bible spoke of the sun moving around the earth. Most people had so much respect for the Bible that they felt it would be wrong to question *any* detail of it.
3. People's everyday experience seemed to confirm the view that the sun revolved around the earth. Consider the following story, which illustrates this point.

One bright summer morning, a famous professor at Cambridge University was out walking with one of his young students. The student remarked that all those people in times past who believed that the sun moved around the earth were morons.

The professor stopped, looked up at the sun shining in the sky above them, and replied: 'Really? And just what do you think it would look like if the sun did rotate around the earth, as they believed?'

The point is that it would have looked the same. It would seem that the earth stands still while the sun moves around it. After all, the sun rises in the east and sets in the west.

Galileo is generally credited with ending widespread acceptance of this model, which places Earth at the centre of the universe. However, his work was itself based on the discoveries of two earlier scientists – Copernicus and Kepler.

Questions

1. What is an *astronomer*?
2. What did Aristotle teach about the earth and the sun?
3. Briefly state three reasons why people accepted Aristotle's explanation of the sun revolving around a stationary Earth for so many centuries.

Copernicus

Nicolaus Copernicus (1473–1543) was the first to challenge the accepted view of the universe. He was a Polish priest who published a book entitled *The Revolution of the Celestial Spheres* in 1543.

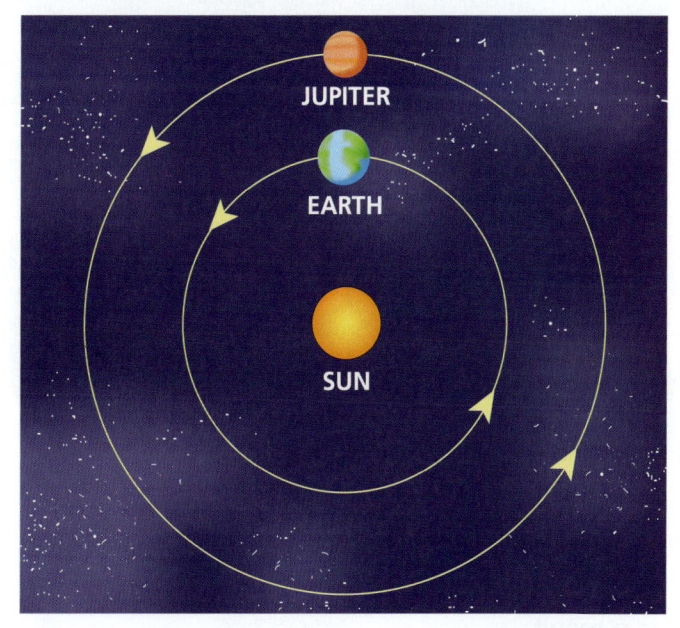

Copernicus' theory presents the sun as the centre, not Earth.

Religion and Science: The Origins of the Conflict   **225**

He argued that the earth and the other planets revolved around the *sun*.

Copernicus' book was written in Latin and it was neither widely known nor read. Further, he was careful to say that he was just putting forward a *hypothesis* (a possible explanation). He did *not* say that it was a fact that the earth revolved around the sun.

Copernicus did not want to challenge the Catholic Church, which at that time taught that the sun revolved around the earth.

Kepler

One person who read Copernicus' book was Johann Kepler (1571–1630), a German astronomer. He agreed with Copernicus in all but *one* aspect. He showed that whereas Copernicus thought that the planets moved around the sun in circular orbits, in fact the planets moved in elliptical orbits.

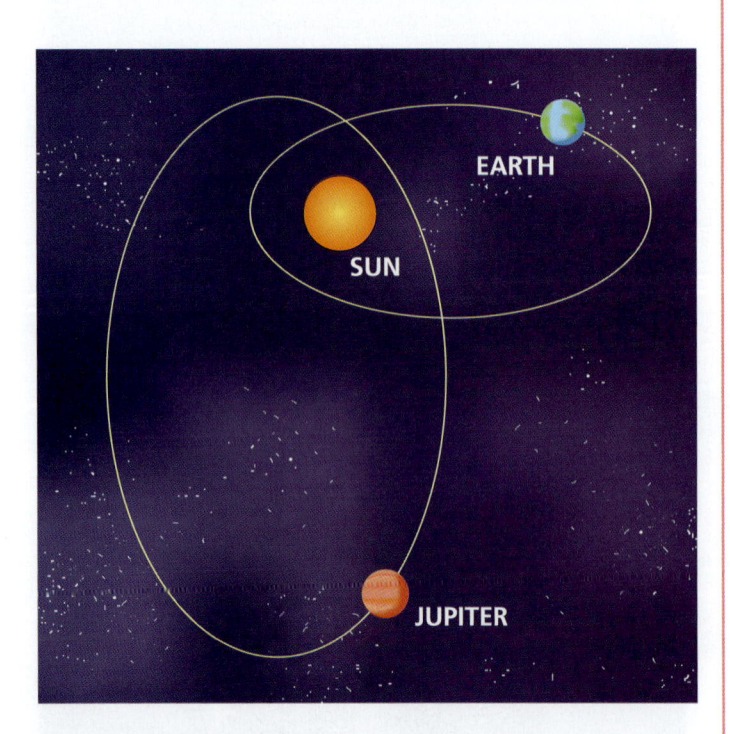

Kepler's model showing the planets in elliptical orbits around the sun.

Kepler openly challenged the Catholic Church's teaching and was expelled from his university post as a result.

Galileo

Galileo built on the discoveries of Copernicus and Kepler. While a professor of mathematics at the University of Padua in 1609, he heard about an invention by a Dutch scientist named Lippershey, called the *telescope* (from the Greek, meaning '*to see afar*'). Galileo copied it and improved upon it. He used the telescope to make a careful study of the planet Jupiter. He noticed four objects near it. He came to realise that these objects must be moons of Jupiter because over a few nights he saw that they were *orbiting* that planet.

Galileo's observation of the moons of Jupiter clearly demonstrated that not everything was orbiting the earth. He argued that the old model based on Aristotle, the Bible and our everyday experience was incorrect.

Copernicus had been correct. *The earth orbits the sun* and *not* the other way around.

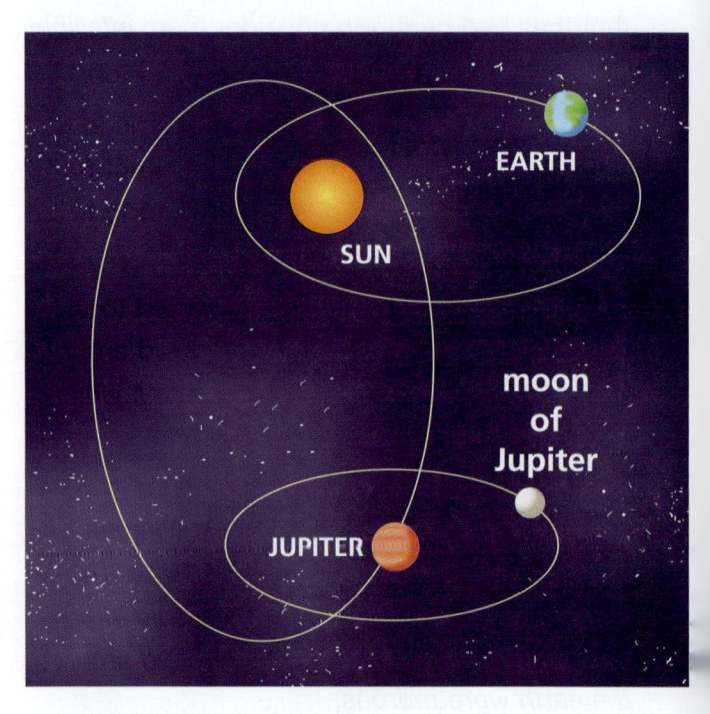

Galileo's model of the solar system.

By then, some important figures in the Catholic Church were becoming very worried about these new discoveries. The Church had taught for

226 All About Faith

centuries that the *earth* was the centre of the universe. Now, Galileo was publicly revealing that the Church's leaders had been mistaken on this matter. These churchmen feared that people's confidence in them as guides to finding the truth would be badly damaged. They acted out of fear and embarrassment. They ignored the wise guidance of the Church's greatest thinkers of the past and made a serious error. Indeed, one leading churchman of the time remarked that 'the Bible tells us *how* to get to heaven, *not* how the heavens go.'

In 1616, the Catholic Church banned the study of Copernicus' writings in its schools and colleges. It ordered Galileo to teach that his discovery was only a hypothesis and that it could not be proved. Reluctantly, Galileo agreed. Later, he decided he would not go along with this.

In 1632, Galileo published his findings in *A Dialogue on the Two Great World Systems*. He made it quite clear that, in his view, all the evidence pointed to only one conclusion: *the earth and all the other planets orbit the sun*.

The following year, Galileo was put on trial in Rome by the Catholic Church's authorities for *contradicting* what they taught. Galileo was confident that he could prove his theory. However, the arguments he put forward were not as conclusive as he believed. In fact, it was only after Galileo's death that Isaac Newton proved him to have been correct. Galileo's opponents used any flaws in his work against him and the court found him guilty of heresy. Under threat of torture, Galileo was forced to *recant* (publicly take back what he had said). Galileo was not put in prison. He was allowed to move back to his country estate near Florence, where he resumed his writing.

This is a sad chapter in the history of the Catholic Church. Its leaders were afraid of new ideas and completely overreacted.

Although this incident happened centuries ago and the Catholic Church has since apologised and accepted Galileo's findings, memories of this event live on.

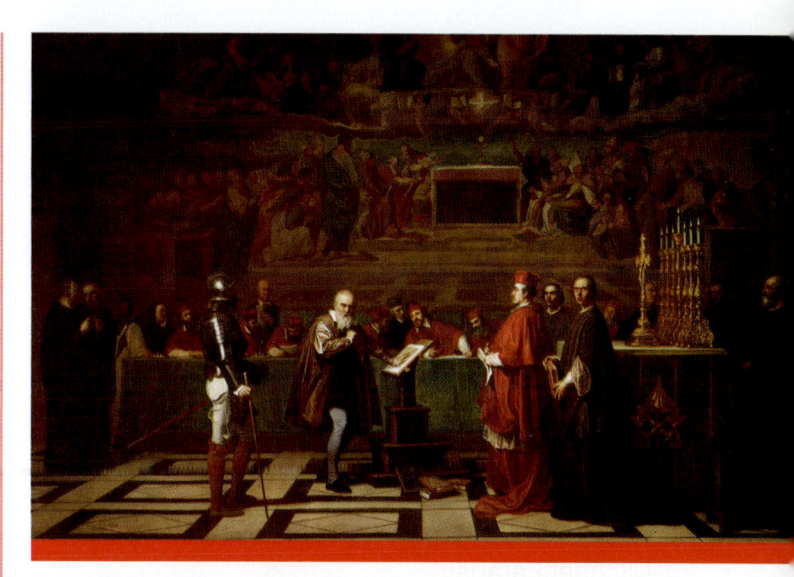

Galileo Galilei before Members of the Holy Office in the Vatican, 1633 by Joseph-Nicolas Robert-Fleury.

Questions

1. What did Copernicus discover?
2. Name the instrument used by Galileo to support Copernicus' theory.
3. How did the Catholic Church authorities react to the discovery that the earth orbits the sun and not the other way round?
4. (a) What did Church authorities order Galileo to do in 1616?
   (b) How did he react to this?
5. What book did Galileo publish in 1632?
6. What conclusion did Galileo put forward in this book?
7. How did the Catholic Church authorities react to Galileo publicly contradicting what they had taught?
8. Were Galileo's arguments to support his claim that the earth orbited the sun as conclusive as he believed? Explain your answer.
9. Explain this statement: *Galileo was forced to recant*.

Religion and Science: The Origins of the Conflict

Christians and science

Unfortunately, the condemnation of Galileo served to encourage the view that religion is opposed to science and that science is the enemy of religion. Nothing could be further from the truth.

It is important to remember that many great scientists were Christians, such as:

- Robert Boyle
- Gregor Mendel
- Michael Faraday
- Louis Pasteur.

They did not see the need for any conflict between religion and science. They realised that *each has something to offer*.

Sadly, narrow mindedness and an unwillingness to listen to other people have plagued the religion/science debate over the centuries. It has done much harm, confusing and misleading people.

Many people still believe that religion and science should be rivals. In fact, as we shall see in Chapter 39, there are very good reasons why religion and science should be seen as partners in the search for truth.

Questions

1. Name three famous Christian scientists.
2. What unhelpful attitudes have plagued the religion/science debate since Galileo's time?

Chapter Thirty-eight

Interpreting the Bible

Creation

Introduction

Until the mid–nineteenth century, most Christians still obtained all their information about the creation of the world from reading the Bible. Most people believed that what they read in it was *literally* true, i.e. that the words meant exactly what they said.

The creation account

Earth as seen from space.

The story of the creation of the world is found in the book of Genesis. It opens as follows:

In the beginning God created the heavens and the Earth. Now the Earth was formless and empty, darkness was over the surface of the deep, and the Spirit of God was hovering over the waters. And God said 'Let there be light,' and there was light. God saw that the light was good, and he separated the light from the darkness. God called the light 'day' and the darkness he called 'night'. And there was evening and there was morning – the first day.
(Genesis 1:1–5)

It continues:

- On the *second* day, God created the oceans and the sky.
- On the *third* day, God created the land and the plants.
- On the *fourth* day, God created the sun, the moon and the stars.
- On the *fifth* day, God created everything that lives in the sea and the birds in the sky.
- On the *sixth* day, God created the animals and human beings.

'Let us make man in our own image, in our likeness, and let them rule over the fish of the sea and the birds of the air, over the livestock, over all the Earth, and over all the creatures that move along the ground.' So God created man in his own image, in the image of God he created him; male and female he created them. God blessed

them and said to them, 'Be fruitful and increase in number; fill the Earth and subdue it. Rule over the fish of the sea and the birds of the air and over every living creature that moves on the ground.'
(Genesis 1:27–28)

On the seventh day, God rested.

Dating the creation

Prehistoric landscape: Ten-foot-tall predator bird, South America, one million years ago.

Some Christians attempted to use the Bible to figure out *when* the creation had occurred.

In 1656, an Irish Protestant archbishop, James Ussher, claimed that he had worked out the exact date on which God had begun creating the universe: *it all began at nine a.m. on Sunday, 23 October 4004 BC.*

However, scientists later began to arrive at a very different date.

In the early 1800s, geologists who were studying how the earth was formed began to discover *fossils* (hardened remains preserved in rock) of creatures long since *extinct* (had died out completely).

Scientists began to piece the fossilised bones they found together. In some cases, they reconstructed the skeletons of huge creatures, which they called *dinosaurs* (meaning '*terrible lizards*'). These extinct creatures were believed to have lived on Earth millions of years ago.

Today, most scientists believe that:

- The universe began over 18 billion years ago in a gigantic explosion called the Big Bang. This sent matter and gases out in all directions which, as they cooled, formed the stars and the planets.
- The earth was formed 4.5 billion years ago.
- The first living things appeared on the earth about 3 billion years ago.

Archbishop Ussher was clearly mistaken when he claimed that the world was created only 6,000 years ago. Earth is *far older* than the Bible seems to indicate.

Questions

1. What does it mean to say that a written account of an event is *literally true*?
2. In which book of the Bible can the story of the creation of the world be found?
3. What is the order of creation as set out in the Bible?
4. According to Archbishop Ussher's calculations, when did the universe begin?
5. What is a *fossil*?
6. How did the discovery of fossils challenge Ussher's date for the creation?
7. What do scientists now believe about the origin of the universe?

Evolution

Charles Darwin (1809–1882).

Wildlife on Galapagos Island.

Most people were surprised to discover that the world is far older than the Bible seems to indicate. However, they were generally shocked by what scientists had to say next.

In 1859, Charles Darwin published a book entitled *On the Origins of the Species*. It has proven to be one of the most influential books ever written. The book is an attempt to explain how the rich variety of plant and animal life he had witnessed on the Galapagos Islands in the eastern Pacific had come about.

Darwin came to the conclusion that *all* life – plant, animal and human – had *evolved* (gradually developed) over millions of years through a process he called *natural selection*. By natural selection Darwin meant

> *a process in which certain plants and animals adapt (change) to suit their environment (the world around them).*

Those that do not adapt are *unable to survive* and so become *extinct*.

In the introduction to his book, Darwin wrote:

> *I see no good reason why the views given in this book should shock the religious feeling of anyone.*

Darwin was being too optimistic. His theory of evolution challenged the long-accepted literal reading of Genesis. Many Christians were deeply confused by what Darwin had written. They wondered if the Bible had anything worthwhile to say to people today.

Interpreting the Bible   231

Initially, most leading churchmen, both Catholic and Protestant, completely rejected Darwin's theory. Later, however, scientists revised certain aspects of Darwin's work, and today most Christians accept some form of the theory of evolution. They have come to realise that it offers them an opportunity to grasp the *real* meaning and purpose of the creation account in Genesis.

The meaning of Genesis

The Creation of Adam by Michelangelo.

The creation story in Genesis chapters 1 and 2 was written by devout Jews who believed that God had created the world. Their account was *inspired* by God, but it was *not* dictated to them by God.

They did *not* write a scientific account of how the world began because they were *not* scientists. The creation story was *never intended* to be read as a straightforward, literal account.

The creation account in Genesis is written in *poetic* language. As such, it needs to be carefully read to discover the important religious teachings contained within the story. One will not find out what it means by reading it in a literal way (word for word).

The Genesis story is intended to convey some very important religious teachings:

1. **God created the world from nothing.**
   This was written to make clear that the *world* had a beginning. Some ancient religions taught that the world had always existed.

   The authors of Genesis wanted to show that *time had a beginning*. Some ancient religions taught that time just goes around in an endless, pointless circle. The Genesis account makes it clear that time goes *forward* to the completion of God's plan for the world. *Life has a purpose*.

2. **God's world is good.**
   Some ancient religions taught that the world is *evil*. They viewed life on Earth as a kind of prison sentence.

   The authors of Genesis believed that since God is good, whatever God created is *good*. They presented life on Earth as a *challenge*, not a prison sentence. Life is all about growing closer in friendship with God.

   The story of Adam and Eve disobeying God and eating the fruit when tempted by Satan (Genesis 3:1–24) contains an important message – human beings, *not* God, brought moral evil* into the world. *God can only do good*.

3. **God created human beings.**
   The authors of Genesis believed that God is *the Father of the whole human race*. Since all men and women are God's *children*, this means that we *all* belong to the one human *family*. People should view each other as brothers and sisters in God's family. We should *respect* each other and *care* for each other as God wishes them to do.

4. **God has given human beings a special place in the world.**
   God has given human beings *abilities* that no other creatures on Earth have been given. Human beings can *think* and make *choices*. With these abilities come *responsibilities*. People are responsible for their actions. We must *care* for the world God has given us.

*Moral evil refers to such acts as murder, rape, torture, theft and so on.

232 All About Faith

Comment

The authors of Genesis did *not* seek to answer the question of how the world was made. Rather, they wanted to explain why it was created by God.

As important as it is to know *how* life began, it is even more important to know why it began if we are to understand *the meaning and purpose of life*.

In brief:

○ The theory of evolution explains *how* life began.

○ The Genesis account in the Bible explains *why* life began.

There should be *no conflict*. Science asks *how* – religion asks *why*. Each tackles a *different* question.

Questions

1. State the title of the book written by Charles Darwin and published in 1859.
2. What did Darwin mean by saying that *all life had evolved*?
3. What is meant by *natural selection*?
4. Describe the reaction among most Christians to Darwin's theory of evolution.
5. If the creation story in Genesis 1 and 2 was never intended to be read as a literal, straightforward account, then how was it intended to be read?
6. Briefly state the four important religious teachings contained in the Genesis *story*.
7. If the authors of Genesis did *not* seek to answer the question of how the world was made, what did they intend to do?

The Miracles of Jesus

A *miracle* has been defined as

a marvellous or wonderful event which occurs solely as a result of God's direct action.

Christians believe that Jesus of Nazareth had miraculous powers and worked miracles, such as:

○ calming a stormy sea
○ feeding 5,000 people with only a little food
○ giving sight to a man born blind.

The miracles were an essential part of Jesus' message. He worked them to deepen the faith of those who already believed in him. He did *not* work them to win people over by extraordinary displays of power.

Of the many miracles reported in the Gospels, the greatest miracle was Jesus' resurrection from the dead.

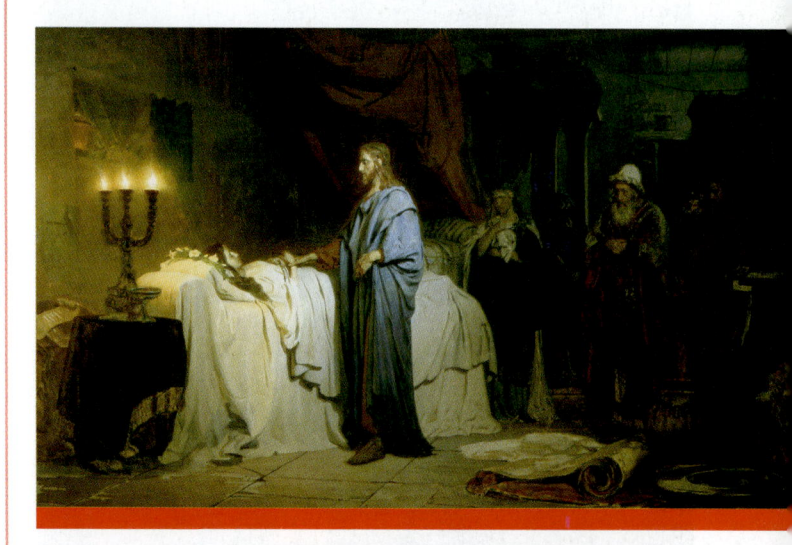

The Raising of Jairus' Daughter by Ilya Efimovich Repin. It was by a simple word of command that Jesus restored Jairus' daughter to life.

Science and miracles

While Christians believe that miraculous events occurred during the ministry of Jesus, they also

Interpreting the Bible

admit that it is hard for people today to identify or explain in scientific terms exactly *what* happened during these events.

This difficulty has led some people to think that modern science says that miracles cannot happen. This is *not* so. Consider the following points:

○ The laws of science describe what it is reasonable for one to expect, i.e. *what normally happens*.
○ However, by its very definition, a miracle is *not* something that normally happens.
○ Science *cannot* guarantee that things can never be different from the way they normally are.
○ Therefore, science *cannot* exclude the possibility that rare and extraordinary events such as miracles can happen.

Rare events

Jesus Gives Sight to One Born Blind by Siegfried Detter Bendixen.

Some people wonder why God does not work miracles to end human suffering or even prevent it from happening in the first place.

Christians believe that God *does* directly intervene in certain situations. They say that there are well-documented cases where people have been cured from diseases that doctors had pronounced incurable and fatal.

However, before deciding if a cure is miraculous, the Catholic Church asks the following questions:
○ Was the disease serious?
○ Was the cure sudden and unexpected?
○ Is it a complete cure?
○ Has it lasted at least three years?
○ Has it been proven by medical investigation?
○ Was the cure achieved without the aid of any medical treatment?

Only if the answer is *yes* to all these questions will a cure be declared *miraculous*.

However, Christians believe that such miraculous cures are *very rare* for good reasons:

○ Miracles reveal that God's power is *not* limited by the laws of nature. They give people glimpses of God's greatness and help to strengthen their faith.
○ However, miracles must remain the *exception* rather than the rule if God is not to become a puppet-master who controls the world and makes all the decisions for human beings. That would deprive us of our freedom to make choices.

Questions

1. What is a *miracle*?
2. '*Modern science says that miracles cannot happen.*' How would a Christian respond to this claim?
3. In what circumstances will the Catholic Church authorities declare a cure to have been *miraculous*?
4. Why do Christians believe that miraculous cures are *very rare* events for good reasons?

Chapter Thirty-nine
Religion and Science in Partnership

Introduction

The different paths to truth.

Some people still think that science will one day do away with people's need for religion altogether. They are often led to believe this by the way in which science has proven so successful in improving the quality of people's lives.

Science has discovered much about the nature of the universe. It has solved many problems in areas such as architecture, medicine, transport and so on. However, there are limits to what scientists can explain.

The different kinds of knowledge

There are many things that cannot be examined under a microscope, calculated by a computer or viewed through a telescope. The scientific way is not the only way of understanding something.

Consider *music*. Scientists can tell that:

○ Music is caused when a voice or an instrument gives off certain vibrations (invisible waves of energy).
○ These vibrations travel through the medium of air.
○ They are picked up by a listener's ear. There the vibrations are converted into electrical impulses.
○ These electrical impulses travel to the brain and the listener hears a musical sound.

How a person hears a musical sound.

But *music* is *more* than this physical process. Music also has the power to calm, console, disturb, entertain or inspire people.

Consider *human beings*. Many different kinds of thinkers can contribute to our understanding of humanity. For example:

1. A *biologist* might say that a human being consists of:

    ○ FAT enough for seven bars of soap
    ○ LIME enough to whitewash one chicken coop
    ○ PHOSPHORUS enough to tip 2,200 matches
    ○ IRON enough for one medium-sized nail
    ○ MAGNESIUM enough for one dose of salts

Religion and Science in Partnership **235**

- POTASH enough to explode one toy rocket
- SUGAR enough for seven cups of tea
- SULPHUR enough to rid one dog of fleas.

While this is true, *there is much more than this to be said about being human*.

There's more to a human being than meets the eye.

2. A *psychologist* would say that a human being is a creature with:

   - emotions, i.e. feelings that inspire or disturb
   - ideas, i.e. thoughts, plans, imaginings and solutions.

   This too is true, but there is yet more to be said.

3. A *sociologist* would say that people need other people. Human beings need to live in *communities* and each person plays a particular role in his/her community.

   By combining what each of these three scientists has to say, we can build up a more complete picture of what it is to be a human being. But *there is still more to be said*.

4. A *religious thinker* would point out that human beings have very special qualities. They can experience *love* and have an inbuilt desire to *worship* something higher than themselves.

   These are *spiritual* matters and they are explored by religion.

Consider what we have learned. We have identified *four* different kinds of knowledge:

- biology
- psychology
- sociology
- religion.

Each says something important about human beings. Each *adds* something to the sum total of our knowledge about people. Thus, they *complement* each other. Religion and science need each other if the *full* story is to be told. *Together*, they build up a fuller picture of what it means to be a human being.

Science and belief

Louis Pasteur in his Laboratory by Albert Gustaf Edelfelt.

236 All About Faith

Religion and science may have more in common than is often realised. *Belief* (accepting something as true) has a role to play, not only in religion, but in science *too*.

Science is based on a number of *assumptions* (starting points it takes for granted) about the world. These are the beliefs that:

○ human beings are capable of knowing the world as it really is and of figuring out how it works

○ the world itself has an order and a pattern to all its events that can be detected and explained in scientific laws.

Scientists may think that they have good reasons for accepting these assumptions as correct. However, they *cannot* be completely certain about them. Yet they *must* start out believing these things, otherwise science itself would be *impossible*.

Conclusion

Religion and science should *not* be in conflict. They are not rivals. Rather, they are *partners* in the search for truth. Each answers important questions, but *each answers different kinds of questions*.

Religion and science *need* each other; they *complement* each other. As the great civil rights leader Dr Martin Luther King once said:

> *Science investigates; religion interprets. Science gives us a knowledge which is power; religion gives us wisdom which is control.*

Allegory of the Creation of the Cosmos by Domenicus van Wijnen.

Questions

1. Identify the *four* different kinds of knowledge that help us to build up a more complete picture of what it means to be a human being.
2. How does each of these four different kinds of knowledge help us to understand what it means to be a human being?
3. What does it mean to say that *belief has a role not only in religion, but in science too*?
4. Read again the statement by Dr Martin Luther King on the relationship between religion and science.
    (a) What point is he making?
    (b) What important role does he believe religion can play?

Religion and Science in Partnership

Chapter Forty

Religion in Contemporary Society

Introduction

Each of the major world religions offers detailed guidance as to how people can live good lives and find lasting happiness.

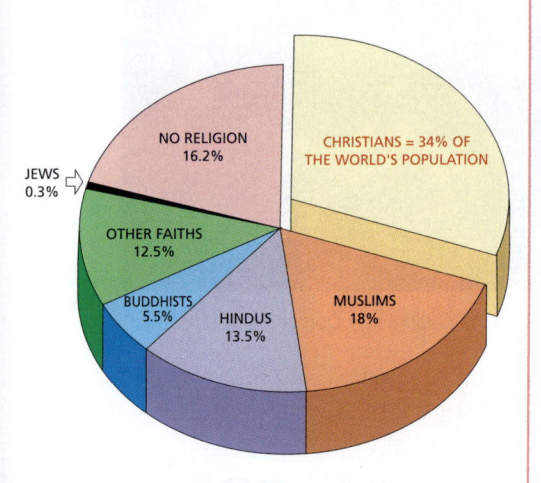

The world religions.

Pie chart: CHRISTIANS = 34% OF THE WORLD'S POPULATION; NO RELIGION 16.2%; JEWS 0.3%; OTHER FAITHS 12.5%; BUDDHISTS 5.5%; HINDUS 13.5%; MUSLIMS 18%.

In some countries, however, organised religion no longer occupies the central role in people's lives that it once did. Consider the map opposite.

Secularism

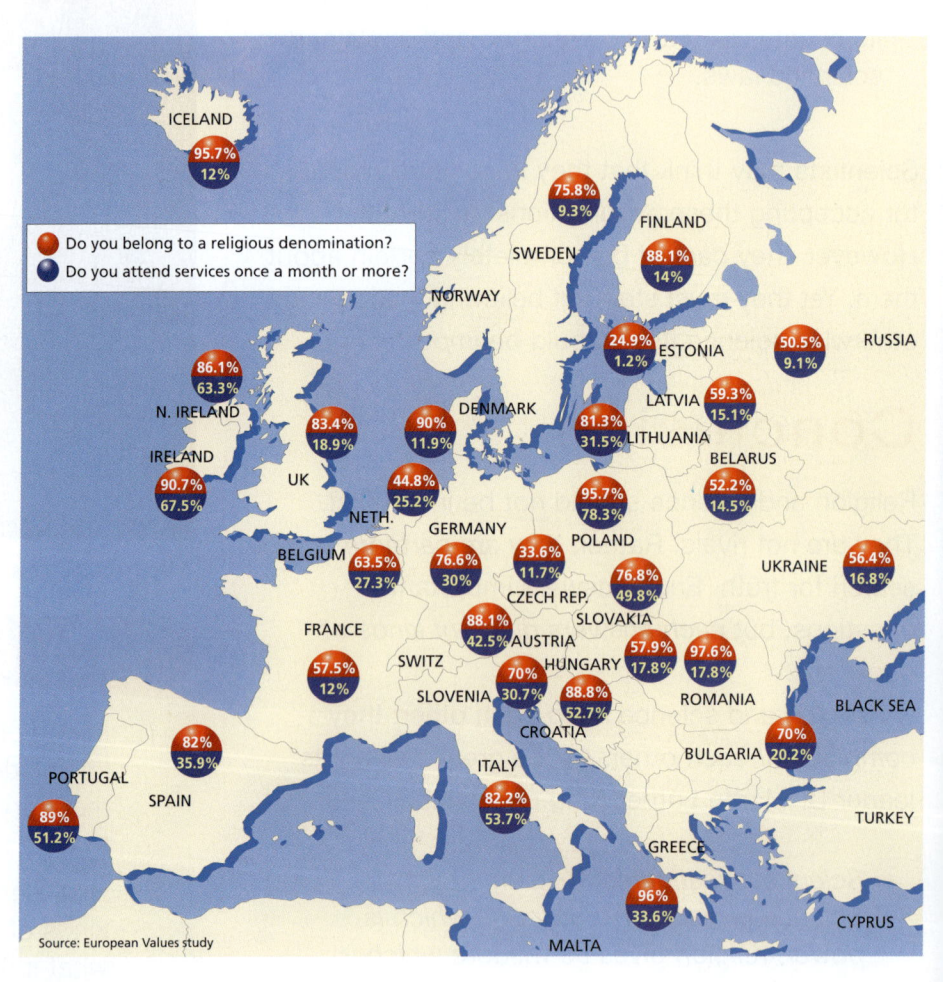

Map of Europe — Source: European Values study. Red: Do you belong to a religious denomination? Blue: Do you attend services once a month or more?

- ICELAND 95.7% / 12%
- NORWAY 75.8% / 9.3%
- FINLAND 88.1% / 14%
- ESTONIA 24.9% / 1.2%
- RUSSIA 50.5% / 9.1%
- LATVIA 59.3% / 15.1%
- N. IRELAND 86.1% / 63.3%
- DENMARK 90% / 11.9%
- LITHUANIA 81.3% / 31.5%
- BELARUS 52.2% / 14.5%
- IRELAND 90.7% / 67.5%
- UK 83.4% / 18.9%
- NETH. 44.8% / 25.2%
- GERMANY 33.6% / 11.7%
- POLAND 95.7% / 78.3%
- UKRAINE 56.4% / 16.8%
- BELGIUM 63.5% / 27.3%
- CZECH REP. 76.6% / 30% *(placement: Belgium 63.5/27.3; CZECH REP 33.6/11.7)*
- SLOVAKIA 76.8% / 49.8%
- FRANCE 57.5% / 12%
- SWITZ / AUSTRIA 88.1% / 42.5%
- HUNGARY 57.9% / 17.8%
- ROMANIA 97.6% / 17.8%
- SLOVENIA 70% / 30.7%
- CROATIA 88.8% / 52.7%
- BULGARIA 70% / 20.2%
- PORTUGAL 82% / 35.9%
- SPAIN 89% / 51.2%
- ITALY 82.2% / 53.7%
- GREECE / MALTA 96% / 33.6%

Until recently, the majority of people in Europe attended some form of religious service and generally accepted the guidance of their religious leaders on moral issues. Many still do, but a large number do not.

This decline in active membership of organised religion and the lessening of religion's influence on many people's values is called *secularism*.

238 All About Faith

> ## Questions
>
> 1. What is meant by *secularism*?
> 2. Read the following statement: *The growth of secularism in Western society can be seen in the way Christian festivals such as Christmas have been used as commercial opportunities by big business.* Do you agree or disagree? Explain your answer.

Humanism

Bertrand Russell, a noted humanist.

Humanists do not consider the growth of secularism to be regrettable. On the contrary, they see it as a positive development. Humanists are either agnostics or atheists. They do *not* believe in God.

Humanists believe that:

- morality is a code for living invented entirely by human beings
- people can be happy and fulfilled without any religious dimension to their lives
- religion acts as a barrier preventing human progress.

To support this claim they point to the harm done by members of the different world religions throughout history.

Response to humanism

Jews, Christians and Muslims respond to humanists by stating that:

- religion is *a trustworthy guide* to leading a good life
- religion is a great force for *good* in the world.

1. A trustworthy guide

In modern society there are many conflicting opinions on moral issues such as abortion, race relations and so on. How is it possible for people to know what is right and what is wrong?

If, as humanists say, morality is a purely human invention, then it may be open to influence by threat or force, opinion polls or simply how the majority of people feel at a particular time.

Humanists believe that morality should be decided by human reason alone, without any reference to God.`

Jews, Christians and Muslims profoundly disagree with humanists. They say that something *more* than human reason is needed to guide people in matters of morality. In contrast to humanists, they believe that:

- God exists
- God loves human beings
- God's plan for living a good life can be found recorded in their sacred scriptures

Religion in Contemporary Society

- these holy books contain guidance of great wisdom as to what makes life worthwhile and what constitutes a good person
- the way to lasting peace and happiness is to be found in faithfully following the teachings of one's religion.

2. A force for good

The Parable of the Good Samaritan by Domenico Feti.

The five major world religions – Hinduism, Judaism, Buddhism, Christianity and Islam – have certain things in common. That is why each of them is called a *religion*. However, each of these religions has its own unique identity and particular set of teachings about God and the meaning of life.

Sadly, the differences between the major religions have been a source of conflict over the centuries. Members of the different religions have committed terrible deeds while claiming to be 'doing God's work'. Newspapers and television reports often mention how religious disagreements can lead to confrontation.

It is important to realise, however, that religion is only *one* element of such conflicts. Other sources of conflict are frequently overlooked, such as:

- poverty
- unemployment
- disputes over land ownership
- lack of education
- ethnic or tribal hatred.

Usually religious difference is simply one more ingredient thrown into a *mixture* of unresolved disputes laced with fear and suspicion. The result can be a time bomb that leads to death and destruction if set off. Consider the horrors of Bosnia, Israel, Rwanda, Iraq, Sudan or indeed, Northern Ireland in recent times.

Mohandas Ghandi.

The great Hindu holy man, Mohandas Gandhi, was once asked if he believed religion was to blame for some of the terrible crimes committed in history, such as the Nazi Holocaust. Gandhi responded by stating that when people hurt, subjugate or kill others in the name of their God, they are distorting rather than representing the true teachings of their particular religion.

Gandhi said that all the major religions encourage their members to:

- love and respect one another
- avoid selfishness in all its forms
- promote peace and harmony between people.

He warned people to be on their guard against unscrupulous and wicked individuals who would *abuse* religion to justify their actions and use it as a smokescreen to hide their own selfish purposes.

He ended with this remark:

> *'The terrible crimes of history are the fault not of religion but of the ungovernable brute in human beings.'*

Questions

1. List *six* sources of conflict between people in today's world.
2. Read Mohandas Gandhi's comment on where the responsibility for history's great crimes lies.
   (a) Why did he reach this conclusion?
   (b) Do you agree or disagree? Give reasons for your answer.

Questions about God

St Patrick's Cathedral, New York City is one of the most noteworthy examples of the Gothic revival style of church architecture in the US.

The three main monotheistic religions – Judaism, Christianity and Islam – are all based on faith in God.

The question we must now deal with is *does God really exist*? There are three possible answers to this question:

- *theism*
- *atheism*
- *agnosticism*.

Does God exist?

Theism	Yes – there is a God.
Atheism	No – there is no God.
Agnosticism	Don't know – it is impossible for human beings to answer this question.

Most people believe that there is a God of some kind. They do so initially because they are brought up to believe it, but when they become adults, many *choose* to believe it because they are convinced that it is true.

Some people sincerely doubt that there is a God. They may remark:

How can I be asked to believe in something I cannot see?

This is an understandable reaction, but religion *depends* on the belief that there is far more to life than meets the eye. Religion claims that *beyond* the natural world which can be observed, measured and explained, there exists an invisible, *supernatural* being who knows the answers to life's mysteries. This being is called *God*.

Judaism, Christianity and Islam teach that people should not expect to see God, at least *not directly*. They do so for two reasons:

1. **They believe that God is *a mystery*.**

    They teach that it is simply *beyond* our human capacity to ever fully know and understand God.
    God is not like a crossword puzzle that can be figured out and then filed away, marked '*solved*'.

    People can only gradually grow in their knowledge and understanding of God by devoting their lives to prayer, study and doing good deeds.

2. **They believe that God is unique.**
    God is not like anything else in human experience.
    God is a *pure spirit*, i.e. God does not have a physical body. Therefore, God *cannot* be directly seen or touched.

    N.B.
    It is important to bear in mind that while God is often referred to as *He*, Christians believe that God is neither male nor female.

Reasons for believing

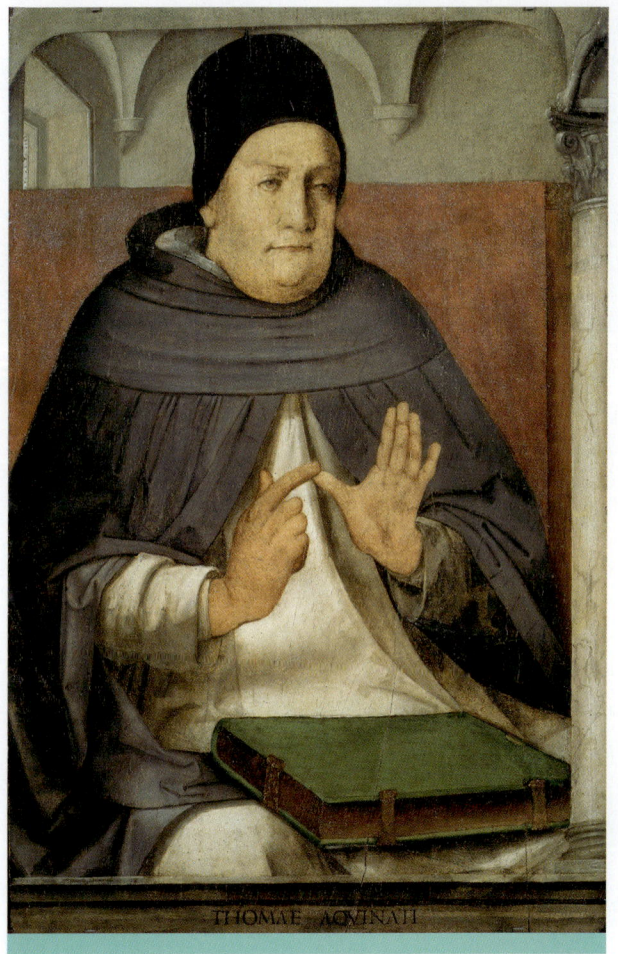

Portrait of St Thomas Aquinas by Joos van Gent and P. Berruguete.

All About Faith

What reasons do people have for believing that there is a God?

There is no direct, visible and straightforward evidence that there is a God. However, religious thinkers like Thomas Aquinas have argued that there is *indirect* evidence of this. They argue that if we look closely at the world around us, we can find this indirect evidence. It points to God's *invisible presence* behind all things.

We will now consider three examples of this evidence.

1. **Things do not just happen.**

    Experience shows us that things do *not* 'just happen'. An event does not happen of its own accord – it is *caused* by someone or something.

    For example, suppose you walk into an empty room on a dark winter evening. There is an electric light already shining in the room. Either *someone* or *something*, e.g. a timer, has switched on the light before you arrived. It did *not* switch itself on. Someone or something had to *cause* the light to turn on.

    Similarly, religious people argue that the universe could *not* simply have started by itself. Its existence can only be explained by saying that it was *created*, i.e. mysteriously made out of nothing, by God.

2. **Someone had to design this. It could not have happened by accident.**

    It is not unusual for people to occasionally stop to admire the beauty of the world: the colours of a sunset, the sound of birdsong or the scent of a flower. But if you examine the petal of any flower, you will see that it is vastly complex, made up of billions of atoms so tiny that they cannot be seen by the naked eye.

    Again, consider the delicate balance of gases that make up Earth's atmosphere and make life possible.

    Religious people argue that such everyday wonders *cannot* just come about by accident. They can only be explained by saying that they were *designed* by God.

The Thinker by Auguste Rodin.

3. **Where do human beings get their sense of right and wrong?**

    The sense of right and wrong is found in all people, everywhere. It speaks to astronauts orbiting Earth as well as to doctors treating their patients. This inner voice is not limited to any particular time, place or race of people. It is a *universal* thing.

    Human beings are the only creatures on Earth with an awareness of right and wrong and the freedom to choose between them.

Religion in Contemporary Society 243

Where did this come from? Why should human beings have it?

Religious thinkers claim that it has been given to human beings by *God*.

Questions

1. Explain the following terms: (a) *theism* (b) *atheism* (c) *agnosticism*.
2. What belief does religion depend on?
3. In each of the following, explain why religious people believe that:
   (a) *God is the creator of the universe.*
   (b) *God is the designer of all life.*
   (c) *God is the source of our sense of right and wrong.*

Part Ten

MORALITY

Chapter Forty-one

Introduction to **Morality**

Introduction

Human beings are *social* creatures. The average person spends two-thirds of each day in the company of others. Humans need to *live in community*, i.e. share their lives with others, whether it is working, playing, talking or worshipping together.

This fact raises a very important question:

How should people behave towards one another?

This is the question that *morality* seeks to answer.

The meaning of morality

Morality may be defined as

a set of beliefs which offer people guidance about the rightness or wrongness of human actions.

Two elements of this definition need to be explored:

○ what is meant by a *human action*
○ how people come to hold certain *beliefs* about what is right and wrong.

Introduction to Morality **247**

Human actions

Human actions can be grouped under two headings:

- *moral* actions
- *non-moral* actions.

To understand the difference between them, consider the following examples.

1. A person accidentally trips and falls down a flight of stairs.

In this case the person does *not* make a choice. This is something that simply *happens* to him/her. The person is not in control here. It is an *accident*.
This is a *non-moral action*.
It is *neither* morally good nor bad.

2. A person jumps into a river to save someone from drowning.

In this case the person *does* make a choice. The person *knows* what he/she is doing and freely *chooses* to do it.
The person *is* in control here.
It is done *deliberately*.
This is a *moral action*.
It is a morally good one.

To summarise:

A moral action is one that is deliberate, freely chosen and under the control of the person doing it.

It follows that people are *responsible* for the consequences of moral actions. They can be *blamed* if their actions are bad and *praised* if they are good.

Questions

1. What is *morality*?
2. Explain what is meant by a *moral action*.
3. In each of the following examples, state whether it is a *moral* action or a *non-moral* action.
   (a) A man who chooses to drive his car when he suspects that he has consumed alcohol above the legal limit.
   (b) A woman who is late for an important appointment because a national bus and rail strike has cancelled all services at very short notice.
   (c) A man who damages a water pipe while working in an area in which he had been assured was safe to dig.
   (d) A woman who goes to visit an elderly relative who has been admitted to hospital.

Learning how to behave

From the moment of birth, human beings begin learning. The way in which people learn how to behave towards others is called *socialisation*.

At first, people generally learn things from their immediate family. As they grow into adulthood, however, they come under a wider variety of influences on their *values*.

Values

We may define a *value* as

anything or anyone considered to be good, desirable, important or worthwhile.

Everyone has values. A singer values his voice and protects it. A sportswoman values her fitness and trains to preserve it.

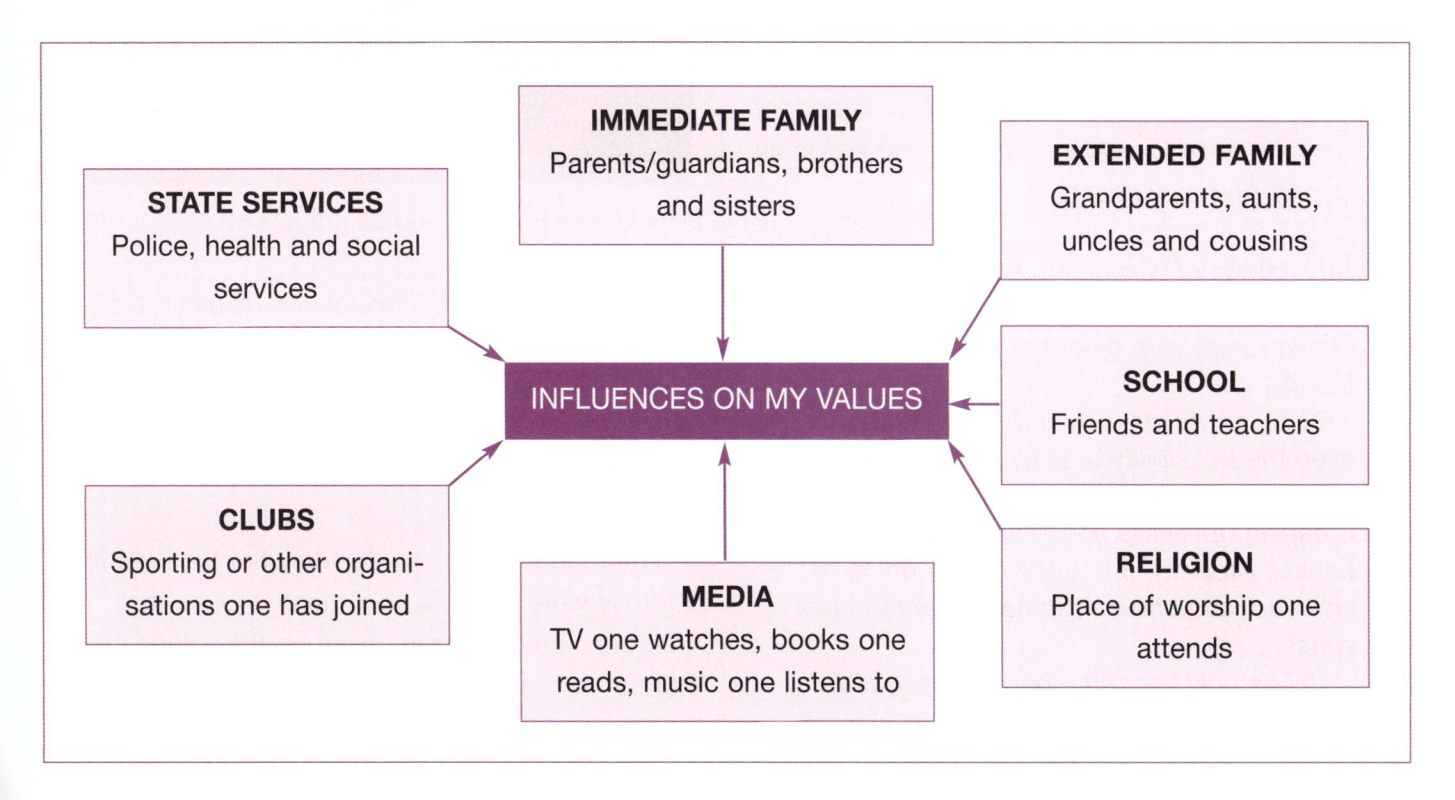

INFLUENCES ON MY VALUES

- **STATE SERVICES** — Police, health and social services
- **IMMEDIATE FAMILY** — Parents/guardians, brothers and sisters
- **EXTENDED FAMILY** — Grandparents, aunts, uncles and cousins
- **CLUBS** — Sporting or other organisations one has joined
- **MEDIA** — TV one watches, books one reads, music one listens to
- **SCHOOL** — Friends and teachers
- **RELIGION** — Place of worship one attends

Introduction to Morality

People gradually acquire a set of values as they grow up by:

- following the *example* set by people they trust
- learning from the *consequences* of their own actions and those of others
- accepting the *rules* laid down by their family, school, religion and society.

Friendship

Outside their own families, perhaps the most powerful influence on people growing up is their own circle of friends among their *peers* (people of the same age group). Their influence is so important because *the need to belong* is very strong in human beings. As Andrew Lascaris writes:

> An analysis of suicide rates indicates that life becomes meaningless without positive relationships with other people, without friendship.
>
> Going on holidays by oneself without even the possibility of talking about it with someone else later is no fun at all. Cleaning out one's house and feeding oneself properly, if nobody is ever going to visit you, somehow does not seem to make sense.
>
> Things only happen – become real, alive – when people are together.

Depending on the kind of people they are, friends can have either a positive or a negative influence on a person's values. Genuine friends are those who share a *mutual respect* and have a real concern for what is in each other's *best interest*.

Such friendships can help people to:

- feel wanted and valued, and so build up their self-confidence and self-worth
- be more considerate of the needs of others and so encourage them to be more generous and sharing
- develop character by giving support and encouragement when facing an important decision.

The role of values

The values a person holds influences him/her to act in certain ways.

For example, high examination results are a value for some students because the better the grades they achieve, the greater their job opportunities will be. Therefore, they will do certain things and avoid certain things in order to obtain good results.

When people have to decide what the right thing to do is when faced with a moral choice, their decisions are generally based on the values they hold.

As a person matures morally, it is hoped that he/she will move away from being preoccupied with *material values*, such as possessions and wealth, and appreciate the greater importance of *spiritual values*, such as God, love and friendship.

Questions

1. What is *socialisation*?
2. What is a *value*?
3. How do people acquire a set of values as they grow up?
4. List five qualities that you consider to be the most important in a genuine friendship. In each case explain your choice.
5. George Washington once offered this advice:

   Be kind to all, but intimate with few, and let those few be well tried before you give them your trust and confidence.
   True friendship is a plant of slow growth, and must undergo and withstand the shocks of adversity before it is entitled to the name.

   (a) What does Washington mean when he says that people should be 'intimate with few and let those few be well tried'?
   (b) Why does he describe true friendship as 'a plant of slow growth'?
6. Consider the following sources of values. In each case state whether it is encouraging the development of good values or bad ones. Explain your answers.
   (a) A *neighbour* who organises a sponsored marathon to raise funds for charity.
   (b) A *student* who encourages his classmates to use illegal drugs.

Questions

   (c) A *parent* who teaches her child to pray.
   (d) A *judge* who sentences a convicted murderer to a life sentence in prison.
   (e) A *team manager* who encourages his players to deliberately injure the star player of a rival team.
   (f) A TV *commercial* that aims to convince people to buy expensive cosmetics that do not actually do what they claim.
   (g) A *priest* who encourages his parishioners to become involved in voluntary work to help people in need.

Morality and religion

Traditionally, people have accepted one or other of the major world religions as a trustworthy guide in helping them to develop good values and make the right decision when faced with a moral choice.

If one reads the sacred texts of the major world religions, one will notice how they all agree on what is called *the Golden Rule*. Here are different versions of it:

- Buddhism: *Hurt not others in ways that you yourself would find hurtful*.
- Judaism: *What is harmful to you, do not to your fellow men*.
- Christianity: *In everything, do to others as you would have them do to you*.

However, this is not meant to indicate that the major world religions all agree as to how this Golden Rule should be applied when dealing with specific moral issues. In fact, there are *significant differences* between the responses of the major world religions to issues such as abortion, capital punishment and war.

Sources of guidance

Each of the major world religions offers its members its own particular set of *moral principles*. We may define a moral principle as

a basic belief about what is good and what is evil that the members of a religion must accept as true.

These moral principles shape the *moral vision* of the members of a particular religion, giving them their *distinctive* understanding of who they are, how they should relate to other people and treat the world they all share.

Most religions have some form of leadership which offers guidance as to how their members should live their lives. In the Catholic Church, this is the role of the *Magisterium* (see Chapter 29).

Questions

1. State *one* version of the *Golden Rule*.
2. Do all the major world religions *agree* as to how the Golden Rule should be applied? Identify any two issues upon which they disagree.
3. What is a *moral principle*?
4. In what way does a religious person's moral principles shape his/her moral vision?

Chapter Forty-two

Love One Another

Introduction

Once, during a discussion with another Jewish rabbi, Jesus was asked this question:

Which of the Commandments is the most important of all?

Jesus gave this reply:

The most important one is this: You shall love the Lord your God with all your heart, with all your soul, with all your mind and all your strength.

This is the second: You shall love your neighbour as yourself. (Mark: 12:29–31)

Jesus' central message can be summarised as

Love God and love your neighbour.

This provides us with the key to understanding the importance of the Ten Commandments.

The Ten Commandments

The Ten Commandments* are as follows:

1. I, the Lord, am your God; you shall have no other gods besides me.
2. You shall not take the name of the Lord your God in vain.
3. Remember to keep holy the Sabbath day.
4. Honour your father and your mother.
5. You shall not commit murder.
6. You shall not commit adultery.
7. You shall not steal.
8. You shall not bear false witness against your neighbour.
9. You shall not covet your neighbour's wife.
10. You shall not covet anything that belongs to your neighbour.

*Source: R.P. McBrien (ed.), Encyclopedia of Catholicism.

The Ten Commandments summarise the Old Law that God gave his chosen people, the Jews. In bringing the New Law, Jesus gave the Ten Commandments even more force by challenging us to make our entire lives consistent with the values the commandments represent.

Judaism, Christianity and Islam teach that God gave the Ten Commandments to Moses. They provide human beings with a *code* (a set of guidelines for living) which applies to all people, at all times.

Jews, Christians and Muslims are called to put the Commandments *into practice* in their daily lives. When doing so they must remember that:

○ Genuine love of God is spelled out in the first three of the Ten Commandments. It means making sure that God is the most important thing for people in every aspect of their lives.

○ This is not possible, however, without keeping the other seven Commandments, which say that people must love and respect one another.

He who does not love his brother or sister, whom he has seen, cannot love God whom he has not seen. (1 John 4:20)

The meaning of love

The word '*love*' means different things to different people. The Christian understanding of love, however, can be found in the New Testament. It identifies four different kinds of love:

○ *Storgé* (pronounced stor-gay)
This is a warm, general affection or fondness for a thing, e.g. a favourite sport, or place, e.g. the area in which a person grew up.

○ *Eros* (pronounced ear-ros)
This is a physical attraction to and strong romantic desire for a member of the opposite sex.

○ *Philia* (pronounced filly-ah)
This is a strong, intimate love for and loyalty to close family and friends.

○ *Agapé* (pronounced aga-pay)
This is unconditional love for other people, *not* just those who love you and are close to you. It involves acting in the best interests of other people and helping them *without* expectation of personal gain.

Questions

1. Summarise Jesus' central message.
2. What do Judaism, Christianity and Islam teach about the origin of the Ten Commandments?
3. What do the Ten Commandments provide for human beings?
4. (a) Which of the Ten Commandments centres on our relationship with God?
   (b) Which Commandments centre on relationships between ourselves and other people and vice versa?

Questions

5. Match the explanation in column B with the word in column A.

A	B
Storgé	A strong, intimate love for and loyalty to close family and friends.
Eros	An unconditional love for other people, not just those who love you and are close to you.
Philia	A physical attraction to and strong romantic desire for a member of the opposite sex.
Agapé	A warm, general affection or fondness for a thing or a place.

6. Read the following extract and answer the questions below.

Dr Martin Luther King (1929–1968).

The great campaigner for civil rights, Dr Martin Luther King, explained the meaning and importance of agapé in the following way:

Agapé is more than romantic love, it is more than friendship. Agapé is understanding, creative, redemptive goodwill to all people. Agapé is an overflowing love that seeks nothing in return. Theologians [religious thinkers] would say that it is the love of God operating in the human heart. When you rise to love on this level, you love all people, not because you like them, not because their ways appeal to you, but you love them because God loves them. This is what Jesus meant when He said, 'Love your enemies'. And we're glad that He didn't say 'Like your enemies', because there are some people that we find it very difficult to like. Liking is an affectionate emotion, and we can't like anyone who would bomb our home. We can't like anyone who would exploit us. We can't like anyone who tramples over us with injustices. We can't like them. But Jesus reminds us that love is greater than liking. Love is understanding, creative, redemptive goodwill towards all people.

(a) Explain the difference between *liking* and *loving*.
(b) No one would like to be assaulted or robbed. How might a Christian *love* someone who had done this to him/her?

Love One Another 255

Love and sex

As young people grow and mature into adulthood, interest develops into the relationship between love and sex.

- The word 'sex' is usually understood as the physical act of sexual intercourse (see pages 257–8).
- The word 'love', however, is used to refer to the entire personal relationship between a man and a woman, which *includes* their sexual relations.

Developing a loving relationship

There are five stages in the development of a loving relationship:

1. **Attraction:** You are attracted to someone. If the attraction is strong, you will try to meet and get to know that person.
2. **Acquaintance:** Once you become acquainted with someone, the attraction may quickly fade away. But if the acquaintance continues, the attraction may grow and friendship may blossom.
3. **Friendship:** Becoming good friends is a special time. You may begin to see the other person in a very romantic, idealistic way. You may see him or her as 'the perfect person' – the only one for you.
4. **Affection:** At this stage, a real caring or affection develops between a man and a woman. This true affection is based on recognising and accepting each other's limitations while still caring deeply about that other person.
5. **Love:** Real love between a man and a woman is a growing thing. It is part of a process. Paul described this love as

always patient and kind; it is never jealous; love is never boastful or conceited; it is never rude or selfish; it does not take offence and is not resentful. Love takes no pleasure in other people's sins but delights in the truth; it is always ready to forgive, to trust, to hope and to endure whatever comes. Love does not come to an end.
(1 Corinthians 13:4–8)

Real love is concerned with the *inner* person, not just appearances. It means caring about the other person as much as oneself. It means working for the other person's welfare and happiness, rather than using him/her as a means of selfishly satisfying one's own needs or desires.

There is *no shortcut* to the development of a truly loving relationship between a man and a woman. You *cannot* reach the fifth stage of the process without growing through the other four stages.

Questions

1. What are the qualities that you would find attractive in a member of the opposite sex?
2. (a) What factors cause the initial attraction to sometimes quickly fade away?
   (b) What factors cause the initial attraction to sometimes develop into friendship?
3. The third stage in the development of a loving relationship is sometimes called the 'starry-eyed' phase. It is a wonderful time to experience, but if people get married without having developed their relationship beyond this stage, what kind of problems can it cause *after* they are married to each other?
4. Read the fifth stage once more. Do you think that it is possible to fall in love at first sight? Give reasons for your answer.

Human reproduction*

Human reproduction occurs when a male sex cell (the sperm) fertilises a female sex cell (the ovum) after sexual intercourse.

Sexual intercourse is seen by Christians as the highest form of lovemaking. It is where a man and a woman make a total commitment to each other in a married relationship.

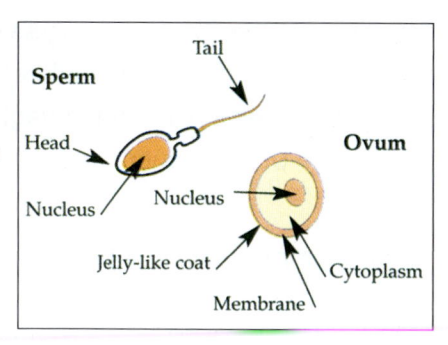

Sperm: Tail, Head, Nucleus
Ovum: Nucleus, Jelly-like coat, Membrane, Cytoplasm

Male reproductive organs

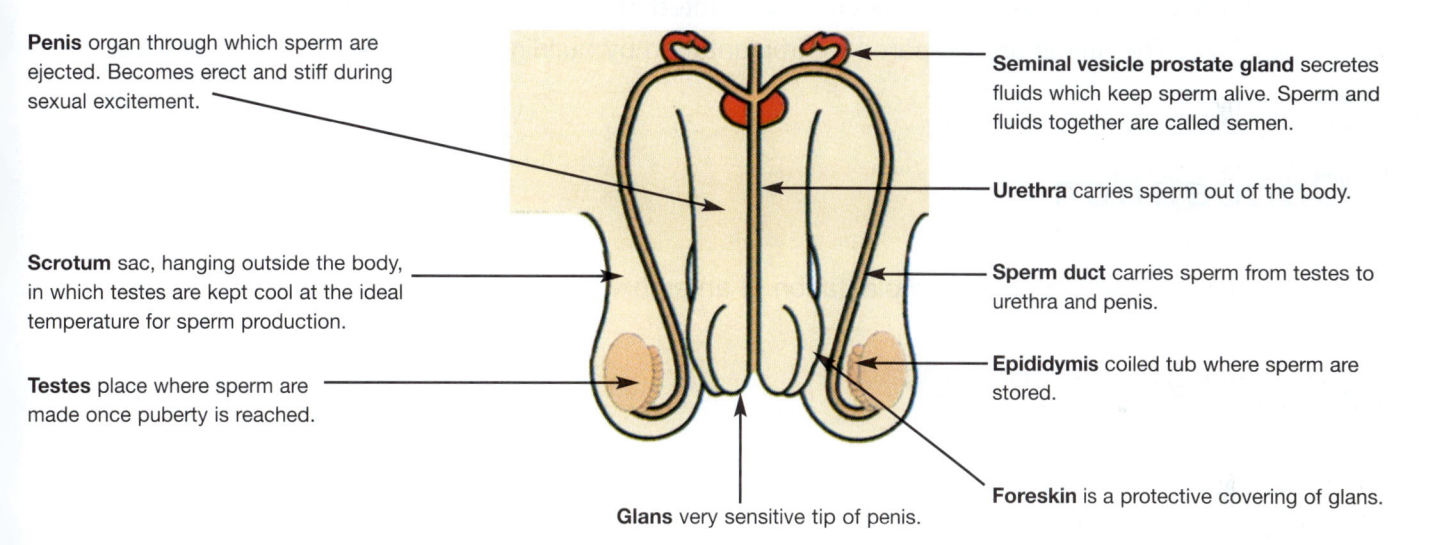

Penis organ through which sperm are ejected. Becomes erect and stiff during sexual excitement.

Scrotum sac, hanging outside the body, in which testes are kept cool at the ideal temperature for sperm production.

Testes place where sperm are made once puberty is reached.

Seminal vesicle prostate gland secretes fluids which keep sperm alive. Sperm and fluids together are called semen.

Urethra carries sperm out of the body.

Sperm duct carries sperm from testes to urethra and penis.

Epididymis coiled tub where sperm are stored.

Foreskin is a protective covering of glans.

Glans very sensitive tip of penis.

Female reproductive organs

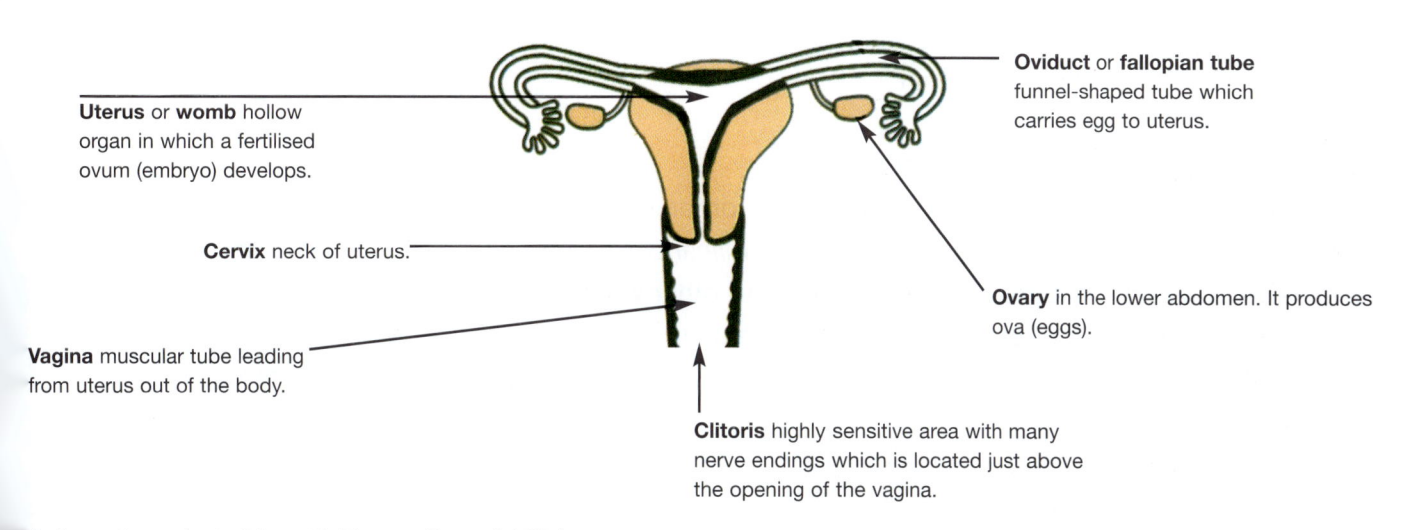

Uterus or **womb** hollow organ in which a fertilised ovum (embryo) develops.

Cervix neck of uterus.

Vagina muscular tube leading from uterus out of the body.

Oviduct or **fallopian tube** funnel-shaped tube which carries egg to uterus.

Ovary in the lower abdomen. It produces ova (eggs).

Clitoris highly sensitive area with many nerve endings which is located just above the opening of the vagina.

*Information adapted from R. Treays, *Essential Biology*.

Love One Another 257

Sexual intercourse

Sperm enter the female during *sexual intercourse* when an erect penis is inserted into the vagina. Movement of the pelvis stimulates nerve endings in the penis. This sets off a *reflex action*, which results in semen being ejected into the vagina. This is called *ejaculation. Orgasm* is the name given to the intense experience of excitement and pleasure which occurs at the climax of sexual intercourse.

Fertilisation

Sperm swim from the vagina to the oviducts. If they meet an ovum, *fertilisation* can take place. One sperm head penetrates the ovum and the two nuclei fuse. This forms a *zygote*, the first cell of a new baby.

The zygote travels to the uterus and becomes implanted in the uterus wall. After this happens it is called an *embryo*. The uterus has prepared for implantation by building up a thick lining, rich in blood vessels.

Conception

Conception includes fertilisation and implantation of an embryo in the uterus.

Pregnancy

The time between implantation and birth is called *pregnancy* or *gestation*. In humans it lasts about thirty-eight weeks. The growing embryo, called the foetus from the eighth week onward, becomes surrounded by *amniotic fluid*, which protects the foetus from knocks.

The foetus needs food and oxygen in order to grow. At first these come directly from the blood vessels in the uterus wall. After a few weeks, however, a special plate-shaped organ develops, called the *placenta*. The baby is connected to the placenta by a cord, called the *umbilical cord*. The foetus receives food and oxygen from the mother's blood, and releases carbon dioxide and other waste matter into it.

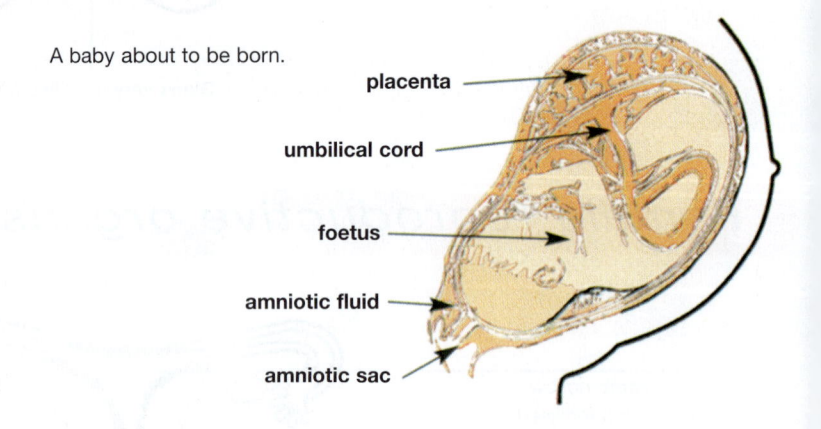

During the last few days of pregnancy, the baby moves so that its head is near the cervix. Finally, the baby is squeezed out through the vagina by strong contractions of the muscles in the uterus. This is called *labour*.

A baby about to be born.

Catholic teaching on sex

In the Old Testament account of the Creation it is written:

> *Male and female God created them. And God blessed them, and God said to them, 'Be fruitful and multiply…'*
> (Genesis 1:27–28)

It is repeatedly stated that God looked upon his creation and said that *it was good*. As a result, the Catholic Church teaches that:

- Sex is a *gift* from God that should be used in a loving and respectful way, as through the sexual act a man and a woman express their total love for and commitment to each other.
- Sex can create new life and so concerns more than just the man and woman involved, bringing with it responsibility for *another* human life.
- Sex is the language of *love*, *commitment* and *responsibility*, because in it a man and a woman tell each other that the other is the 'one and only love'. As a result, sex can only find its true expression within a *married* relationship, i.e. where two people commit themselves to one another.
- Sex outside of marriage is an act of deception, because those involved are not deliberately and unreservedly committing themselves to love and care for each other, both now and for all the years to follow.

Questions

1. Explain the following statement: *Sex is the language of love, commitment and responsibility*.
2. Why does the Catholic Church teach that sex outside of marriage is *an act of deception*?

The meaning of marriage

Christian marriage is seen as a threefold partnership involving husband, wife and God.

A couple busily planning their wedding often find that, absorbed in the exciting and hectic preparations for their big day, it is easy to lose sight of what this event *really* means.

Love One Another   259

Some people think that the words *'marriage'* and *'wedding'* mean exactly the same thing. They do *not*.

- A *wedding* is the *ceremony* in which a couple are married on a particular day.
- A *marriage* means *more* than this.
- A *marriage* is the *relationship* that a couple *begins* on their wedding day.

The *rite* (ceremony) *of marriage* in the Catholic Church usually takes place as part of the Mass. Before witnesses and in the presence of the priest, the bride and groom begin by answering in turn a series of questions.

- *Have you come to give yourself to each other, freely and without reservation?*
- *Will you love and honour each other for life?*
- *Will you accept children lovingly from God?*

The couple publicly declare that they *understand* what it is they are doing and that they are *freely consenting* to marriage.

Then, the bride and groom exchange *vows* (solemn promises to one another). In turn, each says:

I take you as my husband/wife, for better or for worse, for richer or for poorer, in sickness and in health, 'til death us do part.

It is essential that the priest is present in the Catholic marriage ceremony. He represents the Church and accepts the *mutual consent* of (agreement of both) the bride and groom. He says to the couple:

What God has joined together let no one pull asunder.

It is not the couple who have joined themselves in marriage but *God* who has made their union complete. This is why the Catholic Church regards marriage as a *sacrament*.

Next, the priest blesses the wedding rings, and each partner in turn places a ring on the third finger of the other's left hand and says:

Wear this ring as a sign of our love and fidelity. In the name of the Father, and of the Son and of the Holy Spirit.

The endless circle of the wedding ring *symbolises* (stands for) the couple's commitment to love one another in a relationship that is *permanent* (life-long) and *exclusive* (admitting no other partners).

The priest ends by blessing the couple, emphasising how they must be loving and faithful in all the days ahead.

Questions

1. What is the difference between a *marriage* and a *wedding*?
2. (a) State the three questions the couple are asked by the priest.
   (b) Why are they asked such questions?
3. What does it mean for the couple to *exchange vows*?
4. Why does the Catholic Church regard marriage as a *sacrament*?
5. What does the *wedding ring* symbolise?

Why marry?

Traditionally, marriage has been considered a *good* thing because it was accepted as providing the ideal context in which people could:

- freely commit themselves to love and care for each other for the rest of their lives
- bring up children in what should be a secure and loving home

- direct the sex instinct towards the most constructive purpose, i.e. to show mutual love and build a happy home
- give and receive companionship and love, both in good times and in bad.

Making marriage work

The Holy Family with a Little Bird by Bartolomé Esteban Murillo.

In the Old Testament account of the Creation it is written:

> *A man leaves his father and mother and is united with his wife, and they become one.* (Genesis 2:24)

This was written to show that marriage is part of God's plan for human beings. It sets a high standard for marriage: the relationship which a husband and a wife should seek to build is to be so close that these two people *become one*.

God's love should be reflected in the love a husband and a wife have for each other. For a couple to achieve this and for their marriage to succeed, both husband and wife must continually work at their relationship.

According to experienced marriage counsellors, *both* partners must show:

- genuine commitment
- willingness to talk to each other
- close friendship
- respect for each other's privacy
- shared basic values
- readiness to put their relationship ahead of everything else
- sensitivity in settling disputes
- willingness to seek and offer forgiveness
- consideration towards each other in practical ways
- realistic expectations regarding sex.

It is important to remember that *most marriages succeed*, even though they have to face many pressures and challenges today.*

It is advisable for couples intending to marry to attend marriage preparation courses. It is important for a couple to know if they have what it takes to sustain a loving relationship.

> *Guidance counsellors state that for a marriage to succeed, *both* partners must:
> - appreciate and understand the kind of pressures they will have to face, e.g. money, housing, work *and*
> - be prepared to support each other through whatever crisis they may face, e.g. illness, bereavement.

Questions

1. It is recommended that when people wish to marry, they should only do so *with their eyes open*. What does this mean?
2. Why is it advisable for couples intending to marry to attend marriage preparation courses?

Love One Another

Chapter Forty-three

Discipleship

Introduction

Read any interview with a person who is deeply committed to working with the disabled, fundraising for orphans, caring for the elderly or campaigning to preserve the environment. All of them have the same thing in common: they all share a deep conviction that this is the work they were meant to do. They all have a sense of being somehow *called* to do this work.

Vocation

Following Christ in today's world.

This sense of being called by God to do something worthwhile in life is referred to as a *vocation*.

Members of the Catholic Church and other Christian Churches may fulfil their vocations in any one of the following ways:

○ as a single or a married layperson

○ as a monk or a nun in a religious community

○ as a member of the clergy,* e.g. a priest or a bishop.

Each vocation has an important role to play. None is more important than another. This is because bishops, priests, religious and laity are *all equal members of the one family of God*. All are called to be *disciples* (followers) of Jesus.

Discipleship

Jesus told his first small band of followers that to be his disciple meant not merely learning his teachings, but also following his example.

In the *Sermon on the Mount*, Jesus set out his extraordinary, challenging moral vision of what this would mean for his disciples.

○ They should be known for their good works (Matthew 5:13–16).

○ They should go further than the Jewish law commands. For example, they are to love their enemies (Matthew 5:38).

○ They should always act with sincerity and without outward show (Matthew 6:1–18). Jesus was concerned only with inner goodness.

---

*N.B.
The ordination of women

The Catholic Church and the Orthodox Churches have stated that they will *not* ordain women. Both continue the traditional practice of accepting *only men* as candidates for the priesthood.

Among the mainstream Protestant Churches, Anglicans, Methodists and Baptists have women ministers.

LAY PEOPLE ARE CALLED TO

EXPLAIN THE PRINCIPLES WHICH CHRIST TAUGHT BY	READING IN CHURCH	MISSIONARY WORK	TEACHING
DEFEND CHRIST'S TEACHING THROUGH	HOPE PRAYER	FAITH	LOVE
APPLY CHRIST'S TEACHINGS TO THE PROBLEMS OF OUR TIME	VIOLENCE	DRUGS	CRIME
	FEED THE HUNGRY	HOUSE THE HOMELESS	HEAL THE SICK

○ They should not condemn others. It is for God to judge others. People should first assess their own behaviour and not live dishonestly with double standards.

○ The *golden rule* should always be their guide: *do unto others as you would have them do unto you* (Matthew 7:12).

When Christians today are baptised and/or confirmed, they are anointed to *share* in the work of Jesus himself. They are called to *give witness*, i.e. to faithfully put Jesus' teachings into practice in their daily lives and, by their example, lead other people to God.

Questions

1. What is the meaning of *vocation*?
2. State the three ways in which a member of the Catholic Church may fulfil his/her vocation.
3. What is meant by calling someone a *disciple of Jesus*?
4. Identify three challenging things that Jesus demands of his followers in the *Sermon on the Mount*.
5. What does it mean for a Christian to *give witness* to Jesus Christ in his/her daily life?

Discipleship

Giving witness as a layperson: The Samaritans

Rev. Chad Varah.

The Samaritans was founded in 1953 by Reverend Chad Varah, Rector of St Stephen's Anglican Church, Walbrook, in London. He had discovered that befriending by 'ordinary' people was often more acceptable than professional counselling for those who were considering *suicide*. This befriending service is now available twenty-four hours a day, every day of the year and has spread across the globe, with over 22,000 volunteers in some 200 branches.

All Samaritans obey the same strict rules:

○ *Absolute confidentiality*: The Samaritans guarantee complete secrecy about the identity of callers and anything they discuss. For instance, even if a husband and wife or a parent and child contacted the Samaritans about the same matter separately, each can depend on total confidentiality.

Any request for information about people who avail of the service is refused. Answers to letters are in plain envelopes and do not mention the Samaritans. Personal callers are not acknowledged 'outside' by the volunteers if they encounter them in order to preserve their privacy.

○ *Non-interference*: The caller is always 'in charge' and will never be contacted by the Samaritans or mentioned to any other agency or person unless he or she specifically requests it – and then only if the Samaritans' intervention is clearly needed by the caller.

○ *Acceptance of the caller's own beliefs and standards (no preaching)*: The Samaritans have no 'message' except that there is somebody ready to listen and befriend you, day or night, whenever you need it.

The Samaritans seek to offer sympathetic and concerned friendship to callers. Although their name comes from the Gospel story of the Good Samaritan, not all of the volunteers are Christians.

The volunteers are ordinary people from all walks of life – from those in their twenties to senior citizens – who give up some of their free time to befriend others. Usually only their immediate family know that they are Samaritan volunteers, and they are known to callers and volunteers only by first names followed by a number, such as Michael 24, Sarah 6 and so on.

Primarily, the Samaritans are there to help those who are suicidal or feel overwhelmed by feelings of loneliness and despair. *There is no problem that they will refuse to discuss.*

The Samaritans offer callers *time*, treat them with *respect* and take what they say *seriously*. They do *not* offer material help in cash or in kind, but will help people to contact those organisations that do provide such help. They do *not* try to minimise people's problems, nor do they offer vague assurances that things will work out easily. However, they do believe that talking things over in absolute confidence and privacy with someone who accepts you as you are can either help you to solve problems or else to discover new ways of living with an insoluble situation.

The Samaritans believe that by really listening to another human being in distress, they can help that person increase his/her sense of self-worth, help him/her to gain insight into the situation and reduce feelings of isolation and despair. They aim to help people see their problems in a new light and encourage them to find answers or to develop new attitudes that may help them to cope with their problems.

Questions

1. (a) Who founded the Samaritans?
   (b) Why did he do so?
2. (a) What do the Samaritans offer?
   (b) What don't they offer?
3. What are the three strict rules that the Samaritans obey?
4. What is the importance of the service provided by the Samaritans?

Religious communities

In the Catholic, Orthodox and Anglican Churches, some people believe that they are called to follow a different path in serving God in their community rather than as a married or single person. They choose to enter *religious life*. This means that a man may enter a monastery and become a *monk* (either a *priest* or *brother*), and a woman may enter a convent and become a *nun* (also referred to as a *sister*).

Each monk or nun belongs to a specific religious order. These religious orders can be grouped under either of the following headings:

- *Apostolic communities*: These religious orders were founded with specific work in mind, such as teaching, nursing or missionary expansion.

- *Contemplative communities*: These religious orders devote their whole lives to prayer, study and physical work. They rarely leave the confines of their communities. Often they are only allowed to speak at particular times of the day. They may spend up to eight hours of each day at prayer.

The idea of religious communities has its origins in the early Christian Church in Jerusalem (see Acts of the Apostles 2:44–47).

In all religious communities, monks or nuns live under an arrangement known as *the rule* of that particular order. This rule offers detailed guidance as to how they can best live out their *vocation* (calling) as monks or nuns.

The best-known and most influential monastic rule is *the Rule of St Benedict*, set down in the sixth century.

St Benedict (pictured on the left) by Sodoma.

Upon completion of their training, all monks and nuns must take the same three basic *vows* (solemn promises):

- *Poverty*: A monk or nun must not be tied down by possessions, but 'hold everything in common'.
- *Chastity*: A monk or nun may have no sexual relationships. He/she must seek intimacy with God alone.
- *Obedience*: A monk or nun must be completely dedicated to serving God and the community.

Questions

1. What does it mean for a man or a woman to *enter religious life*?
2. Explain the difference between an *apostolic* religious community and a *contemplative* religious community.
3. What is the best-known and most influential monastic rule?
4. Explain the purpose of a monastic rule.
5. State the *three basic vows* all monks and nuns must take upon completing their training.

Giving witness to religious life: Mother Teresa of Calcutta

When Mother Teresa came to London she found people dying in the streets, and even in their own homes, unloved. 'Here you have a different kind of poverty in the Western world,' she said, 'a poverty of spirit, of loneliness, and that is the worst disease in the world today, worse than tuberculosis or leprosy. We have to love.'

This extraordinary woman was born in 1910 of Albanian parents. She trained for a year with the Mercy Sisters in Rathfarnham, Dublin. Then, she

Mother Teresa of Calcutta.

was sent to teach geography in a school for high-caste Indian girls in Calcutta and eventually became its principal. Gradually, though, she became aware of another vocation within her. She believed that God was calling her to serve Him in the poorest of the poor.

She always remembered 10 September 1946 as her 'Day of Decision'. It was then that she asked permission from her religious superiors to work in the slums of Calcutta.

When permission was granted she went first to Patna for intensive nursing training, returning to Calcutta at the end of 1948. She was given permission to open her first slum school and the following year a Bengali girl joined her to form the nucleus of a new order, the Missionaries of Charity. These sisters in their white saris edged with blue stripes were soon to become a familiar sight, not only in Calcutta but also in slums throughout the world – Venezuela, Ceylon, Tanzania, Rome, Australia and in London too. Their work today is done with an unforced joy and enthusiasm which are a perfect expression of Christian love – *agapé*.

Mother Teresa did not want people to focus on her own life. The work she did was Christ's work, serving him in the poorest of the poor and the circumstances of her own life were unimportant.

Look again at *the parable of The Sheep and the Goats* (Matthew 25:31–46). It was often quoted by Mother Teresa and was the basis of her own understanding of her work. As she tended to the dying, cared for lepers and rescued newborn babies from dustbins, she was seeing Christ in the outcast. Her love for them was God's love, flowing through her.

She never worried about money; when needed it seemed to arrive. Mother Teresa saw this as God providing for her work. When the Pope visited India he gave her the white limousine he had used in his travels. She raffled it and made enough money to start a leper colony. She won many international awards for her work, including the Nobel Peace Prize. All prize money went into projects to help people.

She was perhaps best known for her care of the dying. This work started when she picked up a woman from the street who was being eaten alive by rats and ants and the hospitals refused to take her in. Places could only be spared for those with hope of recovery, so she asked the city authorities to provide her with a building where she could take such people. They offered her a disused Hindu temple, which she gratefully accepted. Today it is perhaps the best-known home for the dying in the world. Many thousands have been taken there to die in peace, surrounded by love. All must first have been turned away from hospitals.

Mother Teresa never lost her love of teaching. She started a school in the Calcutta slums. They had no building so they met in a compound belonging to a slum family. On the first day she had five pupils. Now the sisters have over 500. Children are taught to read and are given lessons in elementary hygiene – a far cry from teaching geography to middle-class girls.

Work among lepers has also grown from the five who first came to the sisters in 1957 to the many thousands they care for today. If the disease is diagnosed early it can be cured in less than two years. The sisters run a rehabilitation centre to help those who have been cured and offer loving care to those where the disease has gone beyond such help.

In the early days, people were sometimes patronising about this woman who went off to serve the poor in the slums. What difference could such a tiny drop in the ocean make to the problems of world poverty? She herself pointed out that the ocean would be smaller without that drop. Eventually even the hard-bitten came to recognise her great influence for good. For Christians caught up in the confusions of life in the twenty-first century, Mother Teresa stands out as a reassuring example of the truth of the Gospel.

When she died in 1997, her passing was mourned by countless millions. They saw in her life what can be achieved when Christ is taken at his word and followed in simplicity.

Adapted from Diana Morgan, *Christian Perspectives on Contemporary Issues*

Questions

1. What were the kinds of poverty Mother Teresa identified in a busy Western city like London?
2. When was Mother Teresa born?
3. Why did Mother Teresa decide to ask permission to work in the slums of Calcutta?
4. Name the religious order Mother Teresa founded.
5. Identify the kinds of people she helped.
6. Name one international award Mother Teresa won.
7. Why did she become involved in caring for the dying?
8. (a) Why were people sometimes patronising about Mother Teresa's work?
   (b) How did she respond to them?
9. When did Mother Teresa die?

Saints

Jesus Washing Peter's Feet by Ford Madox Brown. This painting shows Peter, having first protested against it, now submitting to having his feet washed by Jesus. His folded hands and bowed head are expressive of Peter's complete submission to Christ.

Jesus calls on his disciples to live according to very high standards.

> *You must be perfect, as your heavenly father is perfect.* (Matthew 5:48)
>
> *Love your enemies. Do good to those who hate you.* (Luke 6:27)

Jesus' teaching sets forth an *ideal*, i.e. a high standard which people should strive to achieve.

To live as Jesus lived demands great faith, courage and love. Indeed, the challenge Jesus offers is *so demanding* that few people, either now or in times past, have been able to follow his teachings completely.

However, throughout the history of the Christian religion there have been many extraordinary men and women who so devoted their lives to doing good and leading others to God that they have been declared *saints* (people of great holiness).

A Christian can only be considered worthy of being declared a saint *after* his/her death. In the Catholic Church a special commission is appointed by the pope to investigate whether or not the person was indeed a saint. Once it submits its report, a final decision is made by the pope. This decision to honour a person with the title of saint is called *canonisation*.

Questions

1. Explain the following statement: *Jesus' teaching sets forth an ideal*.
2. What is a *saint*?
3. Describe the process by which a person is declared a saint.
4. What is *canonisation*?

Giving witness: Maximilian Kolbé, the Saint of Auschwitz

In July 1941 three prisoners escaped from the Nazi concentration camp of Auschwitz. In reprisal, the Nazis picked ten prisoners who were to be deliberately starved to death. One of the men was Franciszek Gajowniczek. When he realised his fate he cried out, 'My wife, my children, I shall never see them again.' It was then that the unexpected happened. From the ranks of watching inmates, prisoner 16670 stepped out and offered himself to take this man's place. Then the volunteer was taken with the other nine condemned men to the dreaded bunker, an airless underground cell, to die slowly without food or water.

Prisoner 16670 was a Polish Catholic priest named Maximilian Kolbé. He was forty-seven years old. Before the war he had founded one of the largest monasteries in the world. He had also travelled as a missionary to the Far East. In 1939 he began helping Jewish refugees.

Above Auschwitz.
Left St Maximilian Kolbé.

However, in 1941 Father Kolbé was arrested by the Nazis and sent to prison in Warsaw and then deported to Auschwitz. Auschwitz was a terrible place. Human beings were treated in the most inhuman ways imaginable. Thousands died every day from beatings, floggings, torture, disease, starvation and in the gas chambers. Father Kolbé dedicated his life in Auschwitz to helping his fellow prisoners. He would console them, share his food with them and organise secret Church services. He tried to show others, by his own example, that even in such a hellish place God still loved and cared for them.

An eyewitness of these last terrible days of Father Kolbé's life tells us what happened.

'In the cell of the poor wretches there were daily prayers and hymn singing, in which prisoners from neighbouring cells also joined. When no SS men were in the block I went to the bunker to talk to the men and comfort them. Fervent prayers and songs resounded in all the corridors of the bunker. I had the impression I was in a church. Father Kolbé was leading and the prisoners responded in unison. They were often so deep in prayer that they did not hear that inspecting SS men had descended to the bunker; and the voices fell silent only at the loud yelling of their visitors. When the cells were opened the poor wretches cried loudly and begged for a piece of bread and for water, which they did not receive. If any of the stronger ones approached the door he was immediately kicked in the stomach by the SS men, so that falling backwards on the cement floor he was instantly killed; or he was shot to death...Father Kolbé bore up bravely; he did not beg and did not complain but raised the spirits of the others.

Since they had grown very weak, prayers were now only whispered. At every inspection, when almost all the others were now lying on the floor, Father Kolbé was seen kneeling or standing in the centre as he looked cheerfully in the face of the SS men. Two weeks passed in this way. Meanwhile one after another they died, until Father Kolbé was left. This the authorities felt was too long; the cell was needed for new victims. So one day they brought in the head of the sick quarters, a German, a common criminal named Bock who gave Father Kolbé an injection of carbolic acid in the vein of his left arm. Father Kolbé, with a prayer on his lips, gave his arm to the executioner. Unable to watch this I left under the pretext of work to be done. Immediately after the SS men with the executioner left I returned to the cell, where I found Father Kolbé leaning in a sitting position against the back wall with his eyes open and his head drooping sideways. His face was calm and radiant.'

In 1982 the Catholic Church declared Maximilian Kolbé a saint.

Source: Catholic Truth Society

Questions

1. Who was Maximilian Kolbé?
2. What was Auschwitz?
3. Why did Maximilian Kolbé volunteer to take the place of a fellow prisoner in the death cell?
4. How did Maximilian Kolbé die?

Chapter Forty-four

Making Moral Decisions

Introduction

It is Saturday morning at a busy shopping centre. A shopper accidentally drops his wallet on the ground without realising it, leaving it behind. It contains €200 in cash. If someone finds it, what should they do?

Consider how these three people respond to this situation:

- **Alan** puts the wallet in his pocket. He says, 'OK, so it's not mine, but the owner should have been more careful. Finders keepers!'

- **Susan** thinks that no one has noticed her picking up the wallet, so she decides to keep the money. She says, 'Hard luck for the owner, but I could really use this money.'

- **Michael** finds the wallet. He says, 'I could really use the money, but it's not mine to keep.' Michael takes it to the centre's management office and leaves it for the owner to claim.

Both Alan and Susan know that what they have chosen to do is *wrong*. Michael could have easily pocketed the money just as they did. However, unlike them, Michael values *honesty*. He realises that to keep the money would be stealing. He hands it in for the owner to reclaim. Michael chooses to do good rather than evil.

People often remark that someone like Michael *has a conscience*.

The meaning of conscience

Conscience may be defined as

> *a person's ability to apply his/her values to a particular moral problem and make a decision about what is the right thing to do.*

Normally, a person's conscience operates with such remarkable speed and efficiency that he/she is rarely aware of how it functions. Let us look at a slow-motion example to illustrate how one can apply a general moral principle to a particular moral problem.

- *Problem*: I enter a shop. The counter is unattended. I am tempted to take a bar of chocolate without paying for it.

- *Principle*: But it is wrong to steal.

- *Conclusion*: Therefore, if I take this bar of chocolate without paying for it, I am doing something wrong.

Making Moral Decisions 271

- *Decision*: A good person would then say, 'I wish to help people. I do not want to cause harm to another person, so I will not steal this item. If I want it and if I can afford it, I will purchase it.'

The development of conscience

People's families and all those who influence their values as they are growing up have an important role to play in the development of their individual consciences.

This is why all the major world religions place great emphasis on parents' responsibility to develop children's consciences by the *example they set*.

However, each individual also has a role to play in the development of his/her own conscience by:

- *praying*
- *learning about moral issues*
- *doing good deeds*.

The importance of honesty

Person swearing an oath to tell the truth in court.

Honesty involves:

- being truthful with oneself, God and other people
- recognising one's obligation to do good and avoid doing harm
- rejecting lying, cheating and the desire to succeed at any price.

Frequently, people ask '*Why be honest?*' Jews, Christians and Muslims offer this response:

1. God demands honesty in the eighth Commandment.
2. Honesty is the basis for all genuine human relationships. Without honesty, relationships disintegrate due to lack of trust.
3. Dishonesty creates situations that tempt people into inventing more lies to cover up the ones they have already told, thus making a bad situation even *worse*.
4. Dishonest acts, such as shoplifting, taking bribes and committing fraud, lead to higher costs, which affect everyone in the community.

Questions

1. What is meant by *conscience*?
2. Identify three ways in which a person can develop his/her own conscience.
3. What does *honesty* involve?
4. How do Jews, Christians and Muslims respond to the question '*Why be honest*'?
5. Read the following statement: *Some people believe that our society is becoming so obsessed with wealth and pleasure that an honest person like Michael in the opening story is the exception today.* Do you agree or disagree? Explain your answer.

Making a moral decision

What follows is a checklist of questions people should ask themselves before making an *important* moral decision.

- What exactly is the problem facing me?
- Do I have all the relevant facts?
- Where can I find good advice?
- What does the law say?
- What does my religion teach?
- What are my motives for choosing to act in a particular way?
- Which method is the correct one for me to use?
- How will my actions affect other people?

Only *after* going through this process of careful reflection about what the right thing to do is should a person act according to his/her conscience.

People should always try to:

- act in accordance with their values
- do everything possible to fully inform their consciences
- follow their consciences when confronted with a moral decision.

No one should be forced to act against his/her *properly informed* conscience.

Difficulties in moral decision making

People need to be aware that certain things can *cloud their judgment* and make it difficult for them to know what the right choice to make is.

There are four main areas of difficulty:

Don't just blindly follow the pack. Think before acting.

1. *Where people do not understand the true nature of the problem facing them.* This can be because they either could not or would not get the advice or the information needed to understand what is at stake.

2. *Where people allow their emotions to have too great an influence on the decisions they make.* For instance, just because something makes a person feel good does *not* ensure that it is the right thing to do.

3. *When people only choose to do something in order to win favour with others.* Just because the majority of people are for or against something does *not* guarantee that it is right.

4. *Where people make a mistake in their reasoning*, such as:
   - *Problem*: War involves killing people.
   - *Principle*: It is always wrong to kill another person.
   - *Conclusion*: Therefore, war is wrong.

The difficulty here is that it is sometimes necessary and correct to take a life, for example in self-defence when there is no other course of action available.

Making Moral Decisions

Moral maturity

A morally mature person is one who:

- thinks before acting
- honestly evaluates the situation
- considers the consequences of his/her actions
- tries to do what is right, even when he/she has nothing to gain and when this might be to his/her disadvantage.

Questions

1. This is a list of questions a person should ask when faced with a moral decision. They have been jumbled up. Rearrange them into the correct order.
   - What does the law say?
   - Where can I find good advice?
   - How will my actions affect others?
   - What does my religion teach?
   - Do I have all the relevant facts?
   - What are my motives for choosing to act in a particular way?
   - What exactly is the problem facing me?
   - Which method is the correct one for me to use?
2. Identify four areas where it can be difficult for a person to make the right choice when faced with a moral decision.
3. Imagine you are a member of a group campaigning against the emissions from a nuclear power plant.

   There is some evidence that it may be causing damage to the health of the local people and slowly destroying their environment.

   Your group leader declares that swift, violent action is necessary to stop this. He claims that a small explosive device placed inside the main control room would disable the entire plant and end the emissions.

Questions

Some members of the group think that this kind of action is the only solution, but you doubt if this really is the best course of action. Before deciding to accept or reject the idea of going ahead with the plan, consider the following:

A. Examine the *consequences* of the group leader's plan for:
   - Your group – this action is against the law.
   - The employees – what about their jobs?
   - The local community – could the explosion cause harmful material to escape into the air and cause widespread illness or death?
   - The local environment – will it make matters better or worse?

B. Can you suggest a *better* way to end this pollution *without* using violence?

Human weakness

Knowing what is the right thing to do is one thing. Actually *doing* the right thing is something else.

Generally speaking, human beings find it hard to do the right thing. As Paul wrote about his own experience:

> *I cannot understand my own behaviour. I fail to carry out the things I want to do, and I find myself doing the very thing I hate.* (Romans 7:15–16)

When confronted with a difficult moral choice, every human being experiences this pull in opposite directions: to stand one's ground and do what is right, or to turn away and do what is wrong. It is difficult to choose and follow the path of good; it is much *easier* to take the path of least resistance and give in to some passing desire. It takes *courage* to think differently from others, to choose to live by different values, to believe what others may dismiss and to do the right thing.

Original sin

The Expulsion of Adam and Eve by Giuseppe Cesari.

Christians acknowledge that *all* people find choosing and doing good instead of evil to be a real challenge.

Christians do *not* believe, however, that God created human beings with some kind of built-in tendency to do bad things. Rather, they believe that God can only create what is *good*. Therefore, all people are created good. Yet experience shows that people find it difficult to do good and avoid evil. Why?

The key to answering this question can be found in the Old Testament book of Genesis 3:1–21.

This tells the story of *the Fall*, i.e. of how Adam and Eve gave in to temptation, deliberately disobeyed God and as a result were banished for ever from the Garden of Eden.

We should *not* consider Genesis to offer a literal historical account. Whatever its actual historical details, however, this is a very important story which contains a profound message.

- The story of the Fall tells how the first humans deliberately chose to disobey God and do what they knew to be wrong. As a result they brought *sin* (wrongdoing) into the world.

- These early humans acted out of pride and selfishness, and *fell away* from the state of innocent goodness in which God had wanted them to live.

- This first sin by the first human beings is called the *original* sin. It affected all of human society. The effects of this original sin were passed on from one generation to the next down through history. It is because of this that human beings are *weak* in their resolve to do good and avoid evil.

Our earliest ancestors turned away from God and threw away the gift of perfect happiness, which Christians believe can only be found by living the way God wants people to live.

Source of hope

Christians believe that God did *not* create human beings and then just leave them to flounder in this world. On the contrary, God *rescued* this world by becoming a human being in Jesus of Nazareth.

Consider the following:

- Jesus has shown people the way that God always intended them to live and the way in which they can achieve peace with God and with one another.

- Jesus invites people to follow him, but does not force anyone. The choice is up to each individual to make.

People cannot live good lives, however, purely by their own efforts. They need God's *grace* (freely given, loving strength) to help them to do good

Making Moral Decisions

Christ Blessing by El Greco.

and avoid evil. Here the Christian Churches teach that they have a vital role to play:

> *Baptism into the Christian community signifies our acceptance of, and frees us from, Original Sin; but we are still weak. We need the daily strength of the Holy Spirit to conquer that weakness, and the support of each other. That is one important reason why we need to belong to the Church, the community of believers.* (Rowanne Pascoe and John Redford, *Faith Alive*)

Questions

1. By what title is the story of Adam and Eve in Genesis 3:1–21 known?
2. Why is the sin first committed by our earliest ancestors known as *original sin*?
3. What has been the effect of this *original sin* on all human beings since then?
4. What do Christians believe about the role of Jesus in their struggle to live good and worthwhile lives?
5. (a) What is meant by *God's grace*?
   (b) Why do people need it?

Chapter Forty-five

Sin and Forgiveness

Introduction

Human beings are by nature social creatures. Our lives largely consist of a complex web of relationships with other people. If these relationships are to succeed, people need to meet their *obligations* (duties) towards one another by treating each other with compassion and respect. However, whenever people *selfishly* disregard their obligations to others, they enter the realm of *actual sin*.

Actual sin

Cain Killing Abel by Italian School.

We may define *actual sin* as

> *any freely chosen, deliberately intended and selfish action whose consequences one desires, which inflicts harm on one's neighbour and oneself.*

In damaging one's relationship with another person, one damages one's relationship with *God*. The degree of damage depends on the *seriousness* of the sin committed.

> **N.B.**
> Actual sin is *different* from original sin, yet *related* to it. It is because human beings have to struggle within themselves to do good and avoid evil that they are prone to commit actual sin.

The types of actual sin

The Catholic Church distinguishes between two kinds of actual sin:

○ *venial sin*

and

○ *mortal sin*.

Venial sin is

> *any wrongful action a person commits that weakens his/her relationship with God.*

It is a refusal to live as God intends people to live and usually stems from pride and selfishness.

Sin and Forgiveness

Venial sin can lead a person to gradually move away from God and so can lead to the eventual breakdown of a person's relationship with God.

Mortal sin is

any seriously wrongful act by which a person destroys his/her relationship with God.

To be guilty of mortal sin, a person must freely, deliberately and with full knowledge of its consequences commit a very serious offence against both God and other people.

The Kiss of Judas, fresco by Giotto di Bondone in Scrogenin Chapel in Padua, Italy.

The ways of committing sin

A person can commit a sin in either of *two* ways:

1. By *commission* – when one deliberately does something one knows one should not do.
2. By *omission* – when one deliberately *neglects* to do something one knows one should do.

Sin by commission

In 1854, the passenger ship Artic was crossing the North Atlantic when it struck an iceberg. The ship began to sink. There were not enough lifeboats for everyone on board, so the captain gave the order, 'Women and children first!'

However, most of the crew disobeyed his command. Some of them broke into the ship's armoury and seized weapons. These crew members then held the women and children at gunpoint while they took control of the lifeboats.

Most of the crew survived the sinking, but none of the women or children survived.

T. Deary, *True Disaster Stories*

Sin by omission

The funeral of Francis McNamara, seven, who lost a two-day fight for life after a crayon lodged in his windpipe, will be held on Monday.

The boy died last Thursday night at a hospital. He swallowed the crayon on his way home in a school bus. Motorists drove by while the bus driver frantically waved for help.

Finally, in desperation, the bus driver jumped in front of a motorist who was forced to stop. But the man refused to take the youngster to a hospital, saying he would be 'late for work'.

The bus driver, seeking a quicker trip than the bus could make, waved down another driver, who took Francis to Fairlawn Hospital in nearby Worcester. There a doctor quickly opened the boy's chest and massaged his heart to keep him alive.

Dr Chang Kim then ordered surgery, but it was too late. Doctors said the boy died from brain damage suffered during the minutes his heart had stopped beating.

Adapted from M. Link, *Man in the Modern World*

N.B.
It is important to remember that Christians believe that all people are sinners to a greater or lesser extent. No one has the right to feel superior. One may condemn the *act* but *not* the *person*. No one has the right to condemn another.

The need for courage

Oskar Schindler.

In contrast to the two cases examined above, consider the *courage* shown by Oskar Schindler when faced with a great moral challenge.

Courage has been defined as

the ability to make a moral choice to do good, even if it is in opposition to other people who have power over you.

Schindler risked his own life on numerous occasions as he sought to save the lives of over 1,000 Jewish men, women and children who worked in his factory. He prevented them from being murdered by Hitler's SS. Schindler used every possible trick and resource he could think of to save those people.

This took enormous courage at a time when most people around him either actively or tacitly supported the mass murder in the concentration camps. Had Schindler's activities been discovered, he would surely have been put to death, yet he was willing to take the risk. He believed that it was a risk *worth taking* and he had the courage to take it.

Questions

1. What is *actual sin*?
2. Explain the difference between (a) *mortal* sin and (b) *venial* sin.
3. Using the two stories set out above, explain the difference between (a) *sin by commission* and (b) *sin by omission*.
4. What is *courage*?
5. (a) What did Oskar Schindler do during World War II?
   (b) Why do you think he did what he did?
   (c) Why didn't more people do the same?

Sin and Forgiveness

Forgiveness

During his earthly ministry, Jesus called on people to

Repent and believe the Good News!

He said that God had unlimited love for even the worst offenders and forgave the sins of all those who genuinely wanted to reform their lives.

In the *Our Father*, Jesus taught his followers to pray:

Forgive us our trespasses [sins], as we forgive those who trespass against us.

We will now examine the two aspects of this prayer.

The Return of the Prodigal Son by Benjamin West.

Forgive us our trespasses

The story of the *Prodigal Son* (Luke 15:11–32) is familiar to most people, but this familiarity can often blind people to its true significance.

Jesus wished all to know that, like the wayward son of the story, if people are genuinely sorry and want to reform their lives, God will forgive their sin. Though they may turn their backs on God and walk away, God remains loving and forgiving, offering them the chance to repair the damage they have done to their relationship with God and with those around them.

Some people, however, cannot understand a feeling of guilt. They have so dulled their conscience that they apparently have no guilty feelings at all. When they are brought to court for a violent crime, they will insist that either (a) *they did not do it* or (b) *the victim forced them to do it*. Sometimes they will even try to convince themselves and others that their victims *wanted* them to harm them. This pattern of behaviour is quite common with violent criminals. Unlike the prodigal son, they cannot admit either to themselves or to others their responsibility for their evil actions. The admission of personal responsibility for having harmed another person is the first vital step towards finding forgiveness.

As we forgive those who trespass against us

Jesus said that if people want God to forgive them, then they too must be prepared to forgive those who have offended them.

Consider the parable of the *Unforgiving Servant* (Matthew 18:22–25):

The parable has three main characters: a king and two servants. One servant owes the king a huge amount of money: in today's terms, several million euro. He tearfully promises to repay it and pleads for more time. The king feels so sorry for him that he cancels the entire debt. But the servant learns nothing from his experience. On his way home he meets another servant, one who owes him money, a paltry sum of about twenty euro. His colleague pleads with him for time to repay it, but he will have none of it; instead, he has him thrown into prison.

When the king hears what has happened, he summons the unforgiving servant and tells him angrily, 'I cancelled your huge debt out of compassion. Should you not have done the same?' Then the king has him thrown into prison until he can repay the debt in full.

In the parable, God is the king and we are the servants. Like the first servant, we beg for mercy and He grants a total pardon. God is the great forgiver. But, like the first servant, we take forgiveness for granted. We can forget how merciful God is to us and fail to show that mercy to others, just as the first servant failed to show compassion towards his colleague. But the message of the parable is clear. Just as God is generous with us, so too must we be generous with one another. Indeed, we must forgive each other if we expect God to forgive us.

Source: *The Sunday Message*

Forgiving those who have offended or harmed us can often be far from easy. It can demand great courage and strength.

Consider the story of Gordon Wilson:

On 6 November 1987, at the cenotaph in Enniskillen, an IRA bomb killed eleven people, including three couples, and injured sixty.

Gordon Wilson and his daughter Marie, a nurse, were buried in the rubble. She stretched out her hand to him. 'Is that you Daddy?' 'Yes, dear. Are you all right?' He repeated the question four more times before she said – her last words – 'Daddy, I love you very much.'

Interviewed the next day, he said, 'I bear no ill will…She was a great girl. She's in heaven now. We will meet again.'

What Alf McCreary, Mr Wilson's biographer, later revealed is that originally he did not forgive his daughter's murderers. He only said he had no ill will towards them. Forgiving them took time and effort and constant prayer.

Source: *Irish Independent*

Forgiveness does *not* mean letting people walk all over us. Each person is entitled to justice and for those who have caused harm to be held accountable for their actions.

However, Jesus taught that to refuse to forgive and to seek revenge will only destroy a person from within. Forgiveness is vital.

Jesus makes clear that if people want to receive God's forgiveness, they must show:

○ a genuine sorrow for what they have done
○ a readiness to forgive those who have offended them
○ a willingness to change their way of life and to make amends.

The sacrament of Reconciliation

The sacrament of Reconciliation celebrates the loving forgiveness of God.

The ceremony for individual confession consists of the following.

- *Confession* — The *penitent* (the person seeking forgiveness) declares his/her sorrow for any sins committed and admits responsibility to the priest, who is the representative of the Church.

- *Penance* — The penitent must be prepared to make up for what he/she has done. Penance may be a prayer or an act designed to help the person overcome his/her selfishness, such as helping to care for an elderly relative.

- *Act of Contrition* — This is a formal prayer said by the penitent which expresses his/her sorrow and a firm commitment not to sin again.

- *Absolution* — The priest says: *I absolve you of your sins in the name of the Father, and of the Son, and of the Holy Spirit. Amen.*

Confession by Edwin Longsden Long.

The sacrament of Reconciliation is so-called because *it reconciles people with God and with each other*. It expresses the belief that through the power of God's Holy Spirit and the actions of the priest, forgiveness of sins may be given. It reminds Christians that they can return God's love by living good lives.

Questions

1. What does the parable of the *Prodigal Son* say about God's forgiveness?
2. Summarise the parable of the *Unforgiving Servant* and explain what it says about forgiving others.
3. Read the story of *Gordon Wilson* once more. If more people followed his example, how could that help to resolve conflicts between people and nations?
4. What are *three* things that Jesus said are required to receive God's forgiveness?
5. What is a *penitent*?
6. Why is the sacrament of *Reconciliation* known by that title?
7. What is the purpose of requiring a person to do *penance*?

Chapter Forty-six

Law and Morality

Introduction

On First Avenue at Forty-Sixth Street in New York City stands a massive building of glass and marble. It is the headquarters of the United Nations. Outside it flutter the flags of its member states. We may define a *state* as

> *a community of people organised under a government.*

The role of the state

Christians and non-Christians agree that:

- the state has a duty to protect the *rights* of its citizens, i.e. *those basic entitlements which people need to promote and defend their dignity as human beings*
- the state must maintain peace and order among its citizens.

The state does these things by setting out *laws* and insisting on its citizens obeying them.

Law

The figure of Justice, Dublin Castle.

We may define a *law* as

> *a rule set out by the state authorities permitting some forms of behaviour and prohibiting others, which its citizens are obliged to obey.*

All laws should be designed with the aim of protecting the rights of *all* members of a society. Those who break the law should be punished.

Laws and rights

Freedom of speech is a fundamental human right.

> *Everyone has the right to freedom of opinion and expression; this right includes freedom to hold opinions without interference and to seek, receive and impart information and ideas through any media and regardless of frontiers.* (Article 19, Universal Declaration of Human Rights)

Law and Morality 283

Every state should protect freedom of speech in its laws.

In a democracy, people are free to think and speak as they choose. However, people do *not* have an unlimited freedom of speech. The law of the state imposes certain *limits* on the freedom of speech in order to uphold the common good.

For example, the following are against the law:

- Making false statements about someone that damages his/her reputation. When written this is called *libel*, and when spoken it is called *slander*.
- Using abusive or threatening language or behaviour intended to incite racial or religious hatred.

Questions

1. Explain the following terms: (a) *the state* (b) *human rights* (c) *a law*.
2. What is meant by *freedom of speech*?
3. Give two examples where it might be necessary to *limit* the freedom of speech in the interest of the common good.

Obeying the law

It is important to distinguish between *law* and *morality*. Generally speaking, people are obliged to obey the law of the land. Where an *illegal act* is committed (the law is broken), the person who has done so is held responsible and, if caught, will be put on trial. If found guilty, he/she will be punished.

However, simply because a law of the state says that certain behaviour is unacceptable does *not* automatically make it morally wrong.

For example, a person may be obliged by the law to join his/her country's armed forces in time of war. However, a person would be *morally* obliged to refuse military service if he/she was a committed pacifist; for example, members of the Society of Friends are opposed to all forms of violence.

Some people think that the law of the state should be the *only* standard by which people decide what is right and what is wrong. However, the law can sometimes be used to *deprive* people of something to which they are rightfully entitled. What is legal may *not* necessarily be moral. Consider the following example.

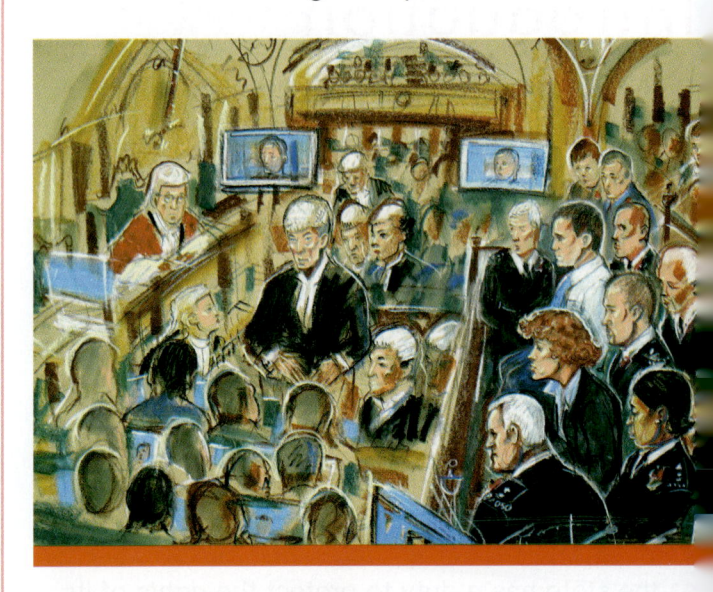

Case study: apartheid

Apartheid was a system of segregation (dividing people) that came into operation in South Africa with the Population Registration Act of 1948. Every citizen was given a racial label – white, coloured, Asian, Chinese or black – and each black person was classified according to tribe.

Every inch of the country was divided into segregated districts and it became illegal (against the law) for non-white people to live or work outside their allocated areas.

More than 3.5 million people lost their homes and businesses through the Group Areas Act of 1950, which allowed the whites to take possession of the prime residential and business areas and to set up a system of racially segregated transportation, education, leisure facilities and even public toilets. Some jobs were advertised as being 'for whites only'.

The movement of black people between the areas was controlled by the notorious Pass Laws. Black workers had to carry a pass at all times and would be allowed or refused entry into a district only after showing this document. The most serious restrictions on freedom came in 1956, when black and coloured voters were removed from the electoral rolls.

By 1969 the South African government had passed a series of laws enabling it to suppress all criticism of its racial policies. The police could arrest and detain citizens without trial, withholding their right to see a lawyer and prohibiting them access to their own families.

This catalogue of pro-white, anti-black legislation created an atmosphere in which violent protest became inevitable. A long, hard struggle was fought before civil rights for all citizens were reinstated in the 1990s.

Frank McLynn, *Famous Trials: Cases That Made History*

Whites-only beach in South Africa before the end of apartheid.

Law and morality

Christians believe that people should respect and obey the laws of the state, but they should *not* do so blindly. People are only obliged to obey a law if it is morally right to do so. Jesus said:

> *Render to Caesar the things that are Caesar's; and to God the things that are God's.* (Luke 20:25)

Christians believe that the state does *not* have the final say as to what is right and what is wrong. There is a *higher* standard, which is *not* set by human beings. It is for this reason that the Catholic Church teaches:

> *God's law continues to bind no matter what the civil (state) law says.*

A person must remember this when making a moral decision.

Questions

1. What is meant by an *illegal act*?
2. Give an example of where a person might believe that disobeying the law of the state is the morally *correct* thing to do.
3. Consider the South African experience of *apartheid*. What does it say about the view that the law of the state should be the *only* standard by which people decide what is right and what is wrong? Give two examples from the above extract to support your answer.
4. In what circumstances do Christians believe that people should respect and obey the laws of the state?

Law and Morality

Law in Islam

Islamic imams in discussion.

The ideal Muslim society is a *theocracy*, i.e. where a state is governed by laws based on the teachings of Islam.

Over the centuries, Islamic leaders and scholars have compiled an all-embracing code of morality and law called the *Shari'a*, which all Muslims are expected to faithfully observe. This is why in most countries with an Islamic majority, the following things are forbidden and punishable by the law of the state:

- adultery
- consumption of alcohol
- astrology
- gambling
- use of unprescribed drugs
- prostitution
- dancing between men and women.

Muslims strongly defend the *Shari'a* against the charge that it is too harsh. They point out that:

- Statistics for crime and violence are much *lower* in Islamic countries than in non-Islamic ones.
- Non-Muslims living in a Muslim state do *not* have to become Muslims. However, they must abide by Islamic law.

Questions

1. What is a *theocracy*?
2. What is the *Shari'a*?
3. Identify three things forbidden and punishable according to the *Shari'a*.
4. How do Muslims respond to the claim that the *Shari'a* is unnecessarily harsh?

Chapter Forty-seven

Exploring Moral Issues

1. Abortion

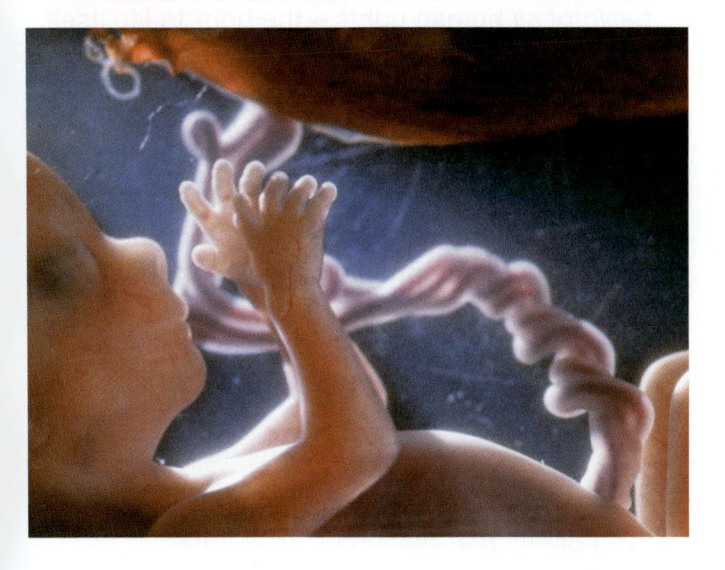

An abortion* may be defined as

> *any procedure that deliberately ends a pregnancy and causes the death of an unborn child.*

In an abortion, the unborn child is removed from the womb usually *before* he/she is capable of life independent from his/her mother.

The *methods* used to carry out an abortion may involve the use of either *surgery* or *drugs*, or a combination of both, depending on the stage the mother's pregnancy has reached.

*N.B.
An abortion must be distinguished from a *miscarriage*, i.e. where an unborn child is *spontaneously* expelled from a mother's womb *without* any outside intervention.

Reasons for Abortion

1. Where a woman is poor and fears that she will be unable to support a child.

2. Where powerful pressure is put on the woman by others who persuade her not to have the child.

3. Where a woman becomes pregnant due to rape or incest.

4. Where there is a fear that the child will be born with a physical and/or mental disability.

The morality of abortion

Although abortion is legal in many countries today, the Catholic Church and most of the other Christian Churches have always held abortion to be morally *wrong*.

The early Christian collection entitled *The Didache* (*The Teaching of the Twelve Apostles*), written in the second century AD, states:

> *You shall not kill the unborn by abortion nor cause the newborn child to perish.*

However, the belief that abortion is unjustifiable *pre-dates* Christianity. The Hippocratic Oath, sworn by Greek doctors from the sixth century BC onwards, states:

> *I will neither give a deadly drug to anybody if asked for it, nor will I make a suggestion to this effect. Similarly, I will not give a woman an abortive remedy.*

The Catholic Church today opposes abortion for the following reasons:

- Human life begins at *conception*, i.e. when a man's sperm and a woman's ovum unite after sexual intercourse to form a new, unique, individual living being.
- Though tiny at first, this new life is *human* in all the stages of his/her development.
- As a member of the human race, he/she is entitled to the same respect and protection due to any person.
- Abortion denies the unborn child his/her *most basic* of *all* human rights – the right to life itself.
- As such, abortion violates the fifth Commandment.
- Human life is *sacred*, i.e. worthy of total respect. Each human being's life is a gift from God, which should be protected from the moment of conception until his/her natural death.

Questions

1. What is meant by the term '*abortion*'?
2. Identify *four* reasons why women sometimes choose to have an abortion.
3. (a) What is the *Hippocratic Oath*?
   (b) What does it say about abortion?
4. Why does the Catholic Church oppose abortion?
5. What does it mean to say that *human life is sacred*?

Challenges

Where there is a medical crisis

Since *both* mother and unborn child are human beings, it is a doctor's duty to regard *both* of them as *patients*. If a medical crisis arises, the doctor must try to sustain the pregnancy as long as there is a reasonable prospect of saving the lives of *both* the mother and her unborn child.

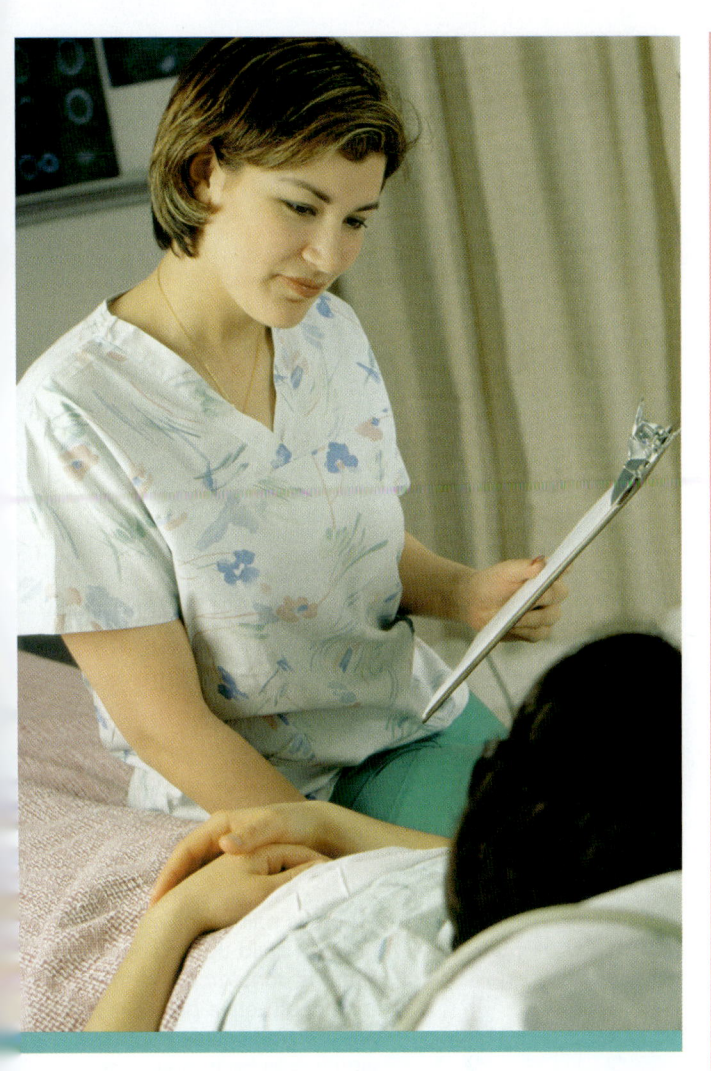

The Catholic Church teaches that essential medical treatment should always be given to a pregnant woman, for example chemotherapy for breast cancer, which tragically occurs in an estimated one per 1,000 pregnancies. This treatment may be given even if it results in the death of the unborn child, *provided* that two conditions are met:

i) the death of the unborn child is *not* a directly intended consequence of the treatment given

and

ii) there is *no other* effective way of managing the treatment of the woman successfully.

Where the woman is a victim of rape

Rape is a horrific crime. The victims of rape need support, sympathy and understanding. Many need skilled help, not just immediately, but for a long time after the event to try to heal the emotional damage they have suffered.

The victim of rape has a right to seek medical help with a view to *preventing* conception. This is done by removing the rapist's sperm *before* fertilisation occurs. This medical procedure is *not* an abortion because conception has not yet happened. The Catholic Church teaches that such action is morally right. It is part of a woman's legitimate resistance to the rapist's attack.

Although pregnancy after rape is *rare*, it does sometimes happen. The Catholic Church teaches that this is a situation which requires great sensitivity with a careful balance of compassion for the victim and protection of the unborn child.

The child developing in the woman's womb is a *new human being*. As such, his/her life must be protected. This child is *not* responsible for what has happened. The child *cannot* rightly be made to pay with his/her life for the man's crime in violating the woman.

Where there is a threat of suicide

Studies show that:

○ suicide in pregnancy is a rare event

○ suicide is more common in the *post-delivery period*, i.e. after the baby is born

○ women are more likely to commit suicide *after* an abortion than during pregnancy

○ a threat of suicide by a pregnant woman is *a desperate cry for help*. There are people willing to answer this call.

Exploring Moral Issues **289**

CURA

CURA offers information, advice and counselling to any woman, married or single, faced with the dilemma of an unwanted pregnancy.

CURA's experienced counsellors seek to help a woman explore the various options and reach an informed decision about her pregnancy. Help offered includes accommodation and medical treatment, at no expense to the woman herself, during the pregnancy if she is prepared to allow the baby to be born and not aborted.

CURA also offers help to women who have had an abortion, but who have later come to regret doing so.

Contact numbers for CURA's confidential telephone service can be found in local telephone directories.

Questions

1. Explain the teaching of the Catholic Church regarding treatment of a pregnant woman suffering from cancer.
2. What medical treatment should a victim of rape seek as soon as possible after suffering such a horrific crime?
3. Why does the Catholic Church oppose abortion in the case of a woman made pregnant as a result of rape?
4. What do studies reveal about suicide and pregnancy?
5. Give a brief account of the services CURA offers a woman facing a crisis pregnancy.
6. In each case below, state the consequences of each choice for (a) the woman and (b) her child.

Questions

A woman discovers that she is pregnant

```
                    CHOICE
                   /       \
         She can have    She can have an
           the baby         abortion
             |                  |
           CHOICE               ?
          / |    \
     Keep  Keep the baby but   Give the baby
     the   have him/her        up for
     baby  fostered for a time  adoption*
      |         |                  |
      |         ?                  ?
     / \
    If   If
  married single
    |     |
    ?     ?
```

*There *is* pain involved in giving a child up for adoption. But it is *constructive* rather than destructive pain. There are many childless couples who would be happy to adopt a child.

2. War

A Russian woman cries over the body of her husband.

Politics has been defined as

the art of solving problems without the use of violence.

When politics fail, people often turn to violence to settle a dispute. Violence can take many forms, ranging from verbal abuse to physical harm.

War is the most destructive form of physical conflict and may be defined as:

armed hostilities between two groups in which each side puts people forward to fight and kill.

Those who respect human life cannot be indifferent to the issue of war. Consider the *cost* of war:

- loss of life
- survivors' physical and mental suffering
- refugee crisis
- destruction of property
- enormous debt.

The causes of war

The causes of war are numerous:

1. The desire to overthrow an oppressive and unjust government.
2. The struggle for national independence, i.e. when a people forcibly expel an oppressive *foreign* ruler.
3. The clash of opposing political outlooks, such as between fascism and communism in World War II.
4. The eruption of racial hatred and/or religious bigotry.
5. The lust for power by an individual or group and the subjugation of a population by force.
6. The fear of a threatening, militaristic neighbour launching a surprise attack.
7. The desire for revenge in order to undo a defeat in a previous conflict.
8. One state's economic ambition to seize the natural resources of another.

The just war theory

Last rites being performed for six US airmen killed in Afghanistan.

One influential Christian response to the awful reality of war is known as the *just war theory*. It was developed by two Christian saints, Augustine and Thomas Aquinas. It acknowledges that as an individual person has a right to self-defence, so too must a community or state have the right to protect itself when its basic rights are threatened.

The just war theory aims to:

- identify those conditions whereby a community/state would be morally justified in going to war

and

- put restraints on how people conduct the war so as to limit the harm inflicted.

Augustine and Thomas Aquinas held that moral standards applied in wartime just as they do in peacetime. They set out the just war theory to provide guidance to people when making the difficult decisions that have to be made about war. However, even if all the conditions for a war to be

Exploring Moral Issues 291

termed *just* are met, this in *no way* means that war is ever to be considered either desirable or good.

Indeed, war is usually the result of failures on *both* sides and it is *rare* that one side is entirely right and the other side entirely wrong. We shall now examine the conditions for a just war.

Conditions for a just war

1. **Just cause:** The war must be one of defence against an unprovoked attack.
2. **Right intention:** The aim of those going to war must be to restore peace and achieve reconciliation. It must not be an act of revenge.
3. **Last resort:** All other ways must be explored before going to war. All negotiations must be tried and have failed, and all peaceful alternatives must be exhausted.
4. **Likelihood of success:** There must be a reasonable hope that the objectives for which the war is fought can be achieved. If a country is hopelessly outgunned by the aggressor (the attacking side) and has no chance of victory, then the harm caused by war could be greater than that caused by surrender.
5. **Principle of proportion:** The war should not inflict more suffering than would be experienced by *not* going to war.
6. **Safety of non-combatants:** Civilians should never be the intended targets of the war. Nothing can justify the indiscriminate killing of civilian populations.

Questions

1. What is meant by *war*?
2. In what ways do people *suffer* in wars?
3. Read the following statements. In each case state whether you agree or disagree with them. Give reasons for your answers.

Questions

(a) All wars are caused by power-hungry individuals. If Hitler had not existed, World War II would never have taken place.

(b) People's greed and their desire for material wealth, land and possessions is at the root of many wars.

(c) War, conflict and violence are a part of human nature. Humans are naturally aggressive creatures. Thus, war can never be completely eliminated.

4. Name the two Christian thinkers who set out the just war theory.
5. List the *six conditions* for a just war.
6. Consider the following situations. In each case explain why they would be *against* the conditions of the just war theory.
   - Refusal to enter into negotiations to prevent war occurring.
   - Attacking an immeasurably more powerful opponent in certain knowledge of one's own defeat.
   - Shooting prisoners of war.
   - Bombing civilian targets such as hospitals in order to demoralise the enemy population.
7. Having considered the just war theory, can the use of nuclear weapons in warfare *ever* be justified? Give reasons for your answer.

Jihad

Jihad is often understood by non-Muslims to simply mean a *holy war* against those considered to be enemies of Islam. In fact, it has a broader meaning. The word 'jihad' comes from the Arabic phrase '*jihad fi sabee Allah*', which means '*striving in God's cause*'.

Jihad can be understood as the duty of every Muslim to:

- be faithful to the teachings of Islam in his/her daily life
- ensure that its teachings are spread
- defend Islam against attack.

Jihad *can* take the form of physical violence. The Qur'an, however, forbids Muslims to engage in unprovoked aggression.

> *Fight in the way of Allah, against those who fight against you. But do not begin hostilities. Allah loveth no aggressors.*

Muslims believe that it is their duty to resist any threat to Islam by force if it becomes necessary either by direct action or by supporting those who carry out acts of violence in the defence of Islam.

Questions

1. What is the meaning of the Arabic phrase '*jihad fi sabee Allah*'?
2. What does the Qur'an teach Muslims about war?
3. Muslims believe that *jihad* means they must fulfil certain *duties*. What are they?

Pacifism

Christians who accept the just war theory agree that war is always morally wrong whenever those involved *deliberately* commit such acts as:

- murdering non-combatants, i.e. the wounded, children and the aged
- torturing or executing prisoners

The Peaceable Kingdom by Quaker artist Edward Hicks.

- cutting off food and water to civilian populations
- causing people to die from disease and starvation.

Opponents of the just war theory point out, however, that it is very difficult to avoid causing harm to innocent people in time of war. As a result they reject war of *any* kind.

Those who object out of conscience to all forms of warfare are called *pacifists*. They refuse to fight in wars and try to find other, non-violent ways to solve conflicts between people.*

In times of war, however, some pacifist volunteers serve as stretcher-bearers and medics in an effort to save lives.

Pacifists use non-violent forms of protest to bring about change, such as:

- peaceful demonstrations or sit-ins
- boycotting shops selling products made using child labour
- writing letters of protest to newspapers.

*N.B.
All members of the Society of Friends are pacifists. They are opposed to *all* forms of violence.

During World War I and II, many members of the Society of Friends were conscientious objectors. The Friends Ambulance Units of both the US and British armies were run by pacifists. They did not take part in combat. Instead, they risked their lives rescuing injured soldiers from the battlefield and carrying them to hospitals for treatment.

Exploring Moral Issues

Profile: Mahatma Gandhi

Mahatma Gandhi on hunger strike to persuade Muslims and Hindus to reconcile.

One of the most famous pacifists of modern times was Mohandas K. Gandhi (1869–1948), who became known as the *Mahatma* (meaning '*great soul*'). He was also leader of the nationalist movement that sought India's independence from Britain.

Gandhi developed *satyagraha* (meaning '*steadfastness in truth*'), the theory and practice of non-violent resistance. He believed that the refusal to retaliate or to use any form of violence would eventually defeat any opponent, though it would demand great self-sacrifice and suffering.

In 1920, Gandhi became leader of the Indian National Congress, which adopted a policy of non-cooperation with the British administration. He led protest marches against unjust British policies (such as the 1930 tax on salt) and encouraged boycotting British goods (especially clothing). Gandhi was imprisoned on many occasions.

Eventually, India gained its independence from Britain in 1947. Tragically, Gandhi was assassinated by a Hindu extremist on 30 January 1948.

Peace

Those Christians who believe that war is sometimes tragically necessary or unavoidable *never* accept it as a good thing. Human life can only flourish where there is *peace*.

Peace is neither easily achieved nor maintained. Peace means far more than the absence of war.

Jesus taught that peace can only come about and be sustained when people live according to the new way of life he referred to as the *Kingdom of God*, i.e. where people allow God's love to reign in their hearts and struggle to live according to God's standards.

This means that people must seek to:

- treat one another with *respect*, not contempt
- replace envy and fear with *love*
- promote *trust* instead of distrust
- ensure *fair treatment* for all and end the exploitation of the poor and weak by the rich and powerful.

Questions

1. What does it mean to be a *pacifist*?
2. Why do some people become pacifists?
3. How do some pacifists help reduce people's suffering in time of war?
4. Explain the meaning of *non-violent protest*.
5. What is the meaning of Gandhi's title '*the Mahatma*'?
6. What is *satyagraha*? Explain how it works.
7. Why is *peace* important?
8. What did Jesus teach about how peace can come about and be maintained?

3. Prejudice and discrimination

Prejudice

A Canadian social researcher wrote letters in response to 100 holiday advertisements. In each case he asked the hotel manager to reserve a room for him. He wrote two letters to each hotel, looking for a room on identical dates but using a different name on each letter. One name was obviously *Jewish*, while the other was not.

Ninety-nine per cent of the hotels offered the non-Jewish enquirer accommodation, but the Jewish enquirer was only offered accommodation in thirty-six per cent of the same hotels.

Why did almost two-thirds of the hotels' management react so negatively to the request for a room from the 'Jewish' enquirer? The answer is that they were *prejudiced*. We may define prejudice as

> *the act of making up one's mind before finding out the facts and reaching a decision without good reasons to support it.*

A deeply prejudiced person is one who refuses to change his/her views even when confronted with the truth.

A fair-minded person does not reach a decision about someone or something until *after* considering the facts.

It is often only when one has been on the receiving end of prejudice that one comes to realise how unfair it is and how much harm it can cause.

Discrimination

Wherever people are treated badly or unfairly simply because others are prejudiced against them, it is said that these people are victims of *discrimination*.

People are usually discriminated against on the grounds that they belong to a particular:

- race
- religion
- gender (usually female)
- age (especially the elderly)
- disability (physical or mental).

The Universal Declaration of Human Rights passed by the United Nations states that *every* human being must be accorded the same respect. Sadly, however, prejudice and discrimination are still widespread.

We shall consider two examples of this:

1. racism
2. sexism.

Exploring Moral Issues

Racism

We may define *racism* as

prejudice against people of another race or ethnic group.

Racism has proven to be one of the *most destructive* forces in human history.

Racists believe that all human beings can be divided up into separate racial groups. Most of these groups will be considered *inferior*, while the group to which the racist belongs will be identified as *superior*, perhaps the *only* superior race.

Scientifically speaking, this is *nonsense*. Differences in skin colour, facial structure and so on are of no real significance. *All* people are members of the *same* biological species – *the human race*.

Hostility towards people of other races can range from mild dislike to an extreme hatred, which can be expressed in acts of violence or in passing laws to deprive people of their rights. Where racism is put into practice in this way, it is called *racial discrimination*.

Historical examples of this would be:

- the persecution of Jewish people by the Nazis before and during World War II
- the treatment of the native people of South Africa under the apartheid regime in the twentieth century.

Racism has long been recognised as evil and destructive. In the Old Testament, for example, the Jews were instructed to treat other races with respect:

Do not ill-treat foreigners who are living in your land. Treat them as you would a fellow-Israelite, and love them as you love yourselves. Remember that you were once foreigners in the land of Egypt. I am the Lord your God. (Leviticus 19:33–34)

In the New Testament, Jesus made it clear that the Kingdom of God is open to *all* people. Consider both

- the healing of the Roman centurion's servant in Luke 7:1–10

and

- the parable of The Good Samaritan in Luke 10:25–37.

Sexism

Non-governmental Organizations Forum on Women, Beijing, China, 1995.

Sexism can be defined as

the view that one sex is inferior to the other, in particular, that women are less able in most ways than men.

The term 'sexism' was first used in the 1960s by *feminists*, i.e. those who work to obtain equal rights and fair treatment for women.

Feminists point out that, until very recently, Western society was largely *patriarchal*, i.e. dominated by men, who made all the important decisions without consulting women.

For thousands of years, women were regarded chiefly as possessions, as the personal property of their fathers or husbands. Women were denied the right to choose how to live their lives. A woman could be married off without any consideration for her happiness. Unfortunately, this is still the case in many parts of the world.

Consider how women form more than half the earth's population, and yet:

- Two out of every three illiterate people are women because of their lack of educational opportunities.
- Women work two-thirds of the world's working hours, yet they only receive one-tenth of the income and they own a mere one-hundredth of its property.
- While women everywhere are overburdened in the home, in poor countries they are also the main food producers. But most of the technology, finance and training in agriculture is given to men.
- In Developing World primary schools there are only five girls for every seven boys. Thus, lack of education and heavy responsibilities keep women isolated and weak – unable to get together to take their rightful share.
- Violation of the human rights of women and female children are extensive and severe. Many women are targeted because they are leaders in the struggle for freedom and justice. Others are victimised because they are seen to be vulnerable, because they can be used to put pressure on male relatives or because of the inferior status of women in their societies. Some are imprisoned, tortured and killed simply because they are unfortunate enough to be in the wrong place at the wrong time.
- Some couples choose to abort a female baby because they have a preference for a male child. The Catholic Church has condemned the killing of unborn female babies following gender testing.

However, thanks to many decades of tireless campaigning, feminists have achieved notable *reforms*. In the Developed World, for instance, it is now recognised by law that:

- women over eighteen years of age are entitled to vote
- women can stand for election to the national parliament
- women are entitled to equal pay for work of equal value
- women have equal employment opportunities and cannot be discriminated against on the basis of gender.

Feminists point out, however, that sexist attitudes towards women can still be seen in the way some people use language, such as using the word '*mankind*' when referring to the whole human race, i.e. men *and* women.

Also, many men still assume that certain jobs should *only* be performed by men. They can sometimes place serious obstacles in the way of women, which men would not encounter. It remains difficult for women to achieve positions of influence in society as a result.

The way forward

St Paul Preaching at Athens by Raphael.

Exploring Moral Issues 297

A person's race or gender are unimportant to God. As Paul wrote:

> *So there is no difference between Jews and Gentiles, between slaves and free men, between men and women, you are all one in union with Christ Jesus.* (Galatians 3:28)

All people are God's children. *All* people are of equal value in God's sight.

Perhaps the only way forward for the human race in the twenty-first century is for people to finally accept that they are *all* members of the *one family of God*. People must not try to evade their responsibilities to respect one another and treat each other with compassion and generosity. This is the only way that lasting peace and justice can ever be achieved.

Questions

1. What is *prejudice*?
2. What is a *fair-minded* person?
3. What is *discrimination*?
4. Identify four groups who are often *victims* of discrimination.
5. Explain the following terms: (a) *racism* (b) *racial discrimination*.
6. What is *sexism*?
7. What does it mean to say that, until very recently, Western society was *patriarchal*?
8. What is a feminist?
9. Identify *four* important rights which women are guaranteed by law in Western society.
10. What is perhaps the *only way forward for the human race in the twenty-first century*? Why?

4. The environment

Clouds Passing over Ben More by Henry Bright.

The word '*environment*' means

the world and everything in it.

Jews, Christians and Muslims believe that:

- the environment was created by God
- the environment is a gift from God to human beings
- the environment is *sacred*, i.e. worthy of honour and respect
- human beings have a special responsibility to care for the environment.

Environmental problems

A scene from the film *The Day After Tomorrow*.

In order to survive and thrive, human beings need clean air, water, food, shelter and medicines. The earth can provide for *all* these needs if properly managed. Unfortunately, much damage has been inflicted on the environment by what human beings have done or by what they have failed to do.

Some of the areas of greatest concern are:

- **The destruction of the rainforests.**
  The world's rainforests are being cut down at such a rate that within fifty years they will have disappeared entirely. This would be a *catastrophe*. The rainforests provide oxygen that enables us *to breathe*.
  Unfortunately, most of the countries in which the rainforests are located show little willingness to stop this policy. They owe heavy debts to Western banks and say that they need the money from deforestation programmes to pay off their loans.

- **The threat of global warming.**
  An increase in the production of carbon dioxide and other gases has contributed to an increase in the earth's temperature. It is feared that this may trigger major *changes* in the planet's climate.

- **The danger of nuclear waste.**
  The nuclear power industry produces large quantities of *radioactive* waste. Most of this is stored in special facilities.
  This waste has to be transported to such sites. It will remain highly radioactive and lethal for *thousands* of years. Future generations will have to cope with the consequences of today's decisions.

- **The harm caused by acid rain.**
  Industrialised nations burn large quantities of *fossil fuels*, e.g. oil and coal. These produce *sulphur oxides* that fall as acid rain, killing trees and poisoning waterways.

- **The prevention of future medical breakthroughs.**
  Half of all medicines come from plants, e.g. *morphine* comes from poppies and *quinine* comes from trees grown in the Amazonian rainforest. The ongoing destruction of the rainforests may deprive the human race of cures for serious illnesses in the future.

The delicate balance

More and more people are beginning to realise that the human race can no longer afford to wreak havoc on the earth without experiencing disastrous consequences.

To illustrate, consider the following story.

There was a rule for people who were climbing the mountain that above a certain point no living things were to be killed. The climbers had to carry all their food.

One day someone who was walking on the mountain above that point was caught in a violent snowstorm. For three days he lived in a makeshift shelter with no food in near-freezing conditions. On the third day the blizzard ended. He saw a very fat old rat crawling out of a hole and thought there would be no harm in killing the rat so that he could feed himself and get down the mountain. Somehow he managed to get a stone and kill the rat. He made it down the mountain and did not think any more about it.

Some time later he was called before the tribunal of guides, that is, of people responsible for the mountain and the path. He was called to account for the killing of the rat, an event that by this time he had forgotten. It seemed there had been serious consequences. The rat, being very old, was not strong enough to catch the healthy insects, and so it fed on the diseased insect population. When the rat was killed there was no natural check on the diseased insects. Disease spread through the whole species and they all died off.

The insects had been responsible for pollinating and fertilising much of the plant growth on the mountainside. When the insects died off, without fertilisation, the vegetation started to diminish. The plant life had been holding the soil in place and when the vegetation began to die the soil started to erode.

Eventually, there was a great landslide, which killed many people who were climbing up the mountain, and blocked the path for a long time. All of this the outcome of the seemingly insignificant act of killing the old rat.

Source: *Mount Analogue* by Rene Daumal.

This story illustrates a vitally important point: all living things – humans, animals and plants – are part of a vast, *complex chain* where all living things *depend* on one another.

The loss of one species of animal or plant can have a devastating effect upon the other living things that depend on it. If enough links in the chain of life are broken, then the *very survival* of the human race will be at stake.

There is a very *delicate balance of life* on Earth. Human beings must recognise this fact and act accordingly. To fail to do so is to invite *disaster*.

Stewardship

A *change* in the way most people relate to the natural world is needed.

Environmental campaigners have made it clear that if the human race is to have a future, then people will have to adopt a whole new outlook as to how they *relate* to the fragile environment of this planet.

Christians believe that the basis for this *new relationship* between humans and the two million other species that share our planet can be found in the Bible.

In the Old Testament it is written of the first humans that:

> *God blessed them, and God said to them; Be Fruitful and multiply and fill the earth and subdue it; and have dominion over the fish of the sea and over the birds of the air and over every living thing that moves upon the earth.* (Genesis 1:28)

However, God makes it clear that:

> *the land belongs to me and you are only strangers and guests.* (Leviticus 25:23)

Sacred scripture makes it very clear that human beings are *not* the owners of the world. Rather, they are called to be *God's stewards*.

The word '*steward*' means someone who:

- has been appointed to care for the world on God's behalf
- should not give in to purely selfish interests but be wise and trustworthy
- has a responsibility to hand on the world in a living and fertile state to future generations
- must try to put things right where they have gone wrong in the past.

Human beings must take the responsibility God has given them seriously, before it is too *late*.

Practical steps

The following are some of the practical steps people can take to fulfil their roles as *stewards of the environment*:

- try to be *less wasteful* of food, fuel and resources
- try to *recycle* paper, glass, metals and other products
- use *biodegradable* products, i.e. those that cause no harm to nature
- join *organisations* that campaign to protect the environment, e.g. Friends of the Earth, Greenpeace or the Worldwide Fund for Nature
- use *votes* in elections to support political candidates who are committed to protecting the environment and will actually do something to improve the situation if elected.

Questions

1. What is meant by the *environment*?
2. What do Jews, Christians and Muslims believe about the environment?
3. Identify and describe any three important areas of environmental concern today.
4. What is meant by the *delicate balance of nature*?

Questions

5. Read the following extract and answer the question below.

   All things are connected like the blood which unites one family. All things are connected. Whatever befalls the earth befalls the sons of the earth. Man did not weave the web of life; he is merely a strand in it. Whatever he does to the web he does to himself.

   Chief Seattle of the Duwamish tribe when the US government was forcing him to accept the purchase of his tribe's lands in 1854

   What point does Chief Seattle make about the importance of preserving the delicate balance of nature?

6. Read the following:

   The land belongs to me [God] and you are only strangers and guests. (Leviticus 25:23)

   What point is being made here about human beings and the earth?
7. What is meant by *stewardship*?
8. State four practical steps by which people can act as *stewards of the environment*.

Exploring Moral Issues

Part Eleven

LIFE AFTER DEATH

Chapter Forty-eight

Reasons for Hope

Introduction

Self-portrait with Death as a Fiddler by Arnold Böcklin.

From earliest times, human beings have believed in some form of life after death. Archaeologists excavating Border Cave in southern Africa have found indications that this belief may be at least 50,000 years old. They discovered the remains of an infant buried in a shallow grave. Alongside the little corpse was a small, perforated sea shell. This shell had to have been brought there from another site at least fifty miles away. Perhaps those who buried this infant believed that this little item would be of use in the afterlife, whatever they believed that to be.

Today, each of the major world religions offers its own answer as to what in particular happens after death. What is significant, however, is that despite all the ways in which the major religions may differ on the particular details, they all agree on one central point: death is not the end for human beings.

Death

According to the World Health Organization guidelines, a person is pronounced dead when it has been firmly established that:

○ his/her brain has ceased to control the vital functions of his/her body
○ there is no evidence of muscular activity or blood pressure
○ he/she is unable to breathe without the aid of a life-support machine.

Therefore, we may define *death* as

the permanent ending of all the bodily functions that keep a person alive.

The word '*dying*' refers to the *way* in which a person's life comes to an end.

Most people are anxious about death, often fearful at the prospect of dying. This is a uniquely *human* concern; human beings are the *only* creatures on this planet that know they must one

Reasons for Hope 305

day die. We know that all things in the universe, from stars to snowdrops, have a certain, limited lifespan. Death is an *inescapable fact*.

We shall turn next to consider two *different* religious views on what happens to the human person *after* death:

○ the *Christian* view

○ the *Hindu* view.

Life after death: the Christian view

The source of hope

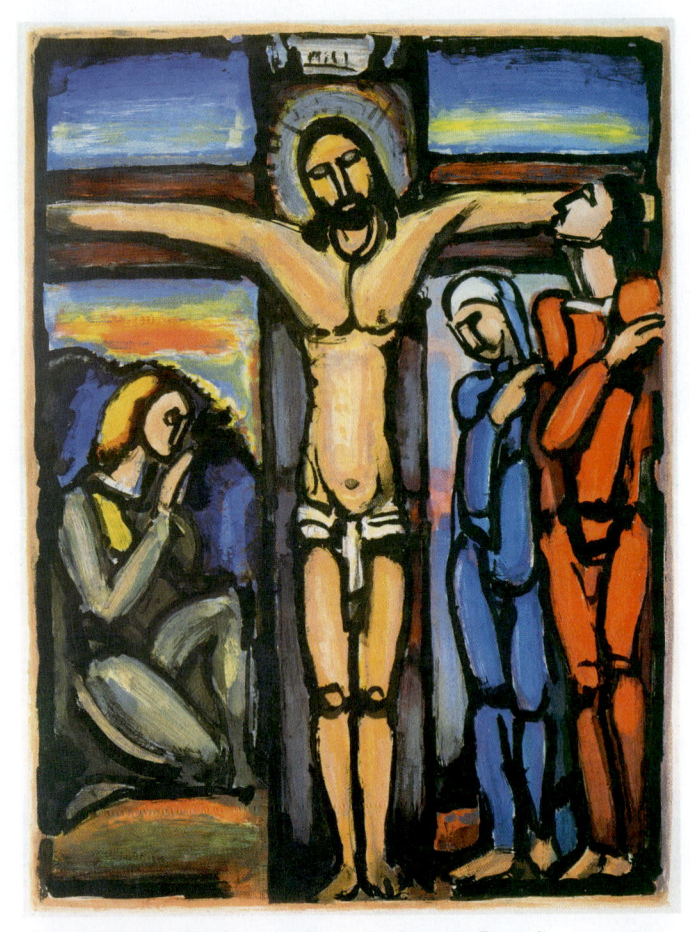

Christ en Croix (Christ on the Cross) by Georges Rouault.

Humanists believe that:

○ God does not exist

○ life in this world is *all* that there is

○ death marks the *final* end for each person.

Christians, however, believe that:

○ God *does* exist

○ God is utterly good and loving.

As such, it would be *completely out of character* for God to give people life, to encourage them to live good lives and then, one day, to simply annihilate them.

The human person

From conception to old age, the soul is the constant, unchanging core of each individual man and woman's personality as he/she goes through life.

Consider what it *means* to be a human being:

○ of all the creatures that inhabit the earth, *only humans* are capable of imagining, choosing, planning, loving and worshipping

○ humans are *unique*

○ the source of these unique capacities in each human being is called the *soul*.

Each person has *two aspects* to his/her nature:

○ a *body* – the visible, *physical* aspect of a human being

○ a *soul* – the invisible, *spiritual* aspect of a human being.

The soul *gives life* to the body.

Christians believe that the soul is *immortal*, i.e. it does not die when separated from the body at death.

However, they also accept that the soul *needs* the body, as it is through their bodies that humans are able to:

306 All About Faith

- recognise other people and be recognised by them
- express themselves and communicate with one another.

As a result, Christians believe that each person's soul will be *reunited* by God with his/her body at the end of time. But to what *kind* of life?

Resurrected life

The Resurrection by Andrea Mantegna.

Christians believe that the risen Jesus reveals what kind of life *after* death is offered to everyone.

- People will *not* merely be restored to their former lives. Rather, they will be *transformed* to live a *new* kind of life.
- This resurrected life will be one *beyond all the limitations of life in this world*. Death will no longer have any power over people.
- Just as the risen Jesus was still recognisably the *same* person the apostles had known *before* his death, so too will *each person survive death with his/her individual identity intact*.
- Death is *not* the end. It should be seen as an *entry* into a new kind of life, one to which *all* people are invited – *eternal life with God*.

Questions

1. What evidence has been found to suggest that human beings have believed in some form of life after death for at least 80,000 years?
2. What is meant by *death*?
3. Why is it said that *death is a uniquely human concern*?
4. Explain the humanist view of death.
5. What is the Christian response to the humanist view of death?
6. Explain each of the following aspects of the human person: (a) the *body* (b) the *soul*.
7. What does it mean to say that the human soul is *immortal*?
8. What do Christians believe will happen to each person's soul *at the end of time*?
9. Describe the kind of *resurrected life* Christians believe Jesus offers them.

Life after death: the Hindu view

Reincarnation

Both Christians and Hindus believe that a human being consists of a body and a soul.

Reasons for Hope

However, they do *not* all agree on how they relate to each other or on what is meant by the soul. For example:

- Christians believe that each person's soul is separate and unique to that person.
- In contrast, Hinduism teaches that a person's soul is *neither* separate *nor* unique.

Hindus refer to the soul as *atma*. They believe that each person's soul is merely a *fragment of Brahman* that has somehow fallen into our world of birth and death. An atma is *trapped* within a human body.

Hinduism teaches that the atma must go through a series of lives and endure a long cycle of birth, death and rebirth. This is called *samsara* (see diagram opposite).

In each cycle the atma takes on a new body and so is *reincarnated*.

Karma

Hindus believe in the Law of Karma, which states:

> *From good must come good, from evil must come evil.*

The word 'karma' can be translated as either 'action' or 'fate'. This is because Hindus believe that an atma's actions in one life decides its fate in the next.

It is for this reason that Hindus have been generally willing to accept the caste system. Many Hindus believe that an atma's caste in its present reincarnation is decided by its *actions* in its previous life. One who has led a good life may be reborn into a *higher* caste. One who has lived a bad life may be reborn into a *lower* caste, or even return in the body of an animal.

When a Hindu dies, his/her body is *cremated* (burned to ashes). The relatives may then scatter the ashes in a holy place, such as the River Ganges, to symbolise their hope that their loved one will be reborn into a higher *caste* or perhaps achieve *nirvana*.

Nirvana

Hindus believe that the atma is trapped in a cycle of birth, death and rebirth, called *samsara*. The only way the atma can escape this is to live a life of such goodness that it can achieve *spiritual perfection*. This is called *nirvana*.

When a very good and holy person dies, the atma finally achieves nirvana. It is released from this world and returns to Brahman. It is then *reabsorbed* into Brahman like a drop of rain returning to the ocean.

[Read this diagram from the bottom upwards.]

The Hindu View of Life

Once a soul has realised these things it does not need to be reborn into the physical world. The soul becomes united to Brahman and does not need a body.

Eventually the soul will be reborn as a person who will be able to live an unselfish life and who will understand that the things of the world don't count because they don't last.

Living a good life will mean that in the next life the soul will be reborn as a person who will be able to understand more about God.

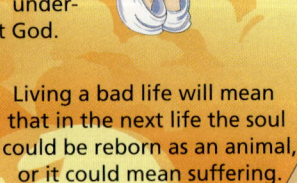

Living a bad life will mean that in the next life the soul could be reborn as an animal, or it could mean suffering.

A soul is reborn many times before it becomes united with Brahman. Your action in one lifetime decides what your next life will be like.

The Hindu doctrine of *samsara*.

308 All About Faith

Questions

1. What do Christians believe about a person's soul?
2. Do Hindus *share* this view of the soul?
3. What is the Hindu name for the soul?
4. What do Hindus believe about the soul?
5. Explain the meaning of *samsara*.
6. What is *reincarnation*?
7. State the *Law of Karma*.
8. Explain the meaning of the term '*karma*'.
9. What happens to the body of a Hindu once he/she dies?
10. What is *nirvana*?
11. What happens to the atma once it achieves nirvana?

Facing death

Most people, whether theists or atheists, are anxious about death. Few people are unaware of the suffering and loneliness it can cause.

Although Christians believe in life after death, this does not mean that they are any more comfortable with the reality of death than anyone else.

As Michael Simpson has written:

> *Belief in the resurrection does not remove the anguish and suffering of death. To pretend that there is no pain in death is to trivialise our human condition.*

The anguish and suffering death can bring is acknowledged in Christian funeral services. While they are sad occasions in which the sorrow of family and friends for the loss of a loved one is recognised, they also contain a strong note of *hope*. Those present are encouraged to trust in Jesus' promise of resurrection and eternal life with him in heaven.

I am the Resurrection and the Life. He who believes in Me will live, even though he dies: and whoever lives and believes in me will never die. (John 11:25–26)

The funeral

Above left When the coffin or ashes are buried, the clergyman reminds people that we came from the ground when Adam was created, and return to the ground at death: 'We commit this body to the ground, earth to earth, ashes to ashes, dust to dust.'

Above right Comforting the grieving.

A funeral service is usually held a few days after the person's death to allow time for contacting people who would want to attend and for making the necessary arrangements for burial or cremation, depending on the wishes of the deceased person.

The body of the deceased person is treated with respect. It is washed, dressed and placed in a *coffin*.

It is then brought to the church, where it is received at the front door by a clergyman.

In the Catholic tradition, a special celebration of the Eucharist, called a *Requiem Mass*, is held. This is attended by the *mourners*, i.e. those who have come to say farewell to their loved one and those who are present to support and express sympathy for his or her family and friends.

Reasons for Hope

Sometimes people attending a funeral wear dark-coloured clothing as a symbol of *sadness*, but this is a custom and *not* a rule of the Church.

The funeral service of all Christian denominations contains a *sermon* in which the clergyman gives thanks to God for the life of the deceased person and for the sacrifice of Jesus, who conquered death and opened the way to eternal life for all people. The *bereaved* (those people who mourn the death of this person) are encouraged to believe that, one day, they will be reunited with him or her in the afterlife.

Following the funeral service, the coffin may be taken either to the graveyard or to the crematorium. Then, the family of the deceased usually holds a reception for those who came to honour and pray for the person who has died. In the days that follow, these people often try to keep in contact with the family and friends of the deceased person and encourage them to talk through their *grief* (feelings of loss and loneliness) and offer support and understanding as they try to come to terms with it.

The Feast of All Souls is celebrated on 2 November, when Catholics pray for those who have died and place flowers on their graves as an act of remembrance and respect.

The priest sprinkles the coffin with holy water to symbolise God's forgiveness of sins.

Questions

1. Explain each of the following terms:
   (a) *coffin* (b) *mourners* (c) *bereaved* (d) *grief*.
2. Why does a priest sprinkle the casket with holy water?
3. What is a *Requiem Mass*?
4. Why do those attending a funeral sometimes wear dark clothing?
5. What is said in the funeral *sermon*?
6. Why is a Christian funeral considered to be both a *sad* event and an occasion of *hope*?

Chapter Forty-nine

The Life Beyond

Introduction

Resurrection of Christ by Master of the Cycle of Vyssi Brod.

Human language is designed to describe life in *this* world. As such, it is of limited value when trying to describe life *after* death. This is because the afterlife is:

- **Spiritual** It is *not* a physical place but a *state of being*, i.e. a life *without* the limits one experiences in this world.
- **Eternal** It is unending life, without a past or a future but only a present, i.e. *an everlasting* now.

The best one can do is to draw analogies as to what life after death is like based on one's experiences of life in *this* world. However, these are only intended to act as helpful images and should *not* be taken literally.

Judgment

Christ, detail of Michelangelo's fresco *The Last Judgement*, 1541, in the Sistine Chapel.

The Life Beyond 311

Christians believe that human life is divided into two phases: life *before* death and life *after* death.

Death does not mark the final end of each person. Rather, death is the moment of *transition* (crossing over) from this life to the next.

Christians trust in the promise of Jesus that they too will experience their own personal resurrection from the dead. They believe that after death, each person will be *judged* (held accountable for his/her behaviour in this life) according to the standards Jesus set.

Read the following Gospel passage.

The Parable of the Sheep and the Goats

When the Son of Man comes in glory, all the nations will be assembled before him and he will separate people one from another as the shepherd separates sheep from goats. He will place the sheep on his right hand and the goats on his left.

Then the Lord will say to those on his right hand, 'Come, you whom my father has blessed, take for your heritage the kingdom prepared for you since the foundation of the world. For I was hungry and you gave me food; I was thirsty and you gave me drink; I was a stranger and you made me welcome; naked and you clothed me, sick and you visited me, in prison and you came to see me.'

Then the virtuous will say to him in reply, 'Lord, when did we see you hungry and feed you; or thirsty and give you drink? When did we see you a stranger and make you welcome; naked and clothe you; sick or in prison and go to see you?'

And the Lord will answer, 'I tell you solemnly, in so far as you did this to one of the least of these brothers and sisters of mine, you did it to me.'

Next he will say to those on his left hand, 'Go away from me. For I was hungry and you never gave me food; I was thirsty and you never gave me anything to drink; I was a stranger and you never made me welcome, naked and you never clothed me, sick and in prison and you never visited me.'

Then it will be their turn to ask, 'Lord, when did we see you hungry or thirsty, a stranger or naked, sick or in prison, and did not come to your help?'

Then he will answer, 'I tell you solemnly, in so far as you neglected to do this to one of the least of these, you neglected to do it to me.'

And they will go away to eternal punishment, and the virtuous to eternal life.
(Matthew 25:31–46)

Comment: If people cannot see God in the people they meet in *this* life, how can they expect to see God in the *next*?

Forgiveness

In this life, it is never too late to repent and to seek God's forgiveness. Consider the story of the *good thief*, who was crucified alongside Jesus.

One of the criminals hanging there mocked him. 'Are you not the Christ?' he said. 'Save yourself and us as well.' But the other spoke up and rebuked him. 'Have you no fear of God at all?' he said. 'We got the same sentence as he did, but in our case we deserved it: we are paying for what we did. But this man has done nothing wrong.' 'Jesus,' he said, 'remember me when you come into your kingdom.' 'Indeed, I promise you,' Jesus replied, 'today you will be with me in paradise.' (Luke 23:39–43)

Comment: God is *always* there, waiting for people to turn towards him. God does *not* force people to behave in certain ways. God gives people the *freedom* to choose how to live their lives. By their moral choices in *this* life, people decide their own fate in the *next* life.

Questions

1. What are the difficulties one faces when trying to talk about life after death?
2. What does it mean to say that people will be *judged* after death?
3. What is the central message of the story of the *good thief*?
4. Why do Christians think it is important to make good moral choices in this life?

Hell

Appearance of Jesus Christ by Francesco Figini Pagani.

Jesus often spoke of *Gehenna*, meaning the unquenchable fire. The Catholic Church follows Jesus' teaching that *hell* exists.

Many people today have difficulty with the whole idea of hell, i.e. an eternity of punishment. They find it hard to reconcile hell with belief in an utterly good and loving God. However, Paul taught the early Christians that:

God wants everyone to be saved.
(1 Timothy 2:4)

Yet this is beyond even the power of God. Why?

The answer to this question is that *God respects human freedom*. God is *not* cruel. God has given human beings the power to choose between good and evil.

Human beings effectively pass judgment upon *themselves* by the way they live their lives in this world.

Consider the following story.

An architect who had worked for a large company for many years and who was soon to retire was called in one day by the board of directors and given plans for a fine house to be built in the best quarter of town. The chairman instructed him to spare no expense, using the finest materials and best builders. As the house began to go up, the architect began to think, 'Why use such costly materials?', so he began to use poor materials and to hire poor-quality workmen, and he put the difference in the cost into his own pocket. When the house was finished, it looked very fine on the outside, but it certainly would not last long.

Shortly after it was finished, the board of directors held another meeting to which the architect was called. The chairman made a speech, thanking the architect for his long service to the company, and as a reward they were making him a retirement present of the house!

If a person *freely* and *knowingly* pursues his/her selfish desires by indulging in a destructive lifestyle, rejecting any involvement in making this world a better place, choosing to cut him/herself off from God and other people, then he/she has *chosen* the alternative to heaven.

Questions

1. Why is it beyond even the power of God for *everyone to be saved*?
2. Read the story of the *architect* once more. Use this story to explain Christian belief about hell.

Purgatory

The word '*purgatory*' is not to be found in the Bible. However, the idea of purgatory can be traced back to the Old Testament (see Second Maccabees 12:45).

Catholics believe that purgatory is required to prepare those people who are not yet ready to enjoy the *Beatific Vision* (to enter God's presence).

Purgatory* is a process of *purification*, where a person roots out or *purges* all those things that prevents him/her from completely loving God and other people.

> '*Before we enter into God's Kingdom, every trace of sin within us must be eliminated, every imperfection in our soul corrected. This is exactly what takes place in purgatory.*' (Pope John Paul II, 1999)

Some people, however, may have *already* done their purgatory in *this* world through their suffering. Others may not. There may be all kinds of barriers in their lives that obstruct their entry into heaven.

As with any experience that helps a person to grow in genuine love, purgatory involves pain, but *not* of a physical kind. The pain of purgatory will be the realisation of how far short one has fallen from loving God and one's neighbour, coupled with a great desire to enter heaven. Once people have allowed God's love to purge those things from their lives that prevent them from loving others as they *should*, God will draw them to share eternal life in heaven.

> *N.B.
> There is no way of knowing how long a person must remain in purgatory. The afterlife does not measure time in the same way as this world. It is beyond our ability to know the answer.

Questions

1. What does it mean to *enjoy the Beatific Vision*?
2. What do Catholics believe about *purgatory*?

Heaven

Triumph of Eternity by Jacopo del Sellaio.

In our twenty-first-century culture, the word 'heaven' conjures up many misleading images – clouds, winged people playing harps and so on. Indeed, the playwright George Bernard Shaw once remarked that people had made heaven sound so dull that no one with a bit of life in them would want to go there.

We need to disregard these popular but *misleading* images of heaven, as they can distract us from developing an accurate, if only limited, understanding of what Christians mean by *heaven*.

When speaking of heaven, people must keep in mind the limitations of human language. As the poet John Donne wrote:

> *The tongues of angels, the tongues of glorified saints shall not be able to express what heaven is.*

Christians believe that those people who have tried with all their heart to love God and their fellow human beings will be brought immediately after death into the presence of God. They will experience the community of perfect love that is heaven.

Heaven is the complete answer to our deepest human longings. There all our worries will be removed, our needs met and our hopes fulfilled. People will enjoy perfect happiness and peace in the presence of God.

This is very difficult for people to grasp here and now, for as Paul wrote:

> *No eye has seen, nor ear has heard, nor the heart of man nor woman conceived what God has prepared for those who love him.* (1 Corinthians 2:9)

Questions

1. Who do Christians believe will be brought immediately after death into the presence of God?

Questions

2. In which experiences of life in *this* world do people catch a glimpse of what heaven is like?
3. Read the following story from China. It explores the difference between heaven and hell.

A small group of people were being led on a tour by a messenger from God.

As they travelled down a long corridor, the messenger opened the first door and told them, 'This is heaven.'

They looked inside and saw a huge banquet table full of delicious foods. All the men and women who sat around the table looked healthy and well fed. And the room was filled with joyful noises. In the hands of all the people were four-foot-long forks that they used to feed one another. Then, the messenger led them to a second door and said, 'And this is hell.'

The door opened. Inside was another huge banquet table filled to overflowing with all sorts of delicious foods. But all the men and women who sat around the table looked horribly gaunt and emaciated. Whining, groaning and angry shouts filled the room. Again, each of the people held a four-foot-long fork, but this time each of them was trying to feed himself or herself.

Christians believe that the kind of person one is or has become at the time of death is the kind of person one *continues to be* in the next life.

How does this story explain the *difference* between those who are in heaven and those who are in hell?

Concluding remarks

Jesus Christ in glory, detail of a mosaic of the early sixth century, SS. Cosmas and Damian, Rome.

I am convinced that there is nothing in death or life – nothing in all creation that can separate us from the love of God in Christ Jesus Our Lord. (Romans 8:38–39)

When someone dies, those who are left behind don't stop loving him/her. Human love refuses to accept division by death. Christians believe that this is all the more true in the case of God's love. They believe that the relationship they have formed with God in this life will *continue* in the next.

God wishes to share eternal life with all people. This is the *destiny* God offers each person. It is an *invitation*, not a command. By their moral decisions, human beings choose their eternal destiny. Yet even if they have spent their entire lives turned away from God, God is ready to forgive, even in the final moments of a person's life. God's love has no limits, it is forever. As Paul writes:

Glossary

agnosticism The belief that it is impossible for human beings to know if God exists or not.

atheism The belief that God does not exist.

blasphemy Any action or statement that displays grave disrespect toward God.

Buddha The title given to Siddhartha Gautama, the founder of Buddhism. Means *'the Enlightened One'*.

Christian Means follower of Jesus Christ, from the Greek word for *'Messiah'* – *'Christos'*.

code A set of guidelines for living offered by a particular religion, which helps people to decide what is the right or the wrong thing to do, e.g. *the Ten Commandments*.

community This exists wherever people:
- live or work together
- share similar interests
- hold broadly similar views about life.

community of faith Where a group of people have a religion in common.

conscience A person's ability to apply his/her values to a particular moral problem and make a decision about what the right thing to do is.

covenant The sacred agreement that God made with the Jewish people.

creed A set of beliefs shared by the members of a religion about God and the meaning of life.

death The permanent ending of all the bodily functions that keep a person alive.

denomination Refers to a separate branch of the Christian religion.

doctrine The official teaching of a religion.

ecumenism The movement which attempts to foster a sense of togetherness across the centuries-old divisions that separate the different Christian denominations from one another.

evangelist Means *'proclaimer of the good news'*. Title given to an author of a Gospel. Refers to Mark, Matthew, Luke and John.

evolution The scientific theory which states that all life – plant, animal and human – has developed from simpler to more complex forms over the course of millions of years.

faith This involves:
- belief in God
- love of God
- belief in the truth of God's revelation
- trust in God's goodness.

formal prayer Can be either a prayer with a fixed format that has been taken from the sacred text of a religion, e.g. the Our Father from the Gospels, or decided upon by the leaders of a particular religion, e.g. the Apostle's Creed.

fundamentalist In the case of a sacred text, this refers to someone who will only accept a *literal* (word for word) reading of it.

heresy What the leaders of a religion consider to be false teachings about God.

human rights Those basic entitlements which each person needs to promote and defend his/her dignity as a human being.

icon From the Greek word meaning '*an image*'. Icons are richly decorated paintings of Jesus, Mary or some other religious figure(s).

idolatry The worship of anyone or anything other than God.

incarnation The belief that in Jesus of Nazareth, God became a human being. Jesus is both fully human and fully divine.

Islam An Arabic word which means '*peace through submission to the revealed will of Allah*'. Name of world's second-largest organised religion.

law A rule set out by the state authorities permitting some forms of behaviour and prohibiting others, which its citizens are obliged to obey.

martyr A person who has died for his/her beliefs.

meditation An inner quieting so that a person can focus his/her whole attention on the mystery of God's love and on how he/she should respond to it.

Messiah Refers to the saviour whom the Jews believed God would send to them.

miracle A marvellous or wonderful event which occurs solely as a result of God's direct action. The Gospels identify four kinds:
○ healing miracles
○ nature miracles
○ exorcisms
○ restorations of life.

monotheism To believe in one God only.

morality A set of beliefs which offer people guidance about the rightness or wrongness of human actions.

moral action Any action that is deliberate, freely chosen and under control of the person doing it.

mortal sin Any seriously wrongful act by which a person destroys his/her relationship with God.

Muslim Name given to member of the Islamic religion. Means '*one who submits*'.

mystery A question to which human beings *cannot* find a complete answer, e.g. *Why do bad things happen to good people*? The major religions help people to gain insights into and grow in their understanding of life's mysteries.

nirvana According to Hindus, this is a state of complete happiness and perfect peace.

oral tradition Important stories and teachings passed on from one generation to the next by word of mouth.

parable An image or story in which a person illustrates some part of his/her message by using concrete examples drawn from everyday life. Examples of Jesus' parables include:
○ The Good Samaritan
○ The Unforgiving Servant.

patriarch This can refer to either:
○ a founding father of Judaism, e.g. Abraham or Moses
    or
○ a leader of an Orthodox Church, e.g. the Patriarch of Moscow (Russian Orthodox Church), the Patriarch of Constantinople (Greek Orthodox Church).

pilgrimage A journey made by a believer to a place that his/her religion considers holy.

polytheism To believe in more than one god.

prayer A conversation from the heart between God and human beings. It is vital for building a strong and lasting relationship with God.

problem A question to which human beings can find a complete answer, e.g. *How is electricity generated*?

prophet A holy man who has received messages from God which he then preaches to people, e.g. Old Testament: Elijah, New Testament: John the Baptist.

religion Belief in and worship of a God or gods.

reincarnation The belief that human beings must endure a long cycle of birth, death and rebirth before they can achieve nirvana.

repent To show sorrow for one's sins and to change one's way of life for the better.

resurrection The belief that Jesus died on the cross on Good Friday and rose from the dead on Easter Sunday.

revelation The way in which God communicates with human beings and tells them things about who God is and how they should live, which they would otherwise not know.

reverence Deep respect for someone or something.

ritual A religious ceremony that:
- gives a regular pattern to people's worship of God
- celebrates the mysterious and invisible presence of God in people's lives through the use of symbols.

sacrament A public ritual in which Catholics recall and re-enact the life, death and resurrection of Jesus Christ. There are seven sacraments:
- Baptism
- Confirmation
- Eucharist
- Reconciliation
- Matrimony
- Holy Orders
- Anointing of the Sick.

sacred Something deserving of people's total respect, e.g. human life and the world people share.

sacred text The holy book or scriptures of a particular religion, e.g. the Bible (Christianity), the Qur'an (Islam).

sacrifice Offering something of value to God in worship.

science This refers to any area of study where knowledge is gained by:
- careful observation of how things work
- conducting experiments to test one's ideas about what one observes
- only accepting or rejecting any explanation if one has good reasons for doing so.

secularism The decline in active membership of organised religion and the lessening of religion's influence on many people's values.

Shahadah The creed that all Muslims are expected to recite: *There is no God but Allah and Muhammad is his prophet*.

Shari'a An all-embracing code of morality and law that all Muslims are expected to faithfully observe.

sign Any concrete image, word or gesture that points beyond itself, but has only *one* meaning, e.g. a green traffic light at a road junction.

socialisation The way in which people learn to behave towards others.

soul The invisible, spiritual aspect of a human being. It gives life to the body and does not die when separated from the body at death.

state A community of people organised under a government.

symbol Any concrete image, word or gesture that points beyond itself and has *more* than one meaning, e.g. the lights on a Christmas tree, a nation's flag.

technology The practical application of scientific discoveries to everyday life.

theism The belief that God exists.

theocracy Where a state is governed by laws based on the teachings of one particular religion.

transubstantiation The Catholic belief that at the consecration during the Mass, the bread ceases to be bread and becomes the body of Jesus, and the wine ceases to be wine and becomes the blood of Jesus.

Trinity The belief that there are three persons in the one God.

venial sin Any wrongful action a person commits that weakens his/her relationship with God.

value Anything or anyone considered to be good, desirable, important or worthwhile.

vocation The sense a person has of being called by God to do something worthwhile in life.

worship Any action by which people show that they recognise the supreme importance of God as the creator and sustainer of the universe.